This series of letters was written by a light infantry officer on campaign, as a lieutenant with the 52nd Light Infantry in Spain and a captain with the 69th Foot in Belgium and France. George Ulrich Barlow saw action at Ciudad Rodrigo, Badajoz, Vitoria, San Sebastian, Nivelle, Nive, and Orthez. He transferred to the 69th Foot as a captain and served with them in Belgium at the battles of Quatre Bras and Waterloo and then remained with the Army of Occupation in France until 1818. His involvement in the fighting and his honest views of some of the famous characters he met during his service are enlightening, including his first audience with Wellington at Freineda in Portugal. There are also interesting asides in his correspondence including his father's difficulties over his governorship of Madras and his brother's involvement in a major riot at the East India Company's Haileybury College.

A former Royal Navy officer, Gareth Glover has now published seventy books in his drive to bring a huge quantity of personal memoirs of Napoleonic soldiers lying in the archives into the public domain.

A Light Infantryman with Wellington

The Letters of Captain George Ulrich Barlow 52nd and 69th Foot 1808-15

Edited by Gareth Glover

Helion & Company

Helion & Company Limited
Unit 8 Amherst Business Centre
Budbrooke Road
Warwick
CV34 5WE
England
Tel. 01926 499619
Fax 0121 711 4075
Email: info@helion.co.uk
Website: www.helion.co.uk
Twitter: @helionbooks
Visit our blog at http://blog.helion.co.uk/

Published by Helion & Company 2018
Designed and typeset by Mach 3 Solutions Ltd (www.mach3solutions.co.uk)
Cover designed by Paul Hewitt, Battlefield Design (www.battlefield-design.co.uk)
Printed by Hobbs the Printers, Totton, Hampshire

Cover: 'British troops Storming Citadel in Peninsular Campaign', watercolour believed to be by Charles Cornwallis Michell (Anne S.K. Brown Military Collection)

ISBN 978-1-911628-10-1

British Library Cataloguing-in-Publication Data.
A catalogue record for this book is available from the British Library.

Contents

List of Plates

Introduction

I am constantly on the search for further invaluable contemporary letters from soldiers serving in the British Army during the Napoleonic wars, however this collection is one I have known about for some time, but one that has waited for me to finally stop procrastinating and to tackle the very difficult handwriting and very faint ink, which means that they may well be lost to us forever soon. The letters are kept in the India files at the British Library and are therefore little known, but finally they will now enjoy the limelight that they so richly deserve.[1]

George Ulric Barlow was born in Calcutta on 8 October 1791, the eldest son and second child of Sir George Hilario Barlow, Governor General of Bengal, and Elizabeth (née Smith) who he had married in India on 16 April 1789. Sir George was then acting Governor General of India from 1805-7 until the arrival of Lord Minto. He had been made a baronet in 1803, a Knight of the Bath in 1806, and Knight Grand Cross in 1815.

A portrait of an officer of the 69th Foot, reputed to be George Barlow. (Kindly supplied by Miles Barton)

Sir George had four other brothers, William who resided in Blackfriars, London or at his country house at Streatham and became young George's 'father figure' whilst in England. Robert served in the Royal Navy and commanded Chatham Dockyard for many years; Samuel had died in 1791; Thomas William entered the clergy and became Vicar of Halberton in Devon. His two sisters, young George's aunts, were Frances Charlotte and Harriet Hilare.

1 British Library Add Mss Eur F176. The individual files reproduced in this work are 55 George Barlow's letters to his father in the Peninsular and Waterloo campaigns, 57 George Barlow's letters to his father from India1822-23, 59 George's letters to his Uncle William 1809-13, 60 George Barlow's opinion on Eton, 62 Letters from George Barlow to Andrew Amos, 65 extract from an unknown officer regarding George's death.

When our George was old enough, he was shipped off to England for his education and he was sent to Eton College. Being separated by so many miles from his family and with an ability to only correspond with his parent via the two great 'India convoys' per year, it was natural that he would build a close relationship with his Uncle William, a trader based in London.

The Barlows were not slow to produce a very large family of fifteen children and George soon had many siblings, with whom he generally seems to have had a close relationship, despite being away from them for many years. Eliza Harriet had been born in 1790 and, following George's birth in 1791, there were William in 1792, Charlotte in 1794, John Henry in 1795, Robert in 1797, Louisa in 1798, Charles Anstruther in 1800, Frances in 1802, Harriet in 1803, Anne Caroline in 1803, Richard Wellesley in 1804, Edward Frederick in 1807, Emma Drury in 1809, and Frederick in 1810. Frederick's birth was to cause huge issues; it was seemingly known later that Frederick was not fathered by Sir George. This led to an acrimonious divorce, citing Colonel George Pratt Barlow, a cousin of Sir George and his aide de camp in India, as the father of this child. The scandal leaked out to the *Times* newspaper and Colonel Barlow set up home with the former Lady Barlow in Kensington until her death in 1836.

George finally left Eton in the summer of 1809 and he wrote a note to his Uncle William, giving him his thoughts on the school and the education that he had received there.

> To William Barlow Esq, Streatham, Surrey
> 13 September 1809
>
> I cannot refrain from passing a few compliments on our alma mater. *There* is still nourished the real enthusiasm of classic learning; there & there alone, does it flourish in its original purity. Can there be a greater proof of the truth of this assertion, than that the best classics *at both* the universities come from thence and bear off all the prizes & laurels to deck the brow of their illustrious parent? In short, every day's experience convinces me, that her system of education is preferable to that of any now in existence. Let the child be first of all placed in one of her seminaries, be *thoroughly* grounded in the first elements. Unless this circumstance is most pointedly attended to all efforts to erect a superstructure, or at least one of any beauty, will be altogether vain. I do not approve of Robert's school in many respects.[2] He however was capable of instilling the first rudiments of the dead languages very well & no further, for his abilities were unequal to the task. Then let the tender shoot be transplanted to Eton, and if it be of the proper genus, no sort is so well calculated for its future growth. This fact however must be carefully ascertained in the first instances. That garden is equally adapted to the culture of the choicest fruits or the rankest weeds. Nowhere does idleness, luxury and vice of every description, meet with more frequent or

2 His younger brother Robert had been born on 24 September 1797. He later served in the Bengal Civil Service and was a senior merchant. He died in 1857.

> better opportunities for exercise, greater success and encouragement & less restraint. Yet on the other hand, I never beheld a finer field for the practise of talent or on which diligence & application were more noticed or rewarded, or where there is a greater stimulus to all the nobler passions. Two of the most heterogenous qualities are there beheld united in the most wonderful manner. It is the best, or the very worst of places. Reflections after nearly five years residence convinces me of this truth and entitle my humble opinions on that head to some degree of credit. I shall take leave of our old nurse with the following pious exclamation used by a fellow partaker of her bounty, 'te sope pus mea lumina votis respicient carum nomen, Etona, vale.'[3]

Now George needed a career, something his father had clearly not failed to provide for; his influence in India certainly helping his rapid advancement from ensign to lieutenant on his very first day in the army, in regiments which just happened to be in India and without purchase! Within three months he had transferred again into one of the most sought-after regiments in the army, after the Household troops, the 52nd (Oxfordshire) Regiment, made famous by its connection to Sir John Moore.

George then served with the regiment for the next four years, seeing much action in Spain and Portugal and being severely wounded on at least two occasions (at Badajoz and at the Nivelle), before he transferred from the 52nd to the 69th (South Lincolnshire) Regiment, with which he served in 1815 at the Battles of Quatre Bras and Waterloo and partook in the subsequent march on Paris.

Returning home to England and a period of half pay, George married his first cousin, Hilare, in 1817 and gained a captaincy in the 22nd Light Dragoons on 17 August 1820 which was then disbanded. On 5 April 1821 he transferred to the 4th (Queen's Own) Light Dragoons on full pay and he soon sailed for India with his regiment and wife Hilare from Tilbury Docks on 31 December 1821. The couple enjoyed two and a half years at the cantonment of Kaira, near Ahmadabad. Unfortunately, however in what seems to have been a major outbreak of malaria in June 1824, which carried away no less than 89 officers and men of the regiment that year: George Ulric Barlow was included in the death toll.

If George had lived to gain his Military General Service Medal, which was eventually issued in 1848 but retrospectively covering all major operations since 1800, he would have been eligible for a medal with five bars, having served at the sieges of Ciudad Rodrigo and Badajoz and the battles of Vitoria, the Pyrenees, and Nivelle. He was also at the action of San Millan and visited San Sebastian whilst the French still held out in the castle which would not have earned him a bar.

We are very lucky that his family avidly hoarded letters as we have not only his fulsome but slightly staid letters written to his father every six months, but a much more regular and lively correspondence with his Uncle William which deal in great detail with his everyday activities, cares, and woes, and also his more jocular and fun-loving epistles to his old school chum Andrew Amos. This does raise the question as to how all of these letters came to reside in his father's correspondence. It is

3 Let the pain of a promise sleep. My lights (or guiding spirits) will look back on your dear name, Eton. Farewell.

clear from the letters, that his Uncle William was sent his sealed letters, addressed to his father in India, to be sent with one of the two India convoys per year. But moreover, there are hints that Uncle William was also forwarding his own letters from George to India once he had read them and it would appear that George knew this and yet he felt honour bound to write his more formal letters to his father as well. How the letters to his friend Amos also appear in these files is anybody's guess, but it is likely that he also chose to forward them to George's father in India after he had read them.

Between them, although there is some inevitable duplication, we gain a very comprehensive and often very unique picture of the life and troubles of a light infantry officer during the Napoleonic wars. He also raises some very interesting thoughts regarding the 52nd, as both an 'elitist' regiment, with John Moore portrayed as someone who actively singled out and recruited officers only of 'high standing' and as regards to its composition, describing it being very much a 'Scottish regiment' in its make-up.

The 52nd Foot are already well represented, having a number of memoirs published from the period of the Napoleonic Wars – not forgetting the correspondence of Sir John Moore himself – including Lieutenant Colonel George Napier (1809-12) Lieutenant John Dobbs (1809-13), Lieutenants Charles and Henry Dawson (1811-14 and 1809-12 respectively) and Ensign William Hay (1810-11). Added to which, I have already anotated those of Captain Charles Kinloch (1806-16) and Captain John Frederick Ewart (1811-12).[4] So, the obvious question must be, does George Barlow add anything else to our understanding? To which the answer is, yes, in spades. From his pretty well unique description of light infantry training at Shorncliffe, to the inner workings of both the 52nd and 69th regiments on campaign, they are invaluable, covering much of the minutiae of everyday soldiering, too often ignored by his contemporaries. I thoroughly recommend his letters to any serious student of the British Army during the Napoleonic wars.

Gareth Glover
July 2018

4 Published by Ken Trotman in 2007 and 2010 respectively.

1

Joining the Regiment

The letters written by George Barlow after he joined the army begin in September 1809 with one written to his Uncle William. This already finds him on route to be a lieutenant in the second battalion of the 52nd (Oxfordshire) Light Infantry, although his path to this position had been a little more convoluted.

In actual fact, he had joined the army on the 4 May 1809 as an ensign (without purchase) in the 22nd Foot (Cheshire), which was then serving in India. However, that very same day (and recorded in the same issue of the *London Gazette*) he was made a lieutenant in the 33rd Foot (1st Yorkshire West Riding) which was also serving in India. This immediate promotion could occur, despite the Duke of York's Army reforms – which set both age restrictions on joining the army and minimum terms of service as an officer in each rank, before they could advance, to remove the possibility of infants becoming commanding regiments – because no minimum term restriction had been placed on moving from ensign to lieutenant. His father as Governor at Madras had obviously engineered this appointment and immediate promotion, both regiments presently serving on the sub-continent.

Such speedy promotion was normally achieved by purchase, but here a death in the regiment, allowed him to step up, which must have been over the heads of a number of ensigns already in the regiment who would certainly have been his senior.[1] The June 1809 Army List shows him correctly as a lieutenant in the 33rd Foot, but the seniority date attached is incorrect (being that of his predecessor). As the 33rd were in India, George certainly never joined the regiment, as on 17 August 1809 he transferred again, this time into the 2nd Battalion 52nd Light Infantry as a lieutenant. The 1810 Army Lists show his correct seniority as a lieutenant as of 4 May 1809.

Having been appointed to this regiment in mid-August, he would have been given one month to prepare before he reported for duty and began his training. This period would certainly not have been one of leisure, for George would have to kit himself out with his full uniform from a London tailor, including his jacket, waistcoat, breeches, hat, sword, and silk sash; moreover he had to have a full supply of shirts, undergarments, socks, materials for his ablutions, towels, bed linen, and a myriad other necessaries. These preparations were very expensive and time

1 Captain Eustace 33rd Foot had died and Lieutenant John Guthrie gained his position, being senior lieutenant in the regiment. This left a gap in the lieutenants which George Barlow transferred into, over the heads of the ensigns of the 33rd Foot.

consuming, but no self-respecting gentleman officer could arrive at their regiment without everything in place. Then, of course, there was the prospect of purchasing a horse and the associated equipment, but that would come later, initially he had to complete his training.

The 52nd was already a prestigious infantry regiment in which to serve, second only to the Guards regiments. Their renown had grown significantly during the last few years, being inextricably linked to their colonel, Sir John Moore, who had been influential in promoting a much more professional attitude to being an officer in the army via the light infantry training programme which he introduced to his brigade whilst based on the south coast of England in 1803 during the height of the invasion scare. He centred this training on Shorncliffe, where an earth ramped redoubt had been sited in 1794 by Colonel William Twiss of the Royal Engineers and barracks built within.[2] It had already been used as a training ground since 1795[3] and had been identified as the perfect spot to site an 'Army of Observation' ready to deal with any invasion force landing in Kent. Moore's brigade then consisted of the 4th, 59th, 1/52nd and 1/95th, the latter two battalions, along with the light companies of the 4th and 59th, began to practise light infantry tactics.

Interestingly, the first trials of the new 'spherical case shot' invented by Major Shrapnel were also carried out by the 24-pounder battery on the shoreline at Shorncliffe. In June 1804 the 43rd Foot (Monmouthshire) was converted to light infantry and sent to join Moore's brigade, replacing the 4th and 59th, leaving the Light Brigade consisting of the better-known establishment of the 43rd, 52nd and 95th. The brigade was eventually split up in 1806, with the 1/52nd proceeding to Sicily and Sweden with Moore, whilst the 1/43rd, 2/52nd and 1/95th went to Copenhagen in 1807, where they served for the first time under Sir Arthur Wellesley, the future Duke of Wellington. The 1/ and 2/43rd, 1/ and 2/52nd and 1/ and 2/95th then served together in the 1808 campaign in Portugal and in the subsequent march into Spain under the command of Sir John Moore and eventual retreat to Corunna.

Just after this campaign ended, Britain sent a huge armada of ships, carrying an army of over forty thousand men to Walcheren, which included elements of the 2/43rd, 2/52nd (five companies only) and the 2/95th. The campaign was disastrous; the army led by the Earl of Chatham was dilatory in its operations and soon got bogged down on the pestilential islands in the mouth of the Scheldt. No more than a couple of hundred men died in the fighting, whereas thousands died of fever (undoubtedly a form of malaria) and thousands more were incapacitated for years to come. Finally, the expedition was abandoned in September 1809, having achieved nothing, apart from killing or ruining the health of over 15,000 excellent troops that could have been used far more effectively in Portugal. It was with this background that George joined his regiment, at their base at Shorncliffe.

Having just graduated from Eton, the first letter gave George's opinion respecting his old school after nearly five years of residence there, but he first informed his uncle of his safe arrival at Chatham on his way to the regiment.

2 S. Summerfield and S. Law, *Sir John Moore and the Universal Soldier* (Huntingdon: Ken Trotman, 2016) Vol.I, p.137.

3 Summerfield and Law, *Sir John Moore*, Vol.I, p.134.

To William Barlow Esq, Streatham, Surrey
Chatham, 10 September 1809

My dearest uncle,
In order to give you a regular detail of my proceedings, I shall begin with informing you of my safe arrival at this place on the Thursday, attended by no other circumstance than that of being ducked in a good hard shower of rain, which overtook me whilst in the act of passing through the dockyard gate.[4]

John has no doubt informed you that we were obliged to chace [sic] with all sail set to come up with our flying prize,[5] which we overtook at the Bricklayers Arms.[6] All the good folks at this place were not a little surprised at my arrival, though some feint hopes of it had been previously entertained, relying as they did on the memorable 8th of September. I was a very welcome guest, being accompanied by the painted cabinet & box of jewels. A thousand enquiries were made about my aunt & yourself respecting the probability of your visit, which I replied was extremely doubtful owing to my aunt's health.[7]

I must now give you the reason for my unexpected delay at this place. In pursuance of my original design I was preparing on Friday last to set out for headquarters & was making the necessary enquiries for a chaise, when all the good folks begged me to postpone my departure from the Saturday till the Monday. My uncle assenting to this opinion, added that he did not see any necessity for such expedition as to go down on the Saturday & proposed that I should remain until tomorrow, when I shall finally take my departure and as I shall set off early in the morning, I shall have arrived without doubt some time at my journey's end ere the present reaches your eyes. I intend to reach *Hythe* by three o'clock tomorrow afternoon. Hythe is only one mile distant from Shorncliffe whither I shall immediately proceed, that place being the headquarters of the detachment of the 52nd and *not Dover* as I falsely told you. This piece of intelligence was communicated to my uncle by a Navy Captain at this place, who has several friends in the regiment. An officer lately passed through Chatham from Folkestone, saying that I am daily expected by Major Hunt who is present commandant of the detachment.[8] You have wisely provided for my wants in the way of money, of which after having laid my

4 He had been visiting his uncle, Captain Sir Robert Barlow Royal Navy, who was Superintendent of Chatham Dockyard from 1808. He eventually rose to the rank of Rear Admiral and retired in 1823. He died in 1843.

5 This must refer to his younger brother John born on 7 December1795. He later joined the Bengal Civil Service and became a senior merchant and salt agent. They were presumably chasing the mail coach.

6 This would appear to be the Bricklayers Arms, Hamilton Road, which stands one mile east of Streatham.

7 William Barlow was first married to Harriet Flemming (died in 1802) and he then married Louisa Harris in 1803; neither marriage bore any children. William died in 1839 and his wife Louisa died in 1860.

8 Major John Philip Hunt, 52nd Light Infantry.

travelling expenses for 43 or 44 miles at 1s 6d the mile, I shall stand in great need. I will thank you therefore to write to me by Monday's post, addressed to Lieutenant Barlow simply and not G[eorge] U[lric] Barlow], Shorncliffe near Folkestone, for this latter is the post town, remitting the necessary sum the amount of which I most cheerfully leave for your determination. My first business on joining the regiment will be to make the best enquiries & from the most authentic returns give you as nearly possible the amount of my annual expenditure, such as my breakfast, dinner, servant, clothes, &c &c &c, in these as well as in everything else, I will conform to the generality of my equals in the regiment, this I know you would wish me to do, so as neither to excel nor yet at the same time, to be at all inferior to my companions. I will also make enquiries respecting the article of horses, one of which with all due deference to General Ross' authority neither I nor yourself could deem unreasonable.[9] Indeed the general himself told me, that the younger officers kept horses & that *there was no impropriety in my having one,* though in conversation with you he *entirely changed his note.* This answer he gave me, when I paid him a visit at his house in Portland Place & when I put him the question about a horse at your desire, *mark this.*

The Guards have arrived at Sheerness though they have not as yet disembarked. A great mortality prevails among them; 500 are sick including in the number their general and several other officers; three of the latter are dead.[10] I conclude that I shall find the whole of the 52nd at Shorncliffe on my arrival there tomorrow. My route thither lies through Maidstone, Lenham & Ashford.[11]

My uncle & aunt desire to be remembered to you, with whom annexing a thousand blessings for you my aunt & all at home. I remain your affectionate nephew G U Barlow

His next letter announced his arrival at Shorncliffe and he began to detail his life in the regiment and the training regime at Shorncliffe.

No 4
To William Barlow Esq, Little Bridge Street, Blackfriars, London[12]
Shorncliffe Barracks, 12 September 1809

My dearest uncle,
As I promised in my last I now proceed to give you an ample detail of my arrival and reception at this place. I left Chatham yesterday morning at

9 This would appear to be Lieutenant General Sir Charles Ross, colonel of the 86th Foot, whose 1st Battalion was in India from 1803-15 although it has proven impossible to confirm his family ties to Lieutenant Colonel Ross of the 52nd.
10 The troops were returning from the Walcheren expedition.
11 Lenham lies halfway between Maidstone and Ashford.
12 Little Bridge Street, London was renamed Pilgrim Street in 1890 and unfortunately the whole area has since been redeveloped.

ten o'clock & arrived at Hythe about 4 in the afternoon. The distance is about 42 miles by one of the best and at the same time most picturesque routes I ever beheld in my life; leaving my baggage at a *horrible filthy tavern,* for it does not deserve the name of an inn, I walked to Shorncliffe situated about 2 miles from Hythe. It was roasting hot; figure yourself a hill as steep, lofty and long as that on which the mill near the miller's tomb at Worthing stands.[13] Without the least exaggeration I think it is equally as high & arduous of ascent. I never in my lifetime mounted such a hill & warm as it was on the beach, yet there was a fine fresh breeze on the hill. We are situated about an equal distance from Boulogne and Beachy Head, both of which may be seen at all times; in short it is the grandest spectacle I ever beheld. I arrived at the barracks a little before mess time which is at five o'clock. Major Gibbs the commandant had gone that morning to Deal;[14] I was therefore obliged to introduce myself to the officers, by whom I was received in the kindest manner & who gave me their advice with regard to a servant, room &c &c and a thousand other necessary particulars. The senior captain was so good as to invite me to his table this morning, until I shall provide myself with furniture and breakfast articles, which will be done in the course of a month or two.

I write the present at an inn at Hythe; whither I have just walked from the barracks, in order to provide a bed and all its necessary apparatus. I am sure you would wish me to fit up my barrack in the same manner as the rest of our subalterns. I propose therefore hiring a carpet, bureau, chairs, washing stand &c &c *but buying the bed;* which will do wherever I may be. I have ordered off the taylor [sic] here two pairs of blue pantaloons & some other necessary articles, of which I have neither time nor space to give you an account and which Captain Currie the present commandant informed me were absolutely necessary.[15] I have also bought some towels & table clothes; these and many other articles (the bills of which I will preserve for your inspection) far, very far, exceed my small supply of cash & are much greater than you can form any idea of. God bless you all whilst in haste I subscribe myself your affectionate nephew G U Barlow

George soon found himself embarrassed for money and he wrote to his uncle urgently requesting funds.

13 John Olliver, a miller at Worthing on Caesar's Hill (now Highdown Hill), arranged for a brick and stone tomb to be built on the top of the hill many years before his death. He died in 1794, aged 84, two thousand people attended the burial and consequent party.

14 Major Edward Gibbs, 52nd Light Infantry.

15 Captain James Hunter Currie; he was killed at the Battle of Vitoria in 1813.

To William Barlow Esq, Little Bridge Street, Blackfriars, London
Shorncliffe Barracks, 24 September 1809

My dearest uncle,
I have to return you my best thanks for the seasonable arrival of the £50, consisting of a £20 & three £10 notes in halves;[16] with regard to the parcels you are so good as to send me, direct them as usual to Lieutenant Barlow, 52nd Regiment, Shorncliffe Barracks. The *coach* which daily sets off from town *at a very early hour in* the morning, will drop them at *The New Inn Hythe*,[17] whither I will send my servant in readiness to receive them. You must of course be the best judge of the method in which those articles are to be sent down; I should think a deal chest or box would be the safest and most convenient.

Give my best love to my aunt for her fine letter; inform her that I do not expect the correspondence between us to be kept up *on her part*; as I am well aware of the uneasy posture she is obliged to assume in consequence. I will therefore beg that she will not in future answer my letters, but reserve her replies until I shall have the pleasure of conversing with her. With my best love to all at home, I remain your affectionate nephew G U Barlow

To William Barlow Esquire, Little Bridge Street, Blackfriars, London
Shorncliffe Barracks, 29 September 1809

My dearest uncle,
Three days are past and still I have not heard from General Calvert.[18] Since no post after today leaves this place until Sunday afternoon, I am unwilling any longer to delay acknowledging the receipt of the hamper which contained the coffee pot, desk, pistols, cocoa, coffee, tea, sugar and the conjuror;[19] but this latter *is of no manner of use* unless you *send me the stand*, the use of which Frederick can explain best to you, and in which consists the whole ingenuity of the contrivance,[20] but *no table clothes or linen of any kind*, came to hand.

General Nightingale commands this part of the Kent district,[21] my acquaintance with him has been & will be of very short duration, for in the early beginning of next week he intends to transfer his headquarters

16 Bank notes were often sent in the post cut in half, the halves posted separately by different methods, so that only the intended recipient would be able to match the two halves.
17 This would appear to be The New Inn, which stood in the High Street of Sandgate, which is between Hythe and Shorncliffe. It was established in 1775 and re-named the Kent Hotel in 1859 and then the Royal Kent Hotel in 1866. It was unfortunately demolished in 1962.
18 Major General Sir Harry Calvert, Adjutant General to the Forces; he became a lieutenant general the following month.
19 This would appear to be a small table on legs that can be packed up.
20 There was no Frederick in the family except his brother born in 1810, which this clearly is not. He was either a friend or servant of his uncle.
21 Actually, Brigadier General Miles Nightingall.

to Dover. However, he invited me to dinner a second time yesterday. These civilities arise from his intimacy with my father, and as to their being in any shape conducive to *my interest*, I have not the least hopes.

I have also met with a kind reception from the colonel;[22] he has not however noticed me more particularly than any other officer in the regiment; *indeed he could not*, and even if we were inclined so to do, it *would be highly improper* to make any such distinction. I am perfectly satisfied with the manner he has behaved towards me and on this head, I could give you many little instances too trifling to be committed to paper; but these as well as a thousand other little trifles will afford as much pleasure for conversation, but are too numerous & could not be sufficiently explained within the narrow limits of a letter. I hope to get leave of absence for about *three weeks* and no *longer* at Christmas, but when *my* turn for the long furlough comes round, I shall be able to stay with you a no less period than five months, which we term the *long leave* & which I shall obtain *this time twelve month* in my due rotation. With regard to the regiments in this neighbourhood, we have the 95th Riflemen at Hythe, as well as a camp of militia on Folkestone Heights. General Stewart is said to be appointed Nightingale's successor.[23] He is to have the Light Brigade viz 43rd, 52nd, 95th. He takes care to keep us in good discipline; every third or fourth day he takes us out in heavy marching order, with our knapsacks, canteens, haversacks, in short equipped as if on actual service and marched us all over the county to keep our legs in practise & to make us accustomed to those long, laborious & rapid marches such always fall to the lot of *the Light Bobs.* He is constantly manoeuvring us, makes us ascend the steepest hills in double quick time & full trot, lay down and fire on our bellies & a thousand similar diverting tricks. In short, he makes us go wherever a human being can possibly set his foot. I do not grudge all this, as I wish to be perfect in every department of my duty whatsoever and this reflection even makes things *agreeable* to me, which are very irksome to others.

I am delighted with reading in yesterday's paper the government orders issued by my father. The manly, firm and energetic language in which it is couched equally struck my mind for the beauties of the composition, as the sentiment. If it was drawn up by his Chief Secretary it does him great credit. The consciousness of a just cause, which cause it most fully explained to my mind, has a right to speak in so determined a tone; it speaks for itself.

How sorry I am to find such dissentions in the Cabinet, this ministry have exerted themselves manfully in the cause of Europe & with the exception of Lord Chatham's appointment which was by no means an unanimous one,[24] I think they have done everything to deserve success & that

22 He refers here to Lieutenant Colonel Ross, not the colonel of the regiment, Major General Sir Hildebrand Oakes, who was then commanding the garrison of Malta.

23 Major General William Stewart.

24 Lieutenant General John Pitt, 2nd Earl of Chatham, had commanded the land forces in the late Walcheren Expedition.

the failure is not owing to them. I like their *measures & their declared sentiments*; and by these two last and not of *persons,* I always form my opinion. I was sorry to hear of Canning's duel.[25] I would sooner see any one of them killed than him. The talents will of course come in now;[26] with love to my aunt, your affectionate nephew G U Barlow

To William Barlow Esq, Little Bridge Street, Blackfriars, London
Shorncliffe Barracks, 2 October 1809

My dearest uncle,
It is with the sincerest pleasure I announce to you the receipt of a letter from General Calvert. He simply states that in consequence of my answer he had applied to General Dundas for the issue of my pay;[27] but that General D[undas] finding I had not been employed or performing any actual duty and besides not being in possession of any certificate of leave, had thought proper to deny my request. I use the term *pleasure,* for although failing in the original object of my wishes, still that failure is not attended with that unpleasant result which I so much apprehended. On this head therefore I am at present perfectly easy.[28]

With regard to linen I will trouble you for six towels ready marked, as also for *four little cloths.* It would be best if these *four last were of a good size* namely such as people generally use at dinner and if you think me not too unreasonable, half a dozen tea spoons and some table ditto with my initials marked upon them. I have also dismissed my rascally servant, who besides my money, helped himself to a pair of blankets. I have felt so much their *pigeoning* that I shall be wiser for the future.[29] A thousand thanks to you for your kind supply of money. I paid off all my bills amounting to £40. The rest I shall spend as frugally as possible & so keep ready for a future contingency. The day after tomorrow we are going to give a grand entertainment to General Nightingale, his staff and all the officers of rank in the neighbouring regiments. We have sent off for some dozen of best madeira and *also for a turtle* from Dover. It is for these matters that I shall keep prepared, as it would be so very foolish to by pennyless [sic] on any such unforeseen

25 In September 1809, Castlereagh, the War Minister, discovered that George Canning, the Foreign Secretary, had made a deal with the Duke of Portland to have him removed from office. Castlereagh challenged Canning to a duel, which was fought on 21 September. Canning missed and Castlereagh hit Canning in the thigh; both men resigned their posts in consequence.

26 The unity government dubbed the 'Ministry of All the Talents' came in to office in 1806 but had broken up the following year over Catholic Emancipation. George obviously believed that another such government would be formed. It did not happen.

27 General Sir David Dundas, most famous for his *Principles of Military Manouevres,* served as Commander in Chief of the Army from 1809 to 1811, during the years of disgrace of the Duke of York, his mistress having been guilty of selling commissions.

28 George had obviously tried and failed to claim wages from his date of appointment in May until the date of his arrival with his regiment.

29 To be pigeoned = duped.

demand. With the articles you were so good as to send me lately, I shall continue to be very snug. We shall now remain here for the winter; these quarters now begin to be very bleak. I had yesterday, a beautiful view of the French shore from Boulogne to Calais. There was not a single cloud on the horizon, the different shades & tints of the verdure were clearly seen on the opposite shore as well as the *foe's buildings, chimney tops & cruisers* off those ports. I sat for some time contemplating these objects through a most excellent glass,[30] fancy yourself on the terrace at Worthing viewing Beachy Head, that between those is exactly the same distance from these cliffs, as the above promontory from Worthing.[31] Beachy Head is very visible from my redoubt; you may fancy therefore how high and exposed we are & shall be in the severest winter months. Privateers are daily seen from hence.[32] The 52nd ought properly to be termed a Scotch Regiment. The officers are almost entirely of that nation; a few Irish and a *still fewer number of English*, make up our regiment. Moore's name attracted all the Scotch nation into this corps; all my acquaintances in this battalion are Scotch with a very few exceptions.[33] All the officers of the regiment behave to one another more like brothers, than any set of men I ever beheld who were utterly unconnected with one another. They are all young without any single exception, even of the colonel & majors & though young in years, are veterans in experience, all of them having seen so much service. I dine today with General Nightingale & will write to share with you direct.
Your affectionate nephew, G U Barlow

Sir John Moore by Sir Thomas Lawrence. (Editor's Collection)

George had written a number of letters to his father in India from Eton (not published here) and he numbered the letters sequentially to help his parents read them in order when they arrived in batches with the trade fleets every six months. Given the hazardous voyage to India in sailing ships and the threat of capture by enemy warships, it also helped them to identify missing letters in the series.

30 A spy glass, or telescope.
31 Beachy Head is around 35 miles from Shorncliffe, whereas Calais and Boulogne are around 25 miles away.
32 Privately owned merchant ships could obtain 'Letters of Marque' from their government, allowing them to arm and to legally act as 'privateers' with the aim of capturing enemy merchantmen and profiting from their sale.
33 An interesting comment, Moore of course having hailed from Glasgow. Looking over the Army List, it is clear that many of the names of officers of the 52nd at this time have a Scottish background.

No 29
Shorncliffe Barracks, 8 October 1809 (Annotated received 16 March 1810, by the *Hector*[34])
To Sir G H Barlow Bart KB, Fort St George, Madras (For *Georgiana* packet[35])

My dearest father,
Having had the misfortune to leave behind at Chatham the book in which I regularly note down the various numbers of my correspondence to my family & friends, I am prevented from applying my usual custom in the present instance. You will not however fail to set down this letter as the first you have received since my entrance into the army. In the meanwhile, I shall send for the above book and in my next, inform you of what number you are to prefix to this.

I have now attained the summit of my wishes, situated as I am in a regiment which if it has its equal is allowed to possess no superior in the British Army. Setting aside all prejudices, I believe there are few, very few corps who have a right ever to presume to the first title. Sir John Moore has the credit of the whole as the regiment was trained under his own special regulations. We have several rules peculiar to ourselves, distinct from any other corps and entirely of his formation; the excellence of which every day seems to confirm. He was also more personally known to the subaltern and inferior officers of the 52nd, than scarcely any other general officer to his own regiment, taking a lively interest in whatsoever concerned their public character, or private happiness; many of which remarkable instances of which I could mention to you. Acting the part of a common drill sergeant when they were originally metamorphosed into a light infantry corps, he was accustomed to put them through the intricate & various evolutions of those troops in person, and this was one of his chief amusements. They

34 There is some difficulty in identifying this ship, as having searched the numerous databases of HEIC ships (which all vary slightly), I have failed to find this ship in any of them. They consistently list three different ships named *Hector* but all of them were in the seventeenth and eighteenth centuries, none in the nineteenth century. I believe that another *Hector* may well have been used by the East India Company in 1809-10.

35 The *Georgiana* was only of 285 tons hence her description as a packet, she served with the East India Company from 1796-1811, initially on hire, but later she was purchased by the company. She made seven round voyages to India between 1796-1811. She sailed from Portsmouth commanded by Captain Leigh, on 4 October 1809 and arrived at Madras on 16 February 1810, before sailing on to Calcutta, where she arrived on 16 May 1810. She arrived back at Deptford on 5 September 1811 on what would prove to be her final voyage to India. She was sold and sent to the South Seas fishery to act as a whaler, where she was one of three whalers captured off the Galapagos Islands on 29 April 1813, by the boats of USS *Essex*. The commander of the *Essex* mistakenly described her as a 'Letter of Marque' ship, he armed her further and commissioned her as USS *Georgiana*. Having successfully helped to capture six other British whalers, she had her guns removed and was sent to America, loaded with three thousand barrels of valuable sperm oil, as she had been deemed 'a dull sailer'. On the voyage home she was recaptured by HMS *Barossa* on 28 November 1813 and sailed to Britain. She continued to sail carrying cargo until February 1818, when she arrived at Funchal leaking badly, she was condemned and broken up there.

accompanied him in all his campaigns, and within these last four or five years, have attended him to Sweden, Sicily, Portugal, Spain & have been in Holland & in short in every quarter of Europe where a British expedition has appeared for some years past. They gained the public thanks of Sir A[rthur] Wellesley,[36] for their conduct at Vimiero,[37],as well as of Sir John Hope[38] at Corunna,[39] where they were present with their lamented colonel.[40] A very large detachment also fought under Sir Arthur in the ever-memorable Battle of Talavera.[41] The whole of the 1st Battalion arrived the very morning subsequent to that glorious victory, though they had made a forced march of 45 miles *in one day* to come up & share in the fun.[42] The 52nd is composed of a greater number of able bodied men than any other regiment in the service. Previous to the above march, they had been journeying from Lisbon to join Sir Arthur in the heart of Spain at the rate of

---

36 Sir Arthur Wellesley was of course the future Duke of Wellington.

37 The 2/52nd under the command of Lieutenant Colonel John Ross and numbering 618 rank and file, had embarked for foreign service at Ramsgate on 16 July 1808. It landed at Maceira Bay on 19 August and was immediately formed as part of Brigadier General Robert Anstruther's Brigade, fighting two days later at Vimeiro on 21 August. Here they helped defeat two attacks, both of which were beaten back by controlled volleys. The 2/52nd apparently lost 3 men killed, 33 wounded and 2 missing.

38 Lieutenant General Sir John Hope, who later became Earl of Hopetoun. With the death of Sir John Moore, command of the army devolved on Hope.

39 The 1/52nd, commanded by Lieutenant Colonel Barclay and numbering 615 rank & file also landed in Portugal at Maceira Bay on 29 August having just arrived from Sweden. The 1/52nd were placed under Brigadier General Anstruther and the 2/52nd joined Brigadier General Robert Craufurd's Brigade. On the retreat to Corunna, the 2/52nd with Craufurd were ordered to proceed to Vigo, where they re-embarked without a problem. The 1/52nd retreated to Corunna with the main army and was involved in the Battle of Corunna on 16 January 1809. The 1/52nd were involved in heavy fighting throughout the day, around the village of Elvina although casualty figures show that only 5 men were killed, with Lieutenant James Ormsby and a further 34 men wounded.

40 Sir John Moore was fatally wounded at the Battle of Corunna and passed away that night.

41 The 1/52nd were refitted immediately after Corunna, taking three hundred and fifty men from the 2nd Battalion to bring them up to establishment (the 2nd Battalion receiving 255 volunteers from the militia), and returned to Portugal, landing at Lisbon on 29 June 1809. Although the battalion did not reach Talavera in time to fight, a detachment of the 52nd was present. When the 52nd Foot had been ordered into Spain with Sir John Moore, four officers (Captain Clement Poole, Lieutenant John Woodgate, Ensigns William Royds and Charles Wood), three sergeants and 130 men were left sick at Lisbon. These were still there having recuperated, and when Sir Arthur Wellesley returned to Portugal they joined him in his march to Oporto and then on to Talavera. Two men were killed and 24 wounded during the battle.

42 This is a more realistic claim than the one made by Napier that the brigade marched 62 miles in 26 hours! The actual distance between Navalmoral and the position of the British army is actually 52 miles, or two miles an hour on average, which is still an extraordinary march for troops with a 60-pound pack on their backs and little water to be had, through a hot sweltering day and a very dark night. Whilst marching to join, news was received that the army was about to engage the French near Talavera and Craufurd ordered his troops to force march all the way there, however they arrived the day after the battle and merely helped to bury the dead.

between twenty and thirty miles daily for some time previous. The officers are equally as select as the commander, they chiefly consist of men of large fortune & the first connections in the kingdom, who have entered the regiment through a love of arms and are determined to continue in it as a profession. The fame of Sir J[ohn] Moore invited the best families to place their sons & relatives in his corps.[43] Although young in years, they are old in experience and I do not hesitate to say, that there is not a single considered who is not only acquainted with the common routine of his duty, but has not also a more extended knowledge of his profession than most of their acquaintances in other corps of the same standing. This as I have said before, is entirely the work of General Moore, who was determined that his officers should be soldiers in reality, so that the subaltern officers are as well acquainted with their common duty as their commander. I use the term common because I do not pretend to denote that they have studied the art of war in its endless extent and various departments, as is the bounden duty of colonels & commanders of regiments.

Colonel Ross in the strength of his person, countenance, character is *tout entirement militaire*.[44]. He is a very young colonel, scarcely 30 years of age. Conceive to yourself a *remarkably* handsome man, with a fine noble deportment & you may form some idea of Colonel Ross.[45] I am under the highest obligation to him for his unceasing exertions in procuring the exchange with Wright,[46] in the course of which I unavoidably gave him a great deal of trouble. No one is admitted into this regiment or allowed to continue in it except men of the strictest principles of honour; or if by some chance one should gain admittance, as was the case with Wright, he is instantly obliged to suit it. In the event of a duel taking place, an enquiry is set on foot & the party which shall appear to have the blame of the affair & to have been the cause is instantaneously obliged to leave the regiment. This is a settled rule; by which everyone is in some measure prevented from being quarrelsome, troublesome or ungentlemanly, and the whole corps acting by this system preserve the strictest & nicest sense of honour, without its leading to any disposition of the above nature. For if on the one hand he is quarrelsome or is the cause of a dispute; if on the other he declines fighting, he is expressly necessitated to walk out of the corps. Moore laid down this rule, and has acted on it in several instances; you are therefore obliged to tread in the direct road of honour & of a gentleman, for deviating on either side, you

43 This is an interesting comment and one little touched on by the histories of the regiment. It is true that many of the names of officers in the regiment at this time indicate that they were the sons of landed gentry and a few more were the sons of dukes etc, but it is quite a claim that Sir John Moore had selected these junior officers because of their wealth and position in society and requires further investigation.

44 French – Everything military.

45 Lieutenant Colonel John Ross transferred to the 66th Foot in July 1811.

46 The *London Gazette* dated 15 August 1809 announced that George Barlow had exchanged with Lieutenant Benjamin Wright, George moving to the 52nd Foot and Wright taking his place in the 33rd Foot.

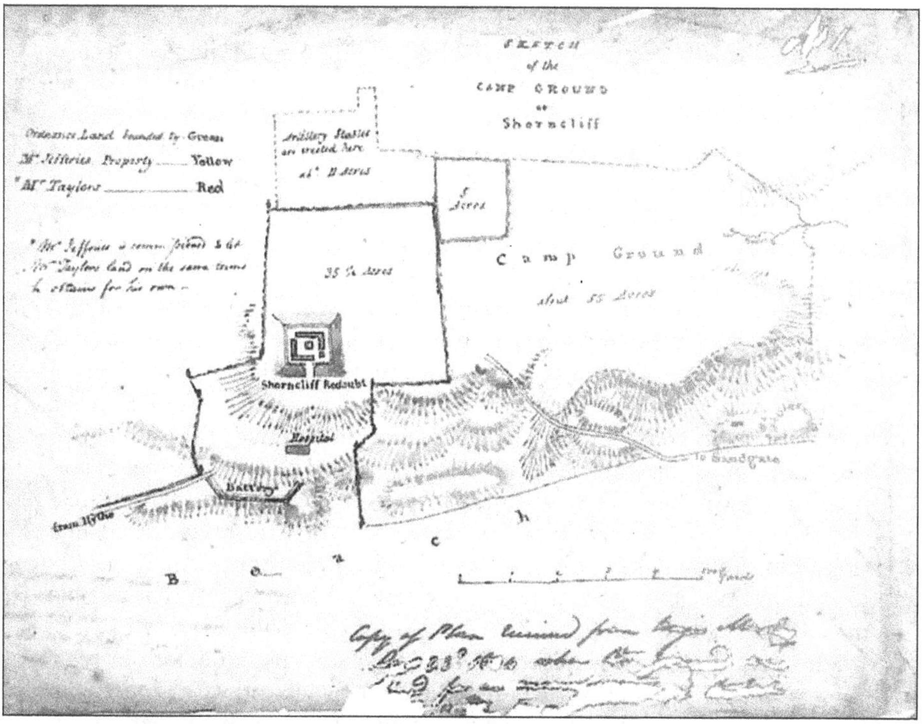

Map of Shorncliffe Camp in 1801. (Public Domain)

fall into an inextricable precipice. Thus, is our conduct regulated towards one another.

As you must know, this regiment is by no means expensive. My pay amounts to £120,[47] which will discharge my journies [sic] to and from Streatham & will also provide me with meat & fruit. My allowance is to be £100 per annum[48] & in case I keep a horse as most of my acquaintances do;[49] I shall have an addition of £60 to the above sum. I shall thus have £100 for clothes, necessaries and private expenses, £120 for my Mess, and £60 for my horse, in all £280 per annum. This arrangement I am sure you will approve.

Shorncliffe is situated at nearly the most southern extremity of the County of Kent; from whence we command one of the finest views of land & Straits that perhaps was ever beheld. On one side we view Beachy Head,

47 He is rounding up, his official pay amounting to £119 2 shillings and 6 pence per annum. See Robert Burnham, *The British Army against Napoleon* (Barnsley: Pen and Sword 2010), p.144.

48 Like most junior officers, he would find it impossible to exist solely on his pay.

49 An interesting statement given Sir John Moore's views. Apparently, the father of a young officer wrote to the general, stating that he proposed to send his son a horse. Moore replied 'that he should be very pleased that the horse should be sent, but that it would be necessary for the father to send with it someone to ride it, for his son would have no time to do so'. Summerfield and Law, *Sir John Moore*, Vol.I, p.156.

a considerable portion of Kent & the greatest part of the County of Sussex, Dover on the left. Every day of my life I behold the French shore; on a clear day houses and other *white* objects on which the sun may happen to shine, are sometimes to be distinguished with the naked eye & are commonly to be seen at all times with the telescope.[50] Yesterday from Folkestone Telegraph with a fine glass, I beheld Boulogne, Ambelteuse, & several towns on the immense line of coast we daily see.[51] The different tints of produce on the opposite hills, trees, privateers at anchor close to the beach, or getting under sail, together with our men of war cruising before their harbours in proud defiance, presented a spectacle at once so grand, that I should scarcely have believed such a report, unless I *had not* seen it myself. The day was beautifully clear & serene; as we are situated within four hours sail of their coast, their privateers frequently pay us a visit, for the sake of bravado, though they do comparatively little mischief to our trade. This cliff with the exception of Beachy Head, is the highest land in the Channel hereabouts. It is extremely bleak in winter & when the day is extremely oppressive in the low lands, ere the Gods above enjoy a refreshing breeze, 600 sick from Walcheren in consequence of so healing a spot, are reportedly recovering. We have been so lucky as to lose but *four men* of that terrible malady, the ague which generally changed into a typhus fever. This is the whole amount of our loss in the late unsuccessful expedition, for our regiment with 30,000 fellow soldiers remained for two months encamped in a horrible marshy island, without firing a single shot & scarcely ever saw an enemy, whilst the remaining 20,000 which composed this noble armament besieged Flushing, such is the result of the endeavours of an army of 50,000 as gallant men as ever wore a red coat and entirely owing to one personage who shall be nameless.[52]

We military men must be extremely shy of dabbling in politics. I have promised to adopt the same rule. I cannot however, as you may plainly see, always keep in my tongue and still retain an itching of the old mania; in truth a soldier ought not to take a prominent part in such affairs.

You good folks in India, will I trust extol Sir Arthur to the skies. I cannot help calling him *Sir Arthur* in spite of his new title.[53] Sir Arthur, adored by the soldiery in this quarter of the [torn- world?] in the same proportion as Nelson was in [torn – the?] Navy. His affable & engaging deportment, and [torn – directing?] all his attention to the wants of the soldiery, have won their affections. He has touched the proper string of their hearts, and in

50 For those that may doubt this statement, Jonathan Leach of the 95th Rifles wrote regarding his time at Shorncliffe in June 1803 'We had no difficulty seeing the immense mass of white tents on the French coast, when the day happened to be clear'. Summerfield and Law, *Sir John Moore*, Vol.I, p.144.

51 The telegraph station was situated on the top of Folkestone cliff.

52 This undoubtedly refers to General John Pitt, 2nd Earl of Chatham, who commanded the army sent to Walcheren, who did not perform well, being far too dilatory and abrasive, arguing fiercely with Rear Admiral Sir Richard Strachan, who commanded the naval forces.

53 Following his victory at Talavera, Wellesley was raised to the peerage as Viscount Wellington.

some measure thereby, stirred the key to render the British troops invincible. Oh, how I should wish to serve under such a commander.

As the *Georgiana* is to sail in a day or two I must conclude with giving my kindest love, to my dear mother & sisters & with every wish for theirs as well as your happiness. I remain your most affectionate son. G U Barlow

George continued to write to his uncle with further requests.

To William Barlow Esq, Little Bridge Street, Blackfriars, London
Shorncliffe Barracks, 20 October 1809

My dearest uncle,
In thanking you for the spoons and the various articles you have been as good as to send me, I must at the same time inform you that I had previously determined upon taking all those necessary precautions which you so strongly enjoin. I have so lately, smarted by experience, that on no account do I trust my trunk, keys or desk to any other guardianship than that of my own pocket. I have every reason to believe that my present servant is perfectly honest and faithful. He is a perfect broad country Scotchman lately arrived from Perthshire and talks like a true highlander. I am well convinced that he has *no gammon* about him, from sundry little trials that I have purposely made of his integrity. [54] He is very diligent, keeps my etceteras in the best order and never wants being twice told the same thing, so that in every little domestic habit or arrangement I may make, I always find him punctually attentive to them. In short, I have every reason to be well satisfied with him this month he has been in my service. I do not however trust him with my keys, neither has he any knowledge of the quarter where my money or other valuables are lodged, determined as I am to throw no temptations in his way. In consequence of his good behaviour, I have rigged him out in a complete new suit of livery, of the Barlow costume, namely a light drab; for this I paid down ready money as you recommend.

I could not exactly understand whether you mention *having sent out* my letter, or whether you intended so to do by the ship that carries out General Brownrigg,[55] but of delicacy to me the subject of the present disputes in India has never been so much as once started at the mess or elsewhere and I of course would not be the first to begin any such discussion where my presence would preclude all freedom of sentiment in the debate.

We have lately made a dash or two to Dover to the balls which are weekly given at that place. The day before yesterday I was at the garrison ball in that town, which was very well attended and was also furnished with some very good partners, who came thither from Canterbury & its neighbourhood which is one of the best in England. I am also one of a party who after our field day on the 25th instant have determined to be present [at] a

54 To be gammoned, was to be tricked or misled out of money.
55 Lieutenant General Robert Brownrigg, who became Governor of Ceylon in 1811.

very elegant entertainment & ball which is to be given on that day by the garrison at Dover to the mayor & corporation of Hythe. Propose eating turtle on that day in the town hall of Hythe so that *we are* obliged to celebrate that anniversary till the 27th instant, when the officers of the Light Brigade consisting of the 52nd & 95th Regiments intend giving an elegant ball and supper. Cards are sent to Canterbury & all parts of Kent for the above days, as there is no display either of 'Bounty or fashion' in any shape in the neighbourhood of Hythe. I would give my cousin William or any of his friends, tickets of invitation, but I fear that Chatham is too distant.[56] If you have any friends or acquaintance in this neighbourhood send me timely notice & I will continue to introduce myself to their acquaintance for the above purpose. I thank you also for your proffered assistance in money which will be very acceptable. These thanks I have also to accompany with another strange request, namely; that if I return you the hamper you sent me some time ago, you would despatch next back again loaded with 9 bottles of good port, nine of claret & six of madeira, in all 2 dozen & deduct it out of the remittance you are about to send me. I wish in return for the invitations of others to give a petit souper [small supper]; this indeed, very seldom indeed but neat & liberal, which will be far less expensive than *a continuance* of lesser entertainments & the time I should be obliged to buy at our mess, would be equally as dear as *the best* table in town and not so good by half. With my best love to my aunt & the little ones I remain your affectionate nephew, G U Barlow

To William Barlow Esq, Streatham, Surrey
Shorncliffe barracks, 29 October 1809

My dearest uncle,
In my last I gave you an apology for the brief manner in which I was obliged to return you my thanks for your supplies, be assured that on this head I feel all those sentiments which I have before so repeatedly and at such length detailed. I trust that the remembrance of them is too well fixed in your mind to need any fresh detail on my part in explaining the nature of them *to you.*

I returned from Dover on Thursday last where I spent a very pleasant evening. General Nightingale has invited me thither for next Tuesday week at the next garrison ball which to be on next Tuesday week; our gala was sported on *Friday last* at Hythe, where we literally tripped on the light fantastic toe and did not give it up until the return of daylight.

I can neither learn either from William's letter,[57] or your own the nature of the Hertford dispute, and am consequently precluded from forming any opinion as to its merits. It must however have been of some importance to require measures of so violent a stature as those which the directors have

56 Cousin William was Uncle Robert's son, he eventually took holy orders.
57 His younger brother William was born on 18 December 1792, he died on 29 July 1811.

adopted. William mentions not a syllable of the matter to me in his letter, with the exception of stating simply that there had been a row and the students had been sent home.[58] I am certainly biased by the sentiments you expressed in your last, namely that 'they had behaved ill'. But though I feel this opinion, I am sure you are too just as not to wish that I should in some degree decide by my own judgement, when I am acquainted with *the real truth* of the whole.

As it is nothing extraordinary or high flying to keep a horse and there are several in this regiment who do, I shall in the latter part of the winter request the performance of your promise. There are several packs of hounds in this neighbourhood; several of our regiment frequently join in the sport, the fox hounds throw off within a very short distance of these barracks, in addition to which there are a pack of very good harriers. You know me too well to think that I shall turn over much attention to these things. It is however a pleasure which I should much wish to enjoy and would fill up the idle hours of a morning, in addition to which it is fine exercise & fit for a gentleman. I have frequently heard you recommend it, in the light I have just mentioned. The frosty weather will commence in the course of two or three weeks which will put a stop to the pleasures of the chace [sic]. It would not therefore be worthwhile to have a horse for that short time, nor *until the beginning or latter end of February,* when hunting will be again resumed & continued till the latter end of April with its usual spirit. If you shall think proper to trust me with one, I will promise to keep my hunter in as good a condition with the allowance you proposed as any of my companions, who may have twice as much.

I should wish much to obtain some staff appointment; an aide de camp is the only post which by the late regulations I am entitled to hold until I gain my company. In the event of this taking place, adieu to all my sporting pleasures, which I would most willingly reign for the attainment of that object for which I entered the army and which I anxiously desire. In that case I must content myself with a good strong hardy charger. If you could by any means effect this staff business you would most inestimably oblige your ever affectionate nephew G U Barlow

58 This refers to the riots at Haileybury College, the East India College founded in 1806. William Baker, a local resident wrote in November 1809, 'There has been a most scandalous riot at the new East India College, in consequence of which several will be expelled. I have not escaped in the general want of discipline and I have been under the necessity of proceeding against three of the students who have intruded upon our premises in a shameful manner, by shooting at pheasants and wounding others immediately under our garden wall. In the Birch Walk and the other plantations. Two of them were convicted on Saturday last and will be obliged to pay a penalty of £20 each. Besides the tax which they have defrauded – the third having been sent home on the dispersion of the College in consequence of the other more serious riots has not yet appeared, but will be had up in a few days and incur the same penalty. It is to be hoped that the new regulations which the Court of Directors will adopt will prevent this establishment from becoming a public nuisance in the neighbourhood'. The College is now a private school.

[PS] Tell William, I acknowledge the receipt of his report, which is just, I will write tomorrow; remember me to all.

His next letter showed that they had moved.

To William Barlow Esq, Streatham London
Fort Pitt, 19 December 1809[59]

My dearest uncle,
At length I am enabled to sit down by a fireside which I can call my own and be master of my own actions; you must know that the quarters in this fort are reckoned the best in this county, but are not adapted for so large a regiment as our second battalion. At this moment there are more than one third of our officers on leave of absence & recruiting, yet in spite of this circumstance we are obliged to *double up*, a military phrase signifying *two in the same room*, as we daily mess two or three and twenty officers. To remedy this inconvenience all the ensigns have been obliged to take up their lodgings in the bomb proof casemates; by this arrangement I am left quiet possessor of a most excellent room in these barracks, as my companion is obliged to descend into his rocky vault in the fosse.

Some of my effects were pilfered on the march excepting a small deal case, containing a tea kettle, jug, and some other things of little value. A soldier of the 9th broke open the chest at Canterbury and fleeced me of those table cloths you sent me down in addition to the above-mentioned articles, but the table cloths were stopped at a pawn brokers at this place, who delivered them back to me, upon my recognizing them as my own. They had endeavoured to destroy the initials but without effect; this proves that the *bible boys* are not so sanctified as their name denotes; for so the 9th Foot are termèd, from their colonel distributing bibles to all the corps and a profusion of these books were found wherever they went.[60]

I find by the Gazette that Robert Coulthard has *purchased* a lieutenancy in the 17th Light Dragoons;[61] the word purchased surprized me much; the 17th are in India and on the Madras station. I suppose he will soon take his departure for India, in which case I shall begin to make up my letters.

William arrived here on Saturday last; my Uncle Robert told me the other day in the course of conversation that he should have been glad to have obtained an internship for him; entre nous it has been well understood that

59 Built in 1805, Fort Pitt was one of a chain of large forts built to defend Chatham from the landward side. The barracks were not within its walls, but sited just to the north and separately casemated, but attached to the fort by a covered way. It became a military hospital in 1828 and is now the site of a grammar school.

60 The 9th Foot (East Norfolk). The regiment has a tradition of being called the 'Holy Boys' but attribute a different, more ethereal reason for the name.

61 Robert Coulthard was gazetted a lieutenant in the 17th Light Dragoons on 23 November 1809.

William has no partiality for a black gown; but I mention this as being the first hint I ever heard at this place to the contrary.

I never was happier in my life than when I beheld the name of Wellesley appointed to front [bench?] of this government;[62] I think you did very right sending a copy of Lord Minto's book to them;[63] it puts the question in a most conspicuous light and confirms your opinion that my father would never have taken so bold a step if he had not entertained the most perfect reliance on the justice of his cause. Has the *Nyaden* yet sailed for the West Indies [?] I have not received a line from William since he went on board her, & should even have been ignorant of the event, if I had not seen my Uncle Robert.[64]

I hope to be able to steal away for a few days to town, as there are many trifling matters for conversation which I cannot sufficiently detail in a letter. With my best love to my aunt and the little ones, believe me to be your affectionate nephew G U Barlow

In his next letter to his uncle, George answered some slight criticism of socialising too much, but also again requested funds.

William Barlow Esq, Little Bridge Street, Blackfriars, London
Fort Pitt, 26 December 1809

My dear uncle,
I could not help remarking in your last a kind of latent uneasiness respecting my mode of spending time; I am perfectly certain that I shall never be tired of dancing; indeed you must be well acquainted with my extreme particularity for this species of amusement as well as of music; but rest assured that in spite of this & every other inducement, I *never, never,* will for a moment lose sight of the ultimate objects of my profession. Objects which first led me to enter the army, will ever keep me in the same line of life and which I shall ever keep in sight until the final attainment of my wishes shall be completed.

Neither am I so destitute of books as you would imagine; I suppose you have forgot the time when you sent me down my three volumes on the whole art & system of war. I will however to satisfy your scruples give you a short specimen of my mode of passing time. I am regularly occupied every day until eleven o'clock on parades and drills; from eleven till two in the afternoon, I employ either in writing, reading or walking, just according to the humour of the moment. From two till three I attend a *third drill*, at a quarter before four I

62 Richard Wellesley, Arthur's older brother, who had been Governor General of India from 1798-1805, was made Foreign Secretary on the resignation of Canning.

63 Gilbert Elliot-Murray-Kynynmound, 1st Earl of Minto, was Governor General of India 1807-13.

64 HMS *Nyaden*, a 36-gun frigate, was the ex-Danish *Nijaden*, captured at Copenhagen in 1807. She was commanded by Captain Frederick Cotterell in 1809 and sailed to the West Indies. William had clearly joined the ship with the influence of his Uncle Robert; he remained a midshipman until his death in 1811.

am on parade, at five we dine, my evenings I must own are frequently passed in the dockyard, but where could I pass them more pleasantly and I may also add usefully. For my Uncle Robert when he has no friends residing with him, generally assembles us round him and takes up a book on chemistry or natural philosophy which he explains to us all; consider that when I am reported perfect and dismissed drill which will be the case in a very short time, I shall be perfect master of the movements of a battalion, whether of heavy or light troops, as also of regimental duty. Indeed, the greater part of this I have known for a long time past, but still it is the basis of everything else, and is rather more difficult to be understood than people generally think it. The duty of a captain or subaltern is as easily learnt as ABC, but that of a colonel particularly of light troops, is more intricate. I intend to apply myself seriously to Euclid & Mathematics,[65] in pursuance of which I have to request you will send me down Simpson's *Elements of Euclid*,[66] without which it is impossible to study geodetics, which is the art of mapping, surveys, reconnoitring & drawing sketches of ground. I have also to request that you will return me by the post a supply of cash; as I am perfectly a bankrupt and our marching this time, in consequence of the jolly dinners we eat on arriving at the inns, very expensive. On referring to your books you will also find that I have not had any receipt since the middle of October, which is now nearly ten weeks. With my love to my aunt and all at Streatham; believe me to be your affectionate nephew G U Barlow

His uncle had clearly asked the reasons for the further request for funds at a difficult time for him and George rowed back a bit, simply asking him for his allowance quarterly.

To William Barlow, Streatham, Surrey
Fort Pitt, 5 January 1810

My dearest uncle,
In reply to your last respecting pecuniary matters, I have only to request that you begin with transmitting me for the future, my allowance by the quarter, or according to your arrangement, £30 in advance at the commencement of every three months. This for many reasons would be most acceptable not to say convenient to myself. I will therefore dismiss this subject by requesting that you will not trouble yourself about my business, till you have made all your arrangements respecting the family at Streatham as well as your concerns in town, which rather I am well aware are sufficient to occupy a considerable portion of your time; until these are settled I will not include myself in your time. I must here add a line to signify that *Simpson's Euclid has not made its appearance or come to hand.*

---

65 Euclid of Alexandria was a Greek mathematician and founded geometry. His *Elements* was the main textbook for teaching mathematics until the early twentieth century.

66 Roberts Simson, a Scottish mathematician published *Euclid's Elements* in Latin and English in 1756.

I cannot help smiling at the farrago of nonsense which daily appears in the newspapers. I cannot help thinking of that forgery (for I cannot suppose it to be anything else) in the *Morning Chronicle* some years past,[67],which contained this paragraph 'poor Barlow is in despair'! And these absurdities are inserted verbatim in every paper & of course are the production of some secret enemy; many of whom my father must have created by his present just, though disagreeable measures. In the *Courier,*[68] *Times, Post, Star,* appeared a long paragraph respecting a mutiny at Pondamalee,[69] or the next day appears the death of Sir G H Barlow & the imprisonment of *Lord Minto Governor General? And that Sir A Wellesley*, mind *Sir A Wellesley*, who is this moment so actively employed in Spain and who could not wish to give up his truly honourable & meritorious post as Commander in Chief of the British armies in the peninsula & who has neither *pecuniary motives*, nor any other wish to go out, is named as his successor. I am persuaded that Sir Arthur's ideas are of a cast superior to such trifles and with the respectable fortune he now enjoys is perfectly content and would not exchange his present situation for the wealth of [torn- the East?] Indies.

My uncle called upon Captain Lautour a few days ago;[70] Mrs L[autour] resides at present with her father in Harley Street and is not to come into these regions until spring. With my love to all my aunt and all at home, I remain your affectionate nephew G U Barlow

[PS] I am in doubt whether I shall write to William or not. Has the *Nayaden* sailed? I should much wish to know this.

George was clearly a serious and determined young man, who avidly sought to gain the accomplishments of an officer and improve his knowledge of every aspect of the army, so that he could eventually gain an appointment as a Staff officer. He did have hopes however, that the battalion might soon be sent out to Portugal to join the first battalion which was already there.

To Sir G H Barlow, India
No 31
Fort Pitt Barracks, Chatham 13 February 1810
(Annotated received 27 September, answered 11 October by the *Montezuma*).[71]

---

67 The *Morning Chronicle and London Advertiser*, was established in 1769 and continued until 1865. It was renamed the *Morning Chronicle* in 1789.

68 The *Courier* published in London cost 6½d per issue in 1811.

69 Poonamallee is now a suburb of Chennai (then Madras). The mutiny mentioned is explained in detail in a following letter.

70 Captain Joseph Andrew Lautour, 1st Foot Guards. He resigned his commission in 1813.

71 This would appear to be the same *Montezuma* that was wrecked on the Atlantic shores of Morocco near Mogadore in 1811; she would have been on her voyage back to Britain from India. She does not appear to have been an East India Company ship.

My dearest father,
In the absence of my memorandum book I have been obliged to send you these letters without adopting my usual custom of prefixing the numbers to each, which are 28, 29 & 30 & which mission you will fill up. A recent trip to Streatham has put me in possession of the above document and enables me to annex the above number to the present.

I little expected in your last that I should have had to address you from this place. Our removal from Shorncliffe to these quarters was occasioned by the shiploads of sick daily arriving from our garrisons in Walcheren & Flushing. Such was the state of these wretched objects that many died in the act of being removed to the hospitals on shore. A march into the interior of the country for the convalescents was therefore totally impossible. This circumstance, combined with the salubrity of the sea air, which is deemed most adapted to the recovery of the patients, contribute to our recent change of cantonments. You may be assured that I am perfectly content; for independent of my uncle's residence at the dockyard I am within five hours ride of dear Streatham. This vicinity to home will be much more agreeable when I am master of a horse, of which most undoubtedly find indispensable of all treasures for a military man. My uncle is at present in reach and will enable me to pay constant visits to the 'alma mater', for such I cannot help considering Streatham. The whole of this battalion is composed of young men of the first birth, rank & connections, a case which is very rarely found in the line.[72] For this circumstance, as I have most amply detailed in a former letter, the 52nd Regiment is indebted to Sir John Moore. Many of my companions keep horses and my uncle, knowing your wish to have me placed on an equal footing with them all, acceded to my request. Behold me then, a character fully independent, possessing a source of the greatest accomplishment and with a small package of necessaries attached to my saddle bag, provided with a conveyance to any quarter of Great Britain. This reflection affords me much pleasure, at the same time though I am about to commence as hunter and sportsman, which are the usual diversions of the army. I then intend to turn a jockey or game keeper, and though fond of those pleasures, I am firmly resolved not to let them engross any larger portion of my time than innocent recreation may partake. I call that recreation innocent which does not occupy too much attention or diverts one's mind from the attainment of objects far more important, useful and honourable. I have been informed of your partiality for such manly exercises, as field sports, in the earlier periods of your life. I will therefore leave your imagination to fill up whatever I may have omitted in this description of my sentiments. Anxious that they are such as you would highly approve of and resemble your own, than which I never wish to have a better criterion of right and wrong.

72 He of course refers to the junior officers.

I am at present entirely employed in going through a course of study, comprising mathematics, fortification, topographical drawing, and every other accomplishment necessary to qualify me for *a Staff officer, and eventually the command of a brigade as a general.* You must be well acquainted with my natural partiality for military studies, in all their varied & complete branches of every kind. This sort of reading and study originally attracted my notice to the army and afterwards rivetted my affections to that line by the firmest ties of regard. Indeed, sensible that amongst my numerous competitors for fame, there are comparatively few, very few indeed, who possess, even in a moderate degree, the requisite endowments of a soldier. This profession is the most intricate of all professions. My humble endeavours shall be exerted to be enlisted among that number. If I am so fortunate as to succeed, my promotion & fame are certain. Every silence comprises a distinct tranche of study, but to the military profession at once the most valuable and sure. All the sister arts contribute their choicest offerings. Analyse it and you will find the most heterogenous ingredients combined together and by the mixture, producing a whole, at once arduous & admirable. The chief of these are Mathematics & particularly that branch of their specialities, Fortification, Gunnery Tables and a knowledge of languages, and all these built upon the durable foundation of classics & history of past times both civil and military. These studies I am at present pursuing and will continue so to do with the most unabated passion, no compromise, no pleasure, in a word nothing in earth shall divert my attention, nor relax my assiduity in following the path I have marked out, as sanctioned by the opinion of the most eminent men in the profession. To be numbered as one of these shall be the principal object of my life, the whole and strength of my mind, hopes, and resources of whatever kind. Grateful am I for your permission to follow my present line of life; I will strive therefore to attain to that eminence which you had designated to me in another station.[73].Reflect, that when you peruse the present, such is the tenor of my life and that I daily make fresh acquirements to qualify me for those high stations, of future advancement, which your interest may be able hereafter to procure me.

In addition to my pay, which accounts (deducting the income tax[74]) to £110 per annum. My uncle has added £120.[75] Since I have joined the regiment, housekeeping & economy will ever find a place in my thoughts & is the regulation of my establishment. I shall endeavour to maintain the appearance of a gentleman, with the least possible extravagance. In the

73 Presumably his father had originally looked for him to gain a high position in the Indian Army or Civil Service.

74 Income Tax had been brought in by William Pitt the Younger in 1799 to help pay for the war effort. It was levied on anyone who earned more than £60 per annum (about £6,000 today) at the rate of 2d in the pound or 1/60th (equating to a rate of 1.66%). It was so hated that it was rapidly abandoned in 1816, but resurrected in 1841 and has never gone away since.

75 In the previous letter he states £100, but the numbers written are very clear.

article of supplies, I have as usual experienced my uncle's liberality and whilst I remain a subaltern, his settlement will be amply sufficient.

We have not as yet received any orders to hold ourselves in readiness for embarkation. Reinforcements however, are to be immediately detached to Portugal. Our first battalion, 1,100 strong, is at present with Lord Wellington at Badajoz in Spain.[76] They lately picked 400 of our best men to fill up their own deficiencies, yet in spite of this defalcation & our losses in Walcheren (which we have experienced less than any regiment in the King's service) our 2nd battalion will carry out 600 men in the course of the spring. A general volunteering from the militia is however expected, which event taking place, we shall quickly be recruited to our establishment, which is 1,100 men, as the 52nd Regiment is a great favourite among the militia and the distinctions of our uniform, as being entirely composed of light infantry, has no little weight in the minds of the vulgar. With my kindest love to my dear mother, Charlotte & little Emma.[77] I remain your affectionate son, G U Barlow

George's next, shows how driven and ambitious he was to succeed in his chosen occupation. He wrote at length in an effort to persuade his father to use his undoubted influence to gain him a captaincy in the 33rd Foot, which still remained in India.

No 32
Fort Pitt Barracks, Chatham, 4 April 1810
(Annotated received 12 October, answered 25 October)

My dearest father,
To anticipate and provide for the exigencies of the future is an object well deserving the attention of one who like myself aspires to the attainment of the higher honours in my profession. This great end can only be secured by a rapid promotion through such subordinate stations. Deprived of this, a military man consumes the prime of his life in the preparatory steps of his advancement to its higher degrees, which at length he only attains when his infirmities in some measure disqualify him from exercising with honour to himself or utility to his country its arduous duties. To provide against

76 His information regarding the first battalion was quite a bit out of date. After the action at Talavera, Wellington's army found itself unsupported by the Spanish troops and threatened in front and rear by the French. The army was moved over to the south of the Tagus river and made their escape by marching to the vicinity of the fortresses of Badajoz and Elvas. The Light Brigade had then marched northwards with much of the army in mid-December 1809, arriving at Pinhel on 5 January 1810 and in early March the Light Division (the brigade had been reinforced and taken from 3rd Division to form the Light Division on 22 February 1810) moved towards the River Agueda, from where they could watch for any movement by Marshal Massena towards the fortress of Ciudad Rodrigo.

77 His sister Charlotte had been born on 29 September 1794 and Emma born on 13 April 1809, were with their parents in India. Charlotte eventually married a Major Balmain and stayed in India, Emma came home with her parents but unfortunately died on 11 August 1818.

so fatal an evil and to secure the above objects, has long occupied my mind & I have at length determined to put to paper a plan, of which I trust you will approve & which your exalted station and interest, will I trust be able to carry into effect.

You must be well aware, that I am not entitled to my company until I have been three years in the service; for Sir D[avid] Dundas added a third year to the probationary period of subaltern.[78] I shall have served my time in September 1811. I am persuaded that your influence with the military authorities in India will enable you to procure me the rank of captain immediately I become qualified. This I dare say will be an object of little difficulty. My next proposition is however more arduous. I wish to be promoted *into the 33rd* Regiment of Foot and this for the undermentioned weighty and important reasons.

1st It is a regiment of a single battalion.[79]

2nd You state it is to have been 16 or 17 years at Madras & that it is the first regiment to be relieved. I wish therefore to become a captain in it, *previous to its being ordered home.* As soon as this event takes place, the promotion in the regiment will become extremely rapid. The captains of the 33rd are generally men of little fortune or interest; they have been so long in India that they are become habituated to that quarter of the globe; their double pay enables them to live with a degree of affluence & comfort which they could not hope for in England.[80] They would therefore wish to remain at Madras & would exchange into other regiments with officers who would wish to return home. If I can gain admittance into the regiment *previous to these exchanges taking place,* (previous to the 33rd being ordered home) I should gain four or five steps and with ease in the course of three or four years, obtain my majority, which is the most difficult of all steps in the army & which is the most favourable time to serve at Calcutta.

3rd Lord Wellington is Colonel of the 33rd Regiment; no doubt on its return to England, he will have interest enough to have a second battalion added to it. This will make an addition to the promotions. I have anticipated as above & such invariably takes place in every regiment on its return from the East Indies.[81]

4th I have a most anxious desire to gain an introduction to Lord Wellington, which would be greatly facilitated by my enlistment into his regiment. He is a man already of the most distinguished character, birth,

78 One of the changes Dundas instigated was to increase the time required as a subaltern officer before you could become a captain from 2 to 3 years, this directly affected George.

79 This meant that there were far fewer officers ahead of him in the seniority list and gave a much greater chance of gaining promotion.

80 Even as late as 1860, it is recorded that officer's serving in India (both Honourable East India Company and King's officers) received double pay for serving there. Why this was I have been unable to discover, it certainly was not danger money as those sent to the West Indies had a much lower survival rate than those serving in the East Indies.

81 When the 33rd Foot did return home from India in 1812, it bucked this trend and never raised a second battalion during the Napoleonic Wars.

influence and connections, a man who is the 'spes patrie matura'[82] and to whom the country will look up [to] in the future perils, with which the overgrown power of France threatens the kingdom. I should wish much to be attached to his person as aide de camp, or some other Staff situation, as he is a man who is always sure to be employed. This last circumstance is merely a speculation of my own, hardly within the bounds of probability. But I am sure that both Lords Wellesley or Wellington,[83] Generals Hewitt[84] or Sir S Auchmuty[85] would readily, out of their esteem & regard for yourself forward the interest of your son by making him a captain.

This letter I conceive to be of so much importance that I shall send a duplicate by another ship of the fleet & recommending the present to your most serious perusal. I shall most anxiously await your answer & remain your truly affectionate son, G U Barlow.

PS The present will most probably reach you in the middle of September. I hope therefore to receive an answer from you upon the feasibility of the enclosed project, by the October fleet. I write thus early upon the matter, that you may *begin early* to pave the ways and be enabled to inform *me some month's beforehand* of the probable result of your endeavours. If I am gazetted into the 33rd at Madras, I shall date my rank the same as if it had been done at home. Perhaps it may be necessary for me to make an exchange from some Garrison or Veteran Battalion before it can be accomplished into the 33rd. G U Barlow.

His next letter to his uncle, was a hurried note informing him that they were rapidly marching on London to prevent rioting.

Dartford, 8 April 1810

My dear uncle,
I have just time to inform you of our arrival at this place on our way to town. We all turned out of bed at one o'clock this morning in consequence of the arrival of an express to march off instantly. We just served out a clean shirt & 60 rounds of ammunition to the troops and marched off at three hour's notice. We left Chatham a little after three this morning for this place, where we [were] ordered to wait for further instructions; expecting of course to make a forced march to town directly we arrived. We have been suffered however to remain quiet this day. An express has however just this instant arrived for us to march at four o'clock tomorrow morning for

82 Latin for 'The great hope for the homeland'.
83 The Duke of Wellington's older brother Richard, the 1st Marquess Wellesley, had served as Governor General of India between 1798 and 1805.
84 Lieutenant General Sir George Hewitt was Commander in Chief in India for a brief period in 1807.
85 Major General Sir Samuel Auchmuty was appointed to command the Madras Army in 1810.

Lambeth Palace, which is to be headquarters, for the purpose of protecting the Houses of Parliament. I have just a clean shirt, pair of stockings & some little necessaries on my back, I must contrive therefore to get them washed at Streatham, as we shall stay for some days in town.

The commissioner [Uncle Robert] is totally ignorant of my departure, I have however left a note to be delivered to him by an officer of the dockyard. I have sent my uncle the key of my stable & delivered to him my horse during our absence, to be taken care of.

Troops are pouring in from all quarters of Kent; we come 1,500 men from Chatham; the horse artillery are likewise on their way from Woolwich, in haste I remain your affectionate nephew G U Barlow

George found himself garrisoning Central London, due to the major riots following the order to arrest Sir Francis Burdett for libelling the House of Commons. Burdett was eventually arrested and the major military presence prevented any serious rioting.

To William Barlow Esq, Streatham, Surrey
Dean Street, Soho Square, London, 10 April 1810

My dear uncle,
I informed you in my last from Dartford that we had been ordered to take up our quarters in the vicinity of Lambeth. An express however met us on the road directing us to proceed immediately to the Horse Guards for further orders. We were then conducted to a large government storehouse for the army. In this street where we are at present all quartered; we are rather confined for room, there being 500 men in this house; all the officers are in one apartment, with our straw & blankets quite comfortable & snug.

There luckily happens to be a coffee room within twenty yards of the barrack, where we dine &c &c.[86] All officers however are prohibited from going beyond the bounds of this street, and the sound of the bugles, so that we may turn out on the first alarm. I shall not therefore be allowed to pay you a visit, until all is perfectly tranquil.

We had four pieces of cannon on this square the night before last with the 15th [King's Own] Light Dragoons. It has been thought advisable to post a large force at this place; as it is close to the vicinity of St Giles & from whence the worst part of the mob came, passing through these streets on their way from Holborne & Oxford Street to the city, which is by far the shortest cut. A large detachment is also posted at Charing Cross so that the communication between the different ends of the city are effectually intercepted. We patrolled all night, Hanover Square and all this quarter of the town. I was posted at the British Museum with 50 men under a captain's orders. This was done in consequence of a riot at that spot the preceding night;

86 This would appear to be *The Crown Coffee House and Tavern* at 20 Soho Square.

but we found no occasion to use any disagreeable measures, though every red-coat is saluted with the polite language of a London mob. All resistance on their part is perfectly useless, as within these two days, General Hope's aide de camp informed Colonel Ross that 25,000 troops of the line & militia had marched into town and patrole the whole metropolis every night, with upwards of 5,000 cavalry and a large body of flying artillery & collected from every situation within 50 miles of the Horse Guards.

I stole away with Colonel Ross for half an hour this morning and called upon the general at Portland Place. He had just learnt our arrival. Mrs Ross was in much agitation respecting their boy, who is at present labouring under some dangerous illness. With my best love to my aunt & all at home, I remain your affectionate nephew G U Barlow

Soon the excitement was over and the regiment returned to Shorncliffe.

To William Barlow Esq, Streatham, Surrey
Ashford Barracks, 26 June 1810

My dear uncle,
You may depend upon a strict observancy [to] the regimen as prescribed in your last for the mare, as soon as we arrive at Shorncliffe; an event which I hope may speedily take place as we are all in a very uncomfortable state, expecting daily to move and not daring to unpack our baggage & effects. I have taken out a few changes of linen and some books and during the cool of the evening scour the country round about, which I think is very picturesque and beautiful, but has no variety of prospect whatever. Everything here is more forward by a fortnight than in Chatham & the adjacent parts of Surrey, strawberries in plenty together with cherries, these last however not so abundant & everything is very reasonable & cheap in the way of vegetables, hay, corn & meat. Unless there is a great pressure of troops, military are seldom quartered here; none have set their feet in this place for a twelvemonth past. Society, there is none, not a gentleman's house in the town, though there are some parks & villas in the neighbourhood, yet unvisited by their possessors. The tradesmen are withal excessively impudent, at which we are particularly sore, as we are so well known & kindly treated in every part of Kent & have never been in these barracks for twelve years. Yet in this as in many other instances the innocent suffer for the guilty; in fact it would be a capital place, to send a regiment of rogues or debauchees to do penance.

There is not the least rumour at present afloat regarding our embarkation; but this is no argument against the probability of such an event taking place; our embarkation & removals frequently happening at four or five hour's notice. I fear much however that our first battalion which is one of Lord Wellington's finest corps, will greatly suffer in the ensuing engagement, as it is in the advanced position. We may be called upon to recruit its ranks by a draft of five or six hundred men & thus at once will perish all our hopes of foreign expeditions.

I see by the papers that the East Indiamen are hourly expected to arrive; I am particularly anxious to know what punishments have fallen upon the mutineers. I had a strange dream the other night about the honours for which Sir G[eorge] B[arlow] is recommended; it was however unaccompanied with any promise of the needful, a realization of which seems to be very far distant, as I find by the papers, that the company propose dividing out five percent and a half on their capital.

I cannot guess from your last whether Fred has bought one or two devils; the one of brass is intended for the girls at Chatham & I will thank you to have forwarded to them immediately. The other for reason which I have before assumed is destined for Streatham. Bye the bye I was glad to hear my uncle at Chatham state that my aunt, was so much recovered as to be enabled to go to church; this is a circumstance of which I was not apprized when last at home. It is the forerunner of a speedy recovery & which I trust your visit to the banks of the Medway will forward. My next will most probably be dated from [torn – Shorncliffe?] where I trust you will soon hear from your most affectionate nephew G U Barlow.

[PS] You will be so good as to remember me on or before the 1st of July. I should much wish to have the greater part of my allowance at first; at all events the more you can spare at once the better.

To William Barlow Esq, Streatham, Surrey
Ashford Barracks, 22 July 1810

My dearest uncle,
I reached this place on Thursday evening and as it is now pretty well ascertained that we shall leave Ashford in the course of the ensuing week, I am desirous of giving you my promised letter previous to our setting out. Shorncliffe is *but a day's march* from hence, a line therefore (which I will take care to send) signifying the *departure* of the regiment, *will be as good* as a notification of *our arrival,* at the seaside.

All our friends were left well at Chatham on the 19th instant; they were much disappointed at my aunt's non-acceptance of their invitation to the launch; the excuse however appeared to me as well as to them, most ample and satisfactory. The spectacle will be as grand as that of the *Queen Charlotte* although the public prints may not puff it off so well.[87] We are to have a jig in the evening; I hope *the next day* to run up to town for a few days, but this depends upon circumstances. At present the colonel whom I have always found most ready to oblige, gives leave to anyone he pleases; but at Shorncliffe we are under the immediate eyes of the commander of the district General Murray,[88] who I understand is a great martinet, very strict & *from whom alone*, all such favours are to be obtained. I went to Chatham

87 HMS *Queen Charlotte* of 110 guns was launched at Deptford on 17 July 1810.
88 Major General Sir John Murray.

on regimental duty, with the intention of staying at most but four days; this term was however extended to *seven* on my applying to the colonel; I propose however, if possible, obtaining a week's leave for the special purpose of seeing you all at Streatham on the 1st of August.

Letters were received yesterday from our first battalion in Portugal up to the beginning of this month; according to the expression of an officer on the spot, '*they are most perilously in the advance*'; at the date of his writing, they were within three leagues of 30,000 men under Marshal Ney who in person with large bodies of cavalry, daily forced back their advanced posts & picquets for the purpose of reconnoitring; the marshal approaching their quarters in such force & in so menacing an appearance & so frequently that they often turned out under arms *by night* as well as by day to receive him.[89] Independent of the above force Marshal Massena & Junot have 50,000 troops besieging Ciudad Rodrigo & its environs,[90] speculating on the inevitable surrender of that place, which was to take place on the very day of the last dispatches, the enemy had thrown his bridges across the Agueda & made every preparation for a general & desperate attack on the British army with his combined force; which by the lowest estimates amounts to 80,000 strong. Sir Arthur was fearlessly waiting the assault in his present position which was very well chosen. His lordship's situation is truly awful, the disparity of numbers most cruel & tremendous; everything however that human skill or valour can effect will be done by [torn – Sir Arthur?] & his brave little army, the position of which under [torn – his?] immediate command does not consist of more than [torn – 30,000?] British & as many Portuguese troops.

There is not at present even any rumour afloat respecting our battalion; in the event of Lord Wellington standing his ground, I have little doubt of its being called upon to supply 500 or 600 men to repair the losses of the 1st in the bloody battle, which I have no doubt, long ere this has taken place. Pritchard with some of the young ensigns left us yesterday morning for Portugal,[91] whither they were ordered to proceed to join the first battalion to which they are properly attached.

And now I have but to [sic] questions to ask, which I will thank you to answer in your next: When does the *Fort William* sail for India?[92] & what is William's address in the West Indies? Now that he is removed onboard the *Sceptre*.[93] With my best love to my aunt & all at home, believe me to be your affectionate nephew G U Barlow

89 Marshal Michel Ney Duc d'Elchingen.

90 Marshal Andre Massena, Duc d'Rivoli; *Général de Division* Jean-Andoche Junot, 1st Duc d'Abrantès.

91 Ensign Samuel Pritchard, 52nd Light Infantry.

92 There were three East India Company ships of this name according to the records, but none officially shown as trading in 1810.

93 HMS *Sceptre* of 74 guns.

Ashford Barracks, 9 August 1810

My dear uncle,
You may easily imagine upon my arrival at this place, what was my first question. The regiment has *received no official orders for embarkation*, therefore Greenwood's account was totally false,[94] whilst that of our officer, whom I met in town, was founded in truth. General Brownrigg received an express ordering his immediate return to town on particular business & it is singular enough that the barracks at Shorncliffe remain unoccupied, although perfectly clean & fit for our reception. Something *is in agitation*, & that is all we know; I am however so sick of being thus repeatedly deceived by reports, that I will *never write* to you on this head until the route actually arrives; until which everything is in readiness. Trusting that this may soon happen, I remain, with my love to all, your affectionate nephew G U Barlow

[PS] I sent your greatcoat to Bridge Street, by the coach yesterday from Chatham.

No 33
To Sir G H Barlow Bart KB, Fort St George, Madras
Shorncliffe Barracks, near Dover, 10 August 1810
(annotated received 19 June 1811 by the *Matilda*,[95] answered 23 July 1811)

My dear father,
I am enabled to affix with precision the above number to the present, having at my elbow my book of correspondence. I fear much, however, that several of my letters to my dear mother as well as yourself will never come to hand, so many captures have been reportedly made by the enemy in the East India Sea. Indeed, I can account for the loss of one or two in this manner with certainty.[96]

So you will see by the state of the present, that we shall remain in England; which is so contrary to the wishes and views of myself and friends. It is natural that a professional man should wish to have practical as well as theoretical knowledge of his intended line of life. The term 'friends' is applied by me to the officers of the regiment. If I recollect right I have mentioned previously in a former letter the mere youth of the individuals who compose this battalion, yet are nevertheless veterans in the service & have seen three or four campaigns in the course of as many years under the

94 The Army Agent, Greenwood, Cox & Hammersley of Craig's Court, London.

95 The *Matilda* was not an East India Company vessel at this time. She was built in 1803 at Calcutta and spent most of her years plying trade between England and India and received two refits in English dockyards. She partook in the operations under Lord Minto to capture the Moluccas and Java, sailing from Malacca on 8 June 1811. She did later serve as a HEIC ship for one round passage to England in 1819-20, but was then wrecked off the River Ganges on 5 March 1822, although all hands were saved by a pilot boat.

96 The only missing letter in the series to his father is No. 30.

tuition of Sir John Moore, who turned them into, the whole regiment, Sir John's, as [he was] accustomed to make particular enquiry into the family & character of everyone who proposed himself as a candidate for it. His interest with people in office was so great, that he was thereby marked to exercise the regiment after his own manner. All were accustomed to look up to him as a superior sort of being & completely under his command. This universal opinion, it took him to effect what no other officer in the British Army dared attempt. We by no means follow thus a daily system for our guide. It has received many numerous & very useful alterations from Sir John & is acted upon in this amended state by ourselves & a few other regiments in the army, chiefly light infantry. The force of discipline & of his judicious instructions & example still flourish in their original purity & vigour although he has long since been numbered with the dead. It animates every individual of the corps, who are expected to persist to the last moment of their lives and disseminate the same throughout the service and looking at the list of officers to choose in the course of time the charge of this valuable body of men will be successfully concluded. I am confident that the 52nd will for a long time remain in their present very superior state of discipline & remain a model for the British Army & loyal to [the] illustrious memory of its author. I will conclude the present with recommending to your perusal the narrative of his late campaign in Spain, by his brother, Mr James Moore.[97] I entered the service much prejudiced against the general on that head. The above book leans with the light of correction. To several of my friends & my uncle in particular, who had imbibed similar prejudices, I advised the same prescription & it is with pleasure I add that they also became its converts. To you therefore who are situated at such a distance from the scene of affairs & take such interest in the busy scene of politics, I would recommend the above book. Equally acceptable for the plain & homely style in which it is penned, as the irresistible mass of truth which it contains.

In a word, if I had a child I would put him into the 52nd Regiment in preference to any other, for the same reason which induced General Ross to place his nephew in it. It is as select as the Guards or cavalry without their experience & it is the corps which for many considerations, as I have repeatedly stated in this & former letters & which in my humble opinion are most cogent, is the best calculated to make a man a fine soldier. Talking of General Ross, I am bound in justice to state, that he has always acted towards me the part of a warm & affectionate friend, ever attentive to my interests & has professed himself ready at all times to afford me any aid or assistance of which I may in future stand in need.

An order was published, a week [or] some, for every regiment in the service to send in a return of their strength. This we conclude is preparatory

97 James Moore, brother of Sir John, published *A Narrative of the Campaign of the British Army in Spain, commanded by His Excellency, Lieutenant General Sir John Moore* in 1809, which was so popular that three editions were published that year.

to sending out a reinforcement to Lord Wellington & which, according to the public prints, he seems much to require. Our condition is superior to that of any regiment returned from Walcheren, both in point of strength of numbers and everything else. In that case we are certain to be among the first. It is a great chance, however when these speculations will be realised, our movements being so rapid & sudden, that a change of quarters from one place to another happens at a few hours-notice and this has occurred during the short time I have joined, on two or three occasions. In the meantime, I am entirely employing the period which remains, until I am qualified to obtain my companion [company?] in September 1811', in my preparations for being thoroughly perfect in the duties of a Staff Officer. For as we are situated at such distant & opposite hemispheres of the world, it is highly necessary that there should be a concert [in] our pleas *long before hand* & by this early & mutual communication rendering of the difficulties & disadvantages of time & space. The following is an outline on my last.

I trust that you have received long ere this two or three others begging that as you had promised with your usual goodness to obtain a company, that it should if possible, be procured in the 33rd Regiment. These were detailed at some length in my preceding number, lest however any mischance should have overtaken them, I will recapitulate them under their several heads as briefly as possible.

1st It is a regiment of a single battalion.

2nd There are in the inferior steps no men of rank or influence so that the promotion may be obtained with little difficulty.

3rd It is Sir A. Wellesley's regiment and thereby I shall gain an introduction to the most promising officer of the age.

4th Sir A. will form a second battalion for it on its return to England, which will access a great advancement.

5th It has been so long in India, that the captains will exchange most probably into other Indian regiments. A company obtained therefore before the regiment is ordered home will ensure me several steps by the above exchanges.

I am at present studying mathematics, gunnery, fortification, military topography & drawing, of French I am perfectly master. My Uncle Robert said that whilst at the Neapolitan Court he acquired a very reasonable knowledge of Spanish, in *three weeks,* even with his limited knowledge of Latin.[98] I propose acquiring *both that & Portuguese in two or three months. In all these* various branches of the military art, I intend being tolerably versed by the end of this year & by April or May next, or eight months from hence, I expect to be perfect in every branch of study, so that if you will be so good as to recommend me to the Great Folks at home here, for an aide de camp's or Staff appointment *on actual service,* I will promise to act with efficiency in any department & not to prove myself unworthy by *irresponsibility*

98 He commanded the 74-gun HMS *Triumph* in the Mediterranean from 1801 to 1804.

or *other vice*, to fill any similarly important station which your interest may obtain for your truly dutiful & affectionate son. G U Barlow

PS I shall expect to hear of your receipt of the present in May or June next year, when your answer will find me as above, perfectly prepared. I propose also, if it is allowed, to obtain leave for an examination & inspection by the staff of Wycombe College & receive a certificate of my capability to fill Staff situations [99]

To William Barlow Esq, Streatham, Surrey
+ *Secret & Confidential*
Shorncliffe barracks, 12 August 1812

My dear uncle,
Fred will no doubt have informed you of our arrival at this place. I hailed with no common emotions of joy, the sight of the well known hill and the beautiful prospect all around us & which forms so great a contrast with our late dismal quarters. Unless ordered abroad, I could not wish for any further change in our situation for this summer & autumn.

You will no doubt perceive ere this reaches your eye, an account of the late sharp action near Almeida; as the public prints however teem with such a variety of false or absurd statements, I will state to you the real fact, together with some interesting particulars collected from the letters of an officer of our regiment, *who was on the spot, is on the staff,* & has access daily to the *very best sources* of information in the army, arising from the high & confidential station which he at present fills.

The assailants were commanded by Massena in person & consisted [of] *10,000* infantry, *50* troops of cavalry amounting to between *4 or 5,000* men with 17 pieces of horse artillery. These were opposed *to the Light Brigade or the 43rd, 52nd & 95th Regiments, about 3,000 men. A detachment of the 14th* Light Dragoons & the 1st German Hussars about 700 strong. In all, 3,700 English to which may be added two battalions of Portuguese chasseurs [cacadores] who behaved very well on the occasion & formed a total of 5,500 men under Brigadier General Craufurd. The enemy as I have above shown were treble their numbers. It was [a] night attack,[100] General C[raufurd] received timely notice of their approach, but [for] reasons unknown to us, determined upon standing fast, although he might have easily retreated across the bridge of the Coa without loss. After a severe action General C[raufurd] retired to the opposite bank & there took up a second & very

99 The Royal Military College had been founded by Colonel John Le Marchant in 1799 at the Antelope Inn, in High Street, High Wycombe. Here pupils were trained in trigonometry, geometry, French language and siege warfare in preparation for becoming Staff officers. The institution moved to Farnham in 1813 and in 1820 it became the senior division of the Royal Military College at Sandhurst. It became the Staff College at Camberley in 1858.

100 The attack was actually made at dawn.

strong position & which he held when the last accounts came away. Our loss in men was very trifling as the newspapers have correctly stated; they have not been so accurate with regard to that of the officers. Instead of *15* officers, we have lost no less than *thirty*, *15* of these belonged to the 43rd, 9 to the 95th and the 52nd came off with the loss of but 5,[101] including however *two* out of our *three* field officers, Colonel Barclay & Major Ridewood.[102] Colonel Barclay was suddenly called upon & having lost his cap, was present during the whole of this affair with his *night-cap* in its place & cut a most conspicuous figure. He is wounded in the foot, but Major R[idewood] has a bullet *through his head.* Although the action was fought at the first peep of dawn, the French riflemen were but too successful, in picking off *our* officers & were I understand equally as well paid in *their* own coin. The conduct of the troops on this occasion, & the admirable manner in which the retreat was made during the *heat of the* contest, in the face of so [torn – superior an?] enemy & over a very narrow & small bridge & which is [torn – the most?] difficult of all military operations, is above all praise. This long description would better suit to be addressed to the editor of a newspaper than yourself. You however be well aware that *I never* intended this for the inspection of *anyone* but yourself & most confidential friends; relying therefore upon your usual discreetness, I will give you from time to time give you the most authentic accounts I can collect, on similar subjects & with confidence I remain your affectionate nephew. Give my love to all at home, G U Barlow

Sir George Barlow, 1st Baronet, by an unknown artist. (Public Domain)

Another letter written from Shorncliffe discussed in detail the difficult situation that his father faced in India. Sir George Barlow had been appointed as Governor of the Madras Presidency in February 1808, after the departure of Lord William Bentinck and Lieutenant General Sir John Craddock, who had been the prime cause of the Vellore Mutiny which occurred in July 1806, having attempted to force the sepoy troops to cut their hair and to discard their traditional headwear.

101 Oman gives slightly different figures, showing 28 officers, 1 on the Staff, 13 of the 43rd, 10 of the 95th and only 3 for the 52nd. Total losses were 333 officers and men killed and wounded.

102 Lieutenant Colonel Robert Barclay was wounded at the Coa and again soon after at the Battle of Bussaco. He died of his wounds on 3 May 1811. Major Henry Ridewood was also slightly wounded at the Coa; he transferred to the 45th Foot as a lieutenant colonel in July 1811.

Unfortunately, Sir George can best be described as a 'cold fish' who managed to alienate local society even further, by insisting on his will being obeyed. He isolated himself within a small circle of officials and appeared remote and out of touch to the majority. His handling of the investigation of the conduct of Mr Sherson, a civil servant in charge of laying in stores of rice for famine years, was inept. He dismissed both Mr Sherson and the civil auditor for declaring his accounts correct and the following court case was thrown out. However, the Court of Directors ordered the reinstatement of both men, severely damaging Barlow's reputation.

There had been unrest within the Madras Army for quite some time because of a difference in their pay in comparison with the officers of the residency of Bengal. This situation was made much worse when Lieutenant General Hay McDowall was promoted to be Commander in Chief of the Madras Army in 1807 and the Court of Directors declined to offer the general the traditional and lucrative office of a seat in council. McDowall saw this as a personal affront and did nothing to hide his views on the subject in front of his officers. It was at this delicate point that Sir George Barlow arrived and immediately embarked on a number of cost-saving reforms, which denied traditional perks to the officers of the Madras Army. To be fair, the new governor was only applying the reforms demanded by the Council of Directors and had been intended to be implemented by his predecessors, but his character was not one for sugar-coating the essential pill and his unpopularity grew even deeper. Colonel John Munro had investigated the perk of 'tent contract' which had been designed to give the commanding officers of regiments money to provide camp equipment when in the field. The money had, however, been paid whether the troops were in the field or in their cantonments and had become a lucrative perk. Munro had been the one to recommend that it should end, commenting that it placed the interests and duty of commanding officers in opposition. The officer corps, angrily seeking redress, demanded that Munro was court martialled for casting aspersions on their good character. The Advocate General ruled that Munro had no case to answer, but McDowall, on the eve of his leaving for England and retirement, had Munro arrested. The governor promptly demanded his release, which McDowall complied with, but he gave vent to his anger in an extraordinary General Order attacking Munro and then promptly sailed for England.

Up until this point in the proceedings, Sir George had acted with great dignity, but he unfortunately chose to reply in a counter-order, with an equally poorly worded rant against the general and his outrageous conduct. Sir George ignored the general's impending resignation and sacked him; and went further by suspending his Deputy Adjutant General, Major Thomas Boles for signing the General Order. Major Boles claimed that it was his duty to sign off his superior's orders and he was seen very much as a martyr by the army officers and a subscription was proposed to compensate him for his loss of earnings.

Three months passed in which McDowall was to find a watery grave as his homeward-bound ship foundered. A memorial had been prepared by the officers during the height of the troubles, but as the upset began to wane, it was decided not to send it to the Court of Directors. Unfortunately however, someone smuggled a copy to them, causing Sir George to react furiously on 1 May 1809, ordering the suspension or removal from command of a dozen senior officers of the Madras Army. This was the final straw for the officers and open mutiny was talked of.

One hundred and fifty-eight officers of the Jaulna and Hyderabad divisions signed an address to the governor, demanding that he repeal the order and restore the officers to their positions 'to prevent the horrors of civil war, and the ultimate loss of a large portion of the British possessions in India, and the dreadful blow it would inflict on the mother country'. The Company's regiment stationed at Masulipatam broke out in mutiny, arresting their commanding officer, and planning to join the two divisions in a march on Madras to remove the government. At this moment, Colonels John Malcolm and Thomas Gage Montresor,[103] amongst other senior officers, recommended leniency and the suspension of the offending order, to placate the officers. However, Sir George had witnessed at first hand the results of acting timidly in such dangerous circumstances, having seen the mess Sir John Shore (Governor General 1793-8) had got into during the officer revolt at Bengal in 1796, whilst he had served as Secretary to the government in Calcutta. He determined on brazening it out and putting down the mutiny with a fist of iron. The new commander in chief at Madras, Major General Sir Samuel Auchmuty, and all the senior officers supported his stance and he could count on the entire loyalty of the King's troops. He also called for further forces from Bengal, Bombay and Ceylon, having determined to take the mutineers on in open battle if necessary. To identify those who remained loyal and almost certainly to challenge waverers, he demanded that all officers signed a pledge to obey the orders and support the authority of the Governor at Fort St George, on pain of removal from their regiments to posts on the coast, but not forfeiture of their rank and pay. The officer corps, seeing themselves as gentlemen, whatever their view of the situation, refused on mass to sign such a declaration and less than 10 percent did sign. The commanders of regiments were ordered to assemble their sepoys and to explain to them that this was a dispute with their white officers and that they should refrain from becoming involved. This was a potentially dangerous act, but it luckily worked with all but the Seringapatam garrison agreeing to maintain their loyalty and to take their salt. The native troops at Seringapatam were fired upon by the King's troops and about one hundred and fifty men killed and wounded. Such energetic action by the governor took the mutinous officers by surprise and they held off breaking out into open rebellion.

They were further assuaged by the Governor General Lord Minto's announcement of his intention of coming to Madras as he had a high reputation for fairness and moderation. On 11 August the Hyderabad Brigade wrote a penitent letter to Lord Minto, signed the pledge and advised their fellow officers throughout the presidency to follow suit. This broke the back of the revolt and the troops returned to their various garrisons. A general amnesty was granted by Lord Minto to the Hyderabad officers for the example they had set the army. In total 21 officers were dismissed or chose to resign, although later all those dismissed were reinstated. The recriminations rebounded for years and after many protests Sir George Barlow was recalled on 21 May 1813, handing over to John Abercromby. His son wrote with nothing but praise for the actions of his father.

103 Montresor commanded at Secunderabad.

No. 34
To Sir G H Barton Bart KB, Fort St George Madras. Per *Barbadoes* frigate[104]
Shorncliffe Barracks, 2 September 1810
(Annotated received 19 January 1811 by the *Matilda*, answered 14 March)
Age 18 years 10 months 23 days

My dearest father,
Though late, yet most sincere and I trust not less acceptable, are my congratulations on the late glorious & successful suppression of the discontents & rebellions of the Madras Army, which have been terminated by you in a manner the most masterly & decisive. Accept then, the effusions of a heart overflowing with joy, which it hastens to pour forth without the least reserve before so kind a parent, which at every stroke of the pen becomes more fixed in a recollection of the past & looks forward to your future fare with the most animated sensations of hope and gladness.

Your proclamations on Mc Dowall's departure, and the subsequent arrest of Boles & Capper reached England in September last and were the first harbingers of any trouble, existing in our eastern empire.[105] Soon after arrival they made their appearance in the public prints at various intervals, in a loose unconnected manner & although at first, from these documents some idea might be collected of McDowall's iniquities, still the more precise details were for some time & for reasons unknown by us, withheld from the public eye. All the same forms of power, placed such entire confidence on the wisdom & justice [of] your measures, that they, in common with myself, awaited with a natural anxiety, though unmixed with the least particle of doubt or fear, the narrative of those transactions & according to the utmost extent of our wishes, does the almost unanimous conscience of the nation pronounce that 'so signal an offence ought to have been expiated by a punishment equally signal' & that it has been acted out by you in exact proportion to the nature of the crime. Matters remained thus until the arrival of dispatches from Governor Maitland at Ceylon,[106] the contents of which never were suffered to transpire even in that demi official manner, by which the nation is generally apprised of the nature of similar communications. In the meanwhile, some of your most inveterate enemy's in a certain street, propagated with too much industry & success these soul [sic] contents. This however, is a most garbled & questionable [statement?]. The *most earnest of sealed enquiries* was immediately made, by your friends &

104 HMS *Barbadoes* commanded by Captain Brian Hodgson was a fifth-rate frigate of 28 guns, which was commissioned into the Royal Navy in 1804, having previously been a French privateer named the *Braave*, captured on 16 March 1803. The *Barbadoes* was wrecked on Sable Island, Nova Scotia, on 28 September 1812. She was carrying $60,000 in coinage when she went down, but it was recovered as buoys had been tied to the money chests, allowing them to be found.

105 Colonels Burnaby Boles and James Capper of the East India Company. Boles died in September 1809.

106 Lieutenant General the Honourable Thomas Maitland, was Governor of Ceylon 1805-11.

the uniform answer desired from the best sources of intelligence, at home in the court, as well as at the Board of Controul [sic] was, that no such accounts had been received by any of those authorities. *Deceived* thus by your friends in office at home, your family denied in toto the whole of what afterwards appeared so true & *positively, boldly & uniformly,* contradicted all reports of mutinies at Hyderabad or Seringapatam. I pursued the same line of conduct & confiding in what I deemed such authentic intelligence, am free to confess that very little anxiety or uneasiness agitated my mind during the whole of what afterwards appeared to have been, so alarming a crisis. Independent of the above considerations, the horrible word 'rebellion' sounded quite unusual to an Englishman's ear, after the dreadful scenes exhibited in France. It appeared a strange phenomenon, a character which I did not think could be generated in a British heart. All the wicked paragraphs in the papers, conveyed to me no other sensations except those of contempt at what I learned, such impotent & ridiculous malignity!

Matters remained in this train until the arrival of the *Rattlesnake*,[107] the latter end of March, when the whole truth stood revealed in all its native deformity. Cheering was the intelligence which served at once to crush the hopes of the ill-disposed, dispel the fears of those who were in the secret & to open the eyes of us all who were ignorant of the real state of affairs. I blessed a thousand times that policy, which had kept our minds in the dark and rendered us insensible to danger until it was past & the whole business was finally settled & with such distinguished credit to yourself, we might almost exclaim with the poet Claudian 'plerique sui praevenet laurea belli'.[108] This line might well be applied to all of us who were *at one* informed of the *beginning & termination* of the late civil war.

Whilst on a visit to Streatham for a few days in August last, my Uncle William put the whole of the original documents and correspondence into my hands for perusal, comprising Lord Minto's letter, your despatches, those of Colonel Davis,[109] Mr Cole[110] and your various subordinate heads in the military and civil departments, as printed and laid before the House of Commons & above all your proclamations during the different stages of the disturbance. In these last, I am at a loss whether most to admire the real & genuine British sentiments of elan and government which they breathe in every line, or the unequalled torrent of argument & eloquence with which these principles are enforced. I do not hesitate to pronounce them superior to anything of the kind I have ever read, either in ancient or modern history, they have been quoted by ministers at the House of Commons in terms of the highest praise & have been noticed with the peculiar approbation of the Court of Directors. It has fallen to the lot of few to contend against greater

107 HMS *Rattlesnake* of 16 guns.

108 Claudius Claudianus, 370-404 AD. The Latin signifies 'Earns most of its laurels by preventing war'.

109 Colonel Henry Davis commanded at Mysore.

110 Mr Arthur Henry Cole was the Residency Secretary at Mysore.

difficulties, to stem the worst torrent of insurrection in which had been accumulating for past years, than yourself; situated amidst an inadequate and factious soldiery & with a number of your civil servants & those too of the highest rank in avowed hostility to the measures of government, threatened with the dangers of war & with the population of the Indian Empire, you have guided the whole in safety through these discordant elements of continual commotion. You have passed through the firey ordeal of difficulty and I trust will attain your due rewards. Both sides of the house are your firm supporters. *In a full,* we all agreed on this one point, your name & deeds have now been emblazoned throughout the British Empire, not the smallest or remotest corner of the wide world will be ignorant of your achievements, nor does there exist one sincere friend to good order & justice who does not hail you as the saviour of the Eastern world.

I have frequently poured [over] all the pamphlets, papers and documents respecting this late business and flatter myself that I could argue the whole case against the keenest disputant in the world. I am sorry that you did not cause more copies of Lord Minto's letter to be printed. We have procured the whole mass of papers laid before the House of Commons & I read with the highest exultation therein the recorded opinions of the Court of Directors in your favour. I declare that had I been their chief secretary, I could not have wished to have penned despatches in more ample terms of encomium, all excepting that paragraph respecting Boles' supersession, an opinion which I am glad to see them recant in their next despatch. I trust that this second letter will follow quickly on the heels of the first, and relieve you from the sensations which I know you must feel, on beholding an unfavourable sentiment expressed against that part of your conduct which you must have been conscious described [with] as great a degree of praise, as any part of your measures through the whole of that affair. I allude to that paragraph in the dispatch, which says 'that the suspension of Boles should have been but temporary and directing him to be restored to his rank'. I will conclude the point with giving you my opinion reflecting Buchan[an]'s pamphlet.[111] Great merit is due to Mr B[uchanan] for the judicious manner in which the whole statement is drawn up and which renders the subject easy and familiar to the most ordinary reader. I have read all the tracts and pamphlets that have been published by the other party and in my humble opinion the above work at one bound sweeps away the whole of the flimsy cobwebs of sophistry, which your accusers have so notoriously wove and now that you may long live to enjoy the honour & fame, when your existing through so many years have most meritoriously perchance, that future rewards & distinctions may await so deserving a possessor is the sincerest prayer of his truly dutiful & affectionate son G U Barlow

111 This was in fact the Reverend Claudius Buchanan, a missionary in Bengal who wrote a pamphlet on the situation there.

His next letter from Shorncliffe to his father, discussed orators at some length, both ancient and modern, having been to the House of Commons to listen to the debates. He also made a few remarks on his brother's new school at Brasenose.

No 35
Shorncliffe, 3 September 1810 (annotated – received 19 January 1811 by the *Matilda* answered 13 March)
To Sir G H Barlow Bart KB. Fort St George, Madras – By *Barbadoes* frigate

My dearest father,
As an attentive perusal of Mr Burke's writings & taking a view of his acknowledged abilities & character, it has frequently been to me a source of wonder that so eminent man and of such universally acclaimed worth, never held a higher station in the ministry of which he was a member, than that of Paymaster General to the Forces,[112] this latter office required more integrity than talents and generally put the lot of those, who were distinguished for family influence or some mere considerations, rather than genius. Mr B[urke]'s auditors begin now to grow scarce; all however allowed that there was one essential flaw in his eloquence, one which Gaius,[113] Demosthenes[114] and all the best orators of antiquity deemed a point of the highest importance, namely *delivery& action*. Mr Burke's *voice* was said to be weak and of little power, neither did his gestures testify the ardour and sublimity of his mind. I should wish to learn from yourself whether this information is correct for such authority in anything relating to Sir B[urke], I hold to be orthodox. This deficiency must in my opinion have greatly injured the effect of such intended eloquence. Figure to yourself any of Shakespeare's best soliloquys or speeches delivered in so insipid tones on the stage, the whole spirit of the passage is utterly lost & sings past idly like the breeze and the same in your closet, when your senses no longer are dumbed with the tortures of a bad actor and you at once are elevated into the regions of sublimity.

Mr Burke's composition & speeches when on paper, possess the latter power in a huge degree and may we with the much-orchestrated efforts of human talent; if this had been accompanied with a suitable delivery, what electric influence must it have [imparted?] on his hearers. To attain force and eloquence in this respect, the labours of Demosthenes are well known; Cicero[115] imitating so illustrious a model, used frequently to contend with Persius the actor, who should less express their ideas on a subject. The reformer by *speaking*, the latter *by action*. Thereby admitting the high value

112 Sir Edmund Burke MP, author of the pamphlet *Reflections on the Revolution in France* in 1790 and also founder of the *Annual Register*. He was Paymaster General for only four months in 1782.

113 Gaius Aurelius Cotta, a Roman statesman and orator 124-73 BC.

114 A Greek statesman and orator, 384-322 BC.

115 Marcus Tullius Cicero, a Roman politician and orator, 106-43 BC.

of the second endearment. Quintilian[116] whom we reckon as the *non plus ultra*[117] of rhetoricians, devotes many pages & chapters of his works to this important article. The word rhetoric signifying a person who taught the act of speaking according to established rules & methods, rather than an actor, for which however it is sometimes corruptly used.

The above opinions flow from what I have personally felt and witnessed in the House of Commons. I naturally expected on witnessing this force & of the learning & talent of Great Britain, to behold some grand spectacle. The first speaker was Mr Windham guess my disappointment at seeing a man whose voice was scarcely audible & whose action seemed rather suitable to a clerk sagaciously acquiring trust & class behind his desk in engaging with a Jew or shop keeper, rather than that of a British senator, animated with the fire of genius, should discussing the most important national questions now & then carve out a bon motte or piece of irony which convulsed the house with laughter.[118] I sat in the rear while yawning and at last went to eat beef steaks at Mr Bellamy's Coffee House.[119] In the papers next morning the speech cut a very good figure and was highly applauded by all.

Mr W[indham] was reckoned a first-rate man in parliament, of what must then the ordinary melee of mere citoyens be comprised. I do declare that our little mock House of Commons at Eton contained speakers better than most of those whom I have beheld attempting to harangue the Great Council of the Nation. In short, I have not the least hesitation in declaring that I was most miserably disappointed. That to us altogether Sir George Canning however, a splendid exception & is an Etonian, and in his oratory, both as to style and action, breathes forth the genuine Roman Playhouse. Next to him may be ranked Lord Grey[120] of the same school and here I cannot refrain from passing a few compliments on our alma mater. There is still nourished the real enthusiasm of classic learning there & there alone does it flourish in its seasonal purity, can there be a greater proof of the truth of this assertion, than that the best classics *at both* the universities come from hence and bear off all the prizes & laurels to deck the brow of their illustrious parents, in that every day's experience convinces me, that his system of character is preferable to that of any man in existence. Let the child be first of all raised in one of his manners, be thoroughly grounded in the first, the only. Unless this circumstance is most pointedly attended to, all efforts to erect an extensive, or at least one of any beauty, will be altogether vain. I do not approve of Robert's School in many respects, he however was capable of instilling the first rudiments of the pure languages

116 Marcus Fabius Quintilanus, a Roman rhetorician 35-100 AD.
117 Latin. 'The last word in, or the best.'
118 William Windham died on 4 June 1810.
119 Mr John Bellamy, Deputy Housekeeper in the Palace of Westminster, ran a coffee house in an upstairs room on the eastern side of Old Palace Yard. A bell fixed in the wall rang if Members of Parliament were required to attend the House to vote.
120 Charles Grey, 2nd Earl Grey.

very well & no further, for his abilities were unequal to the task. Then let the tender root be transported to Eton and if it be of the proper genus, no soil is so well calculated for its future growth. This fact however must be carefully ascertained in the first instance, that garden is equally adapted to the culture of the choicest fruits or the rankest weeds. Nowhere does idleness, larceny and vice of every description walk with more personal or better opportunity to exercise greater success and encouragement & less restraint, yet on the other hand I never beheld finer fields for the practise of talent, or in which diligence & application were more noticed or rewarded or where there is a greater stimulus to all the nobler professions. Two of the most heterogenous qualities are there beheld united in the most wonderful manner. It is the best or the very worst of places. Reflections after nearly five years residence convinces me of this truth and entitles my humble opinion on that head to some degree of credit. I shall take leave of our old house with the following pious exclamation, used by a fellow partaker of her bounty.

> Te safe pus mea lumina artes
> Respicienta carum nomen etona, vale[121]

I think that I have frequently heard you express a wish to have some of my exercises at school in your possession. The three which were deemed fit *'to be sent up for you'* (as the package says) have been sent out to you. That honour was intended to be inserted in No's 1 & 2 (enclosed) the same week. This was not altogether required and Mr Carter saves his choice of No. 1[122] in preference of that of Dr Goodall's for No. 2.[123] It was a source of satisfaction to me the same as if both had received those rewards. Mr C[arter] however soon after litened [sic] upon No. 3. I look back with much pleasure on the moments which have been passed in their company and which I am now convinced have been spent to so much purpose & profit, tracing the successive improvements apparent in each as I became older, and extended my reading and imagination. Those that I like best are marked thus + the enclosed budget contains the best of my later performances.

Classic learning is a most inestimable treasure. Decked in the varied colours of fancy it heightens every scene, improves open thought in all times & certain times of life supplies you with resources of every description as it were from an inexhaustible stream, every fleeting thought and moment, the varied takes of sculpture and art and even chaos and order, are occurrences of life when touched by its magic wand, assume new appearances and shapes, such as are under, except to the eyes of his chosen few. I recommended Henry therefore to lay in as large a stock as possible of this invaluable treasure preceding his entering Brasenose College and above all

121 Latin: 'So you are safe with my enlightening skills, Eton is looking expensive, goodbye'.
122 The Reverend Thomas Carter, Vice Provost of Eton.
123 Dr (of divinity) Joseph Goodall, Provost of Eton.

that he should regularly send you out his compositions & verses.[124] These last are to be at once the best oratories of a boy's diligence, reading Hardy & Genesis are a portfolio to be trusted in this respect, [showing?] the rise and fall of the lead character denoting the true nature of the atmosphere.

And now in pursuance of Colonel Ross's request I beg you will give me in your next line, information respecting his brother in India.[125] The colonel wrote to him some years ago, has received no answer or letter since and if I understand it right, the general & Harriet & his family have been especially unnoticed by him. Any particulars communicated to me, respecting the probable place of abode, or anything which you may conceive interesting to Colonel Ross, will greatly oblige. Your dutiful & affectionate son. G U Barlow

[PS] Perhaps you would wish in preference, to address a letter to the Colonel himself.

In his next letter George revealed that he had developed an infection in his arm and he had a large swelling.

To William Barlow Esq, Streatham, Surrey
Shorncliffe Barracks, 8 November 1810

My dear uncle,
In reply to your last I have to inform you that the swelling in my arm lately increased to an abscess of a prodigious size so as equally to astonish myself & the surgeon. This was attended with such an increased pain throughout that whole side, together with a swelling of that arm, so that I could neither sit, sleep, eat or do anything & I felt much weakened by a fortnight's confinement & want of rest, being obliged to lie always on my back at night. In this state although the swelling was not quite so forward as could be wished, the surgeon punctured it to give me relief. This has been attended with the desired effect & I am now much better & recovering. These cases are however very tedious & it will be ten days or a fortnight yet to come before I can lay aside my sling. You see my writing is now a little more legible & does not give me near so much pain as before. I will rigidly obey your advice reflecting colds at this time of the year. I can form an adequate idea of the difficulties under which you all labour at Streatham; but alas I can only condole with you & of what use is that? I see by the papers that the *Plover* has sailed from Portsmouth on *a cruise*;[126] William has there-

124 This was his younger brother, John Henry Barlow, born 7 December 1795, who became a senior merchant in India and eventually succeeded to the baronetcy. He died in 1841. Brasenose College was founded in Oxford in 1509.
125 I have been unable to identify his brother with any certainty.
126 HMS *Plover*, a sloop of 18 guns, was engaged in capturing enemy privateers in the English Channel.

fore most probably landed at Portsmouth. Perhaps it is an error of the press & she is come round to the Downs. I also read that a *Captain Pellew* (of course Pownoll is here meant) has sailed from *Plymouth* in a sloop of war, to join his ship at Portsmouth.[127] This to me is news but was driven back into *Falmouth* by an easterly wind. I am your affectionate nephew G U B

To William Barlow Esq, Streatham, Surrey
Shorncliffe Barracks, 15 November 1810

My dear uncle,
This last bulletin will announce to you my hopes of a speedy recovery, since puncturing the swelling has continued gradually to decrease. It will be some time however, before it totally disappears, so as to restore me the full use of that arm. In a few days I trust to appear as usual on parade, with the enjoyment of that liberty of exercise, of which till now I never have felt the loss. My confinement having now lasted nearly a month, as soon as these cold winds depart, I propose applying to the sons of Galen for some of their good strong port wine.[128]

I am much concerned at your accounts of Henry; to be expelled at a time when he is just on the eve of leaving Eton would be the height of folly; some allowances are to be made for a boy who is high in school and whose personal qualifications mark him out as a leading man in vows; but it is exactly the reverse with Henry's, neither his rank, stature, or anything else, select him for this dangerous post. He need not make himself conspicuous, but act a passive part and follow with the stream unnoticed. He will become the dupe & cat's paw of the bigger boys, if he pursues a different line of conduct. I shall write to him most fully on this subject, according to your wish, blowing him up, at the same time for not answering my former letter. With regard to the fees, on taking leave £30 will be most ample, £15 for Mr Keate & the like sum for my tutor. I who was in the sixth form gave but £40, you will of course engage him faithfully to pay the above sums, as I well know that it was a practise [torn – for?] some to give but £10 to each of the above persons; reserving the remainder to themselves & Henry I know, may be easily persuaded by specious arguments; to conceive this by no means a dishonourable trick; independent of this it is my father's wish to act with liberality on each occasion & you know that after having provided the means, it would be a great pity that his wishes should be disappointed, by so great a pervertion [sic] of them.

William's last letter to me of the 8th instant, announces his arrival on board the *Royal William*.[129] He states that Pownoll had embarked

127 This refers to his brother-in-law, Captain the Honourable Pownoll Bastard Pellew RN, who by 1812 had switched to a political career, becoming an MP.

128 I presume that he meant Cale, the Romans having called Portugal Portus Cale.

129 HMS *Royal William*, was an ancient warship, having been first commissioned in 1670. In 1790 she was refitted to 84 guns and employed as a guard ship. She was finally broken up in 1813.

at Plymouth with the intention of paying a visit to Admiral Halstead at Gosport & that upon being driven into Falmouth,[130] he had gone ashore & commenced his journey thither by land. I am also given to understand that myself together with twelve others are soon to be created uncles and aunts. William has also promised to come & see upon his landing at Deal; whither I shall also repair to call upon the Pellews as soon as my arm will permit.[131] Bye the bye the mare is very healthy, in capital condition & flesh & continues every day to encrease [sic] her worth in my [torn -stable?]. Indeed, I never heard of an animal so faulty in every respect; with the single exception of carrying her saddle, which I have in some degree remedied *by adding* an additional girth & having it frequently stuffed towards her withers.

You may inform my aunt that I have procured the gloves but dare not risk them by any other conveyance than that of my own pockets. You may therefore expect them together with myself about the middle of next month and now I have only to regret the absence of my Spanish books. Those at present in my possession are most wretched; with this aid however, such as it is, I have contrived to make considerable progress supported by my knowledge of latin, now however I am perfectly at a standstill. I will write to Mr Melbourne a letter of thanks or a [present?] for his bother in procuring them. And now with my love to my aunt & all at home, I remain your affectionate nephew G U Barlow

Eventually George could report that the troops were in movement prior to a deployment.

To William Barlow Esq, Little Bridge Street, Blackfriars, London
Shorncliffe Barracks, 27 November 1810

My dear uncle,
By my last I was left in a state of perfect convalescence & I am now enabled to inform you of my complete recovery. On the 18th instant William's arrival was announced by a letter dated from Deal; this took place on the Monday and for many reasons I decided upon setting off thither the next morning without delay, although my arm was still rather weak. Immediately I paid my respects to the admiral at Walmer & in half an hour afterwards, went off in a gig on board the flag-ship;[132] where my early appearance was by no means expected. My brother appears to be in an excellent state of health, just the same as ever, stout, and I think encreased [sic] in height, although his acquaintance with the young mids was scarcely of 48 hours duration, he was perfectly free & intimate with them all. The next day I went off again

130 Rear Admiral Lawrence Halsted.
131 George's elder sister, Elizabeth-Harriet, born 21 January 1790, had married Captain Pownoll-Bastard Pellew on 1 October 1808. She was pregnant and was due at any moment.
132 This refers to Vice Admiral Sir Edward Pellew who was then commander-in-chief of the North Sea Fleet.

at twelve o'clock, dined in the cockpit by candlelight with his mess, drank grog in the place of beer or water as they all do & took William, with Sir Edward's permission, ashore; where we spent four or five very pleasant days, dining constantly at Walmer. The whole family joined heartily in quizzing him about his fears of the admiral; Sir Edward [Pellew] himself taking an active part. He however ended the business with telling my brother that they should certainly be very good friends. Captain P[ellew]'s address and manners by no means characterize the man he is represented to be; and in spite of the testimony of so many credible witnesses, there must have been a great deal of exaggeration on that head.

And now to the great surprize of all and especially at this time of the year, there is a general movement about to take place throughout the greater part of the Kent district, into that of Sussex. The Light Brigade are to be quartered two or three day's march from Portsmouth; at Little Hampton, Arundel, Bognor &c &c. We are to be stationed at Lewes, for which place the regiment will set out on Friday & Saturday next, through Rye, Winchelsea & Battle. I will not fail to apprize you of our arrival, as soon as it takes place.

I have had a long letter from Henry, who states that all is quiet at Eton; he seems to take it ill that I had suspected him of joining in the rebellion. By his account the mutineers appear to have been suppressed & subsequently expelled; all intention of co-operation is denied on his part & Keate's threats in his opinion seem to have been made with a view of intimidating him from further riot & disturbance in school,[133] rather than in earnest. He wishes me to inform him of the proper amount of fees which it will be necessary for him to give on taking leave. I think £15 for Keate & a like sum to his tutor, would be very handsome for a boy in his part of the school.

If you should happen to call at the vicarage, inform cousin Fanny that Pritchard's letter was sent to Plymouth according to her sister's wish, immediately on the arrival of the last dispatches from Lord Wellington.[134] Give also my compliments to Mr & Mrs Langdale, telling them of my late disaster & informing them that it took place the very day after I had the pleasure of dining with them & that I was thereby unable either to pay my respects to them in person, or even to write a note & when my servant carried thither a message in about five or six days afterwards they were gone from Sandgate.

And now with my kind love to my aunt & all at home, together with a speedy deliverance from all your troubles, the distressing nature of which I can easily conceive & most sincerely lament is the constant hope & wish of your truly affectionate nephew G U Barlow

133 John Keate became Headmaster of Eton in 1809 and took on the task of dealing with the unruly boys, this led to a number of disturbances.

134 Frances Barlow, the eldest daughter of his uncle Robert Barlow, born in 1787; Frances' sister was Hilare Barlow.

To William Barlow Esq, Little Bridge Street, Blackfriars, London
Lewes, 6 December 1810

My dear uncle,
We arrived here yesterday about one o'clock, entering the place with band playing, bugles sounding, in short making all the noise we possibly could. Weather during our march has been very favourable; the roads are however in a wretched state. Our route lay through Winchelsea, Battle, Hailsham and other places of very little note & which were unable to furnish us with a sufficient number of billets. Officers and men were dispersed over the country in every direction & some after finishing the day's march were forced to proceed six, seven or eight miles into the interior through bye lanes almost impassable or wading up to their knees in water whilst crossing the lowlands, which are here inundated to a great extent by the late heavy rains. I was so fortunate as to escape all these disagreeable circumstances. On Saturday we were conveyed from Shorncliffe to Rye & Winchelsea and by the great military canal across Romney Marsh. Sunday was observed by us, as with *all* good Christians, as a day of rest. I took the opportunity of riding over to Hastings, where I met Colonel Halkett,[135] together with the major & his wife opposite Barry's Library.[136] They are intimately acquainted with Colonel Ross & most of our officers & perceiving that my friend & myself were 52nd's they came up to us & we conversed together for some time. At Battle I dined with the 36th and was for the first time introduced to my new tent.[137]

By the above account you will perceive that I have spent very pleasantly my time; my good little grey has had however a deal of work. On Monday the Baggage Guard fell to my lot; on Tuesday I was sent forward by the commanding officer to collect the men quartered in all the bye-villages round about, on all of which occasions I was permitted to ride.

You were no doubt somewhat surprized last week by the arrival of a hamper directed to Little Bridge Street. I forgot to advise you of this in my last or even my reasons for so doing. General Murray informed us one day, that we might expect on *that very evening*, a route for Portsmouth to embark for Portugal. My first step was to send away the cargo of wine; not half of which is yet drank & which I will thank you to preserve for me, until our destination is made known, *six bottles only*, have been drunk out of the 2 dozen, all of which are safely packed in the top of the hamper. All this part of the coast is full of troops as far as Portsmouth so that in a few days, I trust our doubts will be cleared up, at present all is conjecture.

135 Lieutenant Colonel Colin Halkett who then commanded the 2nd Light Battalion King's German Legion.
136 Mr James Barry had opened a subscription library at Hastings on Marine Parade, it was later renamed Diplock's library.
137 The 36th Foot (Herefordshire).

Eliza writes me word that my aunt has lately been very ill; so much so that all the children have been sent to Mrs Platt's; this is a circumstance of which I have been hither to totally ignorant, otherwise I should have been much alarmed. My good fortune has concealed from me this fresh source of uneasiness & this is a mistake, it is old Peter who is dangerously ill. [piece missing- This?] I trust, leaves me now no other tasks than that of rejoicing in her speedy & regained state of health. And now with my kind love to all believe me to be, your affectionate nephew, G U Barlow

Sir Colin Halkett by William Salter. (Public Domain)

George continued to prepare for embarkation, but was beginning to lose faith in it occurring any time soon.

To William Barlow Esq, Streatham, Surrey
Lewes, 16 December 1810

My dear uncle,
The risk of seizure to which the hamper of wine was liable, had not escaped my notice. Two or three days previous to our departure from Shorncliffe I applied to the Excise Officer at Hythe & Sandgate for a permit, which they refused me, adding that I must go to Dover and make an affidavit that I had not more than a dozen or two [bottles] of wine in the hamper; a great deal of form and ceremony must have been gone through, the same as you was about to remove the whole of your stock from Little Bridge Street. There was no time left for a journey to Dover; a route was hourly expected from Canterbury, I determined therefore to make it run the gauntlet of all the swarms of custom house officers & men.

I shall make every exertion in my power to come up and eat my Christmas dinner with you all; but this is everything that can be expected on my part & no more. An air of mystery seems to pervade the actions of our superiors; an officer who lives but *eighteen miles* distance from hence is not allowed to visit his friends, although it is his turn to have leave. What right can I therefore claim for a similar indulgence [?]. Nothing to me is so painful as suspense, in this instance [it is] the more provoking as it detains myself and many others from taking our turn of absence from the regiment, assure us for certain that we are ultimately to go out of the kingdom & everyone would be content. My fears suggest, that this state of uncertainty, will continue until the latter end of February or the beginning of March next, when we shall arrive in time for the opening of the campaign. In the meanwhile, everything is ready prepared to start at an hour's notice. Yesterday we were reviewed on the Downs by Lord Charles Somerset,[138] the most flattering encomiums were paid us on the occasion; but their value was much diminished on a consideration of the bestower, whose praises Sir John Moore had taught us sufficiently to appreciate, when reviewed by him some years ago. The story is too long for a letter, but I will relate it to you on our first meeting. The character & pretensions of the regiment to worth, might be justly disputed, if it rested on no other foundation than Lord C[harles]'s encomiums, who to say the truth is no soldier or *judge* in such matters. Luckily however our reputation is established, by the opinions of more competent men. In short, though Lord C[harles]'s praises were merited, he cannot *himself* form an opinion, whether they were justly applied or no.

It is not in my power to give you a satisfactory reply concerning William, as I have not heard from him since last at Deal. The *Ch*[torn] was only to undergo some temporary repairs and cleaning her copper &c &c and would of course be in dock a few weeks. Whilst this took place, my brother informed me of his intention to apply for leave of absence in order to pay you a visit; he expressed himself in the warmest terms of gratitude & affection to you for your literal conduct at Hertford in the settlement of his bills; owning how deeply he was sorry for the past & how great a sense he entertained of your kindness, on that as well as many other occasions; all of which came from his heart spontaneously & uttered with the genuine candour of truth.

And now give my kind love to all at home, telling my aunt how glad I am to hear that all my alarms were unfounded & believe me to be, your most affectionate nephew, G U Barlow

To William Barlow Esq, Streatham, Surrey
Lewes, 6 January 1811

My dear uncle,
Since writing my last I have been able to obtain the long wished for leave of absence, you may therefore expect to see me by dinner time on Tuesday or Wednesday next. Much depends upon the state of the weather, which will determine also my choice of those two days. Being very low in pocket & not having wherewithal to settle my debts and provide myself with several things of which I stand in need. Necessity has compelled me to break through your rule; I have therefore drawn a bill on you for £47 payable at Messrs Glyn & Co. a liberty, which for the reasons above stated, I hope you will excuse.[139]

---

138 The second son of Henry Somerset, 5th Duke of Beaufort, and brother to Edward and Fitzroy Somerset, both of whom rose to high rank in the army. Charles was also in the army but had a less notable career, being Joint Paymaster of the Forces from 1804-6 and 1807-13; he then became Governor of Cape Colony from 1814-26.

139 A private bank originally known as Glyn, Mills & Co. was established in 1753 and nearly went bankrupt in 1772, when an additional investor meant it became known as Glyn, Halifax, Mills & Co.

As I propose riding up the mare, be so good as to let me know whether you can house my servant? If not, she shall stand at livery at the leaping bar. Perhaps the room in the hay loft is vacant & will do for him admirably. You know that he can assist John in your horses, wait at table or do anything else you may wish. Be so good as to send me a line by Monday evening's post so as to reach me on Tuesday. With my love to all, I remain your affectionate nephew G U Barlow

Finally George was able to inform his uncle of his embarkation.

To William Barlow Esq, Streatham, Surrey
To Be Delivered Immediately
Portsmouth, Friday [25 January 1811?] evening, 6 o'clock

My dear uncle,
The point is just on the point of setting & scarcely leaves me time to inform you of my arrival at this place, having been sent forward by Major Gibbs to give the Embarkation Returns to General Wetham, Governor of Portsmouth.[140] I left the regiment at Chichester where they halt for this night. Captain Pierrepont, the general's Brigade Major tells me that we are to embark tomorrow, the instant we march in at one o'clock in the boats of the fleet on board the *Revenge* of 74 guns & *Argo* of 44 guns & as soon as the 36th Regiment come in on *Monday next*,[141] we shall sail that *very evening*, of the wind continues fair as it now is, so urgent are the orders on this head for dispatch & speed. You see I am in haste & have therefore just time to acknowledge the safe arrival of the portmanteau &c &c but no letter for General Spencer or from yourself.[142] I will come ashore on Sunday morning to the Post Office, for anything you may have to send or write. I am in great hurry, but will write more fully by Sunday's post & have to add, with my dear love to my aunt & all at home, that I remain your affectionate nephew G U Barlow

140 Major General Arthur Whetham was governor of Portsmouth from 1809-10. Captain Charles Pierrepont 20th Foot, returned to the Peninsula in 1811 and was killed in action in September 1812.

141 HMS *Revenge* of 74 guns, Captain Charles Paget and HMS *Argo* of 44 guns, Captain Frederick Warren. George was in error however, as they embarked on HMS *Pompee* of 74 guns, not the *Revenge*.

142 Lieutenant General Sir Brent Spencer, was in command at Gibraltar, when he heard of the Spanish uprising. On his own initiative, he sailed with a force of nearly five thousand troops to Lisbon and joined Arthur Wellesley as he landed his troops at Mondego Bay. He therefore served as his second in command from Rolica through to Fuentes d'Onoro in 1811, before being replaced by Sir Thomas Graham. George was obviously expecting a letter of introduction to him from his uncle.

2

First Time To Portugal

George was finally off to sea with the 2/52nd, 650 men strong, on their passage to Portugal and he was very excited by the prospect. Moorsom's history of the regiment states that the 2/52nd embarked at Portsmouth on 26 January 1811, but George makes it clear that the convoy did not sail until 30 January.

To William Barlow Esq, Little Bridge Street, Blackfriars, London
HMS *Pompee* at sea off the Ramehead 1 February 1811[1]

My dear uncle,
In my last I informed you of our expectations to sail on Tuesday morning; this would actually have taken place, but the wind was so scant that the admiral could not get down to St Helen's until next morning,[2] when we left Portsmouth with a fine stiff breeze at north east, scudding under top sails at the rate of nine or ten knots an hour. We lay too off Plymouth about four hours that very evening, so you may fancy what speed we made; this continued until we had passed the Lizard & had begun to approach Ushant, when a violent northwester drove us back & we have now tacked about & expect to put back again to Torbay this evening. The regiment has frequently been at sea, but all are unanimous in declaring that they never met with a more pleasant set of officers, than that which composes the crew of this ship. All is civility & attention, & our passage is likely to be most pleasant; I am writing the present in the First Lieutenant's cabin; indeed we are fortunate in every respect, for the *Pompee* is the best sailor in the fleet, which consists of eight sail of the line & three frigates; this is going out to Lisbon in style. Nothing has occurred since we left England, excepting the capture of a little lugger privateer[3] which had the impudence to sail through

1 Rame Head is a peninsular in Cornwall, lying opposite Plymouth harbour; the ship was the 74-gun HMS *Pompee,* commanded by Captain Sir James Athol Wood RN.

2 St Helen's, Isle of Wight.

3 It was not a privateer, but the American merchant ship *Canton,* which had been seized by the French privateer *Dantzick* a few days earlier. The French privateers were taken off and she was manned by a British prize crew and sailed into Plymouth.

the middle of the whole *squadron yesterday afternoon & crossed our ship within half a* mile, she was however quickly brought to by the *Ganges.* [4]

It is very possible that we shall anchor for a few hours only, until the wind comes round to the northward & it is my wish to have a letter ready written for the very first conveyance. Independent of this, the sea will not always allow us to write; it blows at present very fresh, with every appearance of a gale for this night, the ship however is now going right before the wind & does not roll so much as to hinder me from writing. You may tell Robert however from me, that in spite of everything I feel as comfortable and as little fear on board as if I was snug in the drawing room at Streatham. There is so much order & regularity, such confidence & such promptitude in meeting every exigency, that to a landsman who has the least knowledge of naval tactics, it must be apparent how little ground there is for alarm & that in storms & tempests which appear to people on shore such terrible things, is regarded by the sailor as of little consequence. He has always a remedy at hand & confident in a due application of it & reckons himself as secure thereby as if on terra firma.

By dint of constantly walking the deck & keeping in the air I have kept off the seasickness; it has affected me in a very slight degree, but neither so as to take away my appetite or spirits. In the wardroom however, some of my brother officers are in a deplorable state. Two or three have been stretched in their cots & bedding the whole of the last two days without stirring or eating a morsel & others are pale & as silent as the grave. Of this last sort you may suppose the number to be pretty considerable in a crew of 1,100 persons of all descriptions. I have just been visiting the lower deck as Officer of the Watch, but however was much surprized to find the soldiers in so much better a state than I could possibly have expected.

Give my aunt a thousand thanks for her [torn – kind?] letter, which I received a few hours previous to sailing; tell the little ones how glad I shall be occasionally to have five or six lines from them in their best handwriting, which I will carefully preserve together with the rest of my valuables & with every prayer for their health & happiness as well as your own & my dear aunt's, I remain your truly affectionate nephew G U Barlow

His next letter found them still in the English Channel ten days later.

To William Barlow Esq, Little Bridge Street, Blackfriars, London
HMS *Pompee,* Torbay, 11 February 1811

My dear uncle,
The morning subsequent to the date of my last, containing an enclosure for William, we again put to sea & after beating about two days & nights the squadron has resumed its original station for the *fourth time* since it left

4 HMS *Ganges* of 74 guns, she became a prison ship in December 1811.

Portsmouth. The whole of us are happy & comfortable enough it is true but are become heartily sick of these delays at a moment, when we are so eagerly desirous of joining the armies. Westerly winds at this season of the year & on this coast constantly prevail so I fear much that we shall never clear the Channel or be detained at anchor for some time to come. This idea is much strengthened by the concurrent opinions of the Torbay-men & those who are supposed to be weather-wise, indeed the weather is excessively mild & warm.

During this last trip, two of our squadron parted company in a thick fog & the remainder steering as they thought for the Berry Head, when the atmosphere became a little clear found themselves making for the Eddystone,[5] so you see we were completely out of our reckoning & were obliged to stand off & on the whole of last night, not being able to reach the bay before dark. Independent of all this lingering work, I am afraid that the troops will become sickly by so long a continuance onboard a ship, crowded together with rainy weather & seas which prevent the lower deck ports from being open, which is the more necessary as 600 men alone sleep in that part of the vessel.

I have written five or six letters to you since we first came to this anchorage. I know not whether you receive them regularly; a man comes off every day from shore, to whom they are intrusted, but whether this is executed faithfully & punctually I cannot ascertain. You may hazard to me a few lines under enclosure to Pownoll, with directions to have them destroyed if the fleet has sailed. There is a cross post from hence to Plymouth & Pownoll will direct them to the *Pompee* if the wind remains foul & if it should come fair he will keep them in his hands & burn them. God bless you all my dear uncle & believe me to be, your affectionate nephew G U Barlow

George's next letter to his father, could announce that the long-desired order to sail to Portugal had finally arrived. He also reported the near loss of a company or more of the regiment owing to the errors of the master of the vessel carrying them.

No 36
To Sir G H Barlow Bart KB, Fort St George, Madras
Torbay, 13 February 1811

My dear father,
Since my last, the long-expected event of our embarkation has taken place, but at present I have neither time nor space to give you the particulars of this period & other transactions which have lately occurred & which were intended to fill up my next number by the spring fleet. It will however suffice to add, that our squadron consists of eight sail of the line and four frigates

5 Berry Head is near Torbay in Devon and approaching this would put the ship close to shore in the lee of the land; Eddystone Rocks are thirty miles to the west, off Plymouth, leaving the ship fully exposed to the heavy seas.

under Sir Joseph Yorke[6] sailed from Portsmouth on the 30th ultimo & proceeded as far as Ushant when adverse winds compelled it to put back to this bay, where we have been at anchor for some days. The China & Bombay ships under convoy of the *Hussar* frigate are arrived close along-side of us [7] On board of the latter is Captain Dawson of the *Piedmontaise* & who goes out as a passenger to join his ship, which if I recollect right, is on the Madras station.[8] He has a brother in our regiment on board the *Pompee* with me & I have accepted Captain D[awson]'s offer to deliver safely to you these few lines. I have heard Sir Edward Pellew speak highly in favour of this young man, as well as several of our East Indian acquaintances.[9] This will most probably be the latest piece of intelligence from me whilst in England. The wind is even now fair for sailing & knowing that it would be highly satisfactory to hear up to the last moment, I determined upon embracing his proposal.

You will I am sure, be rejoiced to know that instead of shipping us in board transports, the government intends discontinuing this practise & for the future prefers sending out the troops in men of war, for which we have seen no unemployment. The dangers attending the former species of vessels & especially at this stormy season of the year, are well known to all, manned as they frequently are so badly & with such unskilful seamen. I could tell you stories about their experience, as astonishing as they are true. A part of our regiment were nearly lost off Portland Bill & the Master nearly carried them into Calais, mistaking it for Dungeness Point. Our ship is a large 74 & carries six companies very well, the officers are a pleasant & gentlemanly set of fellows. From Sir James Wood the captain, I have received much civility & attention, in consequence of recommendations from Sir Edward Pellew & Pownoll who came from Plymouth a few days since and paid me a visit on board. Eliza was very well but expected daily to be confined.[10] I wrote to her on coming here but she was not in a condition to answer it.

6 Rear Admiral Joseph Sydney Yorke commanded a fleet escorting a large reinforcement to Spain, his flagship was the 74-gun HMS *Vanguard.*

7 HMS *Hussar* was a 38-gun frigate launched in 1807. It escorted the India ships home in 1811 under the command of Captain James Coutts Crawford RN.

8 Captain the Honourable Henry Dawson Royal Navy went out to relieve Captain Charles Foote of HMS *Piedmontaise*, which had originally been a 40-gun frigate of the same name in the French Navy. In 1805 she sailed from Brest to Isle de France (Reunion) and had a successful career as a commerce raider in the Indian Ocean, capturing a number of HEIC ships. She was captured by HMS *St Fiorenzo* on 8 March 1808 and served with the British in the expedition to the Banda Islands in 1810.

9 Sir Edward Pellew had served as Commander-in-Chief of the East Indies station from 1804-09 and therefore was well known to the governor of Madras and a sizeable correspondence between the two still exists. He was made commander in chief in the Mediterranean in 1811 and he served there almost continuously until 1816. He became the 1st Viscount Exmouth in 1814.

10 Elizabeth or Eliza was in the final stages of her pregnancy; she gave birth to Edward Pellew the following day, on 14 February 1811 (Edward eventually became the 3rd Viscount Exmouth). The couple later had two further children, Percy, born on 15 April 1814 and

I sent you two long letters, one for my mother & one for Charlotte, in the *Elizabeth* all of which went down on her when wrecked off Dunkirk, together with the greater part of her crew, all those of the dear little children at Streatham, in their best hands, together with some important communications from my uncle, were also lost at the same time [11] I shall prefer my usual vessel, however when at leisure and send it by the fleet which sails in the course of six or seven weeks. The present was only a few lines written to apprise you on the change of our situation & which will come to hand long before the arrival of the above ships.

I have just learnt that we start tomorrow as the wind is northern; before closing the present I must inform you that through my uncle's pressing exertions, letters of introduction have been prepared to Mr Stuart, the British Minister & the first society at Lisbon,[12] and also to General Sir Brent Spencer who is second in command; to Lord Wellington, to the latter at present I have no recommendations but have left it to my uncle's consideration whether it would be proper to apply for them.

The present is a fine opportunity of acquiring the practical parts of my profession & also of learning the languages of the peninsula & as such, I heartily embrace it, but must for the present discontinue the more obtuse and theoretical branches of the science. God bless you, my dear mother, Charlotte, brothers and sisters & all in India & as long as life remains believe me to be, your truly dutiful & affectionate son, G U Barlow

To William Barlow Esq, Little Bridge Street, Blackfriars, London
HMS *Pompee*, Torbay, 14 February 1811

My dear uncle,
Since my last we have put to sea again for a *fifth time* & the wind has as usual, compelled us to return. At the moment I am now writing we are weighing anchor to make a sixth & I hope final attempt. I have nothing to add, excepting the attention & civilities which the letters of Sir E Pellew & Pownoll have procured me from the captain. My opinion of him nevertheless is not changed; in consequence however of his behaviour I have ceased to make any remarks to his prejudice, for which there are so many occasions.

Julianna who was born on 16 June 1816. The marriage was however absolved by act of parliament in July 1820. Elizabeth died in 1833. Pownoll then married the 22-year old Georgina Dick, who gave him another five children. He became the 2nd Viscount Exmouth in 1833, a title he only enjoyed for eleven months before he died.

11 The *Elizabeth* East Indiaman was wrecked on a sandbank off Dunkirk on 27 December 1810. It was carrying 382 people on board, of which only 22 were saved. George was mistaken regarding the loss of his letters, as the *Elizabeth* was on route to Cork when she sank, and his letters duly arrived in India.

12 Charles Stuart was a diplomat and was appointed Envoy Extraordinary and Minister Plenipotentiary to Portugal 1810-14.

I have sent a hasty line to my father by Captain Dawson, who goes out a passenger in the *Hussar* frigate, to join the *Piedmontaise* at Madras, he has a brother in our regiment & is highly spoken of by Sir E Pellew.[13] God bless you all & believe me to be your truly affectionate nephew G U Barlow

Unfortunately it would appear that at least one letter written to his Uncle William has been lost. In this George would have announced that the battalion had finally arrived in Lisbon on 4 March 1811 and that they were fully disembarked by 6 March. However, George was now very unwell and unable to proceed up country with the battalion.

To William Barlow Esq, Little Bridge Street, Blackfriars, London
Lisbon, 19 March 1811

My dear uncle,
You will I am sure rejoice to hear that I am recovering rapidly & daily getting better, by reading the Spanish & Portuguese grammars a good deal of late, my eyes have become a little weak; but it is of no consequence, I am however forbid to read or write. I must however disobey this last injunction as I know you will be anxious to hear from me & within these last two or three days, my eyes have become as strong as ever, so that writing the present can do me no harm. I was preparing a letter of several sheets giving an account of my voyage & misfortunes but dare not continue it at present. You shall however have it as soon as I am able to finish it. I wish you would send me some pounds of good tea & sugar; they make us pay here twelve & 13 shillings a lb for infamous tea, which poor people buy for 7 & 8 s[hillings] in England, from whence every morsel is imported & execrably adulterated; as also 2 or 3 dozens of Madeira, for that wine is strongly recommended to me & what I buy at the Portuguese wine shops is very dear & very bad; I should also like a good Cheshire cheese not very rype [sic] & a file of *Observers,* a *weekly* Sunday newspaper. It is published close to St Clement's Church in the Strand & costs but 7 or 8d.[14] I should wish to have it beginning from Sunday *January 27th* (the day we embarked) if possible. Indeed I *would give anything* for this latter article, or for *a file of papers* from the time I left England. Be so good as to take the *Observer* in for the future for me. All these may come in a hamper directed to Messrs Holford, Gomm & Co. with WB at the corner of the card & I shall know it to be from you. Holford happens to be left behind in Lisbon on command with a party of convalescents,[15] & I have requested him to forward anything of the sort to my quarters & which I have told him he may expect to arrive.

Write directly to me Lieutenant B[arlow] 2nd Battalion 52nd Regiment *Lisbon, to be kept until called for.* I have directed the postmaster who is an

13 The brother would be Ensign Charles Dawson, 52nd Light Infantry.
14 The *Observer* began as a Sunday weekly paper in 1791; it retailed for 6½d in 1811.
15 Lieutenant James Price Holford, 52nd Light Infantry.

English serjeant, to stop all letters for me, as I will send my servant for them as soon as the packets arrive. I am sure thus of receiving everything safe. God bless you all, my dear aunt & all the dear little ones at Streatham & believe me to be, your truly affectionate nephew, G U Barlow

[PS] How is poor Peter [?] You know all letters & parcels must be paid for previously in England or they will not be forwarded.

There is a note on the envelope in his father's hand: 'Think on what a dreadful state he must have been in when he wrote this letter, this written from the hospital it was born[e]. It was lucky we received George's letter of the 7th of May first. GHB'.[16]

To William Barlow Esq, Little Bridge Street, Blackfriars, London
Lisbon, 29 March 1811

My dear uncle,
This present packet will convey to you my promised letter made up into three, having however many an idle moment, I scribble away to fill up the vacancy. The state of my health is progressively & sensibly mending; recovery you know, in all cases of debility & deprivation of the use of one's limbs, is very slow. The surgeon came in yesterday & found me drinking tea at twelve o'clock; I had previously breakfasted at nine. Upon informing him it was my beverage & twice a day, coffee once & that soup formed my fourth & last meal. He said 'Mr Barlow, all you require now is good nursing, all slops must be thrown away'. He then proceeded to recommend jellies, oysters, boiled veal & soals [sic] with fish sauce. Everything in short says he, which is savory [sic] & nourishing & which can induce me to eat flesh. I have employed my servant this morning in procuring the above articles; a course of fattening is, in short, prescribed. Nothing however would tempt him to allow milk for breakfast, for which I begged hard, as a cow is brought every morning to the door & that article obtained hot, unadulterated & of the best quality good wine & Negus is also recommended.[17] Bye the bye I have not been able to afford buying wine for this week or ten day's past. Holford called one day & informed me that his father's partner Mr Lucas could let me have some good wine, upon which I begged that he would let me have a doz[en], purposing to apprize you of the event, in order that the account may be settled with Messrs Holford & Co. in London. He however paid me a visit this morning & says that Lucas will not hear of selling but insists upon making me a present of it. I cannot refuse now without affronting him, though I have all the inclination in the world so to do. Perhaps you

16 This would appear to confirm that all of George's letters to his Uncle William were then routinely forwarded on to his father in India, hence both sets of correspondence having been preserved.
17 Negus is a cocktail, combining lemon, sugar, water and port.

may have correspondents in Lisbon to whom I can apply for that article, as your sending it here is like carrying coals to Newcastle.

I see by the prints that Creevy has been moving for papers;[18] the debate as is usual in those matters was managed by the little fry… so Boles is restored! Pray who of the twelve played the Judas on this occasion? How do matters stand in the India House [?] they were gloomy enough when I left England; I see also that letters are said to have been received announcing Lord Minto's return, pray is this true?[19] The 33rd Regiment is said to be recalled now from Madras; could you ascertain whither those *orders are going out,* or how long they have gone.[20] When you set down to write, you should endeavour to recollect all the news of such a nature (I mean upon family & India concerns) & let me hear them, now we are so far separated & without means of conversing; anything in short that will occupy my thoughts. Fred has a friend in the War Office who can perhaps furnish the desired information. My time is not compleat until the 15th of September next & if the 33rd leave India previous to that month, all hopes of a company in that corps must vanish, which I have much at heart, of this indeed my father is apprized.

And now I must inform you that I am very low in pocket; upon sailing from Portsmouth with so fair a wind we expected to have been but five or six days on our passage to Lisbon, which was lengthened to upwards of five weeks & almost six. Our messing was therefore considerably expensive for so long a period & I paid my share although confined to my cot the greater part of that time, which came to £10 & is at the rate of 5s 6d per diem. After this & every other expense such as buying a mule &c at Lisbon for the carriage of my canteens & saddle bags, an animal which at present is very dear on account of the great demand, I should have had notwithstanding an ample & sufficient overplus even after the regiment had joined Lord Wellington at Celorico, without reckoning upon the guineas. One could not calculate upon my being left sick at this place, with a chance of continuing so for some time to come, *at least,* two or three months. The vicinity of so large an army has caused every article & necessary of life to be dear beyond precedent in Lisbon, particularly are those little trifles of which I stand in need & which are not so common in Portugal as in England. For a glass of calves foot jelly they charge 3s 6d, which with you would not cost more than half that sum.

The king allows me a lb of meat (*bone included*), a lb and a half of bread (the latter hard & four or five days old) per diem. I stew the former into poor soup & poor enough it is. Things to be sure are not so dear as in London otherwise I could not stand it, but such as they are, it falls heavy upon my purse. My signora furnishes me with lodging and candle only, eatables I provide myself with & as I cannot eat solid meat like beef I must furnish

18 Thomas Creevey was a politician and famous diarist. He was very active at this time in trying to continue questioning Sir George Barlow's conduct in India.

19 It was incorrect, Lord Minto did not return to England from India until 1813.

20 Orders were sent out and the 33rd Foot was back in Britain by 1812.

every day a dinner at my own expense, if I follow the surgeon's directions. Give my love to my aunt, God bless her & you all, is the prayer of your affectionate nephew G U Barlow

George was still writing from Lisbon some weeks later, but he still hoped to fully recover and to move up to the army shortly.

Lisbon, 30 March 1811

My dear uncle,
As the spring of the year is now coming on, I should wish that the mare should be separated from any horses with which she might be grazing, as it will bring her into very low & thin condition & that she should be turned into a field wholly amongst mares or by herself. As Mr Patterson has so much ground, perhaps he may be able to effect this. Be so good as to send out in the hamper my saddle & bridle, as I must at all events buy a mule to carry my canteens & saddle bags to the army & I may as well procure one when I am strong enough and able to ride, as at a later period. It will indeed much benefit my health, and as the army is now on the frontiers & the demand for those animals less, I trust in the course of six or seven weeks to be able to procure a tolerably decent one for 50 or 60 dollars. The government also allow all subalterns who possess bona fide a mule, to draw *half bat & forage* or in other [words] half the necessary quantity, the remaining half I must purchase myself. There is amongst my lumber two or three old regimental jackets. Be as good as to take the one with the *broadest skirts* & give it to Powell to make me a new one according to the pattern. I do not want any *wings* with it. Believe me to be your affectionate nephew G U Barlow

[PS] I am also much in want of a cap & feather from Hawkes in Piccadilly.[21]

In his next letter, George admitted that his recovery was so slow that his surgeon had recommended that he return to England to regain his health in full. Reluctantly George had taken the advice and he was awaiting notification of a passage home.

To William Barlow Esq, Little Bridge Street, Blackfriars, London
Lisbon, 6 April 1811

My dear uncle,
I received on Sunday last *the 31st of March*, your letters of *the 18th & 24th of February* with the enclosure for General Spencer. These are the *only ones* which at present have come to hand. The packets on being landed, are

21 The gentlemen's outfitters Gieves & Hawkes started in Brewer Street in 1771 and moved to No. 17 Piccadilly in 1793. They still have a unit at No. 1 Piccadilly.

immediately sorted & within a few hours sent up to the army.[22] Amongst the number of letters & hurry of business, the postmaster neglected to stop mine according to orders. They have consequently travelled all through Portugal to Celorico & back again and were not delivered to me until nearly three weeks after the packet's arrival. *Two* of these vessels arrived yesterday morning, the latter of which brought letters from England dated the 26th of March. My servant went to the office & the answer returned was 'no letter for Lieutenant Barlow'. This I am convinced is not the case, as you have no doubt written between the 24th of February & the 20th of March an interval of nearly a month. The truth is that they have as usual gone up to the army & will not be received [until] a fortnight to come. None of the dear little ones' performances have arrived.

And now I will tell you a piece *of news; you may shortly expect to see me in England.* My surgeon pays me a visit every third morning. On Wednesday last, as usual he waited on me & upon learning that my hip did not feel so well as usual owing to rheumatic pains & weakness, he gave me the following advice in a most serious manner. 'Mr Barlow I never saw such a corpse as yourself upon landing. You are considerably improved, but for your *complete* recovery I recommend you to go to England'. To this I expressed my dislike, adding that I expected to join my regiment in June or the beginning of July. To convince you of my sincere desire to remain in Portugal, I have only to add that I have *twice* refused the offers of *two* different captains of men of war a passage home, actuated by the above motives. 'Anyone but yourself' continued my monitor 'would wish to go home; but to establish a good contribution & health at your age, is most important; when by neglect you may lay the seeds of future disorders: in short' concluded he 'if you remain *here* you cannot expect to join *at soonest the* army *before October next.* It will be a long time before you will be able to lay out in the wet & cold & bear the fatigues of a campaign & there is no further use in fighting against the matter'. Could my dear uncle, any warnings be more solemn or explicit & the consequences arising from a disobedience of them more dreadful? Without health I should become a useless member of my profession; my part in this affair has been open & sincere & I think you will agree with me that I have acted right in following the advice of the faculty. By what conveyance I may return to England is at present uncertain, it is however with the most poignant regret that I am obliged to relinquish all hopes of joining my regiment & friends at Celorico & of serving a campaign in a countryside to which I had been fondly looking for such a length of time.[23]

22 The 2/52nd joined the army before Sabugal on 1 April 1811, missing the combat of Sabugal against Massena's troops and therefore not taking any casualties. Even so the battalion was down to 542 men by 1 May 1811, because of sickness.

23 The fact that his 'opthalmia' an eye condition, had had further complications, indicates that something else has obviously occurred. My great friend Michael Crumplin kindly sought the advice of Margaret Hobson, an expert in rheumatology, for her thoughts. They

My only thoughts are now directed how my stay at home will be rendered comfortable & pleasant to you; I can do everything but get up & downstairs; now if Mrs Beckwith's room had not been occupied, I might have slept in it & walked from thence to breakfast and dinner. My arm is *now perfectly recovered*; my eyes are nearly so & I do not write to my aunt, the little ones or my friends in order to treasure them up, so that I may be able to enjoy reading at home. In the parlour & study I shall be in nobody's way & when in the course of a month or six weeks I am able to walk as usual, I can pay a visit to Devonshire, to Hampshire or study at Woolwich, upon which last I am as anxious as ever so that my six-months residence in England will not have been wholly spent in vain. As my complaint is not in the backbone, but that of the hip & thigh (termed by professional men the osa cochia [os coxa]) sitting in a chair gives me no pain whatever & is my easiest posture & thus I spend the greater part of the day making fly-catchers & gossiping with my signora, not daring to read or write even except to you. I never lie down or sleep in the day in any account & indeed do not stand in need of it; indeed good eating & drinking, the society of my friends are recommended for my cure, as well as the cool air of England. The hot weather, which in Portugal commences about May, being deemed prejudicial to my complaint and give my love to my aunt & all at home, I am your affectionate nephew
G U Barlow

The following small note was included with the above letter:

My dear uncle,
In commencing the present, I must begin with informing you that I have duly weighed & most attentively considered *every cost of* what I now write, & you may rely therefore of the rigid exactness in the truth of the following statement of my case. I write *the present* separate from my letter, in order that my aunt may not be uneasy, which she would be although there is no ground, it tends *for alarm,* destroy it as soon [as read] *my arm is quite well,* my eyes nearly so, though still a little weak, & I am told will keep apace in improvement with the strength of my body & leg. They are so strong, that I *never* wear a shade, excepting when a candle or some glaring light is brought near them. My hip was daily improving, till within this last week, when a rheumatism has flown into it & although that limb does not *improve,* I do not think it gets worse but is at a standstill. When I am in bed lying down, it gives me considerable pain, but *none* whilst I sit in my chair. The surgeon says that the whole of my frame sympathizes with the late inflammation of

jointly conclude that his opthalmia was a uveitis (inflammation of the Iris) rather than a conjunctivitis, because of the apparent photophobia described. The other symptoms affecting the hip and his arm are not direct symptoms of this infection and a secondary cause must be to blame. Because of his eventual recovery without antibiotics it would appear most likely to be a form of Reactive Arthritis (or Reiter's Syndrome), probably triggered by an infection in the bowel or elsewhere.

my eyes & lungs; for my cough was dreadful & lasted nearly a month. In consequence of the above there has been a slight swelling of the liver in my right side; it must have taken place some time back but escaped my notice until two days since when I stripped to wash my legs in some warm water. From the above circumstance & its giving me no pain, it can't be very bad. Upon Mr Cook examining it the next day,[24] he accounted for it in the way I have just mentioned. Upon my requesting to know the real state of the case & my wish to know the danger if there was any, or its fullest extent. He adds that there can be no danger of the liver complaint, as I have always lived temperately & been healthy; and said as my leg & body acquired strength, it would resume its natural size. Adieu, I am well & in good spirits.

I went yesterday & appeared before the Medical Board, they recommend me to come home & I have a certificate from its president to that effect. I was lifted into a chaise & spent the day in driving to every part of Lisbon, commencing [with] the public buildings. Came home & eat [sic] for dinner half a chicken & two large soals [sic] & drank a bottle of good strong porter. You can hardly call me a *sick* man.

The next letter to his father, incorrectly also numbered 36, found young George at Torbay, having been sent back to England to recuperate from his 'opthalmia' which had taken hold during the long passage to Lisbon; not the most auspicious start to his first campaign.

No.36
To Sir G H Barlow Bart KB, Fort St George, Madras
Torbay, 7 May 1811 (annotated received 11th September, answered 4th November)

My dear father,
I landed at Falmouth a few days since from Lisbon having obtained three or four months leave of absence, for the recovery of my health in England. The fleet must have left Portsmouth before my uncle could have been aware of my arrival. By great good luck, they have been compelled to put into this place, by stress of weather, where I have found them at anchor. The place I am now writing from is a small village called Torquay, about seven miles from Teignmouth & Eliza & Pownoll are at present in company with the whole family of the Pellews, whither I shall proceed today. Indeed, I have never had an opportunity of seeing her since she has been in England.

I have much to say, but at present have not time, or even the power of so doing, as my eyes are still very weak and I am forbid both reading & writing. Of course, you have been informed of the nature of my complaint, it was the opthalmia, for which there is no remedy yet known or so effectual as nearly killing the patient by instant & repeated bleedings by physicians

24 Staff Surgeon William Cook (No 1925 in Robert Drew (ed.), *Commissioned Officers in the Medical Services of the British Army, 1660-1960* (London: Wellcome Library, 1968).

& starvation. The disease was very bad, [in] my left eye. I of course had to go through plenty of rough usage of this sort until I became at last so weak, that I was confined three weeks to my bed & thereby lost the use of my left arm & leg. All this took place on board a ship tossing & rolling about in the Bay of Biscay. Indeed, I have suffered much & was not expected to live. From this terrible situation I was soon recovered, from the mild climate of Lisbon. After stopping there three months, having the mortification of seeing my regiment join the army in their operations upon the frontier, I was advised to return to England, the faculty[25] being of [the] opinion that I could not expect to take the field for three or four months, I might as well be at home as in Portugal for the entire period, such is my case. At the moment I am now writing, I am wont to say it improves, I can walk about, eat & drink normally and [am] in good spirits, after having travelled upwards of 150 miles from the Land's End & if I continue to mend as apparent, I shall probably return to the army in July next. My eyes are still a little weak & these are the only traces of my former complaints. God bless you, my dear mother, brothers & sisters & *believe me* to be your only affectionate son G U Barlow

Two months later George was still writing from London, as he recuperated, but he was now back fully on his drive for his captaincy and had clearly received the promise of every support from his father, although not now to join the 33rd Foot, but the Foot Guards. He did also discuss the option of joining the Portuguese army, but he was not happy that the step up in rank which came with it, was purely temporary. He also confirmed that the opthalmia was now largely clear and that he eagerly anticipated re-joining the regiment in Spain.

No 37
To Sir G H Barlow, Fort St George, Madras
Little Bridge Street, 12 July 1811

My dear father,
In your letter of January last instant, the receipt of [No.] 33 is acknowledged, [No.] 34 went down in the *Elizabeth*, off the coast of France.[26] Since that time, I have written twice, in the first instance by Captain Cole[27] of the *Piedmontaise* and the second by Captain Carnegie of the *Baring*.[28] The former would announce to you my departure for Portugal, the latter my safe arrival in this country. Indeed, I felt much gratified at so fortunate an

25 The Medical Board.
26 He was wrong as No. 34 was received and is included in this series of letters.
27 He is mistaken here, he means Captain Dawson.
28 The *Baring* was a large merchantman of 820 tons, built at Deptford in London in 1801 for HEIC service, she made six round passages to India. In 1814 the ship left HEIC service and sailed twice to Botany Bay carrying prisoners. Captain James Carnegie joined the prestigious Society of East India Commanders in 1806.

opportunity for dispelling all your fears on my account, was of a subsequent date to all the correspondence of our family. By attaching 37 to the present one, correspondence will be continued in a regular series, and as it will be conveyed to you by the hands of my cousin, there is so little doubt of its safe arrival.[29]

It is now my duty to return you my warmest thanks for the kindness displayed in every sentence of your affectionate letter, for the interest you take in my position & rank and the liberality shown in the prosecution of this design. The impression made in me is such that whether soon or late the desirable object of a company be obtained, I shall not feel the less grateful for your exertions on my behalf, whatever may be their result. For your past favours in procuring my ensigncy & lieutenancy, I entertain a deep remembrance & will endeavour in my present station so to behave as to deserve a higher [rank] when an opportunity shall offer.

In two months from this time I am now writing, my term of three years will have expired, when I have attained to the rank of captain, it will be a matter of debate whether it would be proper to exchange into the Guards at once.[30] Your strict objection to the 33rd Regiment seems to be the probability of its remaining in India for some time to come. You add (probably with reason) that it would be a loss of time and of the good opportunities which now offer for a man to acquire a knowledge of the military profession. This obstacle, would I think, be removed if the 33rd Regiment was to be ordered home, which I understand *is now the case.*[31] Today, I propose calling for further information at the Horse Guards on this head. It is a single battalion regiment, and the exchanges out of it when recalled to England would advance me pretty high up the list for captains & the addition of a second battalion at home (by no means an improbable circumstance) would almost to a certainty assure me a majority & from thence a lieutenant colonelcy. To be sure, the whole of this future rests upon the truth of the return of that regiment from abroad. I will not however, take any step of this kind without the previous advice of General Ross, upon whose judgement & decision I shall elicit in utmost confidence & in this sentiment I can easily anticipate your most cordial concurrence.

My uncle has of late had frequent interviews with the general on political business, made one of these visits accompanied with me. Your letter of January last on the subject of a company was produced and submitted for his perusal. He read it and merely said that it was very right & proper, that companies were not easily to be had in these times & that it would be right to purchase when occasion offered. Saying this he returned the epistle into our hands & after the strong hint given him, we could not press the matter

29 His cousin William was on route to India.

30 This would almost certainly have to be achieved by purchasing the rank. He could sell his lieutenancy for £550, but to be a captain in the Foot Guards would cost the enormous sum of £3,500.

31 The 33rd Foot did in fact finally sail home from India in 1811.

any further in the scene of intimacy. He made one or two general observations of the nature I have just mentioned, holding out no hopes, indeed he reserves all his interest for one of his nephews who is also a lieutenant in the 52nd Regiment, and who will have served his time three or four months hence.[32] On this head therefore, there is no one else to whom we can apply. In my own regiment, all the seniors will purchase; of these there is a most formidable list.[33] All have money enough, but not interest to have their claims preferred. Indeed, the army is at present so large and of late become an object of so much importance, so many noble families have connections in it, and above all parliamentary influence is of so great weight, that companies when they are to be had, are given to candidates of the above class in preference to all others, and are not to be obtained so easily as you might imagine. I might indeed easily obtain that rank in the Portuguese army, but that is by no means a desirable object, as I should remain a lieutenant in the English service, the same as ever. A company in the King's Army therefore would entitle me to hold a majority in the Spanish & Portuguese service, a circumstance which would afford me the greatest pleasure and in the event of making myself master of the Spanish & Portuguese language (which I intend doing and in which I had made considerable progress previous to quitting England and being afflicted by the horrible opthalmia, which does not allow any application on my part at present). I have little doubt of accomplishing this end once a proposition has been made by our government to organise the Spaniards (if the Dons will allow it) in the same position as Marshal Beresford has disciplined the Portuguese.[34] A knowledge of the languages of the peninsula has been the means to bringing several officers into notice who would otherwise have remained unknown. And it is a quality which so few possess or are determined to acquire, that the paucity of competitors ensures success in the foregoing line & continued practise that [I] have been occupied in explaining such to you the various paths which lay before me & the different tracks that are offered for my adventure & rather than in adopting or chusing [sic] any one in particular, it is right in my opinion, to point out to you this varied military picture, and more especially to particularise its more minute features, which your immense distance from the exhibition will scarcely allow you to perceive,

32 This nephew must be Lieutenant John Wardlaw as he was the only other officer to have a seniority of three years in late 1811, his occurring on 2 November. Unknown to George, Wardlaw had actually achieved his captaincy early, by joining the Portuguese army, which gave him an immediate step in rank. He served with the 4th Cacadores, but unfortunately was killed at the Battle of Salamanca in 1812.

33 In March 1811, there were thirty-three officers ahead of him for a captaincy.

34 When the British landed in Portugal in 1808, the Portuguese army was virtually useless. Major General William Carr Beresford was appointed Marshal of the Portuguese army and he brought forward a range of reforms, 'persuaded' many useless officers to retire, and filled up many vacancies with British officers to help him see through the changes. They received a local step in rank for joining the Portuguese army, but this also gave them greater opportunities for more rapid promotion.

to present it to your view in every shape, before so important a measure, as my future track of life is chalked out.

It will no doubt afford you great satisfaction to hear that my health is now so far re-established that I propose proceeding to Portugal & joining my regiment in the course of next month. My present term of leave expires on the 13th of August & Cline is my advisor.[35] On our first interview he promised me a speedy & certain recovery from my complaint, which was a chronic rheumatism in my left leg arising from [a] cold caught during my severe illness. A good constitution and youth have contributed to restore me to my former state of health with an impressive degree of rapidity. Indeed, I am glad that my sufferings will be past, ere they shall come to your knowledge & that your anxiety will be alleviated by the reflection that I am now well and hearty. They have seed [sic] poor meat & brought me to the point of death, in so much as I was considered past recovery for some days at Lisbon. The letter conveyed to you by Captain Carnegie will give some idea of my complaint and the cause of all my ails. Thank God, few traces of the horrible opthalmia still now remain, excepting a trifling weakness, which time & care will contribute to remove. Such as it appears by even the stoutest, the remedy for this disease is almost as bad as the complaint itself, bleeding and privation till animal nature can hardly rest,[36] forms the only medical advice at present passing and of which our medical men of the regiment, who have been in Egypt most highly approve of. This sort of regimen, with confinement to my bed occasioned the loss of use in my leg, as the bleeding had the same effect with regard to my ails. In this situation a violent cold therefore affected my chest with pain in the side, attended with the most excruciating rheumatism for the space of two weeks when I continued in bed unable to lift myself up, I for three more hobbled about on crutches, a good constitution has however enabled me to weather this storm. I am reviving again to all the delights of health & happiness, growing stout and looking to the future, with the animation of hope & spirits.

I propose keeping a regular diary from the moment of quitting England and transmitting it to you from time to time, as convenience or opportunities may offer. Up to the period of my illness and during my stay in Lisbon, the same measure was adopted on the correspondence with my uncle. These details are however of no interest and are chiefly a recital of my facing of miseries wrote on board of ship & the reception I met with at Lisbon, a reception I shall never forget, as the poet says 'dum memor ipse mei, dum spiritus hos artus agat'[37] the intimate connection which at present subsists between England and Portugal and the reports of our regi-

35 Surgeon Henry Cline (1750-1827), he had also become Examiner to the Royal College of Surgeons in 1810.

36 He means a 'low diet' consisting of milk, tea, rice pudding, sago, bread and arrowroot. No meat, vegetables or alcohol.

37 'While the memory itself is mine; while breath controls these limbs'. It is a slightly incorrect quote from the Aeneid IV 336 'dum memor ipse mei, dum spiritus hos regit artus'.

ment who campaigned with Sir John Moore had rendered me, pretty well acquainted with the characters, manners and customs of the natives of that peninsula and although my own immediate researches were chiefly confined to Lisbon. During my excursion through that city and its vicinity in a post chaise (being unable to walk) my stock of knowledge respecting that now most interesting part of Europe is pretty ample and accurate. It was my good fortune to take up my lodgings at one of the smartest houses in Lisbon. It was occupied by a lady who spoke the English language & most fluently, was well acquainted with the religious evils of that nation, relocating to Lisbon had been educated amongst them, and been in a great degree divested of the bigotry and ignorance which characterises the Portuguese; had in some measure adopted the opinions & customs of our 'Happy Isle', to which her brother & friends had made frequent trips. Indeed, I shall always remember the name of Donna Maria de Campos, for that was the name of my hostess during a residence of nearly two months at her hospitable bound and the provider of every comfort & convenience that her house could satisfy, to which I do attribute in great measure the preservation of my existence; at a time when the regiment was gone up to the frontier and I had not a friend near me. And now with every prayer for your health, honour & happiness, believe me to be, your dutiful & obedient son, G U Barlow

3

To Portugal Again

George was finally well enough to sail back to Portugal in late August 1811 and he now finally looked forward to joining his regiment on active service.

Falmouth, 30 August 1811

My dear uncle,
I have just time to drop you a few lines before this evening's mail is closed, to inform you of my arrival at this place, about six o'clock in the evening. I immediately trudged off to the packet office and have secured a passage in the *Princess Charlotte*, Captain Rutter, which will sail the day after tomorrow or on Sunday morning if the wind is fair. To my great mortification I found that my friend Captain Ball sailed yesterday evening for Lisbon,[1] which was much sooner than anyone would have expected. The box containing my jacket, wings, & map I have opened, as also the packet of letters; which was as follows: one enclosure from Mrs Smith for my uncle in Portugal, Mr Hill's letter to Mr Bell,[2] a plan of Lisbon, as also Mr Cline's prescription, I did not however find any letter from Colonel Fleming to General Burne;[3] this letter would prove a most valuable acquisition as much as my two letters to Sir Brent Spencer are rendered of no effect by his arrival in this country, but owing to what cause the newspapers do not mention. I propose returning them in my small portmanteau with such things as I shall not take out to Portugal, accompanied with a note of thanks to Mr Hugh Baston and Mr Howard, to whom I shall respectively address them under cover. Having come this far without any touch of rheumatism, I trust never to experience a recurrence of it. I do not in the slightest degree feel any weakness or fatigue, from my journey, nor from a want of that regular repose, which my journies [sic] and gaiety at Teignmouth did not allow. I have a *sty* in my right eyelid, but that you know is of very little consequence.

1 Possibly refers to Captain Henry Lidgbird Ball RN.
2 Mr Herbert Hill, became Rector of St Leonards in Streatham in 1810 and held this office until 1829. He had been chaplain to the British factory at Lisbon from 1782-1808, when driven out by the French invasion.
3 I have been unable to identify Colonel Fleming, but he wrote to Major General Robert Burne.

The harbour is full of transports with cavalry for Lisbon; during my residence here I shall call on Mr Sam Pellew, collector of the customs, brother to the admiral and to whom Pownoll has given me a letter of introduction,[4] what with this and with finishing my India letters, which I shall also send up.

George wrote a much longer account regarding his illness and his original abortive attempt to join the army in Portugal. He was also very pleased to have received a letter of introduction from his father to the Duke of Wellington and he completed this letter having arrived safely at Lisbon in much better health than the previous time. He also informed his father of a change of command of the battalion, which meant that his friend Colonel Ross could no longer aid his progress within the regiment.

No. 38
To Sir G H Barlow KB &c, Fort St George, Madras
Off Cape Finisterre, 8 September 1811 – completed 18 September (annotated received 27 June 1812, answered June 1812)
H M Packet Princess Charlotte

My dearest father,
My cousin William would have informed you of my rapid progress in the recovery of health and strength. This favourable state has continued ever since, in spite of two or three rheumatic relapses and I now feel nearly myself again. Some months however must yet elapse before my constitution will return to its full and original tone and before the effects of the late severe illness wholly disappears. This much I have been led to expect from the most eminent of the faculty in London, indeed a few aches and pains on changes of weather, will be most cheerfully borne on my part, provided that they will not as heretofore be of that violent and excruciating degree, so as to take away the use of the limb. For during the period of the rheumatic fits, I am obliged to lay down on a sofa and press the member affected so as to smother the pain, which has been entirely confined to the left leg, whose muscles as well as those of the left arm will require some time before they regain their usual size and strength, debilitated and reduced as they have been by four months confinement on crutches and from such a loss of blood, as it was necessary to draw in order to remove the pain and inflammation from the eyes. This operation was repeatedly performed and to as great an extent as human nature would allow, for in consequence of this treatment and of utter interdiction from food except broths & soups, added to strong doses of physic and confinement to my cot, down in a cockpit, in company with many fellow sufferers, deprived of fresh air & fresh water and rolling about during a tempestuous fortnight in this bay, with all the ports & accesses for air, closely shut down; I was reduced to the last stage,

4 Samuel Humphrey Pellew was a medical doctor but was in charge of customs at Falmouth, he died in 1843. He was brother to Admirals Sir Edward and Sir Israel Pellew.

having been afflicted more severely than any of my friends who soon began to recover. In this state Sir James Wood took me into his cabin & prolonged existence until the squadron reached Lisbon. I was then conveyed through that city in a litter on the backs of four soldiers, muffled as to my head & body with three blankets. In the course of two months, the kindness of my signora and the mildness of the climate, restored me to a degree of strength sufficient to allow of my returning to England. Streatham air to which I shall in future attribute equal efficacy with Cheltenham or any other resort of invalids, and my good uncle's regularity, has wrought wonders. Cline who in so admirable a degree predicted my aunt's recovery and has performed divers other remarkable cases, was called in to my case and under his management I have attained to my present state of convalescence. At our last interview I represented to him the present interesting state of affairs in the peninsula, my anxiety as a professional man, to be present at the scene and requested that he would candidly give me his deliberate opinion & I rejoice to say that I received from him full permission to return to Lisbon and at parting he expressed his sincere conviction of my ability so to do and to use his own words, 'that there was no reason why I should not be able to go on with my official duties as well as any man in Lord Wellington's army by the time I arrived in Portugal, provided that a sufficient degree of ease was observed on my part during the intervening space'. I have omitted no earthly precaution or preventative, which can ensure a non-return of my complaint, such as flannels &c &c and which my situation as a subaltern will admit of being conveyed. For we are only allowed *one mule* between two, for baggage, I shall however be at the expense of having one to myself; all my equipage must therefore be of the most portable nature and having done thus much, the rest must be left to providence. The above is an epitome and I believe, third edition of my illness, from beginning to end. I have laid before you the whole course of my proceedings, perhaps at some length, it forms however so remarkable an era in my life, of one who of late years has known so little of weakness, that it could not be passed over lightly. Once for all I bid adieu to this subject.

To the best of my recollection, I acknowledged in my last, the receipt of the letter you were so good as to favour me with for Lord Wellington. Many thanks for this new proof of your attention & anxiety for my advancement & interests, independent of the advantages which will result from an introduction to so distinguished a personage, it will be a pleasure hereafter to reflect on having been in the company and received lessons of instruction in my profession from undoubtedly the first captain of the present day. The circumstance of having served under him, will be a source of some satisfaction in a more advanced age, if I should ever reach that period, if it pleases God to grant me health & strength, it is my present intention to devote myself for some years to come, to the active duties of my profession. Should our regiment suffer so severely in the course of the campaign, as to require supplying the first battalion by drafts of men from the second & sending the latter home to recruit, I propose volunteering into the Portuguese or

Spanish service; by this means, supposing me a captain in the British army, I obtain the brevet rank of major in the above kingdoms & serving with their troops only. This favour I doubt not, Lord Wellington would grant, for in the event of part of the regiment being ordered home, I must return also & it is my earnest wish to profit by those lessons of actual service and experience, which the peninsula at present so amply affords so fair an opportunity for the British army, in a spot commodiously situated within a few day's sail of our native kingdom and where local advantage can enable & counter balance the innumerable myriads of France has never presented itself, since the War of the United Provinces of Holland[5] & those of George the Second in Hanover and Minden.[6] I have been endeavouring to qualify myself for a [sic] participate in these scenes, by studying the languages of the nations in question and in the small quantum of my baggage Portuguese & Spanish books and dictionaries are not forgotten. My ill state of health during these last six months have prevented me from continuing that application. Never before did I know and appreciate so much the invaluable blessings of sight, sitting as was my custom in a darkened room and for months afterwards unable to apply in the smallest degree and although I have again resumed my usual course of reading, my eyes will not allow of carrying it to the former extent & scarcely at all by candlelight. Such has been the nature of the disease by which my whole system has been deranged and disorganised in the above pursuit. I have found Latin and French great supporters and soon hope in the course of a few month's practise in pronunciation, to be tolerably proficient in these tongues. I propose transmitting to you as often as circumstances will admit a regular account of our proceedings and to observe for the future, a greater degree of method. I shall divide my correspondence with you under two headings, the one on professional matters & military details, the other the journal, together with my remarks in the course of a journey through the country. These will most probably contain nothing of interest or novelty; you may have read them before, in the works of travellers of far greater capacity & leisure for surveys of that nature than the present person. It will however be a sort of excuse for the understanding is a good habit and may perhaps now & then fill up a leisure moment, if you ever should have one on your hands.

My Uncle William was so good as to procure me from two of his friends, two letters to Sir Brent Spencer. That general has however come home and they will consequently be returned on my part. Mr Hill, who has at present the living of Streatham and who has been resident in Portugal the best part of his life or upwards of 30 years as Chaplain at Lisbon, has also feined [sic] me with one to Mr Stewart, the British Minister & Ambassador at the court

5 This refers to the Third Anglo-Dutch War of 1672-4, which essentially formed a part of the Franco-Dutch War of 1672-8.

6 King George II led the British to victory at Dettingen in 1743, the last occasion when a reigning British monarch actually was present at a battle; the Battle of Minden was a great victory fought in 1759 during the Seven Years War.

and which I trust will be the means of introduction to the best society at that place. Such ends as these are essentially necessary for a young man to get through the world, more especially in my profession, where to attain at a proper age of manhood, to its highest honours, requires a rapid progress in the earlier stages. In consequence of Mr Hill's advice, I have left England two or three weeks sooner than was originally intended. Our voyage will just terminate, as the rains in Portugal commence, which generally take place about the fourteenth of September and last till the middle of October; during that period the roads are nearly impassable and all military operations at a stand. When these have ceased, I shall set out to join the army, which at present have a position in the rear of Ciudad Rodrigo and about 270 miles from Lisbon. Our two battalions, together with the 43rd & 95th Regiments form the Light Brigade and are entirely composed of light infantry. They are always in the advance, have the outpost duties, skirmishing &c &c. This is a very pleasant service, in as much as you have always something to do and answers to those troops denominated by the French 'tirailleurs', 'voltigeurs', 'eclaireurs'. General Crawford [sic] who commands the division, is a great martinet and resembles much the German soldier.[7] He has not the act of conciliating the affections of his inferiors, together with the talent of keeping up his dignity & consequence. I am by no means an advocate for laxity of discipline, particularly in a corps which is always under the immediate eye of the enemy. General C[raufurd] has the reputation (for I am not acquainted with him personally) of attending too much to trifles & minutiae, without showing any great degree of talent on the more extended scale of a general's duties; an officer may be an excellent colonel, without possessing the coup d'oeil[8] and other superior qualifications which are required for one entrusted with a brigade.

Since Colonel Barclay's death of the wounds he received at the Battle of Busaco,[9] there has been a great change in our regiment. Colonel Ross who succeeded him and who has always shown me great attention & civility since I have been in the regiment, has exchanged with a Colonel Colborne[10] of the 66th & is going out to Ceylon, as Deputy Adjutant General with General Brownrigg.[11] I dare say Colonel C[olborne] is a good officer, having been so intimate a friend of Sir John Moore; the loss of Colonel R[oss] will however be most deeply and universally regretted by us all. His affability &

7 Major General Robert Craufurd commanded the Light Division until his death at the storming of Ciudad Rodrigo in January 1812. George's views of him are interesting as they obviously emanated from his fellow officers in Portugal.

8 French – a glance that takes in a very comprehensive view.

9 Lieutenant Colonel Robert Barclay was severely wounded at the Battle of Busaco on 27 September 1810, but did not die of his wounds until 3 May 1811 when he had arrived back in England.

10 Lieutenant Colonel John Colborne transferred into the 52nd Foot on 18 July 1811 from the 66th Foot.

11 Lieutenant General Sir Robert Brownrigg became Governor of Ceylon and completed its domination by British forces over the next few years.

gentlemanly conduct has endeared him to every individual, united as it was with that proper degree of discipline and consequence, which it is necessary that every commanding officer of a regiment should keep up and all of which heterogenous qualities, few are able to confine, without intermixing too great a portion either of one or the other.

I have kept this letter open, to inform you of our arrival at Lisbon, which we entered about four o'clock yesterday afternoon. The same packet, which brought me out, returns tomorrow with the mail and will I trust reach England previous to Sir Samuel Hood's[12] departure and give you the latest possible account of my proceedings. I propose gaining exact information respecting the precise commencement of the periodic rains, which will determine the question whether I shall instantaneously set out for the grand army or remain a fortnight in Lisbon, until they shall have ceased. For some people affirm that they commence nearly about the 14th of this month & I am now writing on the 13th; others on the contrary, say that the first week in October is the season for them and that they occasionally vary. Indeed, there are no signs of any wet & as at present by the majority of opinion on this head, my nose will be determined. The army are now in the neighbourhood of Ciudad Rodrigo and operations of some consequence are supposed to be on the tape;[13] as a large reinforcement with Marshal Berthier have lately joined the French army.[14]

And now my dear father, with every wish for your public honour, health & happiness, believe me to be, your most obedient &affectionate son, G.U Barlow.

A second later letter to his father, seemingly sent from Lisbon, is unfortunately missing, but we are lucky to have his regular correspondence with his Uncle William to fill the gaps.

This is now the perfect opportunity to explain what had happened to the 52nd Foot during the previous year of the war, having last left them keeping a protective watch over the fortress of Ciudad Rodrigo in early 1810. On 26 April 1810, Marshal Ney's 6th Corps moved to form a blockade of the fortress and then settled down to progress their siege operations, the Light Division being unable to prevent it as it was heavily outnumbered. The Spanish garrison of over 5,000 men, was commanded by General Herrasti. The French build up was slow, but they eventually formed an effective breach in the walls and on 10 July, the Spanish governor capitulated to avoid a blood bath. With Ciudad Rodrigo now in French hands, securing their base of operations, Marshal Massena launched his invasion of Portugal.

12 Vice Admiral Sir Samuel Hood, he was on route to take command of the naval forces in the East Indies and died at Madras in 1814.

13 As in – lined up at the tape at the start of a race.

14 He is in error here as Marshal Louis Alexandre Berthier did not come to Spain at this time. It is likely that he meant Marshal Jean-Baptiste Bessieres who was given the command of the Army of the North in Spain in 1811.

His first target was the Portuguese fortress of Almeida, which the Light Division was maintaining a protective watch over. Wellington had warned General Craufurd to withdraw his troops over the River Coa, but he had chosen to ignore the advice. On the 24 of July, overwhelming French forces launched an attack with the aim of capturing the bridge over the Coa in Craufurd's rear and thus trapping his force and compelling them to surrender. Despite the numbers, the Light Division fought tenaciously and although forced back, did eventually succeed in getting across the bridge to safety but with some loss. The French elated by their cheaply won success, pushed on too far and were repulsed every time they tried to force the passage over the bridge with even greater loss. During this action, the 1/52nd under Major Henry Ridewood had been in danger of being isolated and cut off, but a counter charge by the 1/43rd caused the French advance to slow and the 52nd escaped. The losses of the 1/52nd this day were light, being only 1 man killed and 18 officers and men wounded.

The division retired to Celorico, when Wellington added two Portuguese Cacadore battalions to the division immediately afterwards. The fortress of Almeida was besieged, when a fortunate French shell apparently rolled right into the cellar of the old medieval castle, which was used as the main ammunition store. The resultant explosion destroyed half of the town and forced the governor, Brigadier General William Cox, to surrender. This allowed Marshal Massena's troops to march south towards Lisbon and forced Wellington's army back by sheer weight of numbers.

Wellington needed a political success to shore up the government at home and in Portugal, he therefore chose to halt on the steep ridge at Busaco and to offer battle on 27 September 1810. Massena attacked without much finesse, sending a series of columns directly up the slopes, only to be devastated by the fire of the British infantry and repelled by a bayonet charge. The 1/52nd saw limited action that day, helping defeat one of the columns by their devastating musket fire at short range. Although their commander was severely wounded, their total losses only came to 3 men killed and 12 other officers and men wounded. Private Alexander Hopkins and Private Harris of the 52nd received pensions for capturing the French *Général de Brigade* Simon that day (Harris was not awarded his pension until 1843).[15]

Despite his defeat, Massena eventually found a route that went around this deadly ridge and his superior numbers ensured that Wellington would have to continue to retreat. Massena's advance was finally brought to a halt by lines of defensive forts which Wellington's engineers had been constructing for more than a year, using thousands of Portuguese labourers, now known as the Lines of Torres Vedras. After some initial probing Massena realised the futility of attempting to punch a hole in these lines and he was forced to settle down for the winter in front of these hills, with no idea how to overcome them. Starvation eventually forced the French army to retire in search of supplies on 14 November and they saw out the winter at Santarem; the British army moving close, but not daring to attack them in such a strong position. The French, overcome by starvation and with little sign of reinforcements,

15 Philip Abbott, *'Every Implement of Destruction was used against Us' The lives of Henry and Charles Dawson 52nd Regiment of Light Infantry* (Privately Published: 2015), p.44, proves beyond doubt that Moorsom identifies the wrong Hopkins.

began to retire into Spain on the night of 5 March, the Light Division in pursuit. In a number of actions, the 52nd lost 1 officer and 12 men killed and 7 officers, 5 sergeants and 70 rank and file wounded.

On 6 March 1811, the 2/52nd had arrived in Portugal, George accompanying them, but whilst in mid-March they began their march to join the 1/52nd, George fell ill and returned to England, as we have seen. Having joined the division at Nabainhos, en route to Celorico, the two battalions were put into the same brigade the 1/52nd then numbering 855 men and the 2/52nd with 565 men on 1 April 1811. The division took part in a number of further skirmishes and small-scale actions as they drove the French army out of Portugal and by mid-April the division was on the banks of the Agueda, keeping a watch over the approaches to Ciudad Rodrigo.

By early May, however, Massena had by some miracle resupplied his army and brought them back on the offensive. Massena attacked at the village of Fuentes d'Onoro and the division was called in to form up with the army. Due to a major attack by the French cavalry on the right-wing of Wellington's extended forces, he drew Houston's 7th Division back to the main position and Drummond's Brigade of the Light Division was sent out to cover their retreat in the face of thousands of French cavalry. This exploit has been heavily over-emphasised by the historian Napier and adherents of the Light Division, but in reality the losses suffered were extremely light, totalling less than 45 men in a brigade numbering over 2,000 men. The division was not involved in the fighting that followed on the third day and the two battalions lost in total 1 man killed and 20 wounded with another 21 missing throughout the battle.

Marshal August de Marmont now took over from Massena and the French army underwent a period of reorganisation, leading to little serious fighting, but much illness, with many succumbing to fevers. The battalions remained along the Agueda all this summer, the 1/52nd now numbering 771 effectives and the 2/52nd 432. These numbers show the significant losses by sickness, but many battalions in the army counted far fewer men.

Wellington's forces had been blockading Ciudad Rodrigo since August, but towards the end of September Marmont combined his forces with *Général de Division* Dorsenne's Army of the North, totalling just under 60,000 men, and launched an attack on Wellington's army numbering about 46,000, but strung out to maintain the blockade of Ciudad Rodrigo. Wellington pulled his troops back and the French successfully communicated with the fortress, but he mistakenly believed that they would not progress further west. When Marmont did attack across the border into Portugal, Wellington's troops were spread out and in danger of being defeated piecemeal. An attack near Carpio was pushed back, but a second attack further south nearly caused disaster for the allies. The French cavalry deployed here heavily outnumbered the allied cavalry and soon broke through, coming upon the 3rd British Division in a dangerously exposed position without support. In a bid to entrap this division, the French cavalry sought to break through near Fuenteguinaldo, but were prevented by the dogged resistance of Colville's Brigade, supported ably by Alten's King's German Legion cavalry. The attacks were driven off and the action is particularly noted for the novel deployment of the 5th Foot, which advanced on the French cavalry in line and defeated them with their rolling volleys of musketry. A turning movement eventually forced Colville to order a steady withdrawal, but enough time had been gained to allow the entire 3rd Division to safely retire to Fuenteguinaldo despite repeated cavalry charges on the British squares which remained solid. At the end of the day, Wellington realised that Marmont had gained an advantage and ordered his army to withdraw to a new defensive position. Marmont however, unaware of Wellington's withdrawal, fearing a counter attack, also withdrew his forces back over the Agueda and the crisis passed. As George states, the battalion was not involved in this fighting at all, but had to march excessively to retire and then re-advance to their original positions as Marmont's troops moved away. It was here on 1 November that George finally caught up with the battalion.

The armies were now settling into their winter quarters, assuming that little would occur before April the following year and with this in mind, George had managed to bring some books with him to continue his education in surveying and set to learning the local languages. He also began to surmise on what the new campaigning season would bring, little realising that it would come early next year. He wrote with feeling on the utter devastation the French armies had wreaked on Portugal (all except Coimbra), leaving little more than a waste ground for hundreds of miles. He continues with a vivid picture of the misery of their quarters, the severe lack of provisions and the soldier's desperate need for new uniforms. Indeed, George betrays a very human concern for his soldiers and their welfare.

To William Barlow Esq, Little Bridge Street, Blackfriars, London
Lisbon, 14 September 1811

My dear uncle,
We arrived here yesterday evening after a passage of eleven days. The weather throughout was remarkably fine; at first our voyage seemed likely to be very expeditious, in the first 24 hours we ran by our log 175 miles & continued at this rate as far as Cape Finisterre,[16] which we reached in two days & a half. We were from thence to this port eight more [days] in coming, a distance which is often run in 60 hours. Constant calms prevented our going more than one or two knots an hour. Three days have we been in sight of this rock;[17] once only have we been alarmed by a strange sail, as he came up, the packet gave him four or five rounds from the stern-most guns. With boarding netting traced up, matches lighted and double-loaded with grape, we all stood ripe for some most ferocious deed, but as soon as the stranger came alongside she proved to be a friend.

Immediately on landing I proceeded to the signora; she has let her house and gone into the country with some of her friends. I burst into her room and found a large and strange family at dinner, they all seem as scared and frightened as if I had been a mad dog. I then proceeded to Barnwell's Hotel, of

16 A rocky promontory on the north-west coast of Spain.
17 The Cabo da Roca is a cape forming the most westerly point in mainland Portugal, it is also known as the Rock of Lisbon.

whom I dare say you have often heard me speak; nothing but pure necessity would have compelled me to take this step, unacquainted as I was anyone in the place. As soon as I have finished the present and made up any packet of India letters, I purpose reporting myself to the Adjutant Generals; I shall then seek out for some of our officers, who I know are in this city and shall confer with them on the best means of procuring mules &c &c. Tomorrow, which is Sunday, I shall employ in putting my baggage into the saddlebags and making all the necessary preparations for my march which is nearly 300 miles, inasmuch as the army have advanced by the last accounts to the neighbourhood of Ciudad Rodrigo. Early on Monday morning I shall go round with my letters to Mr Stewart, Mr Bell and the rest of them, perhaps *today in* Mr Stewart as he lives close by.

This morning I met my old surgeon Mr Cook who attended me during my illness; he was quite surprized to find me so well & strong. I consulted with him about proceeding immediately up the country; he says and so do two or three more, that the commencement of the rains is very uncertain; sometimes not happening till the first week in October and at other periods in the middle of this month. I shall collect as many opinions of those who are qualified to judge, and then determine by the majority whether I shall immediately depart early next week, or remain a fortnight longer in Lisbon; for many reasons I should prefer the former plan, so as to arrive at the Grand army about the period or soon after the rains set in. About that time some business of importance is expected to take place, as Marmont has been reinforced with 15,000 men under Marshal Bessieres and is supposed, will not suffer Lord Wellington to undertake the siege of Ciudad Rodrigo, without interruption.[18]

The weather is still very hot and sultry & not the slightest appearance of rain. The mosquitos & fleas made a fine feast on me last night, so as hardly to allow me a wink of sleep. I am nevertheless very hearty and well. I have got to finish my India letters and the mail will be closed in two or three hours; excuse therefore this [torn – short note?] Should the packet not sail tomorrow I will write to you again; give my best love to my aunt and all at Streatham and believe me to be your truly affectionate nephew, G U Barlow

To William Barlow Esq, Little Bridge Street, Blackfriars, London
Lisbon, 20 September 1811

My dear uncle,
You see we are still detained here and indeed I may with propriety use that term inasmuch as my business was not completed until yesterday when I bought a horse and paid a visit to Mr Stewart. I am now quite ready in every respect and on Thursday next the 25th instant, propose starting for the army, in company with two or three others of our regiment, who have been resident some time at Lisbon for the benefit of their health. On the

18 Marshal Jean-Baptiste Bessieres, Duc d'Istria; it is interesting to note that there was already talk of besieging Ciudad Rodrigo in September 1811.

24th instant I shall receive in full my pay & arrears, a point of some consequence as the army in the field have received not a fraction these last two months. This circumstance combined with the pleasure of travelling near 900 miles in company with my brother officers, who have gone over every inch of the country often before, has induced me to postpone my departure until the above day, when they will also be ready to proceed, in preference to undertaking such a journey in solitude with my servant, or being troubled with conducting a detachment of these last, some are going up the country every week and it will require some manoeuvring on our part to avoid so troublesome a job.

Finding, on coming ashore, that my signora was flown, I applied to the Town Major for a billet, but was not so lucky as in the former instance, being quartered on a poor linen draper, who had a large family and could only spare me one little room. The house consisted of six stories [sic], each of which was occupied by a separate family, who have nothing to do with those who live in the one above or below them. This poor wretch occupied one of these with four rooms and was situated at the farthest extremity of Lisbon, whilst my friends were quartered at Belem, which is on the other extreme; the same distance as Whitechapel or Portman Square, which is I think about four miles. To avoid so uncomfortable a predicament, I have my bed at this hotel, and walk out to Belem for our little mess for my meals. So you see I consult economy as much as possible.

With regard to money matters I have been obliged to draw 200 dollars on account of cattle; a mule cost 80. It has been a year & a half in the service of Colonel Pynn,[19] has been all over the country, is very hardy & stout & just, calculated for the purpose of carrying baggage. He is perfectly sound, warranted to be so, is capable of being rode, has not those obdurate qualities which are attributed to his kind, having been always well treated and really is not dear for his price. My Galloway is also an old campaigner,[20] I purchased him off an officer of the 40th Regiment, with which corps he has actually been *doing duty near* three years, since its first landing in Portugal. It has been to Madrid, and through every species of wear & tear, which these late severe campaigns produced and is only parted with in consequence of its owner being about to return to England. He is an English horse, warranted sound and much resembles your little thick, stout shouldered horse at Streatham, bridle, saddle & all cost me 140 dollars.

I must now proceed to the particulars of my interview with Mr Stewart;[21] he lives at a house called San Domingos about five miles from Lisbon;[22] with

19 Lieutenant Colonel Henry Pynn, commanding the 18th Portuguese Infantry Regiment.

20 The Galloway breed of pony is now extinct. Originally from Scotland and the north of England, it was said to have good looks, hardy and active, with a deep chest and a tendency to pace rather than trot.

21 Sir Charles Stuart was the Ambassador Extraordinaire at Lisbon.

22 This would be one of the villas or summer palaces situated in the Sao Domingos district of Benfica.

great difficulty and through most execrable roads I found him out and upon learning that he was within, was ushered by the stupid servants into his parlour, where he was in the middle of dinner with his suite &c &c. There was I with my dirty boots, covered with dust & heat, with my whole [torn – self muddy?] I marched up however to the top of the table, presented my letter, and apologized for intruding at such an hour as perfectly unintentional on my part being uninformed by his servants that he was at dinner, it was nearly four o'clock and I was supposed to have come upon public business, as I held a letter in my fist. I took my situation however at the lower end of the table and without any ceremony, being very hungry, cut a good dinner, everyone else looking on, for they had nearly finished at the time of my entrance. Though it was a common report, everything was served up in the first style, the wines most excellent. He talked to me a little about Mr Hill; we did not sit long after dinner, as some Portuguese ladies made their appearance, who came to survey the house, which is a most elegant country villa and the museum of curiosities which it contains. I only lament that Mr Stewart does not reside more in Lisbon and thereby afford me opportunities of being more frequently at his house; during the remainder of the evening, the conversation turned chiefly on political subjects from whence I collected some most valuable information and these lights have contributed to alter my opinion & which the world in general entertains, on many recent events. For Mr S[tuart] has resided at Vienna, Berlin and at almost every foreign court; in Germany, Russia & France, he has spent nearly ten years in the various course of his diplomatic life. He is a man of little ceremony; he concluded with giving me a general invitation to his house, whilst remaining in Lisbon. This however signifies but little as in five days more I shall leave the place & on my return he may be no longer in this kingdom: so much for this affair.

Give my love to my aunt and the little ones and with every prayer for your united health & happiness, I remain your truly affectionate nephew,
G U Barlow

George's next letter revealed that he had not left Lisbon as planned.

To William Barlow Esq, Little Bridge Street, Blackfriars, London
Lisbon, 28 September 1811

My dear uncle,
You will probably expect this to be dated from Coimbra rather than Lisbon, upon recollecting the promises of my speedy departure as described in my last. This circumstance has however been delayed by an event that could neither be foreseen or expected. On proceeding to report myself to the commandant of the detachments at Belem, as it is customary for officers to do on setting out for the army, he told me that it was his intention to detain me until the 30th instant or first of October, to take charge of a detachment going up to the grand army. This gives me a good deal of vexation for

several reasons inasmuch as I am obliged to commit my horse & mule to the care of a soldier to conduct them as far as Coimbra, a distance of 135 miles, while I am compelled to embark on board a transport with these men and go round by sea to Figueira [da Foz] town & port situated at the entrance of the Mondego River from whence it is thirty miles to Coimbra. This system of sending supplies & recruits, convoys &c to the grand army is for the future constantly to be pursued; inasmuch as the whole tract between Lisbon and the above mentioned city has been so devastated, consumed & ruined by the ravages & long continuance of so large an army of French, as also by furnishing the necessary requisitions to the allied troops, which in numbers were also very considerable, that the government are willing to spare the few remaining & wretched inhabitants as much as possible.[23] In consequence of this, their cattle teams &c are freed from military service, from a certain portion of taxes & all troops are transported by sea to Coimbra, so as to avoid marching them through those tracts. From that city to Ciudad Rodrigo, where the army are at present encamped, the distance is about 180 miles, so that upon landing at Figueira [da Foz] we shall have 200 only instead of 300 to march.

Today (Saturday) there is always an inspection at the depot for those men, who are fit to join the army; and on Monday or Tuesday next they will be shipped on board. I purpose immediately applying to the commandant to be sent with the first party, as I am quite impatient of stopping here any longer, having been ready to quit it these ten days. On Thursday last I dined a second time with Mr Stuart at his country house at Benfica; whilst at dinner dispatches arrived & were opened at the table; he did not of course communicate their contents but stated that the French had assembled so many thousand in one place & so many in another; that Lord Wellington has concentrated his forces in such & such position. I gave vague hints of that nature by which we could understand that some events of importance are in agitation, but of course he did not give the slightest hint of their tendency. It is a matter well known that the enemy have received considerable reinforcements & that others still more considerable are expected to reach them by the month of November. There will doubtless be a very severe winter campaign. Thank God I am still very well, and if it pleases him to give me strength & health to go through it, I shall be perfectly content & happy. My anxiety to reach the scene of operations is very great and were I my own master, I would go over the ground in three or four days & nights, but my movements are regulated by the will of others & not my own.

I hear by the last packet that the long-expected fleet of Indiamen had arrived from Madras, which place however, Lord Minto had not reached at the sailing of the last advices.

23 This is an interesting statement, confirmed by others progressing up to the army in late 1811. Many historians mistakenly assume that the difficult boat trip up the Tagus and long overland march used previously was the only method used throughout the war.

Give my love to my aunt and all at Streatham & believe me to be your trusty affectionate nephew, G U Barlow

To William Barlow Esq, Little Bridge Street, Blackfriars, London
Lisbon, 1 October 1811

My dear uncle,
At length, all doubts and delays respecting my departure are come to an end and we are finally to embark the day after tomorrow or on the 3rd instant; this piece of information I received with no inconsiderable degree of pleasure at the Commandant of Belem's office yesterday afternoon, when my name was inserted in the garrison orders together with that of eight other officers to take charge of various detachments. Had this not been the case I had rode over to Belem to have an interview with the commandant, purposely to make such a request; relying on the probable state of the winds which prevail at this season, we shall reach Figueira in 24 hours sail and from thence will most probably reach the grand headquarters in the course of ten or eleven days march. Two or three more [days] may perhaps be added, before I can arrive at the Light Brigade, which is considerably in the advance & by the time I have delivered my men over to their respective corps & settled their lists, for to my great regret, I apprehend that there are none of our Light Brigade in the numbers, but of regiments attached to the other divisions of the army.

As two or three days only have elapsed since my last, I cannot of course have anything new to communicate. Accounts have reached Lisbon this morning of the smart brush on the frontiers, in which I hear the Light Brigade were concerned. I propose today going to learn the particulars, as also the names of the killed & wounded. Strange reports are in circulation respecting the manner in which his division, the 1st of the army were attacked, by surprize as report says.[24] I am however unwilling to credit such scandal of military men. Their honour is their only treasure, their very existence; and I should be unwilling to believe such accounts, unless they are fully authenticated, as they certainly are not at present.

You may inform Mr Hall that I waited on Mr Bell and found him not at home; and as neither his Portuguese servant nor I could make one another comprehend, I came away, just as wise as, when I went. I purpose calling on him again as also on Mr Lucas for the purpose of drawing bills of the money which I have received. This sums up the whole of my transactions in Lisbon, of which I am willing to give you an account, as this will be the last at this place and you will probably not hear from me these three weeks since, inasmuch as I shall be nearly a fortnight on my way up to the army, and in the event of our being on the move, or any other operations,

24 The Light Division was not particularly involved in this action. Marshal Marmont launched Montbrun's cavalry against Picton's 3rd Division which was dangerously spread out, but Colville's brigade held up their advance at the Action of El Bodon on 25 September 1811.

another fortnight may elapse before my letters reach Lisbon. The packet is still detained for the dispatches for Lord Wellington, by the time which you receive this, about the 14th instant, I shall probably have arrived at my destination.

As yet I have not had any letters from you, but trust to hear that you are all happy and going on as usual. Remember me kindly to my aunt, Miss Page and all the little ones.[25] I would write to them as well as to you, but unmixed with any society as I have been since my residence in this place & occupied as I have been with mules, horses, billets & such work, there is nothing I am sure that is worth the postage of 2s 4d.[26] I trust however that my journey up the country, will present a greater scope for variety of correspondence. I make this observation, in order that they may not deem my silence to them, as any mark of unkindness or negligence. God bless you all and believe me to be your truly affectionate nephew G U Barlow

Finally, George could announce in his next letter that he had left Lisbon, but he was still far from the army.

To William Barlow Esq, Little Bridge Street, Blackfriars, London
Coimbra, 16 October 1811

My dear uncle,
As the detachment will occupy a day or two in preparing for the ensuing march I think it necessary to furnish you with some particulars of our progress thus far. We embarked from Belem on the 4th instant, sailed finally on the 7th and on the 10th following disembarked in Mondego Bay, on the very same spot where Lord Wellington first landed previous to the Battle of Vimiera.[27] The weather was beautiful & my brother messmates alike accommodating and agreeable. This you must be aware is a point of the first consequence on board a ship. It was a dead calm the day of our coming ashore at Figueira, yet still the swell and breakers were very considerable. Nature has been the best engineer on this coast; a very moderate breeze agitates the surf to such a degree as to prevent a boat living for an instant; the passage moreover into the Mondego, will scarcely admit two vessels abreast & in every other part is full of shoals & sands. In short, along the whole extent of this inhospitable shore, not a single harbour or port is offered to the distressed mariner.

Perhaps it may be needless to inform you that a Portuguese is a character upon which civility & kindness produces no other effect, than a return of insolence & ill usage. You must cure them into good behaviour, this is well known to John Bull after a short trial of residence. He has at first plenty of money and very little head and deports himself with the

25 Miss Page would appear to be the governess.
26 About £5.50 in 2018.
27 Fought on 21 August 1808. This French defeat led to the Convention of Cintra.

usual good breeding & generosity of his country. He is soon compelled to adopt a contrary system. In the distribution of billets, the judge of the town is apt to give himself great airs. One of our detachment in begging the use of a few knives & forks for his dinner was peremptorily refused, the next morning the padrone walked into the room and began to converse & behave in the most pleasing way. This so much incensed the officer, that he sent him *neck & crop* out of the apartment.[28] In the course of the day the Portuguese sent up the above articles without any request whatever on the part of his host.

On the Saturday night, a soldier of the 95th was stabbed by one of the natives; He was walking in company with a brother officer and proceeding to the spot on the first alarm found a man much in liquor on the hill. Upon asking who had wounded him, he replied that he had been struck with a *stick*. I concluded that he had conducted himself improperly & had received a good drubbing for his pains & ordered him to the barracks, whither he marched off as quick as could be expected from a drunken man. It turned out however, the next morning that he had received two severe wounds in the belly but being so drunk at the time did not feel what might otherwise have been expected. All search after the miscreant was in vain and without any redress we marched off for Montemor-o-Velho on the following Monday. Our route lay through a country untainted by French devastation and thickly studded with convents and nunneries.[29] There is scarcely a single town of any consequence which does not possess some of these, especially where the French have not been. Woods of olives and hedges full of aloes larger than any to be seen in England and which grow wild in their country, are everywhere to be beheld; as also fields of Indian corn, which thrives here with scarce any labour or cultivation. The ploughs are wooden; the furrows only a few inches deep and the harvest is sure to equal any which the most laborious & careful farmer amongst you would produce. The roads however are most execrable up to our knees in sand, so as hardly to be passable for carts or vehicles of any description. They almost exceed belief and can only be ascribed to the wretched policy of the country which keeps only two or three intended for the travelling of couriers, to repair & regulate the remainder. At Montemor I was billeted in the country villa of Quintella, a rich Lisbon tobacconist & which had been successively occupied by Junot & Lord Wellington.[30] You must know that this fellow has obtained of the court of Lisbon, the *exclusive* privilege of selling tobacco & making snuff. All Lisbon & Portugal is supplied by him, and no one else is allowed to rend that article. He used to entertain Junot and all his staff in the most sumptuous manner, an incredible

28 Neck and crop – Brusquely and completely.
29 Coimbra and the surrounding country was saved from the ravages of Massena's retreating forces by Colonel Trant's forces barring their entrance into the city at the bridge and forcing them to retreat through the mountains into Spain.
30 The Baron de Quintella.

number of covers graces his table early day. You may form some idea of his wealth, when I tell you that he possessed several other villas equally as good as that at Montemor, which last he had possessed nearly three years and paid but one visit to it during that period. The steward was a nice respectable old fellow, he drank a glass of grog with me in the evening when he communicated the above particulars. He added that the table at which we drank, was that at which Lord Wellington had his first conference and furthermore, find what I was glad to hear, that he had received the same civility and good treatment from every British officer who had lodged in the house, as from ourselves. On the 15th we entered Coimbra about 30 miles from the place of disembarkation, this *city had* a famous university, the students however have at present changed the gown for the sword and their noble halls & colleges are doomed no longer to resound with the lyre, of the muses, or the voice of philosophy, which are changed for the clamours and tumult of a soldier's barrack, or the gardens of a hospital full of sick and wounded men. It is the third city for rank & size in Portugal & of course the *third* in filth & dirt. There are however a number of very good shops & houses, where a man may be supplied with everything necessary for a fitout, it is true at a most exorbitant rate. But this is a point of no consequence, inasmuch as this is the last place at which I understand these articles are to be procured, even the common necessaries, as we strike into the track of the French army, on the first day's march from hence. This town if you recollect, [torn -was luckily?] saved from being sacked by Massena on his late retreat, owing to the extraordinary exertions of Colonel Trant, who with a handful of men, the same description as our local militia; broke down the centre arch of the bridge across the Mondego, which here is very wide. This would have been easily repaired in two or three hours. Lord W[ellington] was however so close at their heels, that they dare not stop even for the short time and being unwilling to risk a battle, they passed along the south bank. Thus was the prey rescued out of the very jaws of the destroyer. Here I also met my horse & mule who had come round by land 124 miles, but were in good condition; as also some officers on leave of absence from the regiment, one of whom had lost the use of his hand & arm by the rheumatism, after the fashion of my late illness. They were all surprized at seeing me look so well, some not having expected ever to meet me again.

17th October. I have delayed, including the present up to the last day of our stay at the place. We are finally to proceed forward tomorrow. Lord W[ellington] and the French have, it appears had another slight bush, the particulars of which came into Coimbra this day. Although, when the infantry retired in square, the French cavalry charged at once, three faces of it; they were beaten off in the finest style. And now my dear uncle with every wish & prayer for your & my aunt's happiness, as well as if those under your good roof, believe me to be your truly affectionate nephew. I hope you received safe my India news, G U Barlow

To William Barlow Esq, Little Bridge Street, Blackfriars, London
Celorico, 26 October 1811

My dear uncle,
We have now got over a good half of the proposed journey and another halt is deemed necessary, to settle the accounts of our men, as well as to secure routes to our various destinations, for here we all separate. I go forward to Ciudad Rodrigo, others to the right & left of the line, upon which the army is at present cantoned, my last [letter] left me at Coimbra. Well, on the morning of the 19th I started, having obtained leave to stop behind an hour from the commandant of the detachment. One matter I had to settle was a dispute between my little Portuguese boy & a shoemaker, for the mending of his boots, the rascally Portuguese charged nearly treble the full value. I went into the shop and paid the fellow just one third of what he asked, indeed I had a great mind to have taken them away without giving him a fraction, did I not recollect that it would be a discreditable story of my nation to have done so. I made a great noise & scared six or seven Crispins[31] who were at work & taking the boots, paid them what I thought reasonable, telling them that a Frenchman would have cut off their heads for such a proceeding. This they knew to be true enough, as the fate of Condeixa [a-Velha], a town six miles from Coimbra. I came to this place in about two hours after crossing the Mondego and here I found the tales of my brother officers at Lisbon, as well as the accounts of the newspapers verified to a degree of accuracy which I could have scarcely believed. A fine town, the noble palace of the bishop and other fine buildings totally consumed. All was a dreary silence & desolation; that [not] a house, except a few base walls left standing. The scene was equally new to me never having been before in a burnt city; the change equally sudden on a two hours transportation from the bustle & noise of Coimbra. Men, women & children merely because they were Portuguese were butchered without exception to an extent & degree scarcely credible, was not the testimony the most respectable. A few poor solitary inhabitants had just commenced to return & remove away the ashes of their ruined dwellings. Leaving this sad picture of misery, I bent my course across the mountains; the roads stony & execrable. The ascent continued for some miles; the sun most intense, not a single tree and what was worse, pathways, for they could not be called roads, branching off in every direction. I took that which appeared the most frequented, after having gone upon this for a considerable length of time, I accosted two muleteers who informed me that I had strayed considerably from the proper route; they conducted me to the proper road & then went [on] their way. I continued my course to Miranda do Corvo; about five o'clock I reached a small village called St Jago, four miles on this side of it. Having come twenty-one miles and tasted nothing except a small roll & cup of coffee at Coimbra the whole day (for by the proper road the

31 A shoemaker, St Crispin being the patron saint of cobblers.

march was but twelve), I sat down near the market house literally faint, for want of sustenance. The villagers came flocking about, and one good young girl brought me some cold fish, bread & water, for which she refused to take any money, although the expense to people in her poor state must have been very considerable. I shall always remember with gratitude the poor hovel of St Jago and must here remark, that in the whole of my progress unattended & alone as I then was during a march of fifty miles, I ever experienced from the *peasantry*, the greatest kindness & hospitality, nay respect, inasmuch as everyone took off his hat that passed, to my British uniform. This however is solely confined to the country people. Well, after being recruited in this way, my strength instantly returned and during the remainder of the journey [I] outwalked the guide. From Miranda do Corvo I continued my route next day 25 miles more. The country is here most sublimely mountainous & grand, this forms the general face of Portugal with some few exceptions. It would however be tedious to recount the names of bridges and mountains. All was one frightful scene of desolation, arches blown up, and every hut & house universally destroyed & provisions of any kind not to be procured, except at the regular magazines of the English commissariat. In a space of one hundred miles thickly studded with numerous villages, I hardly beheld twice as many inhabitants in who chiefly drag a miserable existence on roots & herbs. In one hovel I found a numerous family supping on roasted acorns & water with a little goat's milk. Thus, have the French themselves erected the most insufferable barrier to the subjugation of the kingdom. All the owners of these ruined habitations are become guerrillas, whose hatred & activity is equally great. Not a solitary bullock or house have I seen along the great tract of country but what belongs to the commissariat and would of course be removed on the approach of the enemy. The country is indeed swept to a degree of nakedness & poverty, such as has never had a precedent. This sometimes impelled [torn – making?] detachments to go foraging for what they could find, as it necessarily was for every regiment in the army, some black sheep of course found their way into it. Our commandant however most properly kept up his discipline and bringing them instantly to a court martial at the drum head when caught in the act, they were flogged & several examples of that sort were at first found necessary to produce good order & regularity.

Some English newspapers have been received at the place & it would give me much pleasure to receive a weekly paper at the regiment so as to have an account of all that is going forward. The expense would be but small & I have brought but few books with me and those entirely of a professional nature; and at so great a distance is our division detached from any spot where these articles are to be procured, that they were a considerable, a great treat.

Give my best love to my aunt, Miss Page & all at Streatham, I will write to them as also to the little ones when I join the regiment and with every prayer for the health & happiness of you all I remain, your truly affectionate nephew G U Barlow

Celorico, 28 October 1811

My dear uncle,
We are about to leave this place in a few hours; there is no regular post in this country, but as couriers *sometimes* stop here to take up letters. I write the present on the chance of [it] reaching its destination and knowing your anxiety to receive the first intelligence of my progress. I am in the very best health, although we have been marching for some days past in constant rains, the season for which is now commenced. This place is the grand depot for sick and [are] literally up to one's knees in mud. From hence also the whole detachment separates for different routes, to the various extent of cantonments, which the army [takes] at present. Mine, as having charge of the light detachment, is of course the longest. The regiment is still distant five day's march and is in Spain on the side of the Agueda River and close on the rear of Ciudad Rodrigo, inclining a little to the right. Our route is between seventy and eighty miles across a most difficult country, through the mountainous passes. Today we go to Guarda, about 17 miles, two of which are occupied in ascending to that city, which is higher above the level of the sea than any in Europe & is to be seen from the spot I am now writing. Tomorrow we shall enter Spain at Alfayates [Alfaiates], which in English signifies the town of taylors [sic].[32]

As soon as I arrive at our regiment, I will send you the particulars of our march, this noted down from time to time, as also my journal and other matters. The present I just send you to announce my safe arrival thus far.

I am about going to the commissary to procure bread for the troops and must therefore cut short with a few more hasty scratches. On enquiring for the health and happiness of you all, which often occupied my thoughts; my good aunt, Miss Page, as being invalids, I trust are doing well. We formed a trio of invalids, but I think my name ought now to be struck off the list. Indeed, you may inform Mr Cline that his sick & lame patient marched sixty-six miles, in three days successive, without any inconvenience or difficulty, on setting off from Coimbra. Indeed, I have every reason to be glad that our passage by sea was of so long a delay, as also my stoppage in Lisbon, as it enabled me to gain fully my original strength. By the time I reach the regiment on Friday next, I shall have gone more than two hundred English miles on foot, through very bad roads and most tremendous mountains. It is true I have had regular sleep & meals every day, yet still I cannot help thinking myself as now thoroughly recovered [from] my late illnesses.

I expect to receive letters from you & also from India by the time of my arrival at our destination. Though the army are at present in cantonments, Lord W[ellington]'s intentions are kept so secret and movements are made at so short a notice, that no conjecture of our motions can be hazarded.

32 Alfaiates is still five miles on the Portuguese side of the border with Spain. They would continue from here to cross the border between Aldeia da Ponte and La Albergueria de Arganan. Alfaiates does indeed mean 'tailors' in English.

November is a fine month in the north of Portugal, Lord W[ellington] in a despatch to the regency says that Marmont has near sixty thousand men in his front, and it remains to be seen whether anything of importance will be undertaken during that season. On our part we have ten or twelve engineers with some hundreds of men working hard, at re-fortifying Almeida every day and in reorganising the means for a campaign in the spring. The army has of late suffered very considerably from the agues & intermittent fevers, which it caught in the Alentejo in the neighbourhood of Badajoz & Portalegre,[33] it is a most unhealthy province in the autumn of the year. All cases are sent to this hole of a town and their number must be pretty great, when I tell you that on coming in at a late hour yesterday evening, dripping with wet & on going into a house for a night's lodging, the first thing presented to my view was a dead soldier lying in the doorway, with no one near him & almost every house in the place is full of these wretched objects. God bless you all, I must conclude and with every wish for the health & happiness of you all, I remain your truly affectionate nephew, G U Barlow

George's next letter announced his arrival in Spain, where he had finally joined his battalion.

Martiago,[34] Spain, 5 November 1811

My dear uncle,
I have at length come to the end of my peregrinations by joining the regiment at this place whither I arrived on the 1st instant. We are twenty-five miles beyond the Portuguese frontier and close to Ciudad Rodrigo on the right, which is visible from a small eminence beyond this town. To continue my narrative, I shall go back to Celorico [da Beira], from which place I marched on the 28th ultimo. On the evening of that day our party reached a small village in the mountains towards dusk, four miles from our place of destination; not meeting with an inhabitant, we lost our way in these trackless hills and after wandering about for a considerable time were forced to return to it. The torrents had overflowed the roads, which would scarcely admit of two men abreast; to complete the whole, the rear of the detachment consisting of the Duke of Brunswick's Corps, neglecting to keep so close as they ought, lost their way & separated; the remainder together with myself dripping with wet, took up our abode for the night in a burnt village and here for the first time I lay in wet cloathes [sic] & luckily experienced no injury. The stray sheep however luckily joined the next morning at Guarda. The ascent to this place is nearly four miles & which occupied our party nearly two hours. The road winds in a thousand serpentine directions, wide enough for two carts abreast, along the edge of this most

33 The Alentejo is a geographical region of southern Portugal, its name translating as 'Beyond the Tagus'. Its main towns include Evora, Beja, Estremoz, Elvas, and Portalegre.

34 A small village, three miles south-east of El Bodon.

tremendous precipice; the sides of which are overspread with large woods of olives & dwarf elms. It is indeed a most grand spectacle; the town & castle is evidently Moorish and must have been an impregnable fortress & refuge for that nation in their wars against the natives; to an Englishman who is unaccustomed to mountain views, it is most peculiarly striking. The French took up a position on it during Massena's retreat; there was no attacking them but by that one road, which a few hundred men could defend against thousands. Force of course was impracticable; Lord W[ellington] made a movement to intercept the provisions coming from Spain and they were instantly compelled to abandon it. From thence until the 30th my route lay through a poor impoverished country, every place full of our troops in cantonments. On that morning the sun shone most beautifully & emerging from a thick wood, I passed the Spanish frontier at the village of Albergaria [La Alberguería de Arganan]. It was like magic, the country instantly changes from mountains to a fine level, flat plain full of trees, putting me in mind of old England. I was amongst a new people, new languages & everything changed for the better; the natives a fine, tall, stout limbed race of people; carrying themselves particularly upright and in their garb & look, wearing all that Castillian demeanour & pride for which the Spaniards are so celebrated. The villages are clean & the cottages resembling the neatness of those in England. It is impossible to find so great a contrast, as forcibly strikes the mind on passing the very frontier. The Spanish mantle & hat turned up in front of the natives pleased me much; the antipathy existing between the two peoples is most inveterate. I arrived at the headquarters of the division, just as an express announced the approach of a body of troops to Rodrigo and on reaching this village the next day, I found everything ready for an advance, this took place the next morning. The governor of Ciudad Rodrigo together with a party of dragoons had been surprized by Don Julian's guerrillas, another was appointed in his place, and came down with a more respectable escort of 3,000 infantry and 500 cavalry, together with a convoy of stores.[35] As soon as the brigade arrived within sight of the city it halted and on making a reconnaissance it was found that the whole of them had got in some hours previous to our arrival and that the escort had set off instantly for Salamanca on their return, all this was owing to the spies not sending the intelligence early enough to enable us to intercept them. So, you see my first debut on service was not very fortunate.

The army at present occupies a position in the shape of a semicircle around Rodrigo; our brigade so close that the advanced picquets even see everything that passes in or out. This village is situated amidst the mountains, the weather fine & cold like a frosty November morning. There is plenty of straw for our horses to eat; you must know that the infantry can procure neither oats nor barley for their horses; sometimes not even the cavalry's

35 *Général de Brigade* Reynaud had indeed been captured by Don Julian Sanchez's cavalry under the very guns of the fortress, his replacement *Général de Brigade* Barrie was smuggled in with the successful convoy of 2 November.

hay is an article scarcely known. The cattle live chiefly on grass and what serves as a litter for your beasts in England, forms a good dinner for ours. I often wonder indeed how these animals exist at all. Baggage is carried on the backs either of horses or mules. I have committed but one mistake during the whole of my long journey, I have namely to regret the loss of my famous blue greatcoat and may think myself excessively fortunate that our quartermaster has some blue cloth in his possession where with I may procure another; otherwise I should smart most severely for my neglect, everything else I have managed very well. My baggage is less almost than [torn- that of?] any other officer; very compact and yet combining every convenience in a small pair of saddle bags. I have tortured [my] imagination and provided for every contingency or want so that nothing is left for me to wish or desire. A few more books would be acceptable, yet I cannot carry them, so I must not desire it. I am in excellent health & trust that you all are equally as happy as myself.

I received yesterday morning yours of the 14th of September with General Burnes' enclosure which I will deliver on the first opportunity.[36] General B[urne] is at present in the Alentejo, a long distance from us. I propose riding over to Lord W[ellington's] quarters about 20 miles off in the course of a day or two.

[The rest of the letter is unfortunately lost]

Martiago, 12 November 1811

My dear uncle,
The messenger as usual sets off this day for Lisbon and by this weekly conveyance I always propose giving [you] a line, so that your advices from me may always be up to the latest date, although not worth the Falmouth postage. We all remain in status quo, prepared to move at immediate notice. No man can call any hour his own for a certainty; but should I venture to hazard a guess, it would be that our winter quarters are finally settled in our present cantonment. Nothing is stirring in front, for although on his late advance Marmont brought near 60,000 men with upwards of 40 squadrons of cavalry, he can only compel us to retire on the frontiers of Portugal, where the ground is not so smooth & open as in these parts and then the effectual manner in which our present commissariat is able to remove all supplies and destroy what cannot be carried away, together with the number of strong positions, with which we are so well acquainted, would render us more than a match for him. The main body of the enemy are stationed at or round about Salamanca; guarding the main road which runs from thence to Ciudad Rodrigo. This tract however is terribly annoyed by Don Julian's guerillas who are constantly riding about the walls, so that no one can show himself beyond range of the guns of the fortress. This

36 This must refer to Major General Robert Burne, who was serving as a brigadier in the 6th Division.

famous Spaniard, although merely a partizan and bearing no commission of authority, is obeyed by all the country round about, as much any Spanish or British officer with a regular commission from their governments. He levies contributions &c the same as a general officer and is indeed much more qualified for that rank, than many who at present possess it. He is a farmer, whose family were butchered by the French and for that circumstance he has vowed against them implacable enmity. Moreover, he has kept his word; his troops to look at them, remind me of bandits, they have no species of uniform or dress; they are armed at the expense of fallen foes. Here is an hussar wearing an infantry hat & there a foot soldier with a dragoon's appointments; in spite of this they constitute better irregulars & light troops than any in the British army. The party which amount nearly to a thousand, never remain three nights in any one place, they know every goat's track in the mountains & are ever on the alert, possessing no pay. The French on the most trifling occasion are therefore necessitated to move in considerable bodies. The weather is at present very variable, the night's dreadfully cold & damp, which will probably induce both parties to lay by until spring; when a Russian war will decide, which party will open the campaign on the offensive or defensive.[37] Should however the second battalion be sent home, of which there exists at present considerable uncertainty, I shall be drafted into the first; of this I am very glad, as it would be so mortifying to be sent home in two or three months hence, more especially as I consider myself perfectly recovered from my past illnesses. We have had no news from England for some time past, no less *than four* packets are at this moment due at headquarters and I only fear less some accident at sea should deprive me of some of your letters.

Accompanying this is a letter to the agents merely stating as a matter of form, that having served my time, I am willing to purchase and to tell them where the money is lodged, for a company. God bless you all & believe me to be your truly affectionate nephew G U Barlow

37 It was becoming increasingly obvious that France and Russia were on a collision course. Napoleon was building up a vast army ready to invade Russia. Nobody could have foretold the dreadful consequences for the French army, but it certainly meant that the French armies in Spain were very unlikely to see any reinforcements in 1812. In fact many troops were pulled out of Spain, reducing the French ability to control the areas they held, just when the allied forces in Spain were increasing their resources and Wellington looked to take full advantage.

As I never gave you a list of the towns & distances on our march herein, it is annexed as follows

Leagues		
From Figueira	to Montemor [o-Velho]	3
	to Tentaval [Tentugal]	2½
	to Coimbra	2½
	Miranda do Corvo	+6
	to Moita	+6½
	to Galizes	4½
	to Maceira	3
	to Sampayo [Sao Paio] 3	
	to Celorico [da Beira]	4
	to Guarda	+4
	to Cerdeira	4
	to Aldeia de Ponte	3
	to [Fuente]Guinaldo	+3½
	to Martiago	3½

English Miles = 12 – 4 English miles to a league

The direct road is rather shorter, but in the above account my peregrenations in these days march are included & make the above amount & are marked thus+

PS Will you be so good as to let me know in your next up to what time I have drawn my allowance including of course the amount of money drawn at Lisbon.

4

Watching Ciudad Rodrigo

The Light Division remained at Martiago but continued to keep a wary eye on French movements. Governor Barrie was proving unpopular and supplies were scarce due to the blockade of the fortress, George reported a regular stream of French deserters coming in.

> To William Barlow Esq, Little Bridge Street, Blackfriars London
> Martiago, 19 November 1811
>
> My dear uncle,
> Enclosed I send you a letter for Henry, as I have not written to him since my departure from England. Nothing has occurred since my last of the 12th instant and we remain just as before, anxiously however waiting the arrival of some packets from England, of which there are as no less than five due at present.
>
> The garrison of Ciudad Rodrigo are deserting very fast, they complain much of their new governor who has discontinued issuing their rations of spirits; the Italians especially come in great numbers. The garrison dare not come out of the town for fuel and have begun to pull down the houses of the city for the sake of their timbers.
>
> A Spanish officer who came in the day before yesterday reports that a large convoy, together with a body of troops destined to relieve those at present in Rodrigo, were to leave Salamanca a few days subsequent to his departure; he had escaped from Madrid. This army however at present wants information and for my part, although not one of the Privy Council, I am apt to give little credit to the rumours.
>
> I am at present employed in making out a little narrative for my father, respecting Spain & Portugal. I think it will please him, it is my first attempt and possessing little intrinsic interest, this together with continuing my Spanish & [torn- practising?] military drawing fill up my time. Give my kind love to my Aunt [torn – and all?] at home. God bless you and believe me [torn – to be your?] affectionate nephew G U Barlow

19 November 1811
4 o'clock

My dear uncle,
Since writing to you I find a packet is arrived with letters & papers to the 15th of October; they are not yet delivered out. One of our officers has just returned from General Vandeleur's[1] & having seen the general's papers informs me of Fanny's marriage.[2] I have therefore to trouble you with an enclosure for my aunt at Chatham.

The next letter from George indicated that they had moved five miles in advance to Zamarra and now east of the Agueda River. They were now just six miles south of Ciudad Rodrigo as they sought to tighten the blockade.

Zamarra, 26 November 1811

My dear uncle,
Since my last of the 19th instant some change has taken place in our situation, as well as in our expectations for the future. On the 24th instant, we turned out and marched off at half an hour's notice to this village early in the morning. Here we found our brigade concentrated and on the next day the whole Light Division with a proportion of cavalry arrived on these heights. No apparent cause is assigned for this sudden & most unexpected movement. The whole of the army in the rear has also advanced a day's march. A reconnaissance was made by one of our officers three leagues on the road to Salamanca and no intelligence or account of an enemy could be procured in that quarter.[3] They have not indeed made their appearance; a peasant however from Plasencia, whom I met yesterday, informed me that their force was moving from thence in this direction. So profound a secrecy is observed at headquarters, that no guess can be formed of the tendency of these movements. I hear even that General Craufurd is utterly ignorant of and has made them in conformity only to the orders he has received, without being a bit wiser than ourselves. Appearances seem to indicate, the intercepting a convoy from Salamanca for Rodrigo; as our cavalry are traversing the plains beyond the walls of the city in every direction. This plan however is rendered extremely difficult by the nature of the country of which I will give you some description. Rodrigo stands in the middle of a large plain, fifteen or sixteen miles in circumference. This plain is bounded by a ridge of hills perfectly, for not rising abruptly, but gradually one above

1 Major General John Ormsby Vandeleur commanded the 2nd Brigade of the Light Division from September 1811 to June 1813.

2 This refers to his cousin Frances Harriet Barlow (daughter of Uncle Robert) who married Vice Admiral George Byng, 6th Viscount Torrington, on 5 October 1811.

3 A league differs in length depending on the country, but it generally can be estimated as a distance of three miles.

the other, extending your view to an immense distance. The atmosphere at this cold season of the year is particularly clear & serene, all the roads lead over these hills & approach near each other at Rodrigo & from a very high church steeple, the garrison can observe every movement we make in the direction of Salamanca, to which city there lead but *two* routes. Now the duty of a commandant of a convoy is never to fight, but to scour an immense range of country with his parties, to gain intelligence & never to allow an enemy to come [up] unawares.

In pursuance of this plan the French escort their supplies with 4 or 5,000 men, sending on parties of observation too strong for Don Julian or the guerrillas.[4] Before reaching the heights two or three leagues from hence, they may perceive our videttes or gain intelligence from the peasantry, which may always be done by a liberality of money. The convoy, four leagues perhaps in rear of their advance, becomes acquainted of our being in force about the vicinity of Rodrigo; it retreats & then halts & communicates with Salamanca. Marmont then brings forward an overwhelming force with a great superiority of cavalry & compels you to quit all the open country & retire to the mountains near Alfaiates while the convoy is thrown in. Again, no distant operations can be in contemplation by reason of the weather. Last night, there was a great deal of ice, with as intense a frost as I have ever felt in England. In our present quarter between [torn – these?] the two battalions of the 52nd are crammed together; it is [torn – much too?] small for the health & comfort of the men: our object [torn – must?] therefore be quickly accomplished or not at all. I [torn – remain?] for the present to a miserable hovel; open to all the winds, rains and elements; full of smoak [sic], there is but one apartment, in which ourselves, our servants, batmen & the miserable inhabitants are crowded all together in addition to a large quantity of logs & timber for fire wood. Our horses around me are objects of wonder, they stand together in an open shed without cloths or coverings and I really believe don't possess room enough to lay down, is as much as the town is full of cavalry, their coats are as rough as hogs bridles, they go through heat & cold, hunger & thirst, and are a different species of beings to the sleek, fine, fat animals in your shelter at Streatham.

Letters and papers have been received by us to the 24th of October, none of yours have come to hand, the last & only which I have received is of the 24th of September. Eliza writes to me from Teignmouth; there is however nothing new.

Give my kind love to my aunt and all at Streatham. God bless you and believe me to be your truly affectionate nephew G U Barlow

PS Lord Wellington has just passed through this place to reconnoitre in front, he has with him but one aide de camp & two dragoons.

4 Don Julian Sanchez 'El Charo' was a noted guerrilla leader.

To William Barlow Esq, Little Bridge Street, Blackfriars, London
Martiago, 3 December 1811

My dear uncle,
Soon after I had finished my last to you at Zamarra, the regiment with a suddenness [proceeded] from here to our division, was directed to proceed still further to the front among the mountains. We had scarcely taken up our quarters and arranged the picquets than we received an order to retrace our former steps with equal expedition, to this place. It is conjectured that Lord Wellington had a diversion in view being desirous of making the French recall the reinforcements which they had detached from their army at Salamanca to Galicia, where their affairs are at present in no very favourable track having withdrawn the corps from those parts to oppose us on this frontier.

Two or three days since, I went accompanied by a brother officer, both of us well mounted, to take a close ride of Rodrigo and well knowing that the enemy would not venture beyond their walls, although at the time they had nothing to dread on that score, those of our picquets being then on the plains we rode up to a large convent within cannon-shot of the works. Here with a good telescope we had a most impressive view of the whole place, of the sentries pacing the works, ramparts, the guns, bridge, and in short of anything that was happening in the town. You may form some idea of our distance when I say that we heard all the clocks do the bells chime although there was little or no wind. Although the works are very strong itself, its defence consists in the nature of the soil which is of solid rock & in which trenches and parallels must be cut with much labour and also loss of blood as during the whole night exposed to the fire of the place. It was a fortress of some strength during the wars between the kings of Spain and the Moors and the citadel which stands on the top of a high mound, it puts me much in mind of Windsor castle & just as high a trajectory. A deserter who came in this morning assures me that they are sadly in want of firewood and would not venture beyond the guns to procure a supply of that most necessary article. He adds that he has been two years about from Florence, that he is sick of the French service and has no desire to return to his native country, because whilst he possesses a pair of legs to use he knows Bonaparte will have him be a soldier. The French are I believe most heartily bored of this war; on the body of a captain who was killed in the late affair of El Bodon was found a letter from his father particularly mentioning the young man never to straggle or separate from his men as he would instantly meet his fate from the murdering Portuguese, the picture of his intended was I believe also on him, of whom poor fellow [he] was alas never destined to return. With remarkable resistance we were enabled to beat off the several attacks of the French in that affair under the command of Marshal Marmont himself, whatever good & dry account might hereafter be published in the newspapers.

Lord W[ellington] had reason to send a message to Marshal Marmont, who would not allow the aide de camp to return until the operations then pending should be finished. He accompanied the French chief throughout that affair and when by his side heard him directly commend the conduct of 'that miserable little battalion' as he watched the square formed by the 5th & 77th Regiments.[5] When however these corps prevented the French get possession of the high road to [Fuente]guinaldo and cut off our brigade which was forced to take another road through the mountains, the marshal perceiving the dust occasioned by the march of the column took up his glass & exclaimed 'there is Lord Wellington's lucky star, I see General Craufurd's division is retreating through the hilly passes'. Marmont is now reckoned one of the first officers in the French service though he has been all his life in the artillery, there having not been previously the present opportunities for displaying those talents which are now justly appreciated as being of the first-rate quality[6].

And now I have to request that you will inform me in your next how much I have overdrawn my last quarter's allowance. This I mentioned in a former letter, my passage to Lisbon, as well as my animals which cost me alone 220 dollars, have necessarily occasioned this expenditure. *At Present* I simply want of nothing, it is however necessary that I should *now* order what I may stand in need of three or four months hence & by the opening of next campaign, for even should the commissions which I now give you a list be immediately executed, these things will not reach me at this distance much before that time. The space to Lisbon is very great, there is no conveyance whatever for officer's parcels whatever, the roads most infamous. Packages for several of our regiment have been landed these three months to my knowledge and have not yet come to hand, any one for me would not arrive much before the latter end of March or April.

It is true I am now receiving the new quarter's allowance perhaps or that is paid next, but recollect though I draw them in December, it will be near April before they reach me. Some of these things I cannot purchase in Portugal, others will cost me double their value in England. They are all of a small kind & are packed in my saddle bags which with a smaller portable pair constitute the whole of my baggage although we are idle at present & are as economical as possible and making the best possible use of my time. Every day after breakfast & parade till one o'clock I study Spanish and military drawing. Should the weather prove fine I ride until between four & five. In as much as I like to visit every village and be well acquainted with all the country in our neighbourhood. Our mess consists of but four & is as moderate as possible, we drink little or no wine, take a cup of hot chocolate or tea and generally go to bed by ten or eleven at latest. I seldom

5 This refers to the Action at El Bodon.

6 Marshal Marmont had originally been an artilleryman, but George was mistaken regarding his not having experience with commanding other troops, as he had commanded mixed corps since 1805.

or ever play at cards & when that happens we play but shilling points. Such is the turn of our life at present, I possess however this difference, that I am the only officer who possesses any books & indeed who use them much; as the earlier part of the day is generally employed by them in coursing or shooting, both of which diversions are to be had hereabouts in the highest perfection. God bless you all & believe me to be, your truly affectionate nephew, G U Barlow

NB I have written by this packet to Fred, who has a list of my commissions and with your leave, I dare say, will be good enough to excuse then the expense, together with the bill for my horse at Layton's will take up the greater part of my April's quarter allowance. Should there be any surplus after everything is paid, be so good as to send me the bank notes in eight dollar pieces of Portuguese coin, such as were bought by you for me at Goodbefore's in Cheapside.

I leave you to chuse what conveyance will be best. The packet is the securest & speediest though it is not allowed to send them by those vessels. The *Princess Charlotte,* carried out with me a number of officer's parcels, of course they are smuggled on board. It would not however be proper to run any risk with so valuable a charge. Let it be direct to in Portugal, with the addition

> 'To be left at the Town Major's office Lisbon, until called for' and where I will leave orders for its conveyance up to the army.

[PS] Thursday evening. I have just time to add that papers up to the 12th of November have arrived & bringing me your letter of the 29th of October last.

Martiago 16 December 1811

My dear uncle,
Tuesday being the weekly post day with the Light Division I as usual send you a line, although there is no occasion to make you pay the Falmouth postage & this bye the bye must form a considerable item of your year's expenditure. I will begin by giving you a description of the weather; which at present resembles the season of December in England, with a good deal of rain & sleet has fallen these few latter days accompanied by much snow, this however soon disappears & melts from the vallies [sic], it remains for some length of time on the high mountains with which we are surrounded. All appears quiet and I think likely to continue so, although some vague but persistent rumours of the French army moves southerly towards Plasencia are now afloat, but unless some very necessary and important object is to be attained, no one though, will commence operations at this season of the year. The fords of the different rivers are made impassable by four or five hours of rain or heavy snow, with the exception of a bridge at Rodrigo the

Agueda is not passable for infantry, much less cavalry or artillery anywhere between the bridge of Zamora which we now occupy and that of Barba del Puerco, a tract of near forty miles. Even these are but of wood and could be most effectually demolished in the course of a few hours. It is therefore no light or easy matter to undertake hostilities or to march here and there as I perceive some of your London papers would have Lord Wellington to do. Their geographical exposure in laying down the distance of towns is most truly ridiculous. The *Statement Quadraniega* an evident proof of retreating and so but 70 miles from Oporto when it is as such double the distance. The language of despair used by Cobbett is also most detestable.[7] His lordship has shown himself fully competent to wish any exigency; they will be most fully put to the test in the ensuing campaign. The enemy's force in our front is well known, they are fully employed at present in subduing the south of Spain and are expected to make a simultaneous movement with their army from Rodrigo & to advance from Badajoz to the south side of the Tagus. This has not yet been attempted and will decide forever the practicability of keeping Portugal & those lines on the south side of the Tagus similar to those at Santarem have been constructed and I trust are now completed & that his lordship will be not bely the expectations formed of his past achievements in the minds of his countrymen.

Herein I annex the outlines of General Hill's affair in the Alentejo. It was a most hasty and [hand] made sketch done by the engineer of the division without expressing any of the moves & exceedingly interesting details.[8] I have simply enough copied it with a common pen & which may however enable you to form some slight idea of this well constructed affair & the military act been observed. Sentries let the weather been ever so bad, should have been placed on the hills in the middle of the plain and never ought to have been withdrawn until the whole of the column had commenced his march out of the plain and the movements seen in daylight, such palpable folly has been punished as it deserved.

In addition, the books which I requested to have sent out to me in my last. I wish you would add '*An essay on military reconnoitring including the method of surveying fieldworks with or without instruments by passing on horseback or the eye*'[9] by Captain Malorti de Martemont price 12s 6d as also '*Instructions for officers of infantry by General Friedrich Gaudi with 42 plates*'[10] translated by the same Captain de Martemont into English also

7 William Cobbet, began the *Political Register*; he was imprisoned in 1810 for two years for treasonous libel, but continued to write from Newgate Prison.

8 This must be a copy of the same sketch which is mentioned in Charles Dawson's letter of 10 December 1811. The original sketch was sent to Captain Ewart by an officer present. Unfortunately, Ewart's diary does not record anything about it at all.

9 I have been unable to discover a copy of this work anywhere.

10 *Instructions for Officers of Infantry shewing how to trace and construct all sorts of Field works* by General F. Gaudi, translated into English by Charles Malortie de Martemont, published in 1804. Malortie was an ex Captain in the French Royal Army and Master of Fortification and Artillery at the Royal Military Academy, Woolwich.

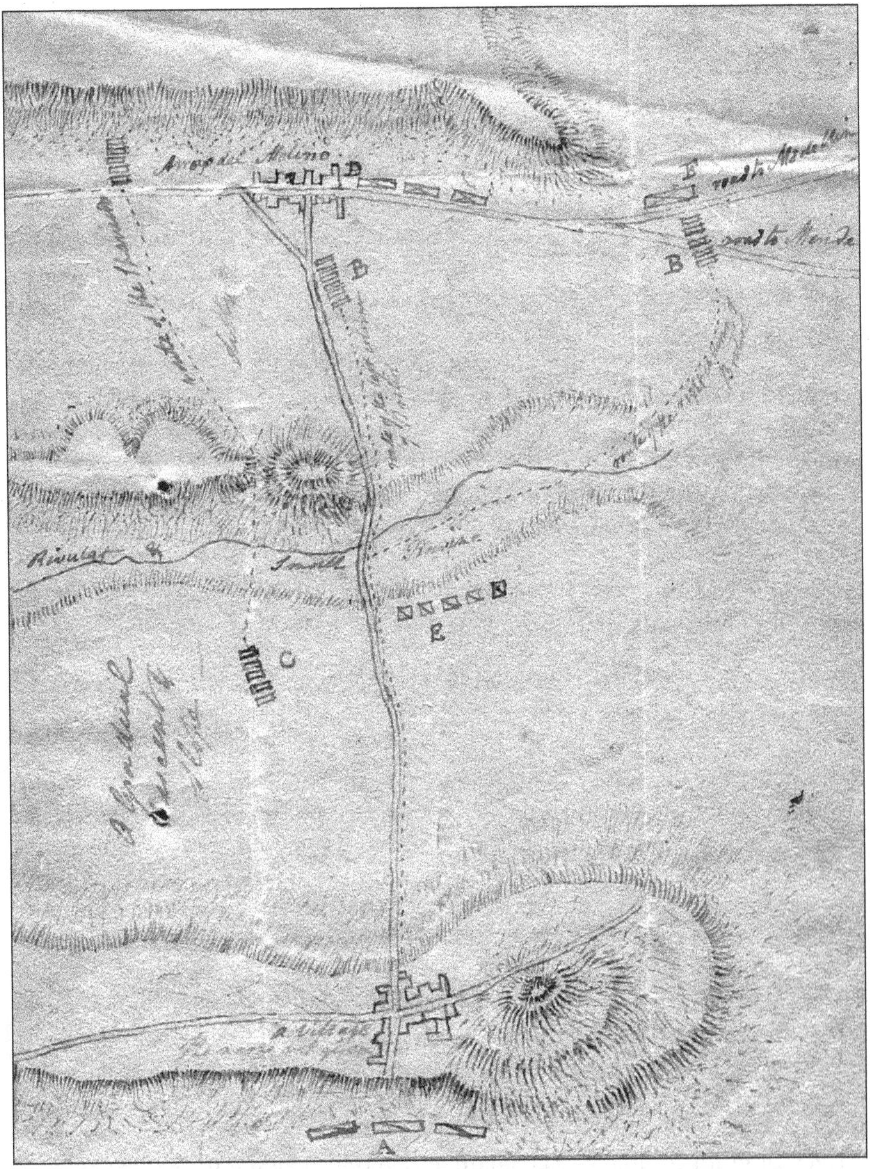

Arroyos do Molinos 28 October 1811 (sketch included with original letter)

Key to Plan
A Position of the allies on the night of the 27th of October behind the hill
B British columns of attack (infantry)
C Spanish infantry
D Position of the French ready to march next morning and in which they were surprized
E The British & Spanish cavalry dispersed on the arrival of the British column
F The point where Girard* attempted to collect about 700 men, but which [unfinished]

* *Général de Division* Jean-Baptiste Girard.

12s 6d '*The Bombadier or Pocket Gunner*'[11] by Captain Adye of the Royal Artillery 4d 6d and '*Principles of Fortification*'[12] by Professor Landmann of the Royal Academy at Woolwich with plates price 2s, thus the whole amounts to no more than 35 shillings & which together with those I have ordered in my last will make complete the complete collection of military books.

I am now fortunately employed and shall continue so during the whole winter at military drawing & Spanish, but this is of no use unless I am in possession of the annexed works which will teach me the art of drawing and surveying distances correctly with the sextant. This together with all my books & my box of colours are easily stowed away, as well the whole of my baggage; for we are now allowed each a mule to carry it and shall therefor manage it well. I am if possible more than content as [to] following my profession and I am sure you will allow me these means of accomplishing this as also those little inconveniences & comforts mentioned in my last and which may be comfortable with my situation. God bless you all and believe me to be yours most sincerely G U Barlow

[PS] I intend riding over to Fuenteguinaldo the first fine day, you may therefore open Lord Wellington's letter & send me a copy of it, your nephew.

To William Barlow Esq, Little Bridge Street, Blackfriars, London
Martiago, 18 December 1811

Though we still remain in statu quo, I have reason to believe that some change in our position will shortly take place. The advanced picquets have fallen back a small distance from Rodrigo, preparatory most likely to a general movement of the whole division to new quarters. Provisions have of late become very scarce; the troops have not received any bread for four days together; and the officers have been obliged to purchase it at the rate of 3s the loaf, much about the same size as the English bakers quarter;[13] and what appears still more incredible the 1st Battalion were unable to procure it at a less price than 5s in a neighbouring village; but purses are not very long at present and a little longer continuance in these parts, as such an expenditure would soon reduce us to beggary. All round Ciudad Rodrigo and our present quarters, the country by no means abounds in corn; the tract for grain commences at Salamanca and its neighbourhood, where the French army have taken up their cantonments. The enemy and ourselves have alternately consumed this spot for miles around; our magazines are a long way in the rear and the supplies must always ford the Agueda in two

11 Published in 1804.
12 '*The Principles of Fortification reduced into Questions and Answers for the use of the Royal Military Academy at Woolwich*,' published in London, 1806.
13 A quartern loaf was a very large loaf, often cut and sold in quarters. The London Bread Act of 1822 stipulated that the loaf before baking had to weigh four pounds fifteen ounces.

Sir John Colborne, by an unknown artist. (Editor's Collection)

parts and pass some dreadful ravines, ere they can reach us. Should however the rain or snow swell the rivers, we must remain hungry, until they subside. The commissary mules have been working so hard during the whole of the present year, that they are pretty nigh done up or at least until they gain some rest, nor can this circumstance be wondered at. Our horses & mules never see corn and subsist on coarse, long grass; which has been thoroughly dried up by the sun and contains no nourishment whatever and should the snow or frost become more severe than at present, they must literally starve.

Colonel Colborne who exchanged with Colonel Ross into this regiment, arrived two or three days since. He was aide de camp & the particular friend of Sir John Moore and as good an officer as Colonel Ross certainly was, it is no disparagement of his merit to assert that his successor is fully his equal. The colonel seems fully inclined to keep up the institutions and antient [sic] system of the regiment, by which it has been brought into its present good state of discipline. He is also an active, middle-aged man and we have therefore every reason to congratulate ourselves on so valuable an acquisition.

In spite of the present state of poverty to which the country is reduced, the brigade have determined upon having a Lord Mayor's feast, after the fashion of John Bull. We have each subscribed five dollars a-piece to this entertainment, such as it will be. An express has been sent to Almeida about 30 miles distant, for pork brine, pretty stuff it will be and we have been scouring the whole country round about for a calf, but have not succeeded in procuring one. The garrison of Rodrigo will I dare say be as merry as ourselves in consequence of the necessary relaxation of the blockade and may perhaps contrive to celebrate Christmas day, with a few ragout of turkey, plenty of which are to be found in Salamanca. Well I will conclude as normal with God bless you all; you see I am hard [torn- put by] shifts to spin out a letter, but being aware that [torn -you?] would wish to hear from me on every arrival, I have taken up my pen & written the present which after all is summed up in the short sentence of 'all is well'. Give my kindest love to my aunt, Miss Page and all the little ones. Believe me to be your truly affectionate nephew G U Barlow

In his next letter, George revealed that preparations were apparently being made for an attempt on Ciudad Rodrigo, but the army believed it to be nothing more than a feint.

To William Barlow Esq, Little Bridge Street, Blackfriars, London
Martiago, 24 December 1811

My dear uncle,
A packet arrived yesterday bringing papers and letters up to the 30th of November but none from you; the last I received [from you] was of the 29th of October. The *Courier* I find complains of the non-arrival of intelligence from the peninsula, during the last three weeks; even General Hill's report had not reached England. Accounts had been received I hear from Lord Wellington dated Freineda 2nd November and on the 4th of the same month, I sent off a packet of *six letters* & should have imagined that they would have been carried by the same vessel. I wrote to you also on my arrival at Celorico and have continued so to do on the Tuesday of every week. This is a constant maxim which I irrevocably have & ever shall observe on all occasions. By referring therefore to the dates, you may easily find out whether any of my letters are missing.

We remain in our old positions, two or three days since his lordship inspected the whole division at Fuenteguinaldo, we did not manoeuvre on account of the quantity of sun which fell in the morning and after an inspection had been made of the men's clothing we were dismissed to our quarters. An order however came yesterday for us to prepare a large quantity of fascines, gabions, and other materials for a siege.[14] In this work, the whole of our division, as well as the first and fourth are at present occupied. By the knowing ones, it is only considered as a feint on our part to induce Marmont to unite a large body of troops which he has detached southwards from Plasencia, to the assistance of the French in the Andalucias, by a show of attacking Rodrigo. It is I believe a pretty correct assertion, that we are incapable of besieging that fortress and opposing the superior force of the enemy at the moment. Should not these preparations succeed in compelling the recall of the above reinforcement his lordship will probably have no course to other means and make a more efficacious diversion by advancing with the army in the direction of Salamanca, which would probably be attended with the desired effect, so that I think we may soon calculate upon being turned out of winter quarters and making a move.

So, I find that a little douceur[15] has been given to Mr Petrie, for his late bitter pill of expulsion from the Madras council.[16] We can of course entertain not a particle of envy at the man's good fortune; our business with him has been most satisfactorily settled to the credit of the Madras Governor. I

14 Fascines were rough bundles of brushwood used for filling ditches, whilst a gabion, meaning a 'bird cage' consisted of a round wicker basket which could be filled with earth, to be used as a protection for artillerymen and sappers.
15 French: A bribe.
16 William Petrie (1747-1816) member of the Madras Council and MP and acting governor until Sir George Barlow arrived in India. Petrie was dismissed from the council in 1810 for his opposition to Sir George, but was rehabilitated in 1811 as governor of Penang.

will therefore only express my joy at finding the spirit of discord & dissatisfaction gradually in the decay. Our opponents in Leadenhall Street have not found themselves strong enough to effect anything,[17] during a season which we had every reason to dread, and I trust that in the course of the ensuing spring he will succeed to the Presidency of Fort William, by the now almost certain valediction of Lord Minto. The ensuing session of parliament will be alike be interesting to the nation & ourselves. I cannot help thinking that the effect of Mr Turnie's [Tierney] will operate to our disadvantage, owing to his connexion with a certain personage.[18]

Tomorrow our Christmas feast, and I have resolved upon going to Freineda on the 26th which is about seven leagues distance. God bless you all and believe me to be your truly affectionate nephew G U Barlow

No. 40
Martiago, Spain, 26 December 1811 (annotated received 2 August 1812, Answered 30 December 1812)

My dearest father,
At length from the ground which I have so often wished to tread, from the Spanish soil I am enabled to address you in the present. Letters from Lisbon would inform you of my arrival in Portugal in perfect health. These I trust were in time either for General Brownrigg or Sir Samuel Hood's departure. As a journal of my route up the country is at present in my preparation I shall confine myself to general remarks on the peninsula and add what will give you the liveliest satisfaction, that I joined the army on the 1st of November, entirely free from the dreadful rheumatic pains to which I have been lately so subject and on the state of the weather and any other circumstances particularly unfavourable to me in the report which occurred in the course of a long march. I consider my strength & constitution to be perfectly established after so ample a trial, so exactly have Mr Cline's predictions and my own wishes been realised, that during a journey of two hundred miles, which I proposed on foot and midst the inclement periodical rains, obliged me to sleep in wet clothes and having marched twenty-two miles for three successive days I found myself as strong and healthy as ever. There was no necessity for treading pedestrian on the occasion, after however so severe an illness I entertained fresh doubt of my powers and determined upon putting them to the trial, which has fully equalled my most sanguine hopes. Health, my good father, is the first of blessings to anyone, but more particularly to a soldier, it is invaluable, and I have expostulated at an unusual length on this feat in order to eradicate every doubt or fear to which my recent service & severe maladies may have given rise.

I joined the army soon after it had resumed their original position previous to the affair of El Bodon. The whole account of this concern, you

17 The Old India Office stood in Leadenhall Street.
18 George Tierney, MP for Bandon.

will see detailed in the public posts, the Light Division were nor concerned in it owing much to the nature of the route by which it retired, through the mountains where the enemy's numerous cavalry could effect nothing, though they closely hung upon the line of march. Our two battalions, with one of Portuguese riflemen were pushed across the Agueda River with sentries watching Ciudad Rodrigo and patrolling within two or three miles of the walls, of course we are the first in advance. The very morning, I reached the battalion, orders came to go in pursuit of a convoy on its way from Salamanca. It had however passed a few hours previous to our arrival on the ground.[19] A few days afterwards the whole army was concentrated and made a slight advance, supposed with the intention of obliging Marshal Marmont to recall the succours which he had detached to the assistance of their Galician Army from Salamanca, we have every reason to believe that the object of our manoeuvre was attained as we shortly afterwards went into these, our old cantonments. These are the only transactions of a public nature since I have joined. During however this temporary season of repose my time is fully occupied and that was in the most useful manner. I have had the precaution to bring up a few books and military works such as the compact nature of my baggage would admit. I am assiduously applying to [learning] Spanish and more particularly military drawing. I further my knowledge of Latin verbs easy enough. The Portuguese is but a dialect of the same branch, though not so pure and elegant as the Castilian. I have written to my uncle particularly for a few instruments to compliment me in the act of surveying and taking distances. This is the branch of the military art in which I am most deficient and in which I am striving to improve myself. This together with a knowledge of the languages of the peninsula, will occupy my undivided attention the whole of the coming winter. I trust that they will be brought into practise and repay my application in the coming campaign. It may appear the height of presumption in so young an officer as myself, who has not yet seen an enemy shot fired to pretend to sending my conjectures, or to offer any observations on so complicated a subject as the probable nature of the ensuing operations. Marshal Marmont & Lord Wellington, with their wisdom and ample means of description have perhaps not yet decided upon it themselves. I hate when a subaltern officer ventures even a guess. With you however, I shall not go near the imputation of vanity. I am impelled by no finer motive but by a desire of discussing subjects of importance, with the view of forming an idea of them, and which time and by practising and by correcting, may instruct and form my judgement, when better levels of information exist to teach me a proper idea of things. Such an attempt, if too great for my present comprehension is not I think the less laudable if kept within proper bounds.

Well after this preamble, I will give you some description of our relative situations. Marmont is expected to open the campaign with between 60 or

19 The large convoy successfully reached Ciudad Rodrigo from Salamanca on 2 November 1811.

70,000 men, including near 10,000 cavalry, and 150 pieces of artillery, in which latter sum of force, the French are always so numerous & so excellent. Lord Wellington has about 35,000 British infantry and between 5 or 6,000 cavalry and it is with great difficulty that the country can feed this number. But should his lordship meditate offensive operations, he may have a further reinforcement of nine or ten very fine and effective regiments of foot ready at present to embark, also four or five more of cavalry. In the event of a Russian war, Marmont's force will not probably secure a proportional reinforcement, more especially of cavalry. We may then advance into the country of Spain and from the populous fertile regions of Salamanca, draw ample supplies. Should however, a proportionate addition so be made of the [French] army, these ideas will be abandoned and reinforcing Almeida, we should take to the mountains of Portugal. Here all our manoeuvres will be confined to two roads [where the] superiority of Marmont will be less felt and should the enemy follow the latter with 50 or 60,000 men, he will be famished in days not years. I can most tolerably compare with my own testimony the assertion of Massena, 'That from Lisbon to Almeida not 2,000, no not 1,000 souls were to be seen all told', no horse, cow, ass or goat, except what was the property of the British commissariat. Lands uncultivated, towns and villages for a length of 270 miles without the smallest exception (saving Coimbra preserved by a remarkable accident) demolished and burnt (a dreary waste or desert are the lot of suffering Portugal), her young men are become savage guerrillas or soldiers, her women are dead or fled, no one knows whither, and her villages be dust & ashes. On the arrival of our party the first concern amongst us was to find a house with a roof, happy were those who could procure one. All was as silent as the grave on entering these abodes of misery. In a word, the whole country on the right bank of the Tagus is swept, and as the enemy, it is supposed, will make a simultaneous movement from Badajoz and Ciudad Rodrigo, the whole tract between the former city and the left flank of that river will be desolated in a similar manner. Lines equally strong as those of Santarem have been constructed on the south side of Lisbon & lie behind passes 'bristling with cannon' (as Massena said), the quarter is provided for.[20] In a word, to conclude, a Russian Tsar will decide whether the campaign on our part will be offensive or defensive. In either case it will be a most active one & if the latter, there will be plenty of employment to the Light Bobs[21] in the mountains, that form the characteristic features of Portugal.

The weather at present much resembles the season of January in England, cold fogs and rains which in a few hours & by the change of wind is converted into snow, has gathered on the tops of the sierras, which are of great height

20 The three lines of defensive fortifications constructed in the hills north of Lisbon on Wellington's orders are now famously known as the 'Lines of Torres Vedras'. It is however, far less well known, that a fourth line of defences were constructed by Wellington on the south bank of the Tagus to protect that city and the ships lying off it from an attack from this quarter.

21 A popular nickname for the light infantry.

in these parts and remain un-melted for a great time, long after the sun has disposed of it in the vallies [sic], which takes place in a few hours, generally after its falling & indeed seldom it lays an hour or more than two. The rivers swell with amazing rapidity, the fords are instantly rendered impassable. The Agueda forms one immense ravine passable at only two bridges, at Zamora & Barba del Puerco is about near upon 30 miles, so it is rather a ticklish matter to carry on military operations at this season, the severity of which would put a stop to the war, without the concurrence of other causes.

Martiago from whence I write the present, is a miserable little village and not the best of quarters. Two of us are huddled in this little hovel, for it deserves no better name. there is no light but which proceeds from the door, above a clumsy roof of tiles from whence the azure itself of heaven may be perceived through the fractures and which admits rain and snow a plenty, indeed we were deluged by it yesterday, and filtering through our walls which as well as the floor are made of earth. My bed a couple of wooden benches with a pair of blankets is considered as [the] most comfortable one amongst us. A tin cup, with a cast [iron] knife, fork & spoon composes the whole of my dinner set, and two pair of saddlebags my wardrobe. This to be sure, is some difference from our mode of living in England. To a man however attached to his profession it is as nothing to him, activity and change of scene, although attended with these little inconveniences is a source of infinite pleasure. I regret however continuance in these quarters, for the sake of the men. They are literally in rags for want of new clothing, which the paucity of bullocks and the still more wretched nature of the roads, added to our current distance from Lisbon of 280 miles, prevent from reaching our division. It has been actually some weeks on the route & in the meanwhile some of our company cannot come to parade on account of nakedness. The country is also pretty nigh exhausted; for four days together, the men have been without bread or potatoes, this however is in some measure the fault of the commissary against whom complaints have been forwarded to the general. The sick were lately numerous but are now recovering and I trust that we shall fully recover our former state of efficiency previous to opening the ensuing campaign. In Ciudad Rodrigo the enemy suffer still more than ourselves and are so strictly blockaded that no picquets are posted beyond the walls at night & seldom show themselves by day. They are obliged to pull down the houses of the town for firewood and are put short rations for the winter. They desert over to us very fast, particularly the Italians. I rode up the other day to a ruined convent, within shell range of their works and with my glass[22] approached near enough to hear the church chime the quarters and had a most accurate view of the whole place. It forms the most venerable appearance of antiquity and possesses some good spires & other public buildings. It was a famous fortress in the wars between the Spaniards & Moors and was built by the Great Rodrigo, King of Leon &

22 Spy glass or telescope.

Castile.[23] The ancient part much resembles the lofty part of Windsor & its structure this day denotes it to have been almost impregnable in the days of chivalry, during the whole time the enemy never attempted to molest it once. Indeed, they are very shy since their governor Reynaud with the greater part of the garrison's cattle were captured by an ambuscade from the famous Spanish guerrilla chief Don Julian, in the open day & actually under the fire of the fortress. They have been surprised in a similar manner when they came to pull down the roof of the convent at which I then was. You cannot conceive how gratifying is the appearance of these patriotic bands. They possess no uniform, nor armed but [from] the spoils of war of other vanquished enemies and wear clothes of every description & colour, [from] their appearance you expect them to be robbers, but their exploits of bravery prove them to be the best soldiers & light troops. Each band of men is animated with hatred of the French for some murdered relative or friend. It was the butchery of his family which caused Don Julian to swear eternal enmity to them and he has truly kept his word. In short they much resemble your irregular Maharatta horse[24] are equally as embarrassing to a large enemy and of all their convoys and stragglers, perpetually on the alert and acquainted with every secret by-road and yet further they slow the country, as all the soldiers of the French army are by this system worn out, but really render their triumph slow indeed, but nevertheless must succeed & complete in the end.

Now after this long military digression, I have to inform you that headquarters did not lay in my route to the army. They have been since proceeding [on] at a spot about 25 miles from hence and I propose taking advantage of the first fine day to ride thither and having delivered my charge I shall naturally give you the particulars of our discussion as soon as I return to the regiment.[25] Accept a thousand thanks for this new proof of your kindness. God bless you my good parent and that every happiness be your lot & in the family & the sincere prayers of your dutiful & affectionate son, G U Barlow

23 Ciudad Rodrigo was converted from a small town into a great walled fortress town by King Ferdinand II of Leon in the twelfth century and was reconfigured with bastions and ravelins in the seventeenth century. King Rodrigo reigned in 750 AD and does not have any known connection with Ciudad Rodrigo.

24 The Marathas had carved out a kingdom in India and controlled these vast lands with hordes of irregular light cavalry, just like the Cossacks on the Russian Steppes or the Mamelukes in Egypt. They had proven formidable enemies to the British in India.

25 Wellington's headquarters were established in the tiny village of Fuenteguinaldo which lies about 20 miles by road from Martiago.

5

The Siege of Ciudad Rodrigo

George's next series of letters report on the siege and the successful storming of Ciudad Rodrigo, which Wellington had suddenly besieged on 8 January 1812. Such a surprise move, at an inhospitable period of the year, caught Marshal Marmont on the hop and leaving him unable to respond quickly with his superior numbers. Speed was therefore of the essence for Wellington. That very same night the Renaud redoubt – often mistakenly called Fort San Francisco in many accounts, including George's below – was captured by a party consisting of two companies from each of the four British and two Portuguese battalions in the Light Division, and commanded by Colonel Colborne, for the loss of 6 men killed and 19 officers and men wounded. George was a member of this attack but luckily came away unscathed. The trenches were begun that same night on the heights known as the Great Teson, the troops of the 1st, 3rd, 4th and Light Divisions were selected to carry out the siege operations, each taking a 24-hour turn of duty in the trenches. When not in the trenches, the men were turned to, to make gabions and fascines. The weather was cold and frosty, whilst the troops had to ford a waist high river going to and from the trenches to their quarters in neighbouring villages (the Light Division was at El Bodon), indeed the weather soon turned colder, forcing the shift changes to be more frequent. Wellington had learnt on the 13th that Marmont was preparing to march from Salamanca to raise the siege, therefore speed was paramount. Three companies of the 40th Foot captured the Convent of San Francisco on the night of the 14th and this caused the French to abandon their other outwork in the Convent of Santa Cruz. Having rapidly constructed four batteries on the Great Teson heights, a sap was carried forward to allow a fifth battery to be constructed on a lesser height known as the Little Teson no more than two hundred yards from the walls and thus rapidly expanding the main breach. By 19 January, a second practicable breach had been formed in the fortress walls and the storming of the breaches was set for that very night.

The attack was set for 7:00 pm and the Light Division was given responsibility for attacking the lesser or second breach. The Light Division formed up for the attack behind the Santa Cruz convent, Major George Napier led the storming party, with Lieutenant John Gurwood of the 52nd – who would be severely wounded – commanding the 25-man Forlorn Hope in advance. Napier did not order the men to load, expecting the men to capture the fortress with the bayonet alone. Unfortunately, the Forlorn Hope went astray in the dark and the main body following up actually reached the foot of the breach first. The lesser breach had not been retrenched and

Wellington's headquarters at Freineda. (Editor's Collection)

the defenders were not numerous, most being called to defend the main breach. There was a heavy loss amongst the senior officers who chose to lead this attack: Craufurd was mortally wounded, Vandeleur and Colborne were both wounded, whereby command of the Light Division devolved on Lieutenant Colonel Barnard of the 95th Rifles. The breach was however taken, the 43rd and 95th immediately turning right to come up on the rear of the main breach to complete the defeat of the French defenders, the 52nd clearing the ramparts to the left.

The casualty list for the regiment was not excessive, the 1/52nd lost Captain Joseph Dobbs and eight men killed and four officers, one sergeant, and 33 men wounded. The 2/52nd, commanded by Major Edward Gibbs, lost one sergeant and three men killed and one officer and five men wounded. Lieutenant Gurwood eventually had the honour of personally capturing the French governor, *Général de Brigade* Barrie.

The army was not allowed to rest on its laurels however, as they soon found themselves on the long march south, with Wellington determined to maintain his advantage of surprise to capture the fortress of Badajoz before the French could react.

Following the regiment's losses from both battle and sickness, it was decided to amalgamate the two battalions of the 52nd and to send the spare officers and NCOs of the 2nd Battalion home to recruit. George should have accompanied them home but was transferred to the 1st Battalion to make up their officer numbers. In total 10 sergeants, seven buglers and 487 rank and file transferred into the 1st Battalion, however, 10 other sergeants, five buglers and 85 men were deemed 'unserviceable' and transferred from the 1st Battalion and sent home. The 2/52nd marched for Lisbon on 25 February 1812.

To William Barlow Esq, Little Bridge Street, Blackfriars, London
El Bodon, 7 January 1812

My dear uncle,
In my last, I informed you of my intention to proceed to headquarters. Major Gibbs had dissuaded me from taking this step sooner inasmuch as there was a great number of generals & other officers assembled as usual during Christmas & his lordship was moreover travelling about the country; although Freineda was nominally his residence where army business is transacted. Mine of course needed a personal interview & could not therefore take place. I told you also that we were employed in making fascines & gabions & other implements for a siege, the object of these is now fully developed and instead of a feint, Rodrigo is to be attacked in earnest. Marmont has left Salamanca with the greater part of his force for the interior of Spain; it must be some very urgent matter indeed that can have induced him to leave that fortress exposed to our assault. The fact itself is however most fully confirmed and a muleteer arrived from Salamanca told me to the same purport; it is generally believed that he is gone towards the East for the purpose of reinforcing Suchet,[1] who is about to attack Valencia & Carthagena.[2] The whole of that part of the peninsula is to be conquered during the winter. All this together with the severity of the season will cost the enemy dear; all their losses will however be recruited in the course of the spring, by the immense reinforcements which we know are hastening to them through France and then they will be enabled to turn their undivided attention upon us and Portugal the ensuing summer. It will be the most desperate effort that they have yet made; as I have already told you his lordship intends profiting by their absence. We left our quarters at Martiago on the 4th instant, in one of the most dreadful storms you can conceive. The wind was very high with sleet & snow beating in your face with uncommon violence, all were instantly soused and with the snow on the ground, twice forded the Agueda on our march hither. Such was the inclemency of the weather that several of our beasts dropped & died on the road with cold, two or three drowned on crossing the river. The trenches are to be opened this night before the town; it is not exactly known which division will be employed in these works, ours, the first, the third, & fourth are mentioned relieving one another alternately. All the army are concentrated in the villages around the place. Lord Wellington arrives this day at Gallegos & also the battering train, which is entirely new and has never been used & is said to be one of the finest ever seen. It consists of guns of the 24 & 32 pounders with thirty mortars of the very largest size. Congreve's rockets

1 Marshal Louis-Gabriel Suchet, Duc d'Albufera, who commanded the French army on the east coast of Spain.

2 Valencia was then a very major city and port on the East coast of Spain whilst Cartagena was a major base for the Spanish navy.

are also to be used,[3] so that either way the poor inhabitants will suffer. A bridge has been thrown across the Agueda near Cesnira [Sexmiro][4] and I hear that we shall make our approaches in two places on both sides at the same moment. The weather is very severe & I fear that it will be our worst enemy and that remaining all night in the trenches will bring on a return of those fevers & agues from which the troops were lately recovering. His lordship however considers it as necessary and one therefore can gamble. The campaign may be considered as begun and important events will soon follow. I have this day been [torn – given?] a bill of thirty pounds by our Dr Maling,[5] we are in arrears of pay [torn – from?] the 24th of October last, and I have not drawn any [torn – money?] since the period of quitting Lisbon.

Our present movements have completely deranged the plan of study which I had marked our for me & I was steadily pursuing; I had nearly completed a set of military drawings and I trust shall yet be able to finish them previous to the arrival of those articles & emoluments which I requested in my former letter, that you would send and when I shall be able to complete myself in the set of plan drawing and surveying with every fulfilment & progress shall be drawn to this object, when finished I will send them to you. I am in good health & spirits and wishing you are enjoying God's blessing on you all. With my kindest love to my aunt, Miss Page and all the little ones, believe me to be your truly affectionate nephew,
G U Barlow

PS I will thank you to have the enclosed letter sent to our *depot* in England, putting in it a five – pound note: it is for my servant's wife & will be delivered to her by our officer commanding at it, you may read it.

El Bodon, 15 January 1812

My dear uncle,
The conjectures stated in my last as to the siege of Rodrigo and the corps of the army to be employed in it have proved correct, they consist of 1st, 3rd, 4th and ours which last have [had] the honour of opening the trenches on the night of the 8th instant. Your kind letter with my aunt's, Miss Page's and Louisa's additions reached us at a late hour on the evening of that day,[6] as the division was halted under the brow of a hill and were

3 William Congreve had experimented in improving the rockets used by the Mahrattas in India for the British army and navy. Despite resistance by Wellington and their very inconsistent trajectory, they did prove useful when bombarding large targets such as cities.

4 This clearly refers to the bridge thrown across the river on trestles at the ford between Sexmiro and Martillan where the siege equipment crossed and moved on to Saelices el Chico.

5 Surgeon John Maling 52nd Foot, he later became a Staff Surgeon attached to the Light Division. (No. 1914 in Drew, *Commissioned Officers in the Medical Services of the British Army*).

6 His sister Louisa born in 1798, she unfortunately died unmarried in 1821 aged only 22.

making arrangements for storming Fort St Francisco [Fort Renaud], which commanded the proposed spot of ground and must therefore first be taken. Lord W[ellington] would not allow of volunteers for this enterprize, saying that he knew the whole Light Division were equally willing and appointed the flank companies of each battalion for that purpose, of ours was one. The redoubt was pronounced by our engineers to be a complete little work of the kind with three pieces of cannon, a ditch fifteen-feet deep and fifteen wide, well palisaded and under the protection of the whole fire of the fortress. Colonel Colborne & Major Gibbs, both of the 52nd commanded, the party advanced in the best order & silence, cut off the enemy's advanced videttes and prevented any alarm. They were however discovered by the sentry on the parapet at the distance of about fifty yards, after receiving one volley from their guns and musketry, the storming party advanced to the ditch and descending by scaling ladders hung upon the palisades, planted them against the parapet on the other side of it. One division took their station opposite the cannon and kept up so hot a fire that the French could not venture to show their heads above the parapet or retard them, which was the saving of many a life; another jumped into the ditch, here the enemy threw several hand grenades which did more mischief than anything else, as it was crowded with our people. A third broke open the gate, upon which they cried out for quarter. Our company composed the rear carrying fascines, under cover. I was however sent forward to Colonel Colborne for orders to what part of the fort they were to throw them in and although amid the confusion of noise I did not succeed in finding him, was present during the greater part of the affair with the attacking party, the night just admitting of distinguishing friend from foe and no more. Three cheers announced to the astonished garrison of Rodrigo and to the Light Division our success by the latter, it was instantly returned, to the no small satisfaction of Lord W[ellington] who was anxiously waiting the result in a neighbouring valley at a large fire. We took 3 pieces of cannon [two cannon and a howitzer], three officers and 50 prisoners.[7] Colonel Colborne's arrangement was most judicious & prompt, for at the time of assault, a further reinforcement was on its way from the city and many more lives could have been lost.

The whole division then came up and broke ground within 600 yards of the place. Our company with several others, were sent forward to cover them, whilst employed in working. Here we lay on the glacis within four hundred yards of their works, on our bellies, in the deepest silence, to be ready for a sortie, and remained there from eight in the evening till five the next morning. The night was terribly cold and frosty, accompanied with dreadful thick dews and we had neither coats nor blankets, as all those encumbrances had been left behind on being ordered with the storming

7 Maj. Gen. John T. Jones, *Journals of Sieges carried on by the Army under the Duke of Wellington in Spain during the years 1811 to 1814* (London: John Weale, 1846), p.105, records in his account that two officers and 43 men were captured and three killed in total. The 52nd lost six men killed and three officers and 16 men wounded.

party. The enemy as soon as they heard us digging, opened the whole of their fire and continued it during the whole of the night; throwing their shells with great correctness, our people however nearly completed the covert way and by morning, when we were withdrawn were pretty well protected. We have thus in one night gained as much ground as Massena did in four days, when he besieged Rodrigo. The governor never dreamt of our attacking the fort by assault & had calculated upon detaining us four days, by making regular approaches when it hardly cost us as many minutes.

Every fourth night we are in the trenches; on the 12th the regiment was employed in erecting the batteries &c. Within four hundred & fifty yards of the place & dragging up the guns yesterday evening they opened to the number of 40 24-pounders, they fire incessantly day & night. The sound is most cheering and gratifying & after having been shot at these last six days without being able to retaliate on the enemy in their own coin. The cannon of the fortress is nearly silenced, as we can see from these hills, by this powerful & well directed fire. The works are however of great solidity and we calculate that it will require four days & nights of incessant battering to make two breaches wide enough for our purpose. Marmont is advancing by forced marches, but we expect that he will arrive a day after the fair, as he calculated that Fort St Francisco would have given us more delay work, more than a quarter of an hour's assault. He is expected to reach Salamanca, about sixty miles distant on the day we propose to storm the place. The garrison were yesterday driven out of the suburbs and are much dispirited by our rapid progress. Never I believe has a siege been conducted with such rapidity as the present and those who are judges assert that our works reflect the highest credit on the engineer's department. I trust that we shall recover the national credit, which received some damage at Badajoz.[8]

God bless you all, I am in the highest health and spirit and believe me to be your truly affectionate nephew, G U Barlow

To William Barlow Esq, Little Bridge Street, Blackfriars, London
El Bodon, 22 January 1812

My dear uncle,
My last of the 15th announced to you the opening of our batteries on the 16th, we took as usual our turn of duty & on this occasion the enemy greeted us with more than usual strength, as the approaches were now advanced within 100 paces of their main bastion. At this spot we worked at the sap day & night, up to our knees in water & mud under the declivity of a hill, down which the whole of the rain had poured. The incessant & well directed fire of our guns had made two practicable breaches on the 19th, when the Light Division was called upon, though out of it's turn for duty, to contribute their aid in the assault; and honour which has cost us

8 Badajoz had been besieged by the British in May 1811, but they were forced to abandon it when Marshal Soult's army approached, leading to the Battle of Albuera.

several brave men. His Lordship had been reconnoitring the whole day; in the evening at dusk, the columns of attack were formed, and at the rising of the moon moved forward. General Picton's Division was directed to the Great Breach on the right, ours to a smaller one on the left. The storming party consisted of 300 men led by Major Napier, and the Forlorn Hope by Lieutenant Gurwood, both of the 52nd. These were closely supported by the whole division in column. The enemy were perfectly prepared, had continued retrenchments on the ramparts & near the breach, so as to enfilade & rake the whole. Their fire did great execution and during the short period of its lasting, was severe. A large quantity of powder took fire at this moment, and blew up numbers of our people, the sight was most awful. Nothing however could resist the impetuosity of the assailants who rushed over every obstacle, scaling two walls & passing as many ditches. The enemy as soon as they came in contact were driven into the Grand Square [Plaza Mayor] of the town at the point of the bayonet. Here they threw down their arms & called for quarter, which to the honour of our soldiers was granted, although in the first fury of the assault, and when none could be expected after so obstinate a resistance, protracted to the last. Indeed, the French confessed that they looked for nothing else than to be massacred, judging from what they themselves would have done. Our loss, you will find by the papers is very heavy; General McKinnon killed,[9] General Craufurd of our division wounded, it is feared mortally, through the body.[10] General Vandeleur, who has this brigade, Lieutenant Colonel Colborne & Major Napier all of our regiment have lost their arms.[11] This enterprize has however been completed in a shorter period, than the most sanguine could have expected and we have accomplished in 11 days, what cost the French twenty-one.

It is impossible to describe the scene that ensued upon the surrender of the enemy. The Portuguese & our people spread themselves all over the town & got at the stores. We entered it about nine at night, consequently until daylight all was a scene of disorder & confusion. Every man had three or four loaves stuck upon the point of his bayonet. A guard was luckily placed over the spirit magazine in time to prevent its seizure. Fifty pipes of good cognac were there found,[12] with a quantity of other commissariat articles; very little booty was however to be gained, inasmuch as the whole town had been deserted by everyone previous to its first occupation by the French, who had pulled down the houses for firewood and our shot has demolished the whole of those nearest the ramparts. The night was

9 Major General Henry Mackinnon commanded a brigade in the 3rd Division and was killed at Ciudad Rodrigo.

10 Major General Robert Craufurd died of his wounds on 23 January.

11 Major General Vandeleur was only slightly wounded; John Colborne was seriously injured but neither lost their arms; Major George Napier of the 52nd Foot was severely wounded and lost his right arm.

12 A Portuguese pipe measured 550 litres. Therefore, the store held 27,500 litres or 6,049 gallons of brandy!

moreover miserably cold & our troops crowded into the ruined houses to make fires. These rotten edifices soon caught the flames and the conflagration became dreadful. Yesterday I rode over to Ciudad with the view of taking a more ample view of this wretched place and during my absence, an hour's notice to prepare letters for England was alone given. Consequently, on my return the courier had started with Lord Wellington's dispatches, which will go home by a man of war & arrive some time before the present, which is conveyed as usual by the packet. So you see it is an accident which prevents you from hearing from me as regularly as usual. In my next I shall send you my India letters, till then adieu, God bless you all & believe me to be your truly affectionate nephew, G U Barlow

Once captured, Wellington turned all hands to repairing the damage inflicted on the fortress, before Marmont could attempt to retake it. Marmont's ability to do so once the repairs were complete were severely hampered by the fact that the French siege train had been captured within Ciudad Rodrigo.

To William Barlow Esq, Little Bridge Street, Blackfriars, London
El Bodon, 28 January 1812

I have nothing particular to mention since my last, we remain the same as before and in my opinion with little chance of moving ever since the fall of Ciudad Rodrigo the troops have been ordered to keep two day's bread & meat cooked in advance, this his lordship has directed to be discontinued, for the future. All hands are at present employed in repairing the breaches of the works, levelling our lines, batteries &c & constructing a new and much stronger work on the site of the Franciscan redoubt, all these matters were going on with unusual activity. When I went into Rodrigo the day before yesterday, for the purpose of attending the funeral of General Craufurd. His remains were accompanied to their last home by all the officers of the division in procession, Lord Wellington & General Graham leading the train procession. The ball passed previously through his arm & then lodged in his chest, he lingered for three or four days & then died, leaving a wife and five children. In losing this officer, the army & our brigade in particular will suffer most severely. He was buried in the great ditch, just at the bottom of the breach by which we entered.[13] His successor is not as yet named; General Charles Stewart, the Adjutant General is however mentioned and I trust that in this instance rumour will prove correct.[14] He was reckoned as good an officer of light troops as any in the British army, even during the

13 It is normally stated that he was buried in the breach, rather than at the foot of the breach in the ditch. Given that the breach had then to be repaired, it seems more likely that Barlow, who was an eye witness, was correct.

14 Major General the Honourable Charles William Stewart, (later 3rd Marquess of Londonderry) was Adjutant General until April 1812 when he returned to Britain and was then sent to join the Prussian forces as a liaison officer in 1813-1814.

lifetime of General Craufurd and under his command the division, will I am sure continue to maintain its such high character.

I am this day going to Castillejo [de Azaba][15] with a detachment of sick & wounded to the General Hospital and am to relieve the officer at present on duty at that place. This business comes to me by rotation; my stay will be of one month's duration, when I shall be succeeded by another. During this period no operations are expected to take place. The nights are very severe and nothing but so tempting an object as Ciudad Rodrigo would have induced Lord Wellington to move from his cantonments. As it is, the army have suffered very much by this cause; and will require a certain portion of rest & recruitment previous to taking the field. I may therefore in some respects consider myself as fortunate on being ordered from the regiment at a time when nothing is going forward & not being in the predicament of two or three brother officers, who were dispatched to the rear to Abrantes, for the purpose of bringing up clothing and stores, the very day we marched to attack Rodrigo and thus saw nothing of that siege. My time expires on this day month, on the 28th of February,[16] I shall most diligently employ it, in the continuation of these studies, which the siege has prevented.

Should headquarters return to Freineda or become stationary; I shall go & deliver my letter to Lord Wellington, at present it is filled with general officers, collected together by the late events, as also with Spaniards. Were I to go at the present moment upon delivery of my charge, I should be asked to dinner. The table would be crowded with many of high & superior rank, with some of whom am I acquainted. Not a word should I be able to have with his lordship; I should depart the next morning and be heard of no more. I possess also scarcely a stitch of cloathes [sic] fit to be seen [in]; and during my absence from the regiment, must take a trip to Almeida for the purpose of rigging myself afresh and must then catch his lordship at some event of leisure opportunity.

God bless you all, remember me kindly to all and giving them my best love, believe me to be, your truly affectionate nephew G U Barlow

In his next letter George was able to report on his long-awaited interview with Lord Wellington. He also advised that he had been transferred to the 1st Battalion and that orders for marching on Badajoz had just arrived.

To William Barlow Esq, Little Bridge Street, Blackfriars, London
Fuenteguinaldo, 27 February 1812

My dear uncle,
On the day subsequent to the date of my last in pursuance of my intention, I started for Freineda, which I reached about two o'clock in the afternoon. It was post day and his lordship consequently occupied in making up his

15 This village is one mile north of Fuenteguinaldo.
16 The end of the three years required before he could become a captain.

dispatches. I could not therefore have an interview, so sending in my letter, by the aide de camp in the waiting [room], I called again in the course of an hour & although not successful in attaining the object of my visit, received an invitation to dinner at seven o'clock, the same evening, when I had the honour of being introduced to his lordship. We mutually bowed & scooped; our conversation was truly laconic & that was soon interrupted by the entrance of dinner. He merely made enquiries of my father, when I had last heard from him, how long since I had seen him, and how long I had been in Portugal. The answer to these were easy and short enough.

During dinner I sat at the bottom of the table & from that moment to their rising & retiring to his own apartment, I did not exchange a single syllable; indeed scarcely two dozen of words passed between us, the whole time I was under his roof. There were none present excepting his family & staff amounting to fourteen in all. His lordship seemed frequently to be deeply immersed in thought & his conversation was chiefly turned towards his Portuguese aide de camp,[17] who had lately been detached to Cadiz with the news of the surrender of Ciudad Rodrigo, on which subject he seemed to express much anxiety. A good deal of talk concerning spies & other military matters occupied the rest of the evening. We sat down at seven & broke up at nine. His lordship is about five feet eight inches or nine in height & possesses an acute & shrewd physiognomy, small eyes, aquiline nose & long chin; and seemed possessed of a most wonderful memory & described several little skirmishes & affairs, with an accuracy truly surprisingly & which I could scarcely have expected in a man whose thoughts are instantly on the stretch & occupied with a quantity of matter, as multifarious as it is important. Notwithstanding my reception did not answer fully my expectations, I am not sorry at having had an opportunity of contemplating [on] thus hearing the opinions of this most wonderful prodigy of the age.

I returned the other day from a tour to Almeida and the quarter part of the country between the Agueda & Coa rivers & found that the long-expected measure of drafting the second battalion into the first had at length taken place; we are now compleated to nearly a thousand strong, and I am transferred from the second to the first battalion. Had this not taken place I should have exchanged duties with some officer of the first & so continued to have remained out here, which step I should certainly have taken for many obvious reasons. Should my father have been able to procure me a company, the appointment will probably arrive in the course of the autumn and the circumstance of my having served a campaign will probably procure a confirmation of it. Independent of this circumstance I am extremely serious to serve a campaign, the present of which as like [to be] the most important that has ever yet taken place.

17 Wellington did not have a Portuguese aide de camp. I believe that he means Major General Miguel Ricardo de Alava, his Spanish liaison officer, whom Wellington held a great regard for. Being a Spaniard, he is much more likely to have been used to communicate with the Cortes at Cadiz.

Tomorrow we commence our march southward for Badajoz, the route came a few hours since and at a very short notice. I have a most wretched pen & must conclude therefore with bidding you all God bless you & believe me to be your affectionate nephew G U Barlow

[PS] Send me a copy of my father's letter to Lord Wellington.

William Barlow Esq, Little Bridge Street, Blackfriars, London
Castelo de Vide, 10 March 1812

My dearest uncle,
We have at length arrived at the end of our march and I am enabled to sit down and give you a more leisure[ly] account of my first proceedings than when I wrote from Guinaldo on the night previous to the commencement of the journey.[18] Nothing particular has occurred during the eleven days in which we have been occupied with it. Our route lay through Castelo Branco and Vila Velha [do Rodao], where there is a bridge of boats across the Tagus to whose left bank reaches the province of Alentejo. On entering it you must ascend a chain of the steepest mountains I have ever beheld; two great hills in particular, each more than a mile in length and of extraordinary raggedness put our cattle to an extreme trial. They however surmounted it pretty well and came off better than many of their fellow species who had proceeded them before with other divisions and had dropped down & men on the road, which was polluted with the remains. I have often heard much of the cruelty with which horses are often treated in England, this country daily exhibits so many more shocking instances of barbarity, that my opinions on this head have undergone some change, though not on the disposition of my countrymen. At this season the grass is scarcely high enough above ground to afford much nourishment and for these last two or three winter months animals have been literally starving having been very hard worked at Ciudad Rodrigo; fifty mules out of five hundred and fifty attached to the Light Division died in conveying ammunition alone to the trenches. Grass is therefore not to be had but a species of it nearly approaching to rushes, corn is seldom or ever beheld; a few days since some was bought at the enormous price of fourteen dollars a fanngue which in Spanish measures pretty nearly answers to our bushel;[19] few are able to afford such extravagance, I however indulged in it, well knowing that a march was pretty nigh at hand and that thirty or forty dollars was nothing when compared with the loss of my beasts and loading my horse. Therefore, with the precious burden, I have footed it all the way, same as when I joined the army near Rodrigo from landing at Figueira. As it is, my animals have

18 The army moved south as far as Portalegre and Castelo de Vide, where they halted until operations against Badajoz commenced. By remaining four days' march from the fortress, Wellington avoided the French getting early warning of his intentions.

19 Actually a fanega, which equalled a bushel.

but three feeds a day, after the end of every long journey and carrying very considerable loads on their back and little or nothing at night. I have the consolation to see that they do their work with cheerfulness & spirit and do not resemble, those shadows of Rosinantes which many officers possess.[20]

Bye the bye I should have informed you at [La Alameda?], a dirty little Portuguese village,[21] I fell in with the very personage of whom you must have often heard me make such frequent & anxious enquiries and whom I never was happy enough to see for a space of so many years, my good friend Russell, Russell when in the hour of pain & after nearly a total loss of sight, so nobly came forward & screened his school fellow from punishment. I have often related the story and my judgement the more it matures, yet more forcibly impressed my mind with a sense of the generosity displayed in such an act, when so severe an accident had overwhelmed my boyish ideas with its enormity and as I had reason to suppose would have had the same effect on Russell.[22] I knew that he was there & payed [sic] him a visit; but for this circumstance I never should have recognized my friend. Both of us were quiet boys since we last met at Mr Roberts[23] & he was now a fine tall, handsome young man. I was probably as much increased in stature & he shook hands ignorant of his salutant, till I called the above circumstance to his recollection. We dined & spent the day together and I left him next morning. Russell received me with every possible kindness and attention. I could not however help imagining that there was a species of reserve & his conduct very widely differing from the sentiments which animated my mind at that moment. Our acquaintance it is true had been stopped as it were for the space of eight or nine years, during which I had never [had] opportunities of seeing him; perhaps he considered this as intentional on my part, or else what I should be very sorry to think time had deadened the recollection of former years & friendships I could not help feeling inwardly rather hurt at this. With anyone else I should be strongly tempted to break off any acquaintance whatever, or at least allow it to subside, a sense however of the irreparable injury which I have unintentionally caused to this young man, for he has never recovered his sight although no outward blemish in that region is perceptible, disarms me of every angry or ill-natured feeling. Indeed, I could put up with anything and although I thought that my pains at finding him out and the length of years of which I undertook was some proof of my esteem, providence will I trust yet enable me to give him some more solid & forcible proofs of it at a future opportunity, when he will be convinced that this former kindness has not been thrown away nor forgotten.

20 Rosinante was the name of the poor worn out horse that carried Don Quixote.

21 I presume that he refers to La Alamedilla which lies on the Portuguese border about 4 miles west of Castillejo de Azaba.

22 This young man whose sight had been impaired by some accident involving George could possibly refer to John William Russell who is listed as being at Eton at the same time as George. Unfortunately I have been unable to discover any further details regarding this man.

23 Mr Roberts was presumably a school master.

Castelo de Vide, our present quarter, is a remarkably neat & what is still more rare in Portugal, a very clean little town. The French never entered it, excepting once or twice & then there remained but a few hours a small party, which came for the purpose of levying contributions. It is about six or eight miles from Portalegre where the 1st, 3rd & 4th Divisions are stationed; the place stands very high, on the top extremity of a most extensive range of hills and commanding a beautiful view of the Alentejo for many miles around. The whole Light Division are assembled here and active operations may of course be expected instantly to commence as his lordship's headquarters are to be at Portalegre this evening. Badajoz we all know is the point of attack, but who is to be employed in the siege & what particular troops at present is not known; some are of opinion that we shall be pushed forward into the interior of Extramadura, to watch the enemy, who it is well known will soon be at hand; his lordship seems to be of [the] opinion that he can attack the place & fight Marmont at the same time. He has a fine body of cavalry, not less than 16 regiments, an arm in which he has been previously so deficient. Whatever may happen I think we shall place a finger in the pye [sic].

A packet has, we know arrived, but headquarters being at present on the move, the letters have not been delivered out. The last from you is dated the 21st of December. I have hitherto delayed sending home my India letters, of which I have written no less than four, as long as two month's since, in hopes of being able to compleat the latter part of my journal.[24] The business of Rodrigo, my journey to Freineda and subsequent march to these parts have prevented me from completing it. I wish however to send another letter to my father and will transmit it home, at any rate by *next week's* post, if I am not in time for this. You must advise them of this circumstance, should my packet not arrive in time for the ships, otherwise it may appear a strange circumstance. I have likewise finished a set of military drawings with some plans & maps, but wishing to keep the first attempts, I shall copy them afresh & send you them home according to what I have before stated.

I am thank God, in the best health and spirits and only await the arrival of those little articles for which I have written to be complete with everything for the next campaign. Give my best love to my aunt, Miss Page and all the little ones and believe me to be, your truly affectionate nephew G U Barlow

No 41
To GH Barlow, Fort St George, Madras
Castelo de Vide, 12 March 1812 (annotated received 29 March 1813)

My dearest father,
The conjectures stated in the postscript to my mother's letter of the 2nd of January last, with regard to the siege of Rodrigo were verified on the 8th of that same month, on which day the Light Division had the honour of

24 It is a major loss that his journal has not been discovered.

storming the redoubt of St Francisco and breaking ground before the place. Some time previous to the receipt of the present you will probably have read the papers of [the] successful accomplishment of our labours, by an assault on the evening of the 19th.

As a portion of my leisure hours are employed in compiling a small journal of our proceedings and which I fear will not be finished in time for the departure of the present packet, I shall content myself with describing the general outlines of this fortunate event, which commenced with the storming of the Franciscan redoubt.[25] Our company composed part of the detachment which effected that service under Colonel Colborne's orders and here I made my debut. The enemy could not have been well said to be taken by surprise, as they were ready *on the* ramparts to receive the assailants. Nevertheless, the attack was wholly unexpected & our appearance before it during the day appeared to them in no other light than a reconnaissance, this we afterwards learnt from the prisoners. The fort has a deep & broad ditch, well palisaded, with three pieces of cannon & was open and within reach of musketry from the walls. Considering these advantages, the defence of the enemy was not good, allowances must however be made on the superior spirit which always pre-animates the attacking party, as also for their fear of being put to the sword, on beholding themselves surrounded & attacked on all sides by escalade. The work was soon carried and quarter granted in the very moment of assault to the vanquished enemy. Our loss consists of three officers & twenty men killed & wounded in all. Three loud cheers announced to the astonished city, as well as to the remainder of the Light Division & His Lordship, who with General Graham[26] and numbers of Staff officers were sitting on the ground near a large fire at a little distance [from] our success. The working parties instantly advanced and broke ground, our company with some others were then pushed forward toward the glacis of [the] place, to cover them from any sortie and here we lay during the whole of a long winter's night in January, from eight in the evening till between four & five the next morning, flat on the ground in the deepest silence, without great coats or any covering whatever, having thrown them aside on being ordered for the storming party at the redoubt. During the whole night the enemy were by no means sparing of their shot or shells, but did very little execution, owing to their ignorance of our precise situation. When the moon got up, we were withdrawn and by daylight the men had worked so incessantly, that all had put themselves completely under cover.

Three divisions, besides our own, being employed in the conduct of the siege, it fell to our turn of course to work in the trenches every fourth night. On the 12th, we were employed in laying down platforms for the batteries and on the 16th in completing the second parallel & commencing the sap. On this day, our batteries consisting of forty 24 pounders opened their fire

25 This confirms that the converted Convent of St Francisco was being confused with the recently constructed Fort Renaud redoubt.

26 Lieutenant General Sir Thomas Graham, commanding the 1st Division.

with great effect. They usually ceased at night, when the enemy's, which was silent during the day, opened in their turn & annoyed us a good deal, as we then were working not more than a hundred yards from the counterscarp of the ditches & the approaches running along the foot of a hill, were filled with mud & water up to our knees, from the rain which had fallen in the morning. The weather was indeed most trying, particularly to those with rheumatic complaints; it has however pleased God to restore me to health again. Many suffered very severely. We lay out every night in the open air. On the 8th but more especially the 16th I was wet through as high as my knees repeatedly in going to & from the trenches, and upon being relieved about four in the morning, lay down to sleep & waking about eight, found my coat & blanket covered with a thick white frost, but experienced no ill effects whatever.

On the evening of the 19th, the incessant and well directed fire of the batteries had caused two breaches; one very large on the right and one smaller to the left in the angle of a tower. Lord W[ellington] had summoned the governor two days previously and received an answer full of 'death & glory' in the usual French style, that he would bury himself in the ruins. An assault was therefore determined upon, by the 3rd & Light Divisions. It was a fine moonlight evening, we assembled under cover of the Franciscan convent in the suburbs, as did General Picton's corps in the second parallel about seven o'clock. The Forlorn Hope was led by Lieutenant Gurwood & the Storming Party by Major Napier, both of the 52nd. These were closely supported by the whole of the 43rd & 52nd Regiments in a solid column. The enemy opened a very heavy fire & made a particularly firm stand at the large breach & on the ramparts were thrown up several traverses which gave them a great advantage. Distracted by both attacks, no effectual resistance was made to either & our people entering both parts of the city at the same instant, carried all before them, upon which the enemy threw down their arms & received as in a former instance, immediate quarter. Just as the column on the right gained the breach, a dreadful explosion from a powder depot near the ramparts took place, which killed & wounded many brave officers & men & considerably augmented our loss, hitherto sufficiently severe.

Thus has his lordship in the short space of 11 days, reduced the very same fortress strengthened with additional fortifications, which occupied Marshal Massena & 27,000 men twenty-nine [days]. The rapidity with which this has been effected, Marshal Marmont in his dispatch to Berthier, presumes 'incomprehensible'. The redoubt and convent of St Francisco, he expected, would have required a regular siege and approaches and 'would have given him at least eight or ten days' to use his own words. They were each carried in about as many minutes. So unaccountably, fail the calculations sometimes of the wisest men. From an intercepted dispatch we learnt that Marmont was hastening every exertion for the relief of the garrison, but that his army could not be concentrated at Salamanca before the 21st, consequently he could not have arrived at our lines previous to the 25th & the place was already taken on the 19th, before the 60,000 men which he had under his orders could assemble even at Salamanca. The garrison at the commencement of the siege amounted to nearly 2,000 under arms, besides 300 sick. They suffered no material loss till the night of the assault and then it fell chiefly on their grenadiers, who behaved very well and had five officers alone in killed. The artillery was as usual, most excellent & served the guns most admirably. Indeed, the majority of the enemy's dead & wounds consisted of these two corps. We paid dear enough for our acquisition. General Mackinnon was blown up & General Craufurd mortally wounded while leading on the Light Division. Colonel Colborne & Major Napier, both of this regiment, lost their arms and the life of the former is yet considered in great danger.

Some degree of confusion must naturally be expected to take place on these occasions, especially in towns carried by a night attack. In expectation of this event, all the inhabitants had fled who were favourable to the cause of the enemy, dreading the vengeance of the allies, of whom the Spanish chiefs Don Julian & Don Carlos were by far the most inveterate.[27] A guard was instantly placed over the depot of spirits, just in time to hinder its seizure by the storming party. About the stores and magazines for eatables we were not so solicitous. The night was moreover very cold and the men careless of the consequences, lighted fires in the ruinous old houses and floors, these soon caught the flames, whilst the sparks carried by the wind communicated similar conflagrations on other parts of the city. On the whole, it was a most motley spectacle. Here might be seen groups of prisoners assembled in all the chief squares & streets and trembling for their lives, expected the same treatment which they themselves had proposed towards the cities of Tortosa & Taragona in the storm of those places.[28] As for myself, tired and weary, I sought an inhabited house and with difficulty succeeding, lay down to sleep in a chimney corner about one in the morning. [After] three hours, my slumbers were broken by an alarm of fire and starting up, found the whole of the upper storey in flames, occasioned by sparks from a neighbouring conflagration, as also a French officer standing in the rooms, who had concealed himself during the first fury of the assault, but was now obliged with me to sally forth into the street & there remain till the dawn of day, which again restored matters to their usual train and our men to their accustomed state of order & discipline.

English papers which have arrived up with the army of a late date convey to us the gratifying intelligence that our late achievements and the beneficial prospects resulting therefrom have been received by the public in that light, of an importance which they so justly deserve. Spaniards as well as English are unanimous in their praise of that penetration which so nicely calculated the moment for besieging and the rapidity displayed in so speedy

27 Don Carlos (as Wellington called him Don Carlos Espagna) was actually General Roger Bernard Espagnac de Ramefort who commanded regular Spanish troops.

28 It was deemed within the ancient rules of war that once there was a practicable breach in the walls of a city or fortress, that they should surrender. If they did not, requiring the besiegers to carry out a costly storming, then their lives were deemed forfeit. Hence the French had warned the defenders and inhabitants of Tortosa and Taragona that they would be put to the sword.

& vigorous an attainment of its object, which compounded the enemy's plans, wrested this, the most important of all the points on the Portuguese & Spanish frontier, their depot of stores, their heavy battering train (an irreparable loss) and this place together with Almeida the grand keys to future invasions of these portions of the peninsula, from their grasp.[29]

With that all animating and efficient activity, which has so eminently marked his military career, Lord W[ellington], has turned our exertions towards a second and equally important scheme, for the benefit of the allied cause. The whole army quitting their cantonments in the Beira and northern provinces about the last week of February for the Alentejo, and more southern districts, have reached Portalegre & its vicinity on their way to Badajoz. From the latter town, Castelo de Vide is removed but four days march. Our halt is only temporary, whilst the necessary reconnaissance's and dispositions for the siege are in preparation. For three or four weeks subsequent to the fall of Rodrigo we have been indulged with a little repose, previous however to marching hither, the men of the second battalion were drafted into the first (together with your humble servant) to make up the necessary compliment of effectives for the latter, and its officers sent home to recruit afresh. We now muster 950 bayonets in a perfect state of readiness for future operations. As for myself, I enjoy thank God, the best health & spirits, after having performed the journey on foot. My horse was on this occasion loaded with a cargo of corn, for which I paid at the rate of fourteen dollars a bushel. During these last two or three months our animals have suffered very much, and many of them died. The snow has constantly covered the ground and the little grass which could be procured resembled a species of bushes and void of nourishment. Neither has the spring verdure yet shown itself above the ground, the beasts have therefore been of late in a state of starvation. The road I knew, in some parts were very hilly; and over the grand chain of mountains between Extramadura and Mondego the above precautions were therefore most necessary, and I have now the pleasure of beholding my animals in as good condition as previous to the commencement of their long and laborious march. I will conclude this military epistle with giving you a description of my interview with Lord Wellington on the occasion of me presenting your letter of introduction. I arrived at Freineda, his headquarters, about one in the afternoon, his lordship was then busily occupied in making up his weekly dispatch for England, and as I was given to understand that he would be so employed till dinner time, I sent in my letter & in return received an invitation for seven o'clock. After waiting a few moments, his lordship entered the room, the 52nd uniform was my only distinction among several other strangers, we mutually bowed. He then advanced and made some enquiries respecting your health, my last advices

29 The fortress of Almeida had been abandoned by the French in May 1811, the French garrison escaping through the blockading forces surrounding it, much to the annoyance of Wellington. Ciudad Rodrigo and Almeida both stood on the traditional northern invasion route from Spain into Portugal.

from Madras and how long since I had quitted Bengal, as also the time of my serving in Portugal. To all these interrogations, the answers were easy & ready enough and immediately afterwards dinner was announced.

The party consisted of 16 persons, in which his family staff was included. His lordship sat at the middle of the table, having on his right, the young Prince of Orange, at present with the army as an amateur.[30] A Portuguese officer had arrived that morning from Lisbon & Cadiz, to which places he had carried the intelligence of the fall of Rodrigo. To him, his lordship's conversation was chiefly addressed, he seemed particularly curious as to the opinion of the public on the late events. I sat near the top of the table & never exchanged a syllable during the remainder of the evening, or indeed had any other conversation than what I have related as above. My attention was therefore immovably fixed in the contemplation of this great man, the glory of England, the pillar of the patriot cause and the genius which has so invariable baffled the most numerous armies & celebrated captains of the present day. A description of his physiognomy in this place would be needless, as it must be already so well known to you. I was however, most forcibly struck with the wonderful acuteness and accuracy of his memory, now particularly displayed in the narration of several little guerrilla skirmishes, whose insignificance would, I have imagined, erased them from his recollection. To me, who am never troubled with care or anxiety, they were well known, I could not however have expected the same minuteness in a head taken up with the cares & concerns of nations & armies.

To conclude, his lordship retired about nine o'clock, after previously having signified to a Spanish officer in the most earnest manner, his desire to have an interview with Don Carlos the next morning at Rodrigo and the remainder of the company followed his example.

It now only remains for me to acknowledge the receipt of your kind letter [dated] the 27th of June last. Two of an earlier date, my uncle states to be in his possession and which he promises to forward by the first opportunity. Alas, my good father, how little must you have been aware at the moment of writing, that your kind solicitudes were then of no avail. Two days previous my poor *brother* finally had left this for a better world.[31] I will not afflict you or myself with a second account of a circumstance which must have reached Madras long ere now, nor harrow up these sorrows which time alone can allay, in that sad hour. Religion whispers to our grief 'that he is gone to those realms of joy & bliss, where tears are no more, nor pain [or] unhappiness can disturb his soul'. But enough.

God bless & preserve you my dear parent, that he may bestow on you every earthly happiness & good, is the constant & sincerest prayer, of your truly affectionate son, G U Barlow.

30 William Prince of Orange, had the rank of colonel in the British army and served as an extra aide camp at Wellington's headquarters and was therefore not an amateur.

31 His younger brother William, born 18 December 1792, had joined the Royal Navy, but died of illness on 29 July 1811.

6

The Siege of Badajoz

On 13 March, the brigade received notice to proceed from Castelo de Vide with only two hours' notice and marched to Badajoz, where they arrived on 17 March.[1] The regiment marched to a position just outside cannon range, due south of Fort Pardaleras on the Torquemada road. That night, a detachment of the 52nd joined the working parties of no less than 3,800 men which broke ground in a rain-storm 150 yards from Fort Picurina. This trek to and from the trenches, proved to be one of the greatest hardships of the siege, having to cross the waist high waters of the Calamon and Rivillas streams –which join just south of Badajoz and join the Guadiana River at Badajoz – in freezing conditions.

On 25 March, 100 men under the command of Captain Ewart headed an attack on Fort Picurina, which initially failed, but they eventually broke through the gate of the palisades and captured the fort, for the loss to the 52nd of 36 officers and men killed and wounded, including Captain John Ewart and Ensign William Nixon wounded.[2] Capture of the fort allowed breaching batteries to be established which could play on the bastions of Trinidad and Santa Maria, however the approach to this face of the castle wall was further protected by a reservoir of water. The following night Lieutenant Robert Blackwood accompanied three sappers, who lay charges to blow the dam, it successfully exploded but unfortunately the water level did not fall by much. This failure would cause the loss of many dozens of lives during the storming of the fortress.

On 6 April three breaches were deemed practicable and at 9:00 p.m. the Light and 4th Divisions formed up silently about a thousand yards from the breaches. Small ladder parties preceded the volunteers of the forlorn hope and were to be closely followed by the rest of the division. Officers of the 52nd who volunteered for the storming party were, Captain William Jones, Lieutenants James McNair and Charles Booth and Ensign George Gawler. As they neared the breaches the inky black silence burst into horrendous life as the French opened up with both musketry and artillery fire at point blank range, cutting swathes through the attacking columns. The two

---

1 W.S. Moorsom, *History of the 52nd Regiment 1755-1816* (London: Richard Bentley 1860), p.160, states that the Light Division marched from Elvas to Badajoz on 27th March, but this would appear to be a typographical error.

2 Captain John Frederick Ewart, 52nd Foot, his diary for 1811-12 has been published by the editor: Gareth Glover, *The Peninsular War Diary of Captain John Frederick Ewart, 52nd Light Infantry (1811-12)* (Huntingdon: Ken Trotman, 2010).

The siege of Badajoz by Leveque. (Editor's Collection)

divisions were checked and every subsequent attack launched by small groups at the breach was soon destroyed by the incessant French fire. For the few who gained the crest of the breach, they found huge planks chained into place, with great iron nails pointing upwards and on the very crest, the gap in the wall was closed by *chevaux-de-frise*, huge logs chained into place with swords and bayonets embedded within, sticking out in all directions. The few brave and lucky souls that reached this unharmed, had their brains spattered by the musket butts of the defenders. It was hopeless, with carnage beyond description everywhere they looked; but still small groups tried valiantly to overcome the obstacles, only to be blasted into oblivion or adding further to the mass of wounded lying at the bottom of the ditch. The retreat was finally sounded and the too few survivors sullenly began to retire as the town clock struck midnight.

However, hope was not abandoned, with Picton's division successfully escalading the still perfect but lightly guarded citadel walls, whilst Major General Sir James Leith's 5th Division also took advantage of the scarcity of defenders in their section, to successfully escalade at the bastion of St Vincente. The success of these two attacks turned what had looked likely to be a dreadful disaster into the successful capture of Badajoz, as the French defenders retired from these two unexpected breaches of the defences. The following day *Général de Division* Armand Philippon, the governor, surrendered the town. The success was a brilliant one, but at a terrible human cost. Nearly 5,000 men of Wellington's army were killed or wounded this night, the Light Division suffering 40 percent casualties. During the entire siege, the 52nd lost 69 officers and men killed and 346 wounded, of which 85 percent occurred in the final storm.[3]

3 The officers killed were, Captains William Jones, William Madden and Clement Poole, Lieutenants Charles Booth and Job Watson Royle. The wounded officers were Brevet

George was severely wounded in the right arm and leg at the storming of the fortress of Badajoz and was close to having the arm amputated. He was eventually given leave to return to England to recuperate.

Armand Philippon Governor of Badajoz. (Editor's Collection)

To William Barlow Esq, Little Bridge Street, Blackfriars, London
Camp before Badajoz, 19 March 1812

My dear uncle,
The days subsequent to the date of my last from Castelo de Vide and when I was absent on a visit to Portalegre, an order came for the march of the division; we reached Elvas on the 10th instant. The following morning crossed over to the left bank of the Guadiana by a bridge of boats, Lord Wellington and the engineers having previously made all the necessary arrangements & in consequence we broke ground & opened the trenches on the very same night of our arrival. The evening was stormy, attended by a high tempest of wind & one of the most uninterrupted & heavy rains, that I have ever witnessed. It was moreover, excessively dark and the elements effectually prevented the enemy from discovering or hearing the noise occasioned by the working parties under these favourable circumstances. On the very first night the approaches were posted within two hundred & fifty yards of a commanding fort, which it has been found previously necessary to attack before anything is attempted against the main body of the city. So perfectly unsuspicuous were the garrison of our intentions that they never interrupted us the whole night with even a musket shot within range of which face our people worked during the whole night. Badajoz is a noble city, of great extent and apparent wealth. It is of an oval shape, against one extremity of which our attack is directed, the other touches the Guadiana on the opposite side of which rises the hill & fort of St Christoval commanding the whole. The garrison amount to nearly five thousand men, composed of the remainder of Girard's corps & some of the best of the French troops. These former, will no doubt [in an] attempt to blot out their recent disgrace & surprisal, render the conduct of

Lieutenant Colonel Edward Gibbs (lost an eye), Brevet Major William Mein (severely), Captains Robert Campbell (severely), Augustus Merry (severely – died of wounds) and John Ewart (severely), Lieutenants James McNair (severely), Charles Kinloch (slightly), Charles Yorke (slightly), Robert Blackwood (severely), Francis Davies (slightly), William Royds (slightly) and George Barlow (severely), Ensigns William Nixon (severely), George Hall (severely) and George Gawler (slightly).

so able a governor as General Philippon, the same man who gave us last year, so warm a reception.

Animated by their former success we may expect a most gallant and determined resistance on the part of the enemy; since it has been in their possession the city has been strengthened by several new & most important outworks and their formidable nature do the highest credit to the skills of their engineers who had rendered the place as strong as it is in the power of men to make it. They are moreover said to have prepared a number of mines for which work the soil is particularly favourable. We on the other part possess a noble battering train of nearly fifty pieces in addition to between twenty and thirty large mortars & howitzers,[4] it being his lordship's intention to show no mercy whatever in the article of shells.

The season at this time of the year is not very pleasant for those who live under canvas; a great deal of rain has lately fallen accompanied with high & tempestuous winds, the camp is moreover very inconvenient in two most important respects. Water must be fetched from a considerable distance & that not of the best; and which in summer must be particularly unwholesome, from being stagnant. It is a considerable distance to the Guadiana and the whole country around a sandy, barren flat, almost as naked as the palm of my hand and almost destitute of wood for fires & cooking; these are indeed two great inconveniences much felt.

I received at Portalegre your numerous & kind letters up to the 15th of February last, by favour of Colonel Halkett & Lieutenant Holford,[5] as also Henry's, Robert's & Charles' together with Lady R[obert] Barlow's enclosures.[6] I will answer them all by the next opportunity as I am at present writing in considerable hurry. I have to return you my best thanks for the trouble you have taken in writing to India about the company, and shall include the present written about noon day with telling you that I am very sleepy, not having had any sleep these two last nights of any nature in camp; on the first being attached to the party which opened the trenches and on yesterday, everyone being sent out with a picquet to watch some roads leading to the bridge of Badajoz, where the enemy have a post and from which duty I have only returned this morning. God bless you all and believe me to be your truly affectionate nephew G U Barlow

4 According to Jones, *Sieges*, p.157, the siege train for Badajoz consisted of 52 cannon in total, including 16 24-pounders, 20 Russian 18-pounders and 16 24-pounder howitzers.

5 Lieutenant James Price Holford, 52nd Light Infantry, who was acting as an aide de camp to Major General Slade.

6 Charles Anstruther Barlow was his younger brother, born in 1800; he eventually became a captain in the Royal Navy and died in 1855.

To William Barlow, Little Bridge Street, Blackfriars, London
Camp before Badajoz, 26 March 1812

My dearest uncle,
Since the date of my last our labours have proven most unremitting and pushed to their utmost extent in carrying on the operations of the siege commenced under such favourable auspices on the night of the, 17th an omen and better known amongst our men as being St Patrick's day. A variety of causes demand such peculiar exertions and some idea of their indefatigable nature may be formed when I tell you that during the first five nights of our operations, one only has passed by me in bed. Two of these were without any sleep and the remaining two, my slumbers lasted only till eleven o'clock each time. Badajoz is nearly thrice the size of Ciudad Rodrigo & its circumference of defence very largely increased by Fort St Christoval and regularly constructed defences in advance, by which it is encircled. Our approaches therefore proportionally increased in extent and but *three* divisions employed in double the quantity of work, which occupied *four* at Rodrigo. This however is required by the confined state of our current directions. General Hill with the 2nd Corps[7] is pushed forwards in the direction of Merida to watch the motion of Marmont's army from Salamanca, whilst General Graham with the 1st, 6th & 7th [Divisions] keeps a vigilant eye to the passes of the Sierra Morena and Marshal Soult at Seville, the area of the enemy, which most effectively prevents by this interposition and can only be affected by a march into the interior of Spain, which it is supposed will afford sufficient time for the reduction of this place. Should they be disposed to risk any battle, with the two covering armies, his lordship is ready to support either of them in case of necessity, leaving a body of men sufficient to blockade the town. A reference to the map indicates this to be his lordship's plan and as far as I am capable of reasoning, a most admirable one.

The governor and garrison are in the meanwhile making most obstinate defence and as therein assisted by several favourable and concurring circumstances. It has constantly rained both by day & night since the commencement of the siege with very few intervals, some of the showers being the hardest I have ever beheld. The trenches are full of mud and water up to the knees and was not the soil of a most favourable nature, it would be impossible to drag up the heavy artillery. The matter at present is one of great difficulty, sixteen bullocks, together with the manual assistance being required to draw such pieces and even then, the opening of our trenches has been delayed nearly two days. We indeed have of late been living in an amphibious state, oftener wet than dry, this inconvenience pursues us to our tents, which are by no means proof against the descending torrents at the moment I am now watching. My baggage during the day is covered

7 Hill's corps consisted of the 2nd Division, Hamilton's Portuguese Division, and two brigades of cavalry.

with oilskin, which at night is substituted for a counter-pane and is indeed absolutely necessary.

As I have mentioned in a former post, General Philippon shows himself very conscious of the important charge committed to his care, strengthening the old & framing every obstacle which art or industry can devise. On the 18th they made a sortie with nearly two thousand men, they reached for a moment, the right flank of the trenches which had been pushed close to the town and carried off a few pickaxes and spades before the coverers could come to the relief of the working parties, the foe was instantly routed and driven back into the town in the greatest confusion under the cover of the guns, since which attempt they have never ventured to show themselves outside the walls.

Everything being ready we opened from six batteries yesterday morning on the town and a very strong fort called the Picurina situated three hundred yards in advance. The garrison answered it with such a superior number of guns, it is difficult to decide whether their artillery or our own was best served, an incessant roar of thunder continued till sunset, with great execution to each other's works. The Portuguese gunners I particularly observed stood to their cannon with equal coolness and directed them with equal precision as the British, often having remained all day in the trenches, our division was relieved about seven o'clock in the evening.

I came back to the camp and hardly finished a hasty dinner when all of us were roused by a tremendous roar of musketry, rockets thrown up as signals of distress and loud shouts indicated a night attack. During half an hour the conflict was most destructive & obstinate. Three loud British cheers soon announced success on our part and we rightly guessed that they proceeded from the storming party against Fort Picurina. An officer of ours just wounded has arrived; he states that it was carried in the most martially and gallant manner.[8] Hardly a man out of 300 which composed the French garrison escaped, about 70 were made prisoners and the remainder bayonetted, they fought to the very last, particularly the officers and were so hotly pursued that several threw themselves into a river which ran close by and were drowned together with some men who sallied out to recover the work. This attempt however was unsuccessful as the former and our success most complete, but attended nevertheless with so severe [a] loss, particularly of officers, one killed, 9 wounded, as indeed is the loss in all storming enterprises where they lead on at the head of the columns. We had one company engaged in the affair, of 120 men out of whom 35 were killed or wounded and among the latter two out of three officers engaged,

8 Both Captain John Ewart and Ensign William Nixon of the 52nd were wounded. It would appear from the evidence of Lieutenant Charles Dawson who also participated in the attack, that Ewart was shot in the fleshy part of the arm very early in the attack and was immediately transported to the rear, so it must have been Nixon who was brought back as described by George.

one I fear mortal with three balls at the same moment.[9] To their lot fell the perilous part of preceding even the storming parties, carrying the fascines to fill up the ditch and the planting the ladders against the parapet by which the others were to mount; noticing [they were] the very foremost of course, they suffered most, for not content with performing the above duties, they fixed bayonets and were naturally the first men who mounted the breach. The engineers have the day been examining the work & declare that had the depth of the fosse and the strength of the place been known to them, they never would have advised the attack, which was made with so much risk & so gallantly succeeded. God bless you & believe me to be your affectionate nephew. G U Barlow.

To William Barlow Esq, Little Bridge Street, Blackfriars, London
Camp before Badajoz, 7 April 1812

My dear uncle,
As you may see by the returns that I am wounded I have thought it necessary to send you a few lines written by a brother officer to dispel any apprehensions which you may entertain. I have not power to give you any details but will content myself with mentioning that the fortress of Badajoz was carried last night by storm with very severe loss on our part. I am wounded in two places, first in the hip & second in the right arm by musket balls, the latter shattered the bone between the elbow & wrist, I am nevertheless doing as well as can be expected & the surgeons say that amputation will not be necessary for the latter, both balls were extracted last night & I propose going to Elvas as soon as my state of body will allow of moving. God bless you all & believe to be your affectionate nephew G U Barlow

To William Barlow Esq, Little Bridge Street, Blackfriars, London
Badajoz, 15 March [annotated – Should be April] 1812

My dear uncle,
Two days subsequent to the date of my last, I was brought into this place, in a litter, Elvas being deemed too great a distance & besides very much crowded. I am thank God, doing extremely well, & my recovery is deemed sure, though slow. I am in the very best spirits & hope soon to be able to sit up & give you a specimen of my left-handed penman-ship. The weather at present is very mild & favourable for invalids & in short everything going on as well as I could wish. I received the day before yesterday, your kind letter of the 14th of March last, in which, you announce having shipped the box of articles, that I had requested, even if possible I would return you more as large. My thanks for this fresh proof of your kindness, conscious as I am that you must have dipped almost into every shop in London,

9 This was Ensign Nixon who survived.

searching for so many & so different articles, besides a certain personage would be as sour as vinegar on beholding so much attention taken off from wine matters.

I am obliged not to trespass too much on the kindness of my writing by entering more trifling detail, my letters will therefore be short and confined to the one good point of my state of health which literally & truly affords me the cheering prospect as above described. Give my kindest love to all at Streatham & that God may bless you all is the innocent prayer of, your truly affectionate nephew, G U Barlow

PS Tell my good aunt how glad I am to find by your last that she is doing so well & how sorry I am to find that Miss Page does not conform to her doctor's instructions as well as I do to mine, otherwise I would venture to say she might yet recover sooner than myself. I have written to Mr Lucas to take care of the box.

To William Barlow Esq, Lower Bridge Street, Blackfriars, London
Badajoz, 18 April 1812

My dearest uncle,
I trust that you will be able to decipher this, my first left-handed and bed written attempt, such as it is.[10] I was incapable of conveying to you the account of my misfortunes, had it not been for the kindness of my amanuensis. God be praised, I am doing remarkably well, the weather is mild and everything favourable for wounded patients; the hot weather not having commenced is indeed a great point. My spirits are in the best state except when they are crossed by reflections on the slaughter which fell on the army, and our devoted regiment particularly, in the capture of this horrible city. The 52nd had nearly 350 men and 23 officers killed or wounded, out of 28 who were present that night. 18 names only appear in the Gazette, the remaining five are but slight cases and they would not put their names into the list thinking it already large enough and not chusing [sic] needlessly to alarm their friends. For your information I send the following particulars of this sad tragedy, which I believe are quite correct.

The night was quite dark, which would render the least confusion & certainty of ill success. This presently occurred by the loss of the two engineer officers who alone knew the way and whilst leading on the advanced parties, fell by the very first volley from the enemy. Our column and that of the 4th Division crossed at that unlucky moment and got mixed and in this state both crowded together to the same breach, instead of each taking its own particular one. This great body of men had to descend a steep counterscarp by five or six ladders only, which as you may suppose, took some time, as four only could go down at once on each. We had then to drive

10 He has forgotten that he wrote previously with his left hand on 15 March.

them out of a demi-lune,[11] and all this close under the noses of between 2 and 3,000 men the greater part of whom had *three* spare muskets each, with people to load them in their rear, and kept up one of the most rapid and murderous fires, such as our oldest veterans affirm they never before experienced. Aim was unnecessary, we stood so thick and crowded on the glacis, and in the ditch, besides the enemy threw amongst us a number of fire balls which enabled them to see our movements as clear as at noon day. The breach would not admit of more than 13 or 15 men abreast and the storming party made a number of gallant though fruitless attempts to carry it. They repeatedly arrived on the summit, but found the entrance filled up with a massy row of chevaux de frise, which it was impossible either to remove, cut away, or even to get over.[12] The slope of the breaches were covered with planks, full of nails with the sharp ends sticking upwards; the interior of the bastions were afterwards found to have been traversed in all directions, ditches and pits fifteen feet deep cut everywhere, into which our people might fall like traps during the darkness of the night; and a new fosse with a rampart thrown up in the rear of all these works.[13] In addition to this, shells and grenades were placed in rows along the parapet to be hurled down on the heads of our poor fellows and a new species of destruction fired out of their muskets, called by us *musket grape*, being a number of slugs bound together, and resembling that sort of cannon shot in miniature; in a word every obstacle which the engineer's art or invention could devise, seems to have been put in requisition by our able foe; in this horrible state we remained nearly three quarters of an hour without being able to retaliate in the least on the enemy. And here I may be allowed to say a word or two respecting the officers of the Light Division, and this with a better grace in as much as your humble servant never got beyond the edge of the ditch. They led on repeatedly their men up to the very muzzles of the enemies [sic] pieces, so as to feel the wadding as well as the ball; when one fell, another supplied his place. It is impossible to describe their feelings on beholding all efforts so vain, this struck them the more as they have been hitherto so invariably successful, the division never having failed at any single object during a long course of service. Excepting myself and one or two others, they all were killed and wounded on the very breach one after another, and in this awful crisis persevered in using their utmost personal exertions, till Lord Wellington, who was on a neighbouring hill, sent us orders to retire, leaving 70 officers in the horrible ditch and nearly 1,000 men.[14] I speak of course only of the transactions of our own division. The whole attention

11 A detached outwork, usually triangular in shape, placed in front of the long curtain wall to protect it from artillery fire.

12 A *chevaux-de-frise* or 'Frisian horse' was a large beam covered with projecting spikes or blades which formed a hedge of points against cavalry or infantry.

13 A fosse, in fortification terms, was a long narrow trench.

14 The Light Division casualties were 15 officers and 163 men killed and 43 officers and 698 men wounded, a total of 919 casualties.

of the garrison had been attracted to the breaches and the castle and other parts left in a comparatively unprotected state; upon which the 3rd and 5th Divisions scaled walls otherwise impregnable and the enemy ran away from the breaches and adjacent parts in all directions; and crossing the bridge (General Philippon accompanying them) took refuge in Christoval and in that fort surrendered next morning. To this circumstance they save[d] their lives, otherwise none would have been spared, a few hundreds of the unlucky hindmost alone being bayonetted.

As for myself, I was first hit in the thigh when the column approached the glacis;[15] the ball carried away a canteen hanging down my back by cutting in two the leather strap to which it was affixed, and taking a downward direction lodged a little below the right hip bone. A poor fellow at that very moment was shot by my side and I concluded at first that in falling he had struck me off my legs. The pain in a few moments decreased however and about a quarter of an hour afterwards as the column moved forwards, I got over the palisades of the ditch,[16] was shown some ladders a little on the left. I turned half round to the men telling them to follow me thither and waving my cap when the second shot struck my right arm, chapeau[17] dropt quick enough as you may suppose and I not being able to hold out any longer, with great difficulty persuaded a couple of soldiers (Portuguese) to help me off. They wanted me to lay flat on the glacis in company with them till the fire which was very heavy should abate a little. To this I would not agree, feeling myself growing fainter every instant from loss of blood. A British soldier coming past with a bearer[18] at that moment, lifted me into it and carried me to the surgeons. Finding the sword and belt galling me much, I requested my Portuguese friends to take charge of it, by the way and whilst under the surgeon's hands, they whipped them off and I have seen no more of them as you may imagine.

Elvas, 22 April

Upon examination it was found that both bones in the arm were broken, one was broke, the other shattered a good deal. The ball in my hip was soon taken out being simply a flesh wound; with that in my arm, two splinters of considerable size were extracted and since then ten or twelve more at various dressings, others the surgeons say are yet to make their appearance and add that it is lucky that the one bone is not shivered like the other, in that case I must have lost my limb.[19]

15 The earthen bank sloping away from the fortifications.

16 A wooden fence or palisade built on the top of the bank of a ditch increased markedly the difficulties of getting out of the ditch.

17 Hat.

18 A stretcher.

19 Although both bones in the fore arm were broken, the one had a simple break and the bone was luckily not shattered, as often happened when struck by a flattened lead bullet. This allowed the setting of the simple fracture, which then acted as a support for the shattered

I began this letter at Badajoz, it has occupied me near three days and you may imagine how well I am doing when you see me finish it at Elvas. I was well enough to bear removing hither yesterday in a waggon, laying on my side, to be sure I was terribly jolted, the roads being very rough, nevertheless I do not feel the worse today. God be praised and you may rest assured that I am doing as well as it is possible to be.

Elvas, 29 April 1812

My dear uncle,
Since my last I have continued to do as well as can be expected from the nature of my wound that in the thigh is mending apace, the improvement in my arm cannot be said to be so rapid, the bone is found to be considerably more shattered than was at first supposed. A splinter has been found of considerable length and nearly working to my wrist, which it will require some time to extract besides the nerves & vessels have been so much injured by the ball passing through the middle of them that the surgeons till now [thought] that I shall not recover the use of the limb & my hand for some months the cure though slow is nevertheless [a] cure. God bless you all & believe me to be your truly affectionate nephew G U Barlow

George was moved back to the hospital depot at Estremoz and reported that the wrist injury was more serious than originally thought, with a second wound having been previously undetected. This was lucky for George as if found during his initial examination the surgeons may well have opted for amputation.

To William Barlow Esq, Little Bridge Street, Blackfriars, London, England
Estremoz, 4 May 1812

My dear uncle,
Since my last of the 20th ultimo my residence has again been changed from Elvas to this place, at present the grand depot for the sick and wounded of the army. I cannot say that much benefit has been derived from this journey, inasmuch as the way waggons, jocularly termed by the soldiers *bone setters* shook my arm all to pieces, the roads in some parts are indeed most execrable, which combined with the nature of the vehicles allotted for our conveyance are well calculated to be the death of the passengers, certainly have occasioned the loss of many a limb.

As I have told you before, my arm is found to be considerably more injured than was at first supposed; about two inches below the musket shot wound is a second of smaller dimensions, apparently made at the same moment by a slug, or as we call them, a musket-grape, which term I have explained in

section in the other bone. As George states, had both bones been shattered, it was almost certain that the surgeon would have felt that immediate amputation was unavoidable.

a former letter. The bone is also here broken and a splinter supposed to be near two inches long, shows itself. The direction has been ascertained, it is very firm and deeply seated, and an incision will it is supposed be required, once the aperture of the small wounds are not sufficiently large to admit of extraction. This operation cannot however be yet attempted.

I have here again to repeat that there is not the slightest cause for any alarm on your part, thinking it proper at the same time to give you the real particulars of my case. The place in my thigh is doing remarkably well & as soon as the cloth works out,[20] will soon be cured. I cannot however dissemble that the recovery of my arm will be far more slow[er]; owing chiefly to the above causes. I have for a time totally lost the use of my hand & fingers, besides three folds of my shirt, a bit of my jacket & also of my flannel waistcoat were carried in by the ball & the latter has only yet come out. None of the faculty have assured me of an earlier return to my duty than three or four months at soonest. It is however a consolation to learn from them, but my constitution & habit are of the very best, but more particularly displayed in the appearance of my wounds which under all circumstances have borne a most healthy, very kind appearance, but more especially considering their severe nature.

Letters have been received from the regiment dated 'El Bodon' our old quarter during the siege of Rodrigo; the army are at present, occupied in provisioning that fortress & afterwards expect to return hither. Two divisions, it is reported will then embark under General Graham & raise the siege of Cadiz, whilst Lord Wellington receiving large reinforcements from England & possessing so fine a body of cavalry will penetrate into the heart of Spain. The bridge of Merida is being repaired & everything promises a most active campaign during the ensuing summer, especially in the event of a Russian war. I am sorry that I shall lose this opportunity of seeing the interior of Spain & be for some months at best unable to have the benefits of military practise & professional experience, which a campaign conducted on so grand a scale must naturally offer.

My hand becomes tired, I must therefore bid adieu. God bless you all & believe me to be your truly affectionate nephew G U Barlow

No. 42
To Sir G H Barlow Bart KB, Fort St George, Madras.
Streatham, 18 June 1812

My dearest father,
My last to you was sent from Castelo de Vide, in which I endeavoured to give a general outline of affairs & our proceedings up to that period, little thinking that such a variety of events were on the 'eve' of occurrence as would constitute a new era in my existence and of which I shall proceed

20 The fear of sepsis from dirty particles of clothing carried deep into the wound with the musket ball was a real concern.

to draw up some account, resuming the thread of my narrative from the above-mentioned town.

On the 13th of March 1812, at little more than two hour's notice, the division quitted Castelo [Branco] and successively passing through Portalegre, Arronches & Elvas, reached the camp ground near Badajoz on the 17th. Report states that it was not His Lordship's original intention to have employed the Light Division in the trenches, but that he was induced to change that determination on the special request of Colonel Fletcher, the Chief Engineer for their services.[21] We arrived about the time that his lordship and the staff were reconnoitring the works of the place, which had been invested that morning by the 4th and 3rd Divisions & on the same evening, as soon as it became dusk, we all set to & opened the trenches under a concurrence of fortunate circumstances. The night was one of the most tempestuous ever known, pitch dark so as to render nothing visible at twenty yards and attended with a most violent storm of wind & rain, which lasted without intermission till daylight, and conveying all sound of the working parties away from the enemy, prevented discovery. Besides the camp was pitched in such a manner as to preclude a guess as to what quarter was the precise object of our attack & they did not chuse [sic] to venture outside their works, thus we broke ground and by daylight established ourselves in a parallel within two hundred & fifty yards of the strong fort, La Picurina. By adopting this method we appeared to attack the city on its strongest side, as independent of this work, there flows a rivulet between it and the body of the place, the course of which has been dammed up & served to make a wet ditch for the ravelin of St Roque and the adjoining bastions. The whole of these defences are commanded by the citadel or castle, whose elevated situation formed as it were, a second tier of guns & the force of which we never could silence and on this side was plied against us with the most decisive effect. A sergeant major of miners however had deserted from the enemy a short time previous, with the intelligence that the whole circumference of the place in other parts (seemingly the weakest) was mined.[22] Our approaches would have been therefore with great loss & what was still worse, much delay. Any attempt against Fort St Christoval was out of the question and consequently no course remained for our choice except that which was followed.

On the 21st, the garrison made a sally with about two thousand men against the right of the trenches, but met with so smart a reception from the covering parties as to be obliged to retire with great precipitation & the loss of three hundred killed & wounded; ours did not amount to one

21 Lieutenant Colonel Richard Fletcher, Royal Engineers. He was slightly wounded at Badajoz and killed at the Siege of San Sebastian in 1813.

22 Sergeant Bonin or Bossin, a skilled draughtsman, had been insulted by his superior and apparently was not given redress by the governor, he fled to the British with his map of the mines around the fortress. Oman had clearly seen this map when he wrote his history of the Peninsula War.

third of that number and rose chiefly from the eagerness of the troops, who followed the enemy too near their works & became exposed to a fire of grape and canister.[23]

Taught by this lesson, the enemy never attempted to molest us any further and our works were carried on with such rapidity, that the batteries were opened on the morning of the 25th. These exertions reflect the greater credit on the troops, in as much as the weather was peculiarly unfavourable & their privations of a very severe nature. During the first week it constantly rained, by day & night, with the utmost difficulty could the heavy artillery be brought up to the camp. It was a clay soil and the trenches filled with mud & water, nor when his toil was over, did the poor soldier retire to the comforts of a dry tent which might protect him from the descending elements. Nevertheless, such was the vigour manifested in the operations, that the French commandant of La Picurina when a prisoner, confessed his opinion reflecting our success, had undergone a most material change upon beholding the surprising progress made during the first three days of the siege.

Well about nine o'clock on the morning of the 25th his lordship having previously, in person, visited the whole of the lines and everything being in readiness, gave the necessary signal, upon which the batteries opened, at the same time the garrison answered with a superior number of guns, the generality of which, especially those in the citadel, were posted on high, & as we term it, *plumped down* into our works. Never has finer practise been beheld, as was this day exhibited on either side. The French artillery is proverbially excellent and on this day fully justified their former reputation; nor was the British in any degree inferior, the Portuguese was equally well served, as I had particularly an opportunity of beholding the excellence of the latter, being stationed near a battery entirely manned with that nation. The captain directed every gun in person and each shot told with the most admirable precision against the ravelin of St Roque as I could well conceive,[24] until a cannonball coming through one of the embrasures terminated his honourable career. This grand bombardment from between sixty & seventy pieces of heavy ordnance continued without any intermission & with considerable speed on both sides. Our shrapnel's bursting over their bastions (as we have heard) with great execution and their fire having considerably injured our works, but the La Picurina on the other hand was completely silenced by two batteries which we had erected within eighty yards of it;[25] such close work the enemy could not endure; notwithstanding

23 George is in error here, as both Sir Charles Oman *A History of the Peninsular War* (Oxford: Charles Chadwick, 1922), Vol. V, p.238 and Jones, *Sieges*, p.161 this to 19 March, the French having lost 304 killed and wounded, the British 150.

24 A ravelin was a triangular defensive structure designed to protect the length of the curtain wall. It was originally termed a demi-lune.

25 Spherical case shot, designed to explode as an air burst at near head height was often called Shrapnel after its inventor.

the fort was built on a sandy rock against which the cannon effected little or no impression, a breach it is true had been made in the salient angle but it was very inconsiderable & from the above mentioned causes not very easy of access. It was nevertheless determined to storm it that evening, our chief placing such a thorough confidence in the tried courage of British troops.

In addition to the above description of its natural strength, it will be necessary to give some further account of the obstacles which opposed themselves to the success of this enterprise, whereby you may be enabled duly to appreciate the merit of those concerned in so gallant an exploit. La Picurina was in the completest state of defence, it mounted six pieces of cannon & was garrisoned with two hundred & fifty men perfectly prepared for the attack.[26] The height from the bottom of the ditch to the top of the parapet was near twenty-five feet, of which the scarp could not be less than eighteen. From this latter projected a most formidable row of fraises the length & thickness of a man's whole leg,[27] in the angles of the counterscarp were places of arms, & the gorge or rear of the work was defended by a triple row of palisades & a ditch, the whole protected by the fire of the place & its covert-way from which the distance was little more than half musket shot.

Every necessary arrangement being made, the assault commenced about half past eight at night in three columns, one of which approached by the breached angle, the other two taking it in reverse & escalading its flanks. Though they advanced in the deepest silence, the enemy quickly discovered them and opened a most rapid & well directed fire, the front ranks having three spare muskets per man, throwing up at the same time some rockets as signals of distress, upon which a sortie was made from the garrison to their assistance. All however failed, nothing could resist the impetuosity of the assailants who carried all before them, the fort was taken after a most obstinate resistance & its defenders were ordered on a neighbouring work, and thus they attempted to make their escape, a few however being made prisoners, whilst their friends who sallied forth from the town were in like manner repulsed by a detachment stationed for that purpose. The working parties were then brought forward & a communication dug with the fort and at the same time ground broke for the second parallel & the breaching batteries. All this was performed under a heavy & well directed cannonade, which was immediately opened upon them by the enemy as soon as our cheering announced the complete success of the enterprise.

On the 30th the breaching batteries opened with thirty-two pieces of cannon, besides ten or twelve howitzers & by the 6th of April made three large breaches. The enemy's fire had in the meanwhile been completely silenced, except that in the castle, which from circumstances I have before mentioned, was out of our power & if possible brisker than ever, blowing up a magazine and subsequently, various boxes of powder. The finale of our

26 Jones, *Sieges*, p.173, states seven artillery pieces.
27 A fraise was a palisade of sharpened stakes set horizontally or at an angle to hamper attackers.

labours arrived however on Monday evening the 6th of April. My uncle informs me that he has sent you a copy of my letter detailing that event, anything further on this subject must therefore be unnecessary.

To compleat [sic] my narrative, it now only remains for me to add that I was carried into Badajoz on the 9th & during a fortnight enjoyed every comfort, which good attendance could desire & our disabled state required. We were then removed to Elvas, and after a similar delay to Estremoz. At the latter place a Medical Board sat on my case, who unanimously recommended me without further delay to proceed to England, as the nature of my wounds would not allow of a return to regimental duty for four months at the soonest. Reaching Lisbon therefore by slow stages, I embarked for old England & landed at Weymouth on the 6th of June. God bless you my kind parent & with every prayer for your health & happiness, I remain your truly affectionate son G U Barlow.

7

Home Again

George stayed at Chatham with his Uncle Robert and family, his Uncle William being unwell. He continued to write a quite legible hand with his left, despite his apologies for writing in 'hieroglyphics'. He attended balls with his cousins (although he was unable to dance) and walked around Chatham viewing the fortifications approvingly with his newly acquired knowledge of military defensive works.

To William Barlow Esq, Streatham, Surrey
Chatham, 28 August 1812

My dear uncle,
Had I not received this morning your letter of yesterday I most certainly should have sat down to fulfil the promise expressed in my hieroglyphics of last night to give you a more detailed account of our proceedings. I will begin therefore with expressing my joy at your being so far recovered from your late indisposition as to be able to go to London as usual and it now only remains for me to regret that yourself and my aunt were not able to come down or partake of the amusements of this place.

The weather has been remarkably fine; the day after our arrival we had a launch & since then two delightful water parties; for the long boat had been previously prepared for your reception & contrary to what I told you it has a deck & cabin where five or six people could dine snug enough with benches, so that my aunt could have partaken of our regattas with great comfort.

The early part of the day I have generally spent in walking round & examining the works, as well as those which are constructing. I view them in a thousand new lights of reflections, which my campaigning in the peninsula throws on such objects and so fully illustrates their various perfections. At other periods I visit the mine saps & trenches which with all the formality of a regular siege, the young engineers are employed in throwing up in front of the lines under Major Pasley a most clever and distinguished officer of that corps to whom I have been introduce & with whom I have dined at their mess.[1]

1 Major Charles William Pasley Royal Engineers.

On Monday evening we went to the Rochester Ball in commemoration of Lord Wellington's victory; the ladies danced till between two & three o'clock, I of course was only a spectator. On Tuesday we went to Lord Darnley's to meet the Duke of Cambridge;[2] who in the course of the evening put several questions respecting my wounds & the affair of Badajoz. He, as well as his brothers in general, is a perfect gentleman in *manners*, very affable & I believe is reckoned the best of the Royal bunch. His R[oyal] H[ighness] appears almost musically mad; one of the party, a Miss Capel played in the most charming style with an execution equal to Attwood or any other performer I have ever heard.[3] The Duke was charmed, sang a great deal with her and afterwards with Hilare & Caroline,[4] whom he accompanied off hand in their glees & songs. He has a most charming voice & went through the various shakes & turns with all the excellence of a professional man; he then took up a violin & accompanied with that instrument. This continued till near one o'clock; we then sat down to supper & came away about three.

At arriving at Strood turnpike we found the gate locked,[5] as also the turnpike house & learnt that the man had run up Rochester in pursuit of a carriage which had previously passed through without paying the toll. The night & dew were very cold & all of us rather sleepy; we waited patiently for a quarter of an hour or twenty minutes expecting his return; at last my uncle and myself jumping out of the carriage made for the turnpike house where we beheld a light burning & a key upon a table inside. This spectacle was too tempting; we gave [torn – the door?] three hearty kicks at the last of which I made a breach, battered the lock to pieces, and shivering the glass, bore away our prize in triumph & unlocked the gate. The toll keeper must soon have learnt from a watchman who stood nigh, who were the assailants, but has not thought proper to call them to an account. My arm is not at all the worse for this raking; I think it exhibits a tendency to heal, which is also Cline's opinion, the latter therefore did not meddle with it at our last interview.

With regard to my plans they are of course subservient to yours. Lady B[arlow] particularly wishes that I would stay here till the 8th of September;[6] in that case I can accomodate both your views & mine of going to Mr Cline's the first week in next month by postponing my visit to the regiment till after our return from Essex; if you will therefore drop me a line signifying when you propose starting I will act accordingly.

2 John Bligh, 4th Earl of Darnley resided at Cobham Hall near Gravesend. He was a huge cricket fan. Prince Adolphus, Duke of Cambridge, was the seventh son of King George III, subsequently Viceroy, and then King, of Hanover.

3 The daughters of the Honourable John Thomas Capel and Lady Caroline (nee Paget). There were five Misses Capel at this time, Harriett, Georgiana, Maria, Louisa, and Horatia.

4 Hilare and Caroline were his first cousins, being two of Uncle Robert's daughters. Hilare later became his wife in 1817.

5 Strood is a town in Kent just north of Chatham.

6 Lady Elizabeth (nee Garrett), the wife of his uncle Sir Robert Barlow.

Give my love to my aunt, Miss Page and all the school room and with the most anxious concern for your health remain your truly affectionate nephew G U Barlow

To William Barlow Esq, Streatham, Surrey
Chatham, 9 September 1812

My dear uncle,
As the ladies are at present most busily occupied with writing letters in all directions, they have requested me to inform you that the desired event has at length taken place and Fanny was this morning about half past two o'clock brought to bed of twins, a boy & girl, the lady preceding as was most proper, the gentleman a few minutes into the world. They as well as the mother are doing remarkably well.[7]

Fanny walked about the garden yesterday as usual without support. Being the 8th we had a party of officers. Fanny ate heartily, in the evening General Lawson & some ladies arrived.[8] The old hands played at quadrille; whilst Hilare & Caroline amused the younger with singing and playing. Fanny sat conversing on the sofa; about eight finding herself not quite so well, she quitted the room & was confined about the time I have mentioned. There was neither bustle nor noise in the house on this occasion & matters are going on in the usual train today.

In conformity with your desires I shall postpone my return to Streatham till you shall judge it expedient. At present my determination is to go down to the regiment the latter end of this week or early in the beginning of next. I cannot say that my stay here has been altogether useless; I generally employ my mornings among the engineers, who are daily practised at mining, sapping and other military exercises and thereby have acquired much valuable information in those branches of the military art; which I afterwards hope to put to good account.

It now only remains for me to repeat my most anxious enquiries after you all and as I hear no accounts to the contrary, I trust that the little patient is in a fair way of recovery. Give my love to Miss Page and all the dear little ones, as well as to my aunt, exhorting the latter to keep up her spirits & to trust in providence that all may yet be right. God bless you & believe me to remain your truly affectionate nephew G U Barlow

George's next letter to his father discussed the latest developments in the politics of India in great detail and gave his own thoughts.

7 I have only been able to discover the birth of a boy, Edward Pellew, in 1811 and suspect that the girl did not survive long.

8 Major General Robert Lawson, Royal Artillery, had served in the American War of Independence and the Egypt campaign; he died in 1816.

No. 43
To Sir G H Barlow Bart K.B, &c &c Fort St George, Madras
Eastbourne, 4 October 1812 (Annotated 'Received 30 March 1813, Bengal')

My dearest father,
Among the numerous publications with which the press has received on the late occurrences at Madras, Malcolm's recent work appears by far the most composed, our respect for the character and rank of that officer are nevertheless quickly obliterated by the abominable egotism which stares us in the face at the very commencement of his publication.[9] This same early acquired nausea accompanies us to the conclusion, occasionally varied with pity at the perversion of so much talent and regret for the absurdities into which such talents have been betrayed, till at length we close the volume though somewhat indignant at the garbled misrepresentation of one who so loudly declaims against partiality in others, yet pleased to hint that the good cause has so little to fear from its most able & crafty foe.

Such, my dear father, is a rapid outline of the reflections to which a perusal of the above pamphlet gave birth. It was my original intention to have followed up the interior details and in a more elaborate performance to have given a wider scope to my sentiments on the subject. With this view and unknown to anyone I carefully travelled through the whole, underlining such parts as in my humble opinion seemed to call for particular comment or exposition. It may at first appear to savour little of discretion that a stripling like myself, unused to literary warfare, should thus present himself on the political arena and for his debut select such an adversary wherewith to break the farce of controversy. This proceeding would argue much in favour of my zeal, but little on the score of prudence. Nevertheless, equipped with those arms which truth, justice and loyalty everywhere is amply and readily provided, I would have taken up the gauntlet and fearlessly entered the lists, had not the shortly expected appearance of such veteran heroes as Mr B[uchanan] and the *Quarterly Review* dissuaded me from the field.[10] To these renowned champions who else would not most willingly resign their respective claims and with confidence commit the management of your cause. Although most fortunately the exertion of my humble efforts was not required in this instance, rest assured that they shall always be kept in readiness. Whenever the period for their being put forth may be at hand; then would I not dread to come in contact with any foes, however numerous and formidable and in the justice of my case, find an

9 Lieutenant Colonel Sir John Malcolm (HEIC) published his *Sketch of the Political History of India, since the Introduction of Mr Pitt's Bill, in 1784, to the present date* in London in 1811.

10 This must refer to the anonymous *Observations on Lieut. Colonel Malcolm's publication relative to the disturbances in the Madras Army*, published in 1812. George believed that it had been written by the Reverend Buchanan. The *Quarterly Review* Volume 5/137 article 8 pp.138-203 by Petrie is titled 'Statement of Facts delivered to Lord Minto, Governor General of India, &c on his late arrival at Madras and other pamphlets and papers on the Madras mutiny'.

ally which might put me on an equality with the strength which a misapplication of power and abilities afford to the attacks of our opponents.

Though it does not fall within my promise to correspond with you on politics, more especially that branch of them which particularly relates to ourselves & family, it might be deemed improper for me to express an opinion on the present set of affairs, I consequently refrain altogether from such topics, though by no means ignorant of what is passing behind the scenes, as well as what is more openly exhibited on the stage. I am honoured with a seat in the Privy Council of our friends, nor is there a single occurrence or subject of discussion or any theme with which I am not most intimately acquainted, with this confidence my uncle has been pleased to entrust me. The strictest silence and caution has as yet been the only return. I cannot however avoid expressing my heartfelt satisfaction at finding our cause yet flourishing in spite of the numerous and repeated attempts made to crush its growth. Notwithstanding the two heads of a certain court are avowedly hostile, no attack has been attempted since that which was accompanied by so signal a defeat on their first entrance into office and from a correspondence with benign authorities, we are given to understand that the cause of justice has its due weight in the minds of those in whom the supreme decision remains.

Such being the case, I should hope that the murmurs of turbulent faction would soon decrease into an occasional whisper, scarcely to be distinguished amid the more commanding tones which the voice of government may be expected to assume should any future crisis demand its exertion at home. For here alone do any seeds of animosity seem to thrive & in your part of the globe, the weed seems to have been thoroughly rooted out and under the present temperature of our Coromandel Government seems little calculated for that soil. If rescued however form the fate of its appropriate dunghill, the noxious plant has been safely conveyed to our shores and in a British atmosphere, afeared to rear its unhallowed head. Partial pruning of its extremities seem but to foster the growth. The Herculean grasp of authority must be applied to the root, ere yet its stem increases to a gigantic size. Nor can such strength be better applied than by continuing that same wise sincere policy, which hitherto has guided their conduct in upholding the Madras government. Your continuance in that presidency for another year or two would be alike beneficial to your public fame and more private arrangements. Faction would thereby be deprived of one of its most specious pretences, namely that of consistency and policy have caused authority in England to satisfy the actions of its representative abroad and thus my good father you would wind up a career of thirty-five year's service, honourable to yourself and advantageous to the public with that distinguished reputation and eclat which has attended you from the beginning till a recent circumstance during these last few years, such applause has been without an exception unanimous. Even then on your side has been the far greater majority, comprising almost an entire proportion of all that is wise and good & virtuous in the land and of whose opinion I know that you are alone solicitous and which reason tells us is alone desirable.

Nay I trust that the period is at no great distance when those whose party spirits have blinded their better judgement and whose resentment in your late at once magnanimous & politic offer of 'allowing the suspended culprits to return' right at least to soften and disarm, shall forego no small share of that inveteracy which the heat of controversy & private interests now no longer clashing with unbiased impartiality have violently raised against you. One or two indeed exist, whom I have in my eye 'quos non longu dies pietas negae mitigate ulla'[11], but the race of these implacable monsters is small indeed and with the chastising rod of power & government is yet held in terrorem over their heads, and give so little encouragement from that quarter, their efforts will rather be harassing and nugatory than decisive or serious. As for Colonel Malcolm's attempts I trust that they be but as the vivid though transitory gleamings of a flame expiring in the socket and beaming with momentary brightness, never more to appear again. Believe me to be your most dutiful & affectionate son, G U Barlow

George wrote again to his father three weeks later. He still remained in England recuperating and had just enjoyed a long sojourn at the seaside with his Uncle William and aunt. He was however, keen to return to Spain and even more anxious now to gain his captaincy, which his father had clearly indicated he was prepared to purchase for him.

No 43 [Should by 44]
Chatham, 26 October 1812 (annotated received 8 May 1813 via Bengal)

My dearest father,
By the arrival of the *Doris* frigate,[12] we have received advices from India of as late a date as the beginning of last July, and among which yours of the 9th of June came to hand, the passage was I believe one of the quickest ever made and the packet reached me at this place, where in company with my uncle and aunt I had arrived the day before on our return from Eastbourne after having spent a most pleasant month by the seaside and during which he and my aunt have derived such benefit, and my leg also some additional strength from my cold bathing.

Alas my good father, the ship was a messenger of joy to all and gladdened every countenance except our own; I could too well anticipate the mournful contents to open the letters with that readiness and pleasure which I always derive at the sight of your handwriting, let me not however renew the dismal prospect of the past, but piously implore heaven that you may be spared the occurrence of a similar trial and surely of our prayers can have

11 Latin: 'Which is not to deny that to mitigate, leads to peaceful days'.

12 HMS *Doris* was a 36-gun frigate, which was built in the East India Company dockyard at Bengal in 1807. Confusingly she was launched as *Salsette* and renamed as *Pitt* in the same year. However, on entering the Royal Navy the following year, she was renamed again as they already had a *Pitt* in service. *Doris* was named after the mythical Greek sea nymph.

any avail, they will in the present instance not on account of ourselves but of him for whom we lift up our hands. For the best and kindest of parents, whom heaven must feel as much inclined to reward in the present as it will most assuredly recompense in the world to come.

My uncle informs me that you are anxiously awaiting the first opportunity which may occur of obtaining my promotion; of your perfect readiness to accomplish this desirable object, from your constant affection and uniform tenor of conduct. I never entertained a doubt; after reflection accuses me of having been too precipitate as well as too pressing in my application for a company in the 33rd Regiment; but believe me this was occasioned by my anxiety to point out to you by what means so desirable an object could be most easily obtained and which I conceived might perhaps have escaped your notice. Hence with perhaps too little attention to delicacy I ventured to descend to particulars & propose certain methods by which my views might be accomplished, coupled as this circumstance was with an erroneous notion which you seemed to entertain, that promotion might be easily gained in England with the assistance of money, which you were good enough to offer for such an occasion. Into whatever eagerness I may have been betrayed, it has been caused by the above motives, encouraged moreover by the rapidity with which you procured my first commissions and my desire to point out a mistake under which you seemed to labour. Your silence under such circumstances I duly appreciate and am most anxious to make reparation for the unintentional indiscreetness of my conduct, by a confession of my error. The obstacles are greater than I had imagined; I shall therefore await with patience, convinced as I am that everything has been done in your power for my interests.

As the ship is to be so shortly dispatched, you see, I am again obliged to put in requisition the services of my left-handed pen, which it now becomes, pretty nearly as ready at a call as the right on most occasions. The latter at present seems likely to enjoy for some time longer a suspension from employment and the final recovery of that limb as had been foreseen will be most protracted. I am at present writing in the utmost agony as you may well imagine from this horrible scrawl, a wager against time. I hope that you will be able to decipher it in as much as so sudden a notice will not allow me to pay the slightest regard or attention to penmanship or enter into any details. I must content myself therefore with stating that my wounds yet remain unhealed in consequence of the exfoliation of the bone. At the same time they bear a most healthy appearance with little or no signs of inflammation; my fingers begin to be a little more pliant and on the whole I have every reason to thank providence for the preservation of my arm under circumstances which have excited considerable surprise amongst the faculty and which I detailed to you in a former letter. My health and constitution have not in the least suffered, on the contrary they have proved conspicuously good under the late severe trials and please God, I trust in the course of two or three months to return to the peninsula with a view to follow up my profession as actively as before, and to which my temporary retirement has if possible only increased my former attachment.

To you my good parent, who are so well acquainted with the sentiments so repeatedly expressed by me on this point will not be surprised at learning that ten month's experience has in no way affected my predilection for the service. Youth, health and strength, render me happy in every situation. Two pretty decent marches on foot, one of two hundred miles on foot in very unseasonable weather, a second of one hundred and twenty southwards, a winter's siege before Rodrigo in January and another of three weeks before Badajoz in the month of March, in which the duty was particularly severe and the rains most heavy, have in no degree changed the bent of my mind; my studies have been particularly directed to the sciences of artillery & engineering; so much so that I should feel myself so capable of assisting in those departments, should any future opportunity like those above mentioned for the future occur.

May God bless you my dear parent, dear mother, brothers & sisters and believe me to remain, your ever dutiful and affectionate son, G U Barlow

George's next was a letter to Uncle William, apprising him that he had temporarily become a student of Captain Malortie's lectures on fortification. It would appear that whilst appointed to Woolwich, Malortie gave private instruction at nearby Shooter's Hill.

To William Barlow Esq, Little Bridge Street, Blackfriars, London
Shooters Hill, 19 December 1812

My dear uncle,
I was surprized the day before yesterday with a visit from my Uncle Robert, on his way to town, as he told me to meet you in Surry Street,[13] as well as to see Mr Grant and Lord Buckinghamshire in succession.[14] I could not however ascertain whether you had brought the young ones to the Norfolk Hotel for a day or two during the Christmas week, according to your original intention, or merely rendezvoused there on account of business. In the latter event I will not come to Streatham till Christmas day, in the former I should wish, if convenient, to join your merry party.

As one of Mr Malorti's scholars quitted him last week,[15] I have changed my quarters and taken his place; lodging at the inn was rather expensive and as economy the most rigid must in future be the order of the day with us, I was induced to take this step; which is far less conducive to my comfort; being posted into a small room with *two* others and our three beds occupying the greater share of the apartment. Everything is very different from

13 Surrey Street in Westminster runs up from the Thames to The Strand.
14 William Grant MP and Robert Hobart, 4th Earl of Buckinghamshire.
15 Captain Charles Malortie de Martemont who had translated a number of works on fortifications.

Streatham, and I cannot give you a better specimen of our situation than by telling you, I am at the moment in possession of the *only chair* that has a bottom; all the rest are kicked through. Two common tin candlesticks such as are used in kitchens stand on the table; and not having a third (for we are each allowed one luminary) a *bootjack* is substituted in lieu,[16] some tallow being poured on the wood and thus is the candle fixed. You may judge of the capacities and ages of my companions, by a question one of them put to me this day, whether when in an action the enemy or us give notice to each other when the firing would commence! They are quite young brats and I will do them this justice, that they are very quiet & orderly seeing I study a great deal and are civil and obliging.

Be so good as to send me a line by a return of post and enclose me a ten-pound note, as I was pennyless [sic] the other day and obliged to borrow that sum off the innkeeper. Direct to Captain Malorti's, Shooters Hill. With my love to my aunt and all at home. Believe me to be your affectionate nephew G U Barlow

Note – £10 No. 5769, dated 25 April 1812, by post

George wrote again from England, via his brother Henry who was sailing for India, informing his father that he was recovering slowly and hoped to return to his regiment at the end of March, before the campaigning season began.

No. 45
To Sir G H Barlow Bart KB &c, Fort St George, Madras
Portsmouth, 29 January 1813

My dear father,
The present number will most probably conclude our correspondence with you in India,[17] and which I trust good fortune may enable Henry to deliver safely into your hands.[18] Nothing particular has occurred since the departure of the Bombay ships last month. We are going on as usual and I must refer you to my brother for a full account of all our ways and proceedings. A thousand minute, though not the less interesting details may be conveyed through the medium of conversation of which neither the limits & nature of a correspondence will admit. The bearer of the present is fully qualified to draw a strong and faithful sketch of the whole family, and as more personal knowledge of which will I trust for the future, repay in some measure your past parental solicitudes & kind wishes.

16 A device for holding a boot at the heel, to ease its removal.
17 Sir George was soon to return to England.
18 His younger brother, John Henry, had been born on 7 December 1795 and was now travelling out to India at the age of seventeen having completed his education, to join the Bengal Civil Service, with which he enjoyed a successful career.

Observation will soon convince you how fully Henry merits my praises on the score of his talents, which it is in my humble power to bestow and I am convinced that there is only need of a corresponding activity and degree of application to render success in the line he has chosen, the certain result. This has always been my favourite opening and how *correctly it has* been formed, time alone can show. He has passed a very fair examination at the college and missed obtaining the prize owing to a temporary cessation in study occasioned by his absence, on account of a disturbance among the students, in which he was though, I really believe in a *very slight degree indeed implicated.*

I trust that the good advice and instruction which it will be in your power to bestow, added to that portion which his friends in the truest spirit of goodwill and sincerity have given him at home, will prevent the recurrence of that or any other fault, which may be an impediment to his progress through the service and I am most anxious therefore that he should make a short residence at Madras and on the spot receive such advice as is most particularly necessary to Griffins on their first arrival in India.[19]

His health has of late been rather delicate, I do not however agree with some who imagine that his constitution is puny, it seems to me at present not to have taken any decided turn; the sea air and fine atmosphere of the southern climate will I hope, enable it to take a bias of the most decided and favourable nature. Temperance and good hours must to a certain degree be invariably practised on board a ship and with such great aids of health, any apprehensions on that line will most probably be dispelled long previous to his arrival at Madras.

With regard to myself, God be praised, my arm is goodly recovered. I have procured a further grant of leave and propose if possible returning after [ink blot- so long?] an absence to Portugal during the latter end of March, previous to the departure of the army from their winter quarters and commencing the campaign. The wounds are not yet however, healed and I am given to understand that some space of time may yet be expected before a perfect cure shall take place and the exfoliation totally cease.

God bless you my dear father, mother and with many a prayer for your speedy and safe return home. Believe me to be, your truly affectionate & obedient son, G U Barlow

During the remainder of 1812, whilst George had remained in England recuperating, his battalion had been busy. Having taken Badajoz, the army was rushed northwards again in mid-April, to counter an incursion into Portugal by Marshal Marmont, who threatened to assault Almeida. The battalion reached El Bodon on 26 April, to find that their march north had forced Marmont to retire into Spain once again.

19 Griffins were inexperienced, akin to the more modern equivalent 'greenhorn'.

The army moved forward in mid-June to the Salamanca area and the 6th Division began the siege of the three forts established there by the French, which fell on 27 June. The 52nd formed part of the covering force being encamped near Aldea Lengua, until the forts fell when they advanced as far as Rueda. Marmont was reinforced and he became the aggressor, forcing the army back to the area of Castrijon. Here Marmont attempted to cut off two divisions from the rest of Wellington's army, but they successfully marched to re-join the main force despite the French threat. This then led to an incredible few days with the two armies marching in parallel, often at no greater range than a thousand yards from each other, both manoeuvring for advantage, without coming to blows. However, when Marmont's army looked to turn Wellington's left on 22 July, the French forces became over-extended and Wellington pounced. The British army won the Battle of Salamanca only after some hard fighting, but the French army eventually fled in rout. The 52nd, as part of the Light Division, formed the extreme left flank of the army and was not involved in the fighting, but led the pursuit after the battle and it did receive the battle honour on its colours. The army marched to Madrid and when in early September, the main army marched on to the siege of Burgos, a detached corps, including the Light Division, remained south of the capital, commanded by Lieutenant General Sir Rowland Hill.

In October, superior French forces broke the siege of Burgos and pursued Wellington's army back to the Portuguese border, Hill's troops retiring at the same time to join them, arriving at Salamanca on 10 November. The army suffered dreadfully on the retreat to Portugal, with terrible weather and virtually no supplies. The Light Division were involved in a rearguard action near the Yeltes river, where the French eventually ceased their pursuit and the Light Division reached Ciudad Rodrigo on 19 November. The retreat was finally over and the army gratefully retired into winter quarters, but with huge numbers of sick. Losses in the 52nd during this long retreat amounted to only three officers and men killed and 33 officers and men wounded, with a further 21 men missing.

8

The Vitoria Campaign

Despite the hardships and failures that had marked the end of the previous year, Wellington's overall position was dramatically stronger going into 1813 as Napoleon was syphoning off forces for his Russian campaign. Wellington now planned an advance that would hopefully drive the French forces completely out of Spain. However, he had to wait for the crops to begin to grow to ensure adequate supplies for his numerous cavalry before he could launch his attack.

The Light Division marched forward, crossing the Agueda on 20 May and proceeded towards Salamanca, forming part of the right wing of the army. This movement was however, merely a diversion, whilst the much stronger left wing under Graham marched around the northern flank of the French defensive lines and proceeded towards Burgos as the French were forced to fall back. Hill's troops were soon marching northwards to join the rest of Wellington's army and by mid-June the Light Division formed the advance guard. To everyone's relief, the French abandoned and destroyed Burgos castle and continued to retire on Vitoria, with the British army in close pursuit.

On 16 June the Light Division came upon a French division at San Millan and took 300 prisoners, the remainder of the French infantry dispersing into the mountains. Five days later, the army found the French formed up in the valley of the Zadorra in front of the city of Vitoria. The Light Division was in the centre of the British line near the bridge at Villodas but hidden from the view of the French. About noon a local farmer led one brigade of the Light Division to the bridge of Tres Puentes which remained unguarded and once across they moved on the village of Arinez, whilst the second brigade, including the 52nd, advanced over the bridge at Villodas to eventually come up on the right of the other brigade. They then advanced towards Vitoria although under constant heavy fire, until the French realised that an attack on their right rear threatened their main route of retreat and they routed, the French losing no less that 151 of their 153 cannon and their entire baggage train, including a huge wealth of plunder. The 52nd only lost Captain Currie and three men killed and Lieutenant Richard Northey and 18 men wounded. The Light Division pursued the retreating French and arrived at Pamplona on 24 June, where they were ordered on a very arduous and ultimately unsuccessful attempt to intercept the retreat of a detached corps under *Général de Division* Clausel. They then marched into the Pyrenees, guarding the area around Vera.

Unfortunately, none of George's letters to his father from the 1813 campaign have survived, although undoubtedly a number of them were sent, given his usual proclivity for writing. Luckily his letters to his Uncle William and his school friend Andrew Amos, do survive so that we can piece his story together. We know that George had sailed for Portugal in March 1813 and re-joined the 1/52nd in Spain in May 1813 just in time for the opening of the campaign. He consequently served with them at the battles of Vitoria on 21 June, the crossing of the Bidassoa on 7 October and of the Nivelle on 10 November, where he was again severely wounded in the foot and he returned home to recuperate. George was ultimately to be awarded a temporary pension on 11 November 1814 of £50 per annum for this injury.

To William Barlow Esq, Streatham, Surrey
Portsmouth, 5 March 1813 Friday afternoon

My dear uncle,
By the place from whence the present is dated, you may judge how useless was all the expedition made by me in leaving town. After being present at Pownoll's christening, I and poor Jose[1] mounted on the top of the coach precisely at five, he clad in the Spanish cloak and myself borrowing Mr Milbourne's great coat,[2] and we reached Portsmouth the next morning about half past ten, a space of seventeen hours and a half. The night was not so cold as that of my last trip; it froze nevertheless pretty sharply and was attended with a heavy fog and dew. About one I took a sail off to the *Ethalion*[3] and dined onboard at the pressing invitation of Mr Humphreville, Pownoll's friend.[4] The officers in appearance seemed to me a set of very gentlemanly young men. Mr H[umphreville] offered me his cabin, which I positively declined & shall therefore swing in a cot. Colonel Way of the 29th,[5] Colonel Martin of the Guards,[6] whom we knew at Chatham and some others go out also as passengers; a Captain Heyward called this morning,[7] he states that it is his intention to start as soon as possible and on the very first change of wind to drop down to Yarmouth roads in order to collect his convoy, which is very large and keep the army officers, of which there are between three or four hundred from being ashore. Jose went on board early this morning, with the baggage, whilst I remain here with a few articles ready at a moment's notice.

Colonel Gibbs and six or eight of our regiment are detained wind-bound, in the same predicament as myself. They have been quartered here between

1 His Portuguese servant Jose had clearly travelled to England with George.
2 Midshipman Charles Robert Milbourne.
3 HMS *Ethalion* was a 36-gun frigate built in 1802.
4 This gentleman does not appear to have progressed beyond the rank of Midshipman as the list of Royal Navy officers, which lists only those of the rank of Lieutenant and above does not list him.
5 Lieutenant Colonel Gregory Holman Bromley Way, 29th Foot was returning to Spain having been wounded at Albuera.
6 Captain & Lieutenant Colonel Samuel Coote Martin, 1/1st Foot Guards; he was killed at the Battle of the Nive on 12 December 1813.
7 Actually Captain Edmund Heywood Royal Navy. He spells his name correctly later.

three or four weeks and are pretty well tired of their situation. It is indeed a glorious harvest for the Portsmouth folks. I have however avoided the George and Crown,[8] and repaired to the Fountain,[9] our old berth, where they immediately recognised me. Mr Carter gave me a call, which I have also returned, but neither had the good fortune to meet the other.

I called again at the Army Medical Board on Wednesday last and was treated with the greatest *civility*, one member only was present. He took down the particulars of my claim in writing and promised an answer the latter end of this week and upon examining my arm pronounced that some further splinters were yet to come forth. The wounds continue to discharge but do not seem the worse for the journey or extraordinary degree of fatigue they have lately undergone.

And now my dearest uncle, it only remains for me to express how sensible I am of the kindness and affection experienced during my long recent stay in England. If it pleases God that I should return, Streatham will probably possess another owner, who although nearer connected by ties of blood can never, as he himself has confessed act more parentally than you have towards him who now addresses you,[10],gave him sincerity for being deeply grateful and with kindest love to my aunt, Miss Page and all the little darlings. Believe me your ever affectionate nephew G U Barlow

[PS] I will write up to the last moment of being ashore.

William Barlow Esq, Streatham, Surry
Portsmouth, 8 March [1813]

My dearest uncle,
As the wind is now within a point or two of being fair, we are all preparing to go onboard at three o'clock this afternoon and will probably be off tomorrow morning at daylight. On Friday last I slept onboard the *Ethalion* and was very well pleased with my messmates, in short everything promises a pleasant voyage.

I am really glad that there is at last a chance of sailing and the sooner we are off the better. However this may be, my determination was previously made to leave shore this day. Living here being so expensive; I have been obliged to draw upon you for seven pounds more at Mr Turners.

God bless you all. We shall stop but three or four days at Lisbon, direct your letters therefore to the *Light Division British Army*, and inform me of

8 I have been unable to discover a George & Crown at Portsmouth and I suspect that he refers to the George Hotel, which stood at 29 High Street and was where the London stagecoach stopped. It had been frequented by Lord Nelson and many others. It was knocked down after severe bomb damage in 1941.

9 The Fountain still exists at 163 London Road although it was completely rebuilt in the early 1900s on the site of the original.

10 His father was to live at Streatham on his return from India.

what success my application to the Medical Board for a remuneration has met with. Mr Milbourne I think promised to call on Greenwood this day for that purpose.

Thank Frederick for his kind letter & beg of him to let me know by what means I may be able to write to you all free of postage. This I should be glad to know, as also to hear from him whenever he may be so inclined.

Give also my kind remembrance to Mr Milbourne, Lord Torrington's franks enclosing a letter from the Adjutant General, one from Cline & one from Shorncliffe duly came to hand.[11]

Adieu then till we reach Lisbon, and with my kindest love to my aunt & all the dear little ones. Believe me your most affectionate nephew G U Barlow

The ship had sailed, but George's ill luck with voyages continued and they were forced to put in to Falmouth.

To William Barlow Esq, Streatham, Surry
Falmouth, 23 March 1813 half past ten o'clock

My dearest uncle,
I have purposely delayed writing till the last moment in order that you might be acquainted with the precise moment of our departure. I left Teignmouth on the day of my writing to Louisa, and next morning the whole fleet got under weigh. As soon however as it arrived in the Chops of the Channel, the wind came foul & we all bore up for this port on Saturday evening.

I have spent two very pleasant days with the Pellews and received from them every civility & attention. I have also been obliged to draw upon him a bill for ten pounds, having paid for my proportion of stock on board the *Ethalion*, and as General Davis went over to Teignmouth expressly for the purpose of seeing Lady Pellew it was also a point of civility to her that I should also go, being on board the same ship.[12] God ever bless you all and believe me your ever affectionate nephew G U Barlow

Finally sailing again on 26 March, he enjoyed a rare swift journey, arriving in Lisbon after only seven days.

To William Barlow Esq, Little Bridge Street, Blackfriars, London
Lisbon, 3 April 1813

My dearest uncle,
By the date of the present you may conclude that our fleet has had a most speedy passage. We sailed with a fine fresh breeze from Falmouth on the

11 George Byng, 6th Viscount Torrington, succeeded to the title in January 1813.
12 This would appear to refer to Henry Davis, previously mentioned then as a colonel in the HEIC Army. He appears to have chosen to visit the army in the peninsula as an observer.

26th which lasted us the whole of the voyage and notwithstanding the delay occasioned by several wretchedly badly sailing ships, landed here on the seventh day, the *Ethalion* putting Colonel Martin of the Guards and myself onboard a transport off the bar. Everything was as comfortable and pleasant as the nature of the service would allow and so indeed could be wished. I paid but sixteen dollars for messing from the period of my first embarkation, of nearly three weeks; reasonable enough as you must allow, when it is considered that we lived so well & wine also being included. A catholic clergyman named Macdonald composed one of our party; I have scarcely ever met in my life a more intelligent man; he was a perfect master of the classics, most of the modern languages, having been educated abroad, but particularly well versed in Spanish, among which nation he had resided several years and upon which subject he gave us a variety of useful information. Captain Heywood was also very civil and attentive in consequence of letters from my Uncle Robert, so that hitherto I have been truly fortunate.

Upon arriving I learnt that all our officers accompanied by their detachments started two days previously. Officers who have recently come down from the army state that the Light Division is in cantonments at Gallegos and its vicinity about twelve miles in the rear of Ciudad Rodrigo. The hussars whom we saw embarked at Portsmouth the same time with poor Henry are yet here in Belem barracks. The Guards are in the rear as far back as Oporto,[13] so that operations are not likely to commence for some time to come on account of the scarcity of forage. Our stay in Lisbon will probably be of no long continuance and that Colonel Martin and myself will be able to travel up together unaccompanied by soldiers in a nice snug comfortable manner. In the meanwhile to save expense, I have taken a billet in a nasty Portuguese house, which has only this inconvenience, that it is in the neighbourhood of Colonel Martin's quarter, where we propose making for ourselves a comfortable little mess.

My first care on landing was to make enquiries about the famous box; it is now in my possession, I have not had time to examine its contents; it appears however not to have been plundered, although the case bears the marks of several attempts having been made to open it. The great coat and overhawls [sic] were at the top and would infallibly have been seized by the Portuguese had they been disposed to finger the contents. The serjeant denies the statement made of his conduct in toto and it would seem that there has been a petit guerre between the underlings of office, who mutually angry with each other have made out each their own story.

I have not had time to deliver my letters but will do so on the first leisure opportunity; you may tell Mrs Clark that I was perfectly innocent of the charge of losing her letter to Colonel Halkett about which she rowed me the last Sunday I [torn – I was at?] Streatham and well I might be so, as it has

13 The 1st Foot Guards were suffering from a severe sickness, causing them to lose numbers of men. Wellington had them sent to Oporto to recuperate and they therefore missed the 1813 campaign.

only come [torn – to hand?] *this morning* and was enclosed in my box of [torn – clothes, which?] was to have been delivered so long ago, I immediately put the same into the fire.

General Davies showed me a work recently published with Marshall's signature entitled '*Observations on the conduct of Sir G. Barlow*'.[14] I do not recollect to have heard you mention any such publication, and therefore imagine it must be one of recent date. Of course you have now purchased it; I have neither time nor space to offer any comments and therefore will only express my opinion that it would be right to *prepare for the worst,* as in numerous passages he plainly tells you that actions will be brought in the court of King's Bench,[15] and also at the '*Bar of the House of Commons*', but more of this in my next.

I have now to conclude by stating that my arm remains in status quo discharging daily as before and the two places remaining open. The surgeon of the *Ethalion* and indeed as I myself can feel, the bone is soft and elastic like a piece of gristle and by no means hard or susceptible of strength and more splinters are yet to come out.

May God bless you my dear uncle, aunt and all the dear little ones, evermore. Direct your letters according to my former request and let me know if any means exist by which I can write to you free of postage & of which I recollect to have heard Frederick make mention; as I have a little journal to send. Believe me your most affectionate nephew G U Barlow

To William Barlow Esq, Little Bridge Street, Blackfriars, London
Lisbon, 9 April 1813

My dear uncle,
This will probably be my last from Lisbon previous to the commencement of our journey which is fixed for an early day in next week and should any opportunity present itself by the way, which probably may occur at Coimbra, I shall write again. Our stay has been longer than was originally intended owing to the difficulty of procuring animals; for good beasts are particularly scarce and their prices most extravagant. Colonel Martin & myself are however tolerably well suited and as reasonably as could be expected in such times as these; we have however determined upon altering the plan of marching, which I communicated to you; and instead of proceeding by ourselves propose joining two other officers, so that with our servants and batmen we shall make a retinue of ten without including Jose and the Portuguese boys. These precautions are rendered necessary in consequence of various bands of robbers which infest the roads leading to the army.

14 Actually, a *Review of Some Important Passages in the Late Administration of Sir G. H. Barlow, Bart, at Madras* published in 1813 by the barrister and MP Charles Marsh.

15 The Court of King's Bench was one of three medieval courts of common pleas still in operation. It sat in the Palace of Westminster. The courts of common pleas were finally combined into the High Court in 1875.

The deserted depopulated state of the country, the numerous mountains and extensive woods are well adapted for these brigands whom rumour also states to be reinforced with deserters and other ruffians from our own and the Portuguese armies. Rumour has probably exaggerated the real accounts. It cannot nevertheless be denied that that it would be impolitic to travel alone as before; several outrages have lately been committed and among others the officer off whom I bought my mule lost all his baggage. Five men overpowered his servant who was straggling in rear of the regiment, tied him to a tree and carried away his paraphernalia; this is not a single instance and although many people arrive in Lisbon who have seen nothing of these banditti, I am convinced that these alarms are not altogether groundless.

I have drawn on you a bill for £24 payable to Lieutenant Layton of the 95th or his order,[16] it is dated I think on the 5th of April and is the amount for a horse saddle and bridle. I have also had 80 dollars from Mr Lucas towards purchasing a mule and perhaps I may be obliged to draw for more but will be as sparing as possible, on the other hand I have a balance in Greenwood's hands due to me of £15 7s 6½d according to a letter which I have received from their house, dated the 22nd of March & which they have placed to my credit. Be so good as to deduct it from whatever I may draw upon you here and I will write them a letter to authorize the delivery of the same into your hands.

I had my arm examined yesterday by one of the faculty; he probed it and tracked a splinter and gave it as his opinion that others had yet to make their appearance; it discharges daily but nevertheless looks healthy and well. He recommends me to save it as much as possible and to be cautious, as any violent blows or accidents would yet render it liable to take an unfavourable turn.

I said a few words in my last regarding Marsh's publication: it would seem necessary to begin already some measures of precaution against the threatened attack by retaining the best legal advice. There appears very little doubt, but that Marsh will be an active instrument both in parliament and the courts of justice to persecute my father, he plainly says as much and this ought not I think to be regarded as an idle threat or the effervescence of passion. Bell, Storey, Kenny, Munroe and several others, who were broke and never can be restored are his intimate friends and yet seek for revenge,[17] whilst those who have been reinstated never will forget or forgive their past humiliation and being aware of his limited fortune, they will endeavour

16 First Lieutenant Jonathan Layton 1/95th Rifles. He left the peninsula in April 1813 and therefore sold his horse equipment to George.

17 These are the names of a few of the officers who were discharged from the HEIC Army following the mutiny of 1809. 'Bell' could refer to Lieutenant Colonel John Bell who had commanded the garrison at Seringapatam or Lieutenant Colonel Robert Bell of the artillery; Major Joseph Storey commanding the 1/19th Native Infantry, Major David Courtenay Kenny; Captain John Munro of the Madras European Regiment and Quartermaster-General.

to ruin him in pocket by lawsuits and harass him in mind by prosecutions in parliament & thus strive to accomplish their ends. I would also suggest the *propriety* of calling Mr Whitbread's, Mr Canning's & Mr Thomas Grenville's attention to this subject and in short of all the leading members of the House of Commons.[18] God bless you my dear uncle, aunt and all at Streatham & believe me your affectionate nephew G U Barlow

To William Barlow Esq, Little Bridge Street, Blackfriars, London
Abrantes, 4 May 1813

My dearest uncle,
We have often laughed about the uncertainty which always attends upon my proceedings and movements, thus instead of proceeding to the army by way of Coimbra, behold me taking the very different route of Abrantes. The circumstance however which occasioned this change in my direction was by no means jocular and to the details of which I shall now proceed without any further preamble. I left Lisbon on the 24th ultimo in company with Colonel Gibbs, who arrived from England most opportunely to rescue me from the detachment which I was ordered to take up to the army, and which circumstance had previously hindered my starting with Colonel Martin. I went up the Tagus in a boat as far as Vila Franca [de Xira], the next stage from thence is Alcoentre, a distance of between twenty-one or two miles. Now you must know that my camp baggage is enough for two animals and possessing a third with the regiment, I proposed walking the journey on foot as in a former instance, but at the end of the first day's march my arm swelled very much and on proceeding next day to Rio Maior a distance of ten miles it became so bad that I found it impossible to proceed any further, quitting therefore Colonel Gibb's party, I hired a bourro and coming across the country by a bye road or rather no road,[19] drenched to the skin, I reached Santarem a little before dark. This is a grand hospital depot and on arriving I showed my arm to an assistant surgeon. He probed it, but his probe was stopped by a splinter which evidently is working out, under these circumstances he recommended me to put my arm in a sling and return to Lisbon. I would not however take such a step without the concurring advice of the chief surgeon upon whom I waited the next morning, telling him that I came to ask a question for my own private satisfaction, whether it would be necessary to return, as in my pocket was an order from Colonel Gibbs to proceed to Lisbon. He did not give it a very attentive examination, seemed at first inclined to doubt whether any splinters could possibly come out of so small an orifice, did not probe it and said that he considered a few days rest would be amply sufficient. Of course, I immediately determined upon an advance, though I doubted much and doubt still whether this gentleman had any grounds to form so decisive an opinion. It appears to me that the

18 Samuel Whitbread MP, George Canning MP, and Thomas Grenville MP.
19 Burro, a small donkey.

sling has been laid aside too soon and that the limb after so long a confinement was incapable of bearing the jolting & journey of so long a march. I resumed therefore my silk handkerchief and after halting four days, came to Golega 18 miles and the day following hither, which was 20 more without feeling any inconvenience in consequence of the above precautions.

I am still eight days of long marches from Fuenteguinaldo the headquarters of the regiment. Tomorrow [torn -we?] cross the Tagus & re-crossing it again at Vila Velha [de Rodao] [torn – & will?] reach Castelo Branco in four days. Hitherto I have travelled thus far by myself, but as the country between this place and the above-mentioned town has of late been much infested by banditti, I shall take along with me two sergeants & five men of the regiment who have been in charge of some regimental stores and who most opportunely received orders this very morning to join the battalion. Had not this been the case I proposed travelling in company with some artillery & engineers men on their route to the frontiers.

Everything indeed announces the immediate opening of the campaign. The men of our regiment were ordered from [Fuente]guinaldo to escort a convoy of new great coats; but a general order has been given to the army, for everyone to leave behind his great coat & to take only a blanket, a pretty sure sign that his lordship intends to try the hardihood of our feet. Marshal Beresford and Sir Thomas Graham passed through here yesterday and a general order arrived from the Adjutant General this morning, to break up this station & for everyone to join immediately. The weather has been very hot and no rain up the country. It has however fallen pretty plentifully within this last day or two and as the grass & forage for the cavalry may now be expected to be pretty abundant, the army will certainly move into the heart of Spain. I met this day our old friend Colonel Hill, who has arrived thus far on his route to join General Hill's Division. He desires to be remembered to you and my aunt, as well as to Mr & Mrs Attee, in common with myself.[20]

On leaving Lisbon I was obliged to draw pretty largely on you at Mr Lucas. This was necessary to pay for my mule, my expenses at Lisbon, and the journey up to the regiment leaving also in reserve a certain sum for the ensuing campaign, when I expect to be advanced into the centre of the country where all communication with Lisbon & England will probably be cut off in consequence of so great a distance from those quarters. The army is only paid up to January last, will probably be kept some time farther in arrears & I can expect no pay for the next four or five months to provide against this unpleasant circumstance I carry along with me some gold and draw larger than usual. You must also recollect that in this sum is included a hundred dollars issued to me by Mr Lucas on coming down from Badajoz, which the latter never charged and which circumstance I mentioned to you when last in England, when you stated never to have received any demand

20 Brevet Lieutenant Colonel Charles Hill of the 50th Foot whose regiment was in Lieutenant General Rowland Hill's 2nd Division.

from Holford's house for that sum. I proposed to have written stating the above particulars last 24th, the day of my quitting Lisbon but was obliged to hurry away without doing the same on account of the tide.

Give my love to my aunt, all the dear little children & Miss Page. Tell that I shall soon write to each; God bless you all lastly and believe me my dearest uncle to be your truly affectionate nephew. G U Barlow

To William Barlow Esq, sent to Blackfriars (forwarded on to Sea Houses, Eastbourne, Sussex)[21]
Fuenteguinaldo, 19 May 1813

My dearest uncle,
My last from Abrantes left me on the eve of starting by forced marches for this place, where I arrived on the 13th instant, having accomplished my journey in eight days as I originally proposed. On reaching Castelo Branco the party halted for a day. During these four stages the weather was invariably bad and the roads across the passes of Vila Velha and in the neighbourhood most dreadful. A large train of pontoons on their way to the army I left fast sticking in the defiles, the draught cattle being perfectly exhausted. This spectacle was alone *satisfactory to me* and knowing that no movement would take place until these stores should reach the frontiers. At Castelo Branco a tolerable sized splinter worked out of my arm & which I believe to have been the cause of all the aches & pains which I experienced on the earlier part of the march. Its appearance was probably quickened by the poultices which were kept constantly applied. Near Sabugal I passed our friends the Life Guards, quartered in some miserable little ruined hovels forming a sad contrast with Whitehall and on Wednesday last joined the regiment who were in no small degree surprized at my appearance, having heard of my disasters by the road & judging therefrom of my probable return to Lisbon. The arm remains in statu[s] quo, but appears to have a tendency to healing at which I am much rejoiced and shall promote such an event by every precaution & care possible.

We are all now in readiness for a start & in the course of the ensuing week events of some importance may be expected to take place. Three hundred artillery horses are now dragging along the pontoons, whose arrival may be expected tomorrow or the day after and will probably be the signal of our march. The division musters remarkably strong and is in very fine order, our battalion amounting to nearly nine hundred very good men.[22] The whole were reviewed on Monday last by Lord Wellington; but the ground being in the neighbourhood of Espeja,[23] a distance of sixteen or eighteen miles and having recently come off from so long a journey, myself and animals were

21 The Sea houses at Eastbourne were later famous as the site where Charles Darwin wrote much of his *Origin of Species* in 1850.
22 On the 25 May 1813, the Official Return shows the battalion with 890 men.
23 Espeja is in Spain, three miles south east of Fuentes d'Onoro.

dispensed with attending. All the hospitals and sick have been dispatched some days since to the rear and an order for advance may now therefore be hourly expected. The French at present occupy Salamanca, but in no considerable force and are expected to retreat immediately on our approach, with the intention of concentrating their forces along the line of the Duero & eventually perhaps on the Ebro, where when joined by Marshal Suchet from Valencia they are expected to assemble in very great force. His lordship it would seem has some more sieges in view; three or four companies of Sappers & Miners are on the march,[24] whilst the heavy train of artillery are gone round by sea to St Andero [Santander] in the Bay of Biscay at no great distance from Burgos & Pamplona, where [torn – it will?] probably be required.[25]

Letters and papers have come to hand from England as late as the 20th of April, but as yet none for me are arrived, save one from my friend Amos.[26] The annual change in the direction appears much in our favour, although I could nowhere find upon whom had fallen the election of the two chairs; what think you of Marsh's pamphlet and let me know whether anything further has transpired regarding the threatened prosecutions. General Davis and myself used often to converse on this subject and at his request I promised to send him an account of anything material that should occur on East India matters.

And now my dearest uncle, you may expect to hear from [me] once a fortnight most regularly, should nothing of consequence intervene, in which case I shall write weekly as before. My present letter is not worth the postage, but as I thought you would wish to hear of my safe arrival & in good health I put my pen in requisition. Give my best love to my aunt and all the dear little children; may God ever bless you all is the prayer of your affectionate nephew G U Barlow

[PS] I have received the last ½ of the draft safe.

This next, the first surviving letter from George to Andrew Amos, announced their advance on Salamanca and the French abandoning the city. It also dealt in some detail with the discovery of the skeleton of Captain Henry Dawson, who had been killed and hastily interred during the retreat from Burgos at San Munoz, it led to

24 Four companies of the Sappers & Miners were in the field during the 1813 campaign. The 8th Company 2nd Battalion under Sub-Lieutenant Turner, was attached to the Light Division. The 7th Company 1st Battalion of Sub-Lieutenant Calder and the 5th & 7th Companies of 2nd Battalion under Sub-Lieutenants Gratton and Wallace, were attached to the Pontoon Train.

25 It is very interesting to note that the movement of the army to the Pyrenees and the subsequent need for the siege train at Burgos and Pamplona was being openly discussed before the campaign actually opened.

26 His former schoolfriend at Eton, Andrew Amos (1791-1860) who was a lawyer and eventually became Legal Member of the Supreme Council of the Governor General of India 1838-42.

deep feelings of melancholy. His mood was not made any lighter by the theft of his mule, but lightened, however, as he described the sights of Salamanca, which he had found time to enjoy, before they had marched to Toro to join the left wing of the army under General Graham.

George also fails to mention that the composition of the Light Division had now changed somewhat. The Light Division, now commanded by Major General Charles Alten, still consisted of two brigades, the 1st Brigade temporarily under the command of Colonel Beckwith consisted of the 1/43rd, 1/95th, 3/95th and the 1st Cacadores. The 2nd Brigade still commanded by Major General Vandeleur now consisted of 1/52nd, 2/95th, 3rd Cacadores and 17th Portuguese Line. The addition of the 17th Line was unusual as these were not trained as light infantry, but they remained with the brigade until the end of the war.

No. 2[27]
3 June 1813, Camp near Morales [de Toro] two leagues beyond Toro

My dear Amos,
According to the conjectures contained in my last from [Fuente]guinaldo two days did not elapse before an order for marching arrived. It was on the 19th about two o'clock on one of May's most beautiful afternoon that we quitted our cantonments, a constant residence during two successive winters had almost naturalized the regiment in the town and without the slightest deviation from truth, I can assure you that its departure was accompanied by the regret *and tears of* many of the people, who were much attached to the troops from their exemplary good conduct. Two or three heroines might also be seen quitting their paternal homes with the resolution of sharing our destinies, whose ardour I thought had got much the better of their discretion. As for my part I marched off with the greatest indifference having had a most valuable week to recruit myself and animals after the recent long march & thinking more of the places upon which we were marching than those which we were about to leave.

It would be needless to give you an account of each day's stage and uninteresting enough when nothing of consequence occurred. It will be sufficient therefore to mention that we passed by the well-known walls of Ciudad Rodrigo & on the 23rd halted at San Munoz, a house half-way to Salamanca is the advanced post of the enemy which quickly retired previous to our approach; here our great chieftain came up during the halt of the 24th. I made an excursion round the environs of the place, which excited some interest and having seen the scene of a pretty smart skirmish between our division & the French advance on last year's retreat, we walked to the spot where one of our poor captains fell & discovered the identical tree but not the spot where during the affair he had been hastily interred.[28]

27 Unfortunately letter No.1 in the series has not survived.
28 George was not of course a witness to Henry Dawson's death and burial as he was then in England.

Bayonets [were] the only tools for scraping a little hole, and scarcely were his remains covered with a little loose earth. After much difficulty his grave was discovered, but oh what a spectacle here presented itself of mortality in its most hideous form. The head of the chest lay in one place, the trunk in a second, the thighs in a third, and the lower jawbone compleat in a fourth, a dozen yards from the remainder of the sad relics. The latter I took in my hand, and by some very particular marks in the lower teeth I was one of the first who identified our unfortunate comrade, to make certainty till more sure, we picked up a ragged shirt & with a little difficulty found the name of the deceased in most legible characters, together with his overhauls & flannel waistcoat. Some wild animals had probably tore up the corpse & disarticulated it and mauled it. We designed therefore to re-inter with more cover, with feelings which you may well imagine, the sad remains of our friend whilst many reflections of the frail state of our nature and on the sad day which we also must sooner or later come pervaded every other and undoubtedly did mine.[29]

My short career was thus easily crossed by a mischance may appear trivial enough in itself, but of no small importance to a campaigning officer. I allude to the loss of my best baggage mule for he was stolen during the night by some rascally Spaniard, owing to the neglect of the sentinel to whose charge it was committed 'Poor Dicks' animal passions were of the most congruous noble nature which occasioned him to be led to a separate tree from the remainder of the herds, hence it may be accounted for his present state of captivity, where he drudges no doubt severely enough under some unfeeling muleteer whose panniers are probably much more unmerciful than those of his original master.

On the fifth day's march we approached Salamanca where General Villattes corps was stationed,[30] two divisions crossed the ford above the town & General Hill's by that of the one a little below. General V[illatte] seems to have stopped slightly longer than prudence justified, seemingly with a ridiculous spirit of bravado, doing so before a force he might have retired without any loss, but on the contrary chose to draw up in squares outside the town. The British infantry made every effort to get up but found it impossible, having already made a forced march of five leagues during the heat of the day. The cavalry & horse artillery however pursued and harassed him constantly till Lord W[ellington] called them off; the latter having pommelled his masses, knocking down some two hundred of them, whilst the former cut off his stragglers & caused him to retreat in great disorder with the loss of much baggage & some provisions.

Hitherto our march had been through a very fine country, well watered & covered with woods, of course not populous but still susceptible of high cultivation. However, the banks of the Tormes, the scene changes, trees are not so thick and through places [well] supplied with corn, whilst the general

29 This refers to Captain Henry Dawson, 52nd Foot, who was killed at the ford of San Munoz.
30 *Général de Division* Eugene Casimir Villatte.

face of the country becomes all rocky with a series of gently undulating hills above & around Salamanca. Next day being a halt, I repaired to this famous city with the intent of purchasing a mule & viewing the curiosities. Even approaching by a fine stone bridge over the Tormes,[31] which is a tolerable wide stream hereabouts the place has a very interesting appearance being built on the slope of a hill with the houses rising one above other, adorned with several beautiful church and convent spires spread among which that of the cathedral, whether considered as to size or workmanship is truly magnificent; several however of these mansions of piety have been totally ruined by all destructive wars: three in particular had been selected by the soldier's eye as posts susceptible of defence; find the reduction of them by the English, the cannonballs had laid low these venerable superstructures while the infernal mine had torn up their lowest foundations.[32]

Having just emerged from the filthy towns of Portugal, Salamanca has the appearance of a most clean & well-built city. The people greeted us with vivas and their joy was no doubt sincere enough, but prudence restrained a too great expression of it, as the French promised to return in the course of two or three weeks and would pillage them again after the manner of last year, on our retreating from thence, for their former patriotic conduct. I approached the cathedral which is one of the most light & beautiful specimens of the gothic which has ever fallen under my view. I had not time to survey it or note down any particulars but it was the most exquisite performance that the mind can conceive. A Grand Te Deum was being chanted and we accordingly entered, the interior fully corresponded with its external magnificence and is worthy of the Grand University of Spain & Lord Wellington, Marshal Beresford, General Castanos,[33] all the staff together with a number of English & Spanish officers attended on the occasion & without meaning to disparage the piety of Salamanca, I think this splendid concourse drew together as a large a congregation as any other motive, the music and singing was very good but more theatrical than religious in tone, at least such it sounded to my ears.[34] Having however little time and much to do, I came out before the service was ended and took a turn before the shops are shut up and the good people go to sleep their siesta; which is the invariable custom for three or four hours during the middle of the day in warm weather.

The smallness of their numbers and the rapidity of their retreat had deterred the French from committing the usual ravages. I entered the Plaza Mayor and found everything just as in time of profound peace.[35] It is a very

31 The bridge over the Tormes at Salamanca consists of twenty-six arches, only fifteen of which consist of the original Roman bridge, the rest being a medieval extension.

32 Three convents had been converted into small inter-supporting fortresses by the French, named San Vincente, San Cayetano and La Merced, with a total of 36 guns and a garrison of 800 men. They were besieged by the British between the 17-26 June 1812.

33 General Francisco Xavier Castanos, Duke of Bailen (1756-1852).

34 The Catedral Nueva de Salamanca, was begun in 1513 and consecrated in 1733.

35 The baroque Plaza Mayor at Salamanca had been completed in 1755.

fine square with a piazza & walk all round like that of Covent Garden. The shops abounded with everything, with cottery and all the usual manufactures of London, not omitting *Windsor soap*[36] and with all the perfumes & more delicate bagatelles of Paris, at a tolerably reasonable price, but no students with gown & or trenchers[37] were to be seen to avail themselves of any advantageous bargains, such a thing is not to be beheld in these times of war & tumult, or when gentlemen of the red cloth are alone & everywhere in fashion. The march of the division being fixed for an early hour the next day, obliged me to quit Salamanca that afternoon without stopping for the theatricals which were to have taken place in the course of the evening.

At Aldea Nueva[38] the division halted two or three days for the purpose of allowing General Graham and the main body of the army time to come up from Miranda [do Douro] in Portugal & cross the Esla. To superintend this operation our indefatigable chief has quitted us & makes a march of forty miles in one day for this purpose, which being done we made a forced march for the banks of the Douro of eight leagues and arrived opposite Toro about twelve o'clock yesterday afternoon. General Graham made a simultaneous movement & ascending from Zamora came up the opposite bank. This was indeed a most masterly manoeuvre of Lord Wellington's & most unlooked for on the part of the enemy. Their side of the Douro is very hilly, completely commanded ours & presents a very strong line of defence, very difficult of attack in front & which gave Lord W[ellington] so much trouble & manoeuvring previous to the Battle of Salamanca last year. This they had intended making a first stand & with that view had blown up the bridge; but a reference to the map will at once show how skilfully Lord W[ellington] crossed the Douro in *Portugal* & coming along the same bank as that occupied by the foe, threw himself on their flank, while the Light & General Hill's Division menaced the front & thus compelled him to fly with the utmost precipitation without any resistance & leaving the castles of Toro, Zamora & all his works uninjured. Such is the nature of the grand stroke already made & assuredly merit predictions of the future successes of the campaign.

Toro is a large straggling town, but possesses a most melancholy lonely appearance, the people having all run away & shut up their houses, in expectation of a fight between the two armies. The French only quitted it yesterday morning, the hussars, the 10th, 15th & 18th Regiments being in close pursuit & who succeeded in catching General Giron's [Digeon's] Brigade of dragoons near this village & upon whom the 10th made a most brilliant charge supplemented by the 15th. They overthrew all before them & made 200 prisoners with very light loss on our side.[39] Adieu & believe me yours most sincerely G U Barlow

36 A scented soap renowned for its excellence.
37 An old term for a mortar board.
38 Aldeanueva de Figueroa.
39 The Action of Morales occurred on 2 June 1813 when Grant's Hussar Brigade came upon Digeon's cavalry brigade drawn up in a strong defensive position. They were charged by the

His next letter to his uncle was penned on the move, written in small sections as time allowed. The shadow of having to besiege Burgos had darkened their thoughts, given their failure to capture it last year. However, huge explosions cheered the army immensely, as it signified that the French had abandoned the fortress and destroyed it.

To William Barlow Esq, Little Bridge Street, Blackfriars, London
Camp four leagues in front of Palencia, 9 June 1813

My dearest uncle,
As this is the first day's halt which we have had since leaving Aldeanueva [de Figueroa] near Salamanca I take the earliest opportunity of sending you a few details, which it was impossible to include in my hasty postscript from Ampudia of the 6th of June.[40] By a forced march of eight leagues we arrived on the banks of the Douro opposite to Toro about four in the afternoon and found that it had been evacuated that very morning by the enemy, who had blown up an arch of the bridge. Our hussars in full pursuit came up with their rearguard at the distance of a league and of which they made a severe example. As soon as the tents were pitched I went into the town, which presented a truly melancholy appearance, most of the inhabitants having shut up their houses and hid themselves. So, I spent the day in viewing the works of the place and at night helped to repair the bridge for the passage of the troops next morning. We then proceeded and on reaching Ampudia were joined by his lordship who on that point concentrated the greater part of his army. This step was the more necessary as Joseph Buonaparte [sic] with the main body of the French army occupied Palencia three or four leagues in our front and here we assembled between sixty and seventy thousand fighting men. On mounting a hill near the skirts of the village you might behold five large camps at the same instant, situated on various parts of these extensive plains which are here bounded alone by the farthest horizon. With his lordship at our head, the hussars & our division moved forward to Palencia and entered it about eleven o'clock, the enemy's rear having quitted about four hours previously. All the streets and windows were crowded and the people showed much joy at our arrival. If we could believe their vivas and shouts which were loud & plentiful enough. Next morning, we started in the direction of Burgos and took up the camp which we now occupy near a little village of the name of Tamara [de Campos].

10th Hussars, supported by the 18th Hussars, causing the French cavalry to flee until they came up with the French rear-guard of infantry. The French lost two officers and 208 men of the 16e Dragons captured, half of them being wounded, whilst the 10th Hussars suffered only 16 casualties.

40 This letter is missing.

13 June, Camp in front of Burgos three leagues,
You see I am obliged to write this in scraps as we keep constantly and rapidly moving. It is now past five o'clock, we are but this moment come in from a long march and the adjutant has just sent us a message that the letters for England must be sent to the orderly tent in half an hour and there is no alternative. I write the present *in a ditch* leaning against the bank for *a table,* in the middle of a wheat field. We have been incessantly marching since leaving Tamara and yesterday in pursuing a strong division of the enemy got under arms at four o'clock in the afternoon, went six long leagues, with the exception of a small morsel of biscuit fasted the whole day and did not pitch our tents or get anything to eat till eight o'clock at night. We came up with the enemy's division in sight of Burgos; but they had most effectually secured themselves from our attack & we could effect nothing more than frighten them a little with our artillery.

This morning however, three or four tremendous explosions were heard in the direction of that city and intelligence soon arrived that the enemy had evacuated the place, blowing up the celebrated castle, together with its adjacent works; thereby much trouble & the life of many a brave man is spared and the event is of so much the more desirable as it was most formidably mined and in such a state of defence as would have cost five or six weeks at the least for its reduction.

Writing in such haste & with so little time, I necessarily must confine myself to dry matters of fact and geographical details in order to give you a succinct account of our proceedings, leaving to more leisure hours, the task of drawing any reflections or remarks. The French amount to near 70,000 men and are retreating to take up their long-meditated position, the right of which is expected to lean upon Bilbao near the seaside & the left upon the Ebro near Tudela & Calahorra, at least such was their disposition about four years ago when obliged to retreat to their frontiers.[41] We shall see how his lordship will contrive to turn them out of this, their last refuge. Our division is now pushing towards the mountains of [the] Asturias, in the neighbourhood of St Andero [Santander], where the enemy will probably give us some trouble in the strongholds and passes of these districts. Our fine & numerous cavalry has given us too decisive a superiority to enable the enemy to fight in the flat country. When united with Suchet's army from Catalonia and Valencia, they expect to assemble 100,000 men and it seems to be the general idea that no means exist of preventing the junction of these latter reinforcements by the eastern route of Spain.[42]

41 This is interesting as there was clearly no thought that the French would stand before reaching the Ebro.

42 The threat of such a force led to Wellington's demands for British forces from Sicily to be landed on the East coast of Spain, but he added the strong proviso, that this force should not be lost in any rash actions, as he needed its very existence to help prevent Suchet from joining Joseph.

Letters and papers have come to hand up to the 18th of May but I have not heard anything from anybody. God bless you all & believe me in great haste, your most affectionate nephew G U Barlow

George's next letters to Uncle William and Andrew Amos are particularly remarkable, given that these long letters were actually penned the day before the Battle of Vitoria. He had been very amused, as many British soldiers seem to have been, by a visit to a nunnery. He also describes the action at San Millan and the belief that they would face the French in battle the following day.

No.3
To A[ndrew] Amos Esq, to the care of James Amos Esq, St Helens Place, Bishopgate Street, London
Camp near Subijana [- Morillas], four leagues from Vitoria, 20 June 1813

My dear Amos,
It has been a common remark that our formidable foe has owed no small portion of his success to an inconceivable celerity and animation of movement. John Bull was always considered to be a more phlegmatic though not less doughty character, a chap always ready for the fun and of tried bottom, but possessing more strength of arm than lightness of heels. Late years have however exhibited the champion in a more scientific light, proved him to be equally matchless in the fight as in the pursuit, with skill to sufficiently prosecute the advantages gained by his superior degree of move.

Baron Duero as we may now most appropriately style (without using Cobbett's vulgar signification) by his recent manoeuvres had totally deranged the enemy's schemes and resolved upon following up these successes without allowing him time to breath or mature further plans into any practicable shape.[43] The elusive king [Joseph] was soon convinced that he had no safety left but in flight. His foe followed with a pursuit not resembling the march of an army, but rather the speed of a post. The country affords him every facility, being extremely flat & open, superabundant in corn throughout these parts, which are called the Plains of Leon, whose extent on every side as far as the eye can reach are lost in immensity of space, at least such was the prospect which offered itself on ascending some gentle eminences rising above the fine city of Palencia, which we entered about eleven o'clock on a beautiful summer's morning, four hours only after the departure of the French & the public joy was manifested here according to the usual custom, by hanging out variegated pieces of drapery upon every window and their patriotism was sincere enough, could explicit reliance be placed on the bawling spirits *which the multitude* gave, or the bouquets which were dropped so fragrant from the balconies by the enthusiastic fair to the British soldiery. Camp was pitched close under the walls and was

43 Wellington had been granted the title Baron Douro in August 1809; Cobbett's vulgarity is not clear.

soon crowded with visitors, tents being a novelty in these parts and a luxury which neither Spanish or French troops enjoy, who are forced to be content with huts made of leaves or straw.

In the course of the day I walked on to make a minute reconnaissance of the town & found there the grand English & Portuguese headquarters, which are alone sufficient to fill up any place and in point of animals and followers are equal nearly to a division of the army's officers & uniforms of all nations flocking in from all parts, activated by the same motives as myself, namely to see the lions,[44] contributed to make a rare scene of hubbub. The cathedral is neat, spacious & well built, but after Salamanca's possesses nothing worthy of remark and the streets tolerably regular though full of mud & stuck up on every quarter with a posting from King Joseph to his well-beloved subjects about receiving guineas at a particular rate to which little attention was paid.

It has been observed that for the first time I entered within the hallowed precincts of a nunnery, a most liberal intercourse with the rest of the world, has and will continue to do away with much of the superstition of the peninsula & has already removed much of that impenetrable secrecy which was thrown around these mansions & their inmates when a packet of British heretics were allowed to behold & converse with the spouses of God. We were ushered into a neat little apartment, in which, behind an iron grating resembling that of the jewellery in the Tower of London, were ranged a dozen of those vestal virgins; our nation & the circumstances attending their entry occasioned us a welcome reception. Cakes were handed around and upon us expressing our wish for some bouquets, one of them went into the garden and plucked some nice bunches of roses. In the course of conversation, we made a request which the usual gallantry of our cloth prompts us to beg of this sex. Stop now, do not be alarmed, it was all innocence itself, in asking them to sing. The toothless grins of the majority however at this proposal soon convinced me that all hope of success in our petition lay in one or two whose mouths & features bore less traces of antiquity. After many hums and hangs and such like full ruminary, clearing of pipes, one of the younger sisters began a doleful quivering ditty as to require the utmost possible compression of the risible muscles to avoid giving offence. The sister however soon found that she had undertaken a task above her power and sinking in the middle of the strain released the audience to their no small satisfaction from so severe a trial upon their gravity & decorum.

To resume however the thread of military events, our march was resumed next morning in the direction of Burgos, we crossed & re-crossed several times a most beautiful canal, with capital locks & called the canal of Castille. It is really a very fore work or beginning near Segovia which is not very far distant from Madrid & passing by Valladolid, Burgos & terminates

44 Lions – the sights.

near the Asturian frontier.[45] This piece of Spanish industry gave me the more agreeable surprize, as I was perfectly ignorant of its existence and in the heart of a country where there are few rivers and still fewer navigable, it must afford so great facility to inland commerce.

Continuing our route with the same unwearied ascending for several days, we arrived in sight of the famous city of Burgos early on the morning of the 12th. Curiosity would naturally extend and anxious eye [sought?] this scene of last year's disasters, 'to the rock (as Bonaparte said) upon which the English was wrecked' & whose solidity was soon proposed trying. Our view was distant, but the fortified castle might be seen very distinctly rearing its head above the other edifices. It is built upon a large rotundal hill, whose sides are [ringed?] with three distinct walls ranged at a certain distance one behind the other and transformed as much as possible into a modern fortification. Above each rises the castle or keep with two venerable turrets at the gate and the whole resembles many such ancient fortresses as are met with in England. Our failure last year was evidently owing to a want of cannon but as you will presently see, they spared us any trouble this season by blowing it up themselves.

Having come up with the rearguard of the fugitive army about three o'clock in the afternoon & given it a pretty smart cannonading, we took up our camp on some rising ground expecting sharp work the next morning. About daylight on the 13th some tremendous explosions were heard, the cause quickly surmised & that the enemy not chusing to risk a general battle had trotted off & destroyed his favourite work. This was quickly ascertained by the advanced parties, upon the return of the latter, his lordship with that admirable decision which so eminently characterises all his measures pushed our division upon the flank of the enemy, whom he amused with a part of General Hill's corps, as they retired slowly along the high road to the strong defiles of Briviesca & Pancorbo & whither they expected us all to follow; but as the proverb says 'they reckoned without their host'. His lordship stole a march by a lateral road towards the Ebro; they soon found this out & that the danger was imminent. Another days' delay and we might interpose ourselves between it & them. Both parties now moved by parallel routes for that river, both putting their best leg foremost to see which could arrive first. Had the foe been thus fortunate, his position would have been impregnable and attacked with great risqué [risk]. You approach it by a terrible defile of a paved road near half a league in length, where ten men can scarcely pass abreast. You cross a small bridge to the other bank, upon which rises a tremendous chain of hills with a road similar to that just described, which would be defensible by merely hurling down rocks or stones. General Graham however crossed on the 15th & took up the

45 The Canal of Castille was begun in 1753 and completed as far as it goes by 1849. It was designed to link the Castillian wheat region with the port of Santander, however it never reached the Bay of Biscay before the railroads superseded it. The canal lock gates have been removed and the waterway is used for irrigation schemes today.

position (if we believe report) just as some of the French staff officers came in sight with a view of reconnoitring & selecting it for themselves. Be as it will, all was done in the nick of time, one of the finest positions for defence acquired without a shot fired & our *heels* accomplishing what our *arms & hands* never could have done.

Matters now began to assume a more serious aspect; Lord Wellington continuing to pursue his unceasing career of success on Vitoria. This latter city stands on the high road to Bayonne, is one of the enemies [sic] grand depots & to cover which his march was directed. The day before yesterday our division, being in front of the advance, came up with General Maucune's corps near San Millan.[46] This general was retiring from Frias on the Ebro & the country being rather hilly continued his route on Vitoria, in ignorance of the Light Division's approach. He was in the act of filing through San Millan when the head of our column appeared, proceeded by some hussars. So defective was his intelligence that he mistook the latter for Mina's guerrillas,[47] but was soon convinced of his mistake by his flankers being driven in and our troops ascending the hills, on which he had hastily formed, with their usual vivacity. So compleat [sic] was our surprize that his baggage was in the middle of the affair and he literally made little or no defence. The 52nd partly skirmished & partly advanced in line and were pretty well blown as to wind by the time they had climbed, for such it really was, these rugged mountains & came up to their enemies, the latter then turned tail and we were so fagged as not to be able to pursue. The 1st Brigade escaped but the 2nd got well pummelled, lost two hundred killed & wounded & three hundred prisoners together with a pretty decent quantity of baggage, amongst which some of General Maucune's & General Montfort's letters fell into my hands,[48] and which I hope some day to show you.

We hear that Joseph Bonaparte & Marshal Jourdan are at Vitoria with between 60 & 70,000 men concentrated for the purpose of fighting, the field officer of the day by the outposts says that Lord Wellington has been on the lookout hills reconnoitring all day the enemies [sic] positions. It is time that they should at length make a stand & our people have some reticence, leaving Salamanca our marches have not known a simple intermission or halt for twenty-two successive days and during this last week, short rations alone have been issued, together with half the usual allowance of bread. The army nevertheless keeps up most wonderfully well & most of our regiment are old hands, tolerably well-seasoned. To give you a specimen, our company mustered eighty-six bayonets on leaving [Fuente]guinaldo and in all, by this day's parade statement, that we have not dropt [sic] a single man

46 *Général de Division* Antoine Louis Popon de Maucune commanded a division of the Army of Portugal

47 Francisco Espoz y Mina was a guerrilla leader and in 1810 the Junta gave him command of forces in Aragon. In 1812 he was promoted to Commander in Chief in Upper Aragon and his forces served under Wellington.

48 *Général de Brigade* Jacques de Montfort commanded a brigade in Maucune's division

during a forced march of more than two hundred miles. As for myself, I like the service very well, enjoy the heart, health and spirits and am perfectly happy to remain. Yours most sincerely G U Barlow

To William Barlow Esq, Little Bridge Street, Blackfriars, London
Camp near Vitoria, 20 June 1813

My dearest uncle,
I take the opportunity of this, our *first* day's halt during more than *three weeks* of incessantly rapid forced marches to give you some further account of our still successful progress. By the papers we see that events of the greatest importance have taken place in the north,[49] and ere long some portion of your attention will be called to the south of Europe. My last left the army in full march for the Ebro, which celebrated river we crossed at the pass & bridge of Puente Arenas; pushing on then through the Asturian mountains, our division arrived at the little stream of Rio Losa and passed it at a small village about thirty miles from Bilbao on the sea coast, we expect therefore shortly to have salt water bathing. Here his lordship made us wheel to the right about and bent towards the left bank of the Ebro, when upon coming within a mile of San Millan, which had been marked out for our quarters, a French division was found passing at that period. Our corps was pushed on & some fine *fun* ensued, I do not abuse the term for there was so little bloodshed on our part (two men of the 52nd alone being wounded) and the whole being a compleat hunt & chivying affair. The enemy were posted along the ridge of some tremendous hills covered with trees & brushwood. Some of the 95th skirmished in front and we in something of a line, climbed the steeps, in some places literally making use of our hands as well as our feet, but without any loss, arrived upon the summit, being protected by the inequalities of the ground, but as you may imagine, perfectly winded and breathless. The French however previously took to their heels & climbed yet another height, worse than the first. We here pommelled them in handsome stile [sic], which they bore most patiently without making any return, but made for a village on the right; our people moving forward on a parallel line with them at the distance of a hundred yards as fast as they could trot, but in some disorder owing to the broken state of the country. Very few however succeeded in gaining it and they were obliged to double back and take to cover in the woods which forms the whole force of these mountains and here they dispersed in the wildest confusion. From the prisoners we find that it was the division of General Maucune and those whom we engaged composed *its second brigade* commanded by General Montfort, who I hear together with his aide de camp was killed early in the affair and to which cause I attribute the

49 The Russians and Prussians were advancing deep into Germany, but news of their defeat by Napoleon at Lutzen (2 May) and Bautzen (20 May) cannot have been received before this comment. Eventually a summer truce was agreed.

unsteadiness and bad defence they made.[50] Their loss amounted to between five or six hundred men and numbers of wounded and stragglers are daily being collected among the woods & rocks.[51] They were so utterly ignorant of our approach as to imagine the first skirmishing to be directed against some guerrillas and had been previously marching the whole morning as well as ourselves when we came across them. Those who escaped must have starved for their good fortune, we took numbers of horses and mules, a vast quantity of officer's baggage and lots of knapsacks well stocked with bread & biscuit for five or six days, which was not the least acceptable prize to our hungry soldiers.

As I have just observed, there was much spoil taken in this affair; some very valuable maps of Spain, of General Montfort's property, some of his letters and others belonging to individuals were picked up by me at the foot of a hill and a most superbly embroidered coat with the star & insignia of the Legion of Honour was offered to me by a soldier for twelve dollars. I longed much to have purchased it & send it you [at] home, but to tell the truth had not the means, being obliged to part with all my spare cash in purchasing a mule at Salamanca to replace that which was stolen, a circumstance I shall frequently have occasion to regret, as preventing me from obtaining several other little curiosities at a trifling value. The letters found however I will send by the post homeward bound.[52]

At the end of yesterday's march our division & the 4th came up with a corps of twelve or fourteen thousand men posted in some strong passes. Lord Wellington immediately ordered an attack, for which the necessary arrangements were being made when his lordship thought proper to countermand the same, although the 4th Division had already commenced in pursuance of the original instructions and dislodged the opponents. Today we halt as I imagine on account of the supplies, which such rapid marching have left considerably in the rear; for two days no bread has been served out to the troops and for *the three* preceding them, but half a pound per man which is little indeed for those who are constantly eight or ten hour's under arms, make rapid marches in these mountainous tracts and have no substitute whatever, excepting a quarter of a pound of flower [sic] & sometimes not even that allowance. As for myself thank God I am in the best [of] health & during the early part of the march about Salamanca & Toro, the heats were very great and by night the dews very heavy and most piercing cold. It is this which is most trying to the constitution and from whence all sicknesses & fevers originate, the blood being greatly heated by active [pursuits?] under a burning sun & the freshness of evening & night so perfectly agreeable. I constantly wear next my skin a flannel waistcoat, find it most serviceable and comfortable and saving a slight rheumatic touch *on*

50 This is an error, as Montfort lived until 1824.

51 Estimates usually refer to around 300 prisoners, but there are very few eyewitness references to the numbers captured.

52 These letters of Montfort's have unfortunately been lost.

my left ribs, owing to laying on damp ground, which however went off in two or three days, have never enjoyed better health and am at this moment, in the best campaigning trim.

I shall now force on your observation some remarks on the late operations, of little value enough, but shall continue to do so from time to time unless my good correspondents give me a hint to the contrary. A reference to the map will show that the plan of this campaign has hitherto been very different from any of the preceding. General Hill's corps & our own moving in two columns, crossed the Tormes simultaneously both above & below Salamanca, which forced the enemy to retire from thence. In the meanwhile, the third body of the army leaving their winter quarters at Miranda & along the line of the Duero, moved up its right bank and by this unprecedented route, crossing the Esla, moved into Spain; on those parts, nature has thrown every obstacle in the way of an invading army, in the shape of formidable mountains, bad roads & poor resources. You may figure to yourself some of the difficulties attendant on this enterprize, when I mention the fact of twenty men belonging to the Seventh Division being drowned in crossing the fords of the Esla.[53] By this admirable manoeuvre, the enemy's line of defence along the Duero was compleatly taken in reverse on the right bank and the 2nd & Light Divisions pushing forward for the same point on the southern, they were compelled to fly with all speed, giving them no time for breathing. His lordship followed close upon their heels with his whole collected forces and by the aid of his fine & admirable body of cavalry, which proved of infinite usage in the flat country, kept them compleatly at a distance & crampt [sic] them to a degree; as to prevent a single reconnaissance on their part to discover our numbers, routes or intentions & in fact they never had a glimpse of the infantry till the day before yesterday. This rapidity of movement prevented Burgos from being supplied or provisioned & in consequence no alternative remained but to blow it up, which they did, and then with their main force retreated to a position a little in its rear upon the high road and whither they expected to be followed, but here again were they completely deceived. Three hours after the explosion was heard, Lord W[ellington] pushed this and some other divisions in the direction of the Ebro, keeping and amusing them in front upon the main road by various manoeuvres, while he stole one or two most valuable marches by lateral roads on their flanks. This was indeed a masterly proceeding, which threw three or four divisions across that river before the enemy could occupy it or march thither any force. Not a single man showed himself, excepting two or three staff officers, who (as I hear from report) came thither for the purpose of examining its banks as to choosing a position for themselves, but found it already in possession of General Graham's corps. So as for the line of the Ebro, upon which

53 The Esla was deep and flowing strongly, requiring the infantry to ford the river whilst hanging onto the horses of the British hussars, between 10 and 20 men were drowned during the crossing.

the enemy had formed so many calculations and indeed about three miles from the right bank, you begin to descend the mountains and for *a mile and three quarters,* the road is a continued defile admitting but eight or ten abreast, tremendously steep, paved, so that horses could scarcely stand on their legs. A bridge was then to be passed and then you entered another formidable defile, similar to the preceding and extending for the space of two miles. Had the enemy been allowed ever so little leisure time, a few ditches cut across the route, two or three trees placed as a barricade, a rock blown up or even mere stones rolled down upon our heads from the craggy precipices above and two hundred men would have stopped any force in the world. We are now traversing perhaps one of the strongest countries in Europe; it abounds with defensible positions, but our adversaries have literally had no time to concentrate in any numbers or organize any regular plan of operations. Tremendous hills whose faces are covered with trees or brushwood, craggy rock & deep ravines cover the whole of this province of Biscay. We now traverse the scenes where the guerrillas have performed so many noble exploits under Mina and Longa,[54] of which we have heard so much in England. Indeed, nature has visibly pointed it out as the refuge of persecuted patriotism, where the valour of a few can baffle all the combinations of the military art & superiority of numbers. I do not wonder that the French have never been able to drive them from such recesses and but for our great captain's celerity, every advantage must have cost us much blood. These present successes would amply have rewarded two or three great general actions, but here you reap them by shear manoeuvring & marching and lose scarcely a single life in a march of three hundred miles from the banks of the Agueda to those of the Ebro. At present the left wing of this army occupies Orduna & we are upon the right flank opposite to Vitoria, which bears nearly north east from our present position. The enemy are now concentrated in great force at the above town where they occupy some very strong ground and report states them at upwards of 70,000 men which I think must be pretty near the truth and King Joseph who is with them, will probably soon have to fight a general battle for his kingdom, of which at present he holds a very small share. Great dissensions are said to prevail among their generals, none of whom ever commanded so great an army before, or anything indeed more considerable than a division. General Reille [who] is the senior officer,[55] perhaps presumes a little upon the importance of this new situation and of which his equals are very jealous. I think that we may rationally augur some good from this divided state of their councils, let them look sharp as

54 Francisco Tomas de Anchia Longa was a Spanish guerrilla in the Biscay region. In 1813 he was appointed a general and commanded the Iberian Division, joining in the march across Spain.

55 *Général de Division* Honoré Reille commanded the right wing of the army at the Battle of Vitoria, composed of elements of the Army of Portugal. The French army at Vitoria was commanded by King Joseph Bonaparte and Marshal Jourdan.

they are opposed to an adversary who has been matched against the best Marshals of France, and who has already given them no mean proof of military talent.

Our good friends in Lisbon, have probably given us over for lost, and stand little chance of seeing for some time to come, their accustomed visitors. Communications from England must in future be by way of Corunna, and St Andero [Santander]. You will probably hear often *of the* army but must not wonder at not receiving regular advices from me. There exists no such thing as an established post in these parts and no means of forwarding letters except through the medium of the Adjutant General, who thus concisely sends round to officers '*Letters for England must be sent to my office in half an hour*'. It behoves me therefore to keep something in hand ready prepared & I will now write in perfect ignorance whether it may go off tomorrow or three weeks hence and only trust that my epistle though slow, come sure to hand at last. I sent *two letters* from Lisbon, *one from Abrantes, one from Castelo Branco,* one from [Fuente]*guinaldo,* one from *Aldea Nueva,* one from near Palencia & concluded near Burgos. Referring to those in your possession, you will see if any have missed from shipwreck, the enemy, or any other mischance. At present not a line from any of you has reached me since leaving Streatham.

Remember me most kindly to all friends and tell my aunt, the little girls and Miss Page, that I will write to them, as soon as we get a little rest. At present, there appears little likelihood of any, today the regiment enjoys a little repose, but *our company none,* as we lie now on outlying picquet & we must continue on the alert during night. The marching bugle sounds generally at four in the morning. We seldom reach the end of our stage, nor does the baggage, which always follows in the rear, arrive much before three in the afternoon. The remainder of the day is generally spent in having our meals dressed &c &c & by eight or nine all turn in to bed. God ever bless you & believe me your most affectionate nephew, G U Barlow

George's next was full of details of the Battle of Vitoria and its aftermath.

To William Barlow Esq, Little Bridge Street, Blackfriars, London
Camp in sight of Pamplona, 24 June 1813

My dearest uncle,
At a very late hour of night, drenched with incessant heavy rain during a twelve hour's march in pursuit of the flying enemy through most execrable roads, I seize the first leisure moment to send you a slight sketch of our proceedings during the three last days, more especially those of the memorable 21st.

In my letter of the 20th I mentioned the probability of our coming in more immediate contact with the French army, then concentrated in our front. We were all apprized of his lordship's intention to make an attack as he spent the whole of the day previous in making a most minute reconnaissance on

The Battle of Vitoria 1813, by Adam Neale. (Editor's Collection)

every part of their position. At half past two the next morning, the regiment marched out and about nine with the remainder of the division, halted beneath the brow of a woody hill whilst the different arrangements for the columns were being formed. These occupied nearly two hours, during which, from our elevated situation we had a most beautiful & distinct view of the enemy's whole position with the exception of a small part of their left, which was allotted to General Hill's corps, extended across the summits of some very high mountains down the opposite side. Stretching from hence to their centre were two or three chains of ravines successively ranged in order one behind the other, very difficult of access, with several lines of troops & well furnished with artillery. In their centre was a wood & village, where passed the grand high road to Vitoria; to enfilade which as well as the place in their front, we planted various batteries with a body of cavalry in square. The right rested on a formidable circular hill, covered with infantry and several brigades of guns and near to which ran a small stream with a bridge bounding the extremity of that flank and whose passages various dispositions were made to defend. Military men were at first sight, of opinion that the position in most respects [was] well chosen, had the great fault of being too confined and showing a very inconsiderable front, consequently most liable to be taken in flank. Lord Wellington's coup d'oeil in the survey of ground has been frequently exhibited, but perhaps was never more conspicuous than on that day. The beautiful manoeuvring from which with such amazing rapidity he drove the enemy out of their chosen position, made the affair seem a contest between master and pupil rather than equal rivals in capacity. He first caused General Morillo's Spanish corps,[56] to advance

56 Major General Pablo Morillo commanded a Spanish division at the Battle of Vitoria.

against the enemy's right [left], which we saw them do in a very handsome style. Much impression was not however made, as the foe stood very firm till General Anson's Brigade came to their support & gained the disputed point.[57] In the meanwhile, the remainder of General Hill's corps advanced and the business became very warm on that side; so much so that the enemy fearing it to be our main attack was seen to detach various strong reinforcements from his centre to that quarter. About one in the afternoon, at the favourable moment, the 3rd Division charged and took the bridge over the little River Zadorra, which the enemy ought certainly to have previously destroyed; this being done, the 3rd & Light rapidly pushed on to take the large circular hill in flank,[58] whilst the 4th simultaneously moved upon the village in the centre.[59] These dispositions decided the fate of the day, from that moment the battle might be considered as certain and our own. It was impossible for the enemy to think of stopping another moment; his mien[60] was infallible and he most wisely drew off before we could close with the bayonet, blazing away very hotly from his cannon, but fighting no longer for victory but retreat. Thus, was the key of the position carried, he then retired to some rising ground followed by the whole allied army moving in most perfect order with contiguous columns. The sight I am told was very fine; at this period a squadron of 18th Hussars attempted a charge; but riding impetuously they came up to the enemy very irregularly in three & fours & got a severe trimming from their infantry's fire. The Light Division now advanced in line to carry a village under a heavy fire of cannon & here it sustained almost all its casualties, their artillery being very well served and every shot telling with effect through our ranks.[61] At this instant the two left hand companies of the 52nd were ordered to clear some coppices & woody ground on the left, ours unfortunately was one.[62] A swarm of tirailleurs were driven out of the lanes and enclosures into a field of corn; we followed them closely into the wheat & in getting across a hedge through some broken down gaps, my poor captain (Currie) was shot through the forehead & never spoke another word. This light infantry work is very sharp, more especially for the officers, who are much exposed in skirmishing through covered countries. Our company sustained a loss of one sergeant & eight men in casualties & I have to mourn the death of one who whether as a friend or an officer I think had not his equal in the regiment. At length the whole army moving en masse arrived close under the walls of Vitoria, while General Graham who had been manoeuvring on the

57 Major General William Anson's infantry brigade of the 4th Division. He is in error however, as it is clear in subsequent letters that the brigade of Lieutenant Colonel Cadogan from the 2nd Division was intended.
58 This is Monte Jundiz near Arinez. This was the observation point for the French headquarters at the commencement of the battle.
59 The village of Arinez
60 Mien – demeanour.
61 The 52nd had advanced on the village of Zuazo.
62 This would appear to be a wood just north of the village of Zuazo.

left, threw himself across the high road to Bayonne, cutting off all retreat in that quarter, became briskly engaged about five in the afternoon. From every church and window in the city might the battle now be beheld and the French by the movement just mentioned thrown into the utmost confusion. Close under the walls a dash was made by the hussars and according to report King Joseph owed his escape to a small mill dam which obstructed his pursuers. He was forced to jump out of his coach (which was taken together with his baggage, servants & retinue, mount a horse & make the best of his way. This circumstance derived much credit from the circumstance of Marshal Jourdan's baton being found & who generally attends his person.[63] Your humble servant in the meanwhile trotting along with a few of the headmost skirmishers through corn fields &c became separated from his regiment & division about half a mile beyond Vitoria and emerging from thence on the skirts of a large plain found himself near the Hussar Brigade opposed to whom in front were a large body of French cavalry, this was indeed the golden moment of victory; their army in the most frightful confusion. But the 10th, 15th & 18th though they made two or three very gallant charges were unable to overpower the superior numbers of their adversaries and by these means I saw two large masses of their infantry who were scrambling off in the wildest disorder, dispersed & scattered over a large plain [to] effect an escape. Had another brigade of dragoons been present, utter destruction availed them in so defenceless a state; mind I do not presume to blame anybody, the presence of our cavalry might have been necessary elsewhere or obstacles might impede their arrival, it is only to be lamented that a greater number were not on the spot.

All the infantry had in the meanwhile closed to the front, the heavy cavalry came up shortly afterwards and the hue & cry became so hot that messieurs turned tail in the most horrible disorder, they had not time to gallop off with their artillery, barely enough to cut the traces & save themselves on their horses, leaving upwards of seventy pieces of cannon (all indeed their army possessed excepting four),[64] the whole of their waggons, ammunition, caissons, hospitals in Vitoria, money chest, magazines of provisions & powder, a compleat battering train of eighty pieces in a wood,[65] all they possessed, in our hands together with many prisoners and thus to Bayonne as I have before mentioned, being intercepted they ran off in the direction of Pamplona, pursued by us two leagues beyond Vitoria until it became quite dark. Never, my dearest uncle, shall I forget the impressions made on me by the adventures of this memorable day. Oh, were it in my power that

63 Marshal Jourdan's baton was captured by the 87th Foot and sent to the Prince Regent. The Prince returned a marshal's baton to Wellington, instantly making him a British field marshal.

64 It is usually stated that the French only got away with two cannon, one of which was captured later.

65 The Army Reserve of Artillery apparently numbered 47 guns, See Oman , *Peninsular War*, Vol.VI p.442.

it had been unclouded by the loss which the regiment and I in particular have to deplore of a most excellent individual. The regiment was under arms near twenty hours and in the course of the day must have passed over near five leagues of ground. Words cannot paint the scene of confusion which pervaded the roads leading from the field of battle. Had there been permission or time, I could have furnished myself with a complete fit out for a campaign. Here lay a broken-down waggon stocked with claret and champaign [sic], but which as officers we could not touch, being moreover ordered to prevent the soldiery from doing the same. In another were hams, tongues, plenty of bread flower [sic] and other most tantalizing objects to hungry soldiers who had fasted nearly a whole day. Portmanteau's full of linen clothes, shoes, casks full of capital brandy, kicking about in all directions and not a few full of money, which the women and followers of the army plundered. Flocks of sheep & numbers of horses and mules were seen to invite a pillagers hand, whilst lots of books & papers excited the attention of the curious and bestrewed our route in all directions. It is inconceivable the quantity of papers be-spread over the face of the country, such indefatigable scribblers are the French. Doubtless many a cheating commissary or swindling paymaster blesses the result of the 21st of June, which has buried in oblivion all traces of his former rogueries. His lordship, without allowing the fugitives a moment's breath, pursued them in the direction of this city, before which I am now writing. Two days of heavy rain has rendered the cross roads half way up to the knees in mud and water. Nevertheless, we have marched four, six and five leagues successively, numbers of houses, waggons &c show his track & mark his precipitate flight. All the villages through which he passes were deserted by the inhabitants, who taking away their little all and abandoning their homes, fled to the mountains to avoid the fury of the enemy, who took special care to burn such, where he had sufficient leisure. This was a most serious inconvenience to our people, who having outmarched the commissariat and all his supplies, were forced to pick up a precarious subsistence during *four days* forced marches [with] only one pound of indifferent biscuit, half a pint of watered rum and four pounds of meat were served out per man. All the shoes moreover worn out by incessant marches during the last fortnight, of which we have never once had a full allowance of bread. These causes must soon cause a halt; in consequence of the result of the Battle of Vitoria, 12,000 men under General Clausel,[66] who were coming up from the Ebro at Logrono to join their main army, were entirely cut off. They then made for Pamplona, but here his lordship was beforehand and again interposed between them and their object. It has indeed been a trial of speed on both sides, General Clausel finding that he could not succeed, has been forced to bend southwards and run down the Ebro to Saragossa where he now halts. Such is a general outline of our affairs. King Joseph has set out for France with his shattered forces,

66 *Général de Division* Bertrand Clausel, commanding the Army of the North.

leaving a garrison of 5,000 men in the citadel of this place, which is one of the strongest in Europe & will require a most severe and protracted siege to reduce it. God bless you my dear uncle, aunt and all the dear little ones under your roof & in great haste, believe me your most affectionate nephew
G U Barlow

9

The Pyrenees

The French had effectively been forced out of Spain, although they retained garrisons at Pamplona and San Sebastian, whilst Marshal Suchet maintained some grasp on Eastern Spain. Marshal Soult had however been given command of the shattered remnants of the French army by Napoleon and he had soon miraculously put them back into order, when he promptly launched an attack to push the British back out of the Pyrenees and to relieve the fortress of Pamplona. The 52nd were only involved in a great deal of difficult marching before the French were defeated at the two battles of Sorauren and forced to retire into France permanently. The 52nd did not suffer a single casualty during these operations.

One hundred and fifty volunteers were then asked for from the Light Division for the assault on the fortress of San Sebastian, the 52nd providing 40 officers and men, of whom one was killed and 16 wounded.

On 7 October, the Light Division advanced on the French heights above Vera which had been heavily fortified. The attack was completely successful for the loss within the 52nd of 12 men killed and six officers and 66 men wounded.

On the night of 9 November, the Light Division was moved silently into position in front of the French fortified heights of La Petite Rhune. The attack at dawn on 10 November, formed a part of the Battle of Nivelle and was entirely successful, the troops having gained the right rear of the French entrenchments, forcing the French troops to flee rather than be cut off from their line of retreat, although the main redoubt did put up a more serious resistance. Colonel Colborne offered a parley and informed the French that if they did not surrender immediately, that he would hand them over to the Spanish: afraid of Spanish reprisals, the garrison promptly forced the commanding officer to capitulate. The battalion lost 32 killed and wounded this day and 6 officers and 202 men wounded, including George Barlow, who was wounded severely.

George's first letter in this period was a rare one, written to his aunt.

To Mrs Barlow, Streatham, Surry
Oronoz,[1] among the Pyrenees, 11 July 1813

My dearest aunt,
Our more warlike operations have of late occupied my uncle's letters and now that they are at a stand-still for a few days I sit down to give you an account of some peaceful transactions. The enemy being entirely driven out from this part of Spain, with the exception of a garrison in Pamplona and the passes of the Pyrenees in our possession, a small respite from fatigue has fallen to the share of the Light Division and of it they may be truly said to stand in need, as scarcely a shoe is left to their feet. After such terrible & incessant marches was it not indeed for a considerable number found amongst the plunder of Vitoria, their condition would be truly deplorable; but we must not grumble as victory and so many brilliant results have been only attended with a great consumption of *shoe leather;* this is indeed purchasing it at a cheap rate, for without joking, success hitherto has been as much owing to our *heels* as our *arms.*

You will all be glad to hear that my health continues so good amidst the various trials and vicissitudes which arise in the course of a campaign. During the early periods of our march, the weather was terribly hot; extreme drought is marked on every feature of the country between Ciudad Rodrigo and Salamanca, the soil being light and sandy and what little verdure there is being quickly parched up by a burning sun. The climate was much the same, though the land very fertile and abounding in corn between that city and the banks of the Douro, the villages were moreover more thickly studded, better built and more populous and so rapid was the flight of the enemy as to leave them no time to commit their usual outrages. The people greeted our entry with numerous vivas and cried out 'matad todos' which in plain English means 'kill them all', but much reliance must not be placed in these sonorous proofs of bawling patriotism as a fine old veteran French dragoon, who was made prisoner at the affair of Toro told me, that they turned about like his hand, first showing me the back of it & then the palm, and that the same tongues which were now so vociferous in praise of Lord Wellington would be equally ready to salute the arrival of any formidable French marshal tomorrow. I am not however inclined to give compleat credit to such an assertion, but in charity am rather of opinion that they are inclined to keep well with both parties occasionally, as they fall sometimes into the power of one, sometimes of the other.

Apropos talking of these French folks, they are indeed a most curious gentry. Notwithstanding we had just arrived from a march of eight leagues, on reaching Toro I immediately went in with my usual curiosity to pry & see what was worth noticing. The people had mostly fled or hid themselves and the greater part of the town consequently deserted. Nothing offered

1 Oronoz is a small village, to be found three miles west of Elizondo.

itself to my researches but 200 of these poor wretches many of whom had been dreadfully sabred and cut about by our cavalry. Notwithstanding their sufferings their national sang froid & impudence had not forsaken them and one of them had the assurance to tell me in the course of conversation that had they been equally numerous (they were in this respect much superior) and as well mounted, there would not have been the slightest doubt of the result being far different.

After a series of rapid marches the division reached Palencia on the morning of the 7th of June, the itinerant king and his court having quitted it but four hours previous. The windows and balconies were much crowded on the occasion and hung with drapery as a sign of their joy. In this instance I believe it was sincere enough as King Joseph had made them undraw their purse strings pretty widely, previous to taking [torn – leave?] of his well-beloved subjects. Here also for the first time in my life I stepped across the thresholds of a convent and saw the nuns who were its inmates. We conversed through the grating made of pretty strong iron work similar to that of the jewellery in the Tower of London. These vestals were generally pretty well stricken in years, with one or two exceptions and these last not particularly good looking. The dress of the order was very old fashioned, with very long waists like as in the times of good Queen Bess. Cakes as usual were handed round to us and what was far more acceptable, a beautiful bouquet of roses apiece with which we took our departures.

The celebrated city of Burgos we passed by without however having it in [my] power to enter, as more important operations were then in train & a trial of speed being then in practise, which should first get to the Ebro. John Bull however wonderful to relate was winner of the race. We crossed that stream at one of the most beautiful valleys extant I suppose on the face of nature. Shut up on all sides by tremendous chains of mountains is situated this perfect little paradise, interspersed with five or six most rural little villages; with peace and plenty smiling all around them. Never shall I forget the impression made on me by the first glimpse of this beautiful spot. It was a heavenly summer's evening, when upon descending from a long and sultry day's march the tremendous precipices which extending for a mile or two on either bank; this romantic little vale burst at once on the astonished soldier. The charming scene of corn and cultivation most agreeably diversified with *hedges,* spreading in all directions (a spectacle most *uncommon,* and therefore doubly gratifying in this country). The gentle Ebro stealing along with its banks margined with the most deliciously cool & refreshing shade of numerous groves and crowned by a rustic bridge, the soft harmony of martial music floating along the glen as passed the various soldiery, the curling smoak [sic] of our encampment, which contributed not a little to the embellishment of the whole, combined with the heartfelt gratification of having obtained so important an advantage in the possession of our enemy's line of defence, all this created a sensation in my breast such as I have seldom before experienced. It was a mixture of all those finer ideas, in which man is sometimes apt to indulge, when left to his own reflection, far from the bustle & noise of the world and left at liberty to contemplate the beauties of nature.

The climate moreover entirely different from the more sultry regions which we had just traversed; everything around bore the verdure of spring, and the rapacious hands of the French had not been allowed to deface a single feature of this beautiful landscape, which successively continued for three or four days march towards Vitoria and as I learn, more [or] less follows the course of the Ebro on both banks.

Gazettes and newspapers will no doubt make noise enough about the business of Vitoria, I will not therefore add my squeaking note to the general clamour but continue my rural descriptions. This may indeed be stiled [sic] the land of plenty, *a four-pound loaf*, being bought for a shilling & very nice wine two pence *a pinta* which answers nearly to the pint and a half of our English measure and everything else in proportion. In such a country *officers* might live with elegance on their pay. The corn is nearly ripe and fit for the sickle. The extraordinary spectacle of *cherries & pears* in season together may now be beheld, together with peas & beans and *cyder.*

I could write a great deal more but must conclude in haste for want of time. God bless you my dearest aunt, as also my uncle and all your little family & believe me ever your most affectionate nephew G U Barlow

George's next found the regiment peacefully occupying Vera, virtually on the French border.

Vera, 16 July 1813

My dearest little Fanny,

You are I believe, the next upon the list of my Streatham correspondents who have not yet received a letter since my leaving England; an accidental enquiry has just furnished the intelligence of a packet being dispatched homewards this evening, in consequence of which I sit down to write, although possessing nothing new to communicate since my last to my aunt at Oronoz. Two days subsequent an order for advancing arrived and we took possession of this town, which is the very *last* in the kingdom of Spain and where rumour states that the army are likely to remain some time, at least during the present operations carried on against St Sebastian.

You are I know, a great reader of Homer and consequently I may venture to introduce here some military observations, which you may report for my uncle's information. We are encamped upon the side of some very steep hills, at the bottom of which runs a steep ravine, whilst opposite rises a corresponding chain of heights occupied by the French troops within half cannon shot of our position, so near that we could upset their dinners, or spoil their slumbers with a few shots whenever we please. Their sentries and our men in some places are not further distant than one hundred and fifty yards. We mutually behave ourselves with the greatest politeness and offer not the smallest molestation to each other. Their position is truly formidable;

imagine one of the steepest South Down hills near Worthing or Eastbourne, along which a man would find difficulty enough to climb without fighting and upon reaching the summit would be so perfectly out of breath as scarcely to be able to stand, the sides moreover considerably more difficult of access than those English mountains, being intersected with numerous ravines and thick woods & you will have some idea of their situation. It commands a most beautiful view of the sea, Bayonne and the adjoining province of Gascony and is exactly situated on the hills where the dotted lines of the map mark the frontiers behind the little stream of the Bidassoa. Our enemies appear very musical as they are drumming and trumpeting all day long. They yesterday found it necessary to quit a hill for a short space of time. We saw the whole regiment move up the defile and leave behind apparently two men as sentries among some bushes and trees. A closer inspection however with good telescopes discovered a curious cheat being practised upon our optic nerves. *Two images* stuffed with straw and dressed as soldiers were seen perched among the coppice and placed as we suppose, to deter our approach. The picquets immediately began to ascend which messieurs spying from afar, they came trotting back at double quick in great force and obliged us to retire. In the meanwhile, all the country in our front is up in arms, volunteers called out, militia trained and everything prepared to give us *a warm* though not friendly reception, should we be disposed to enter the enemies territory, which the knowing ones seem to be of opinion we shall not do.

Letters and papers have been received from England as late as the 22nd of June. I conclude that you are all down by the seaside and enjoying yourselves, and that the amusements of Eastbourne are so numerous and attracting as to leave no time for writing to George. Do not forget to remember me to all our good friends, if there are any, who were at that place with me last year, not forgetting Mr Atlee & your little play fellows, the misses Atlee's. You may tell Miss Page, Louisa (and the other *smaller fry*, to use a *cloak* phrase) that I will send them each an *intercepted letter* by the first favourable opportunity, it would cost too much to send them by post and not having heard from anyone since leaving England, I am ignorant whether Frederick has discovered any method of having my letters transmitted to you all *free* otherwise *Pritchard* I understand soon expects to go home in the capacity of adjutant to the second battalion of our regiment, in which case they shall be sent in his charge.[2] Give my kindest love to my uncle, aunt, Miss Page and all the dear little ones and believe me, my good little girl, your most affectionate brother, G U Barlow

His next letter to his good friend Andrew Amos, covered the whole period from Vitoria (having written to him last on the very eve of battle) up to date, but in particular, he announced the sudden attack made by Soult's forces, which culminated in the two battles of Sorauren, near Pamplona.

2 Lieutenant Samuel Dilman Pritchard did gain the office of adjutant to the 2nd Battalion at home.

No 4
To A[ndrew] Amos Esquire, to the care of James Amos Esquire
St Helen's Place, Bishopsgate Street, London[3]
Camp near Vera, 4 August 1813

My dear Amos,
The temporary calm of the 20th of June was but preparatory to the tremendous storm on the following day about to burst with surcharged wishes on the French army & blast King Joseph's hopes & prospects, whilst the sun which rose upon a body of 70,000, occupying most advantageous positions lined with a formidable artillery, beheld the same at setting driven like chaff before the wind, stript [sic] & despoiled of everything but the very clothes on their backs and an object of derision rather than alarm to their enemies.

Such was the result of the 21st of June, a day which it is to be devoutly hoped has set the seal to the deliverance of the peninsula from the gallic yoke. All the interesting particulars you will probably find detailed long ere this in Lord Wellington's dispatch, I shall therefore content myself with enlarging on a few which fell more minutely within the sphere of my own personal observation. It was a beautiful summer's morning when the attack commenced by a body of General Morillo's corps assaulting a part of the French position, this they did in very handsome stile, but as the foe was well covered with rocks, bushes & the ground much broken, he stood very firm till poor Colonel Cadogan came up & charged with the 71st whose attack they did not await, but retired up a craggy conical hill in the utmost disorder, where it did not enter into our contemplation to follow.[4] The Light Division in the meanwhile was destined for a bonne bouche,[5] in the shape of a formidable circular hill which the right of the French appuyed[6] and which presented a most imposing spectacle, swarming with several lines of troops, it was Massena's expression 'bristling with cannon'. The latter opened upon us on advancing & crossing the Zadora, behind which their infantry were formed in square, and here our guns pummelled the latter pretty handsomely whilst I beheld the shrapnels make them jump about like *parched peas.*[7] Supported by the 2nd [4th] Division & hussars & in conjunction with them, we carried the hill, the key of the position & which they did not stop to defend. The artillery of both armies were now in full volley, although the enemy had commenced his retreat, this movement however was very

3 James Amos was Andrew's father, a merchant trading with Russia. St Helen's Place, a beautiful and grand Georgian terrace still stands between the Bank of England and Lloyds of London.
4 Lieutenant Colonel the Honourable Henry Cadogan commanding the 71st Foot was killed at Vitoria.
5 Bonne Bouche – A delicious morsel, a delight.
6 Appuyer – French, to strengthen.
7 Spherical Case Shot, a shell packed with lead balls, with a timed fuse intended to explode as an air burst, had been invented by Lieutenant Colonel Henry Shrapnel. The name shrapnel has since become synonymous with the mass of flying shards emanating from an explosion.

slow & deliberate on their part, being favoured by the difficult nature of the country everywhere intersected by ravines, presenting a series of positions, one behind the other. The 52nd advanced now against a village,[8] the two left hand companies (of which mine was one) acting as flankers to check the enemies numerous skirmishers. These latter were driven out of the wood & closely followed across an intersected country into some corn fields, when in getting through some gaps of a hedge into the wheat, my poor captain was picked off by a fatal shot & I lost a most estimable officer and friend.

We continued however the pursuit close up to the walls of Vitoria, in which all the good people from their windows might behold the frightful confusion of the enemy and the tide of battle rolling along beneath their view without the least danger to themselves. My little band followed the enemies skirmishers beyond the city till the latter came up with their main body, formed in two solid squares composing General Maucune's Division, our old San Millan friends. These were retiring over a naked plain when I came up to a hedge about one hundred or one hundred & twenty yards distant. But beyond it was not prudent to venture, as on their left was formed a strong body of cavalry to cover their retreat & to chastise importunate intruders. The 15th Hussars now arrived & with their front squadrons executed two brilliant charges, but the disparity of force was far too great, the French dragoons preserved a very steady countenance, till the remainder of the hussars & General Ponsonby's Heavy Brigade came up towards dusk, when they turned back & fled.[9] People seldom complain of a want of light, on the *21 June* the British army however could have wished for *two hours more.* Nox then threw her sable mantle over the fugitives just as we all had well come up with them.[10] The Light Division however did not halt, till near ten at night and having been under arms & marching near twenty hours, when it was no longer possible to discern the road.

It would far exceed my good friend, the annals of a letter to attempt even a description of the various scenes both artful and amazing which presented themselves in the course of this eventful day, they must be reserved for our next meeting. General Graham's successes on the [French] right prevented them from drawing off scarcely a single piece of artillery. One hundred and twenty pieces of cannon with three or four hundred associated waggons were broken & then upset, lay scattered in every direction & horse waggons loaded with money, there [were] others filled of flour, bread, biscuit, on a third 'brandy' *claret & champagne, hams, tongues, flocks of sheep,* horses, mules, everything that a man would wish, or want. Strict orders against pillaging were however given and the officers of the Light Division were so scrupulous in this respect that they touched nothing scarcely even of

8 The village of Arinez.

9 Major General the Honourable William Ponsonby commanded a brigade of heavy cavalry consisting of the 5th Dragoon Guards and the 3rd and 4th Dragoons. He was famously killed at the Battle of Waterloo.

10 Nox was the Roman goddess of the night.

the eatables tantalizingly enough to hungry soldiers who had fasted all the day. While we thus pursued our enemy the rear divisions of the army, the cavalry,[11] *the women, suttlers & host of followers* who are always on the look-out for such occasions, together with hordes of Portuguese & Spaniards plundered the whole in the course of the night & every man took just as much, whatever he liked, and distributing money in *hatfulls*. Such is the case, I have seen two or three similar instances in the course of this short campaign, when those who honourably acted up to these & those who generally fought most notwithstanding the others reaped the fruits of their labours & obtained everything.

With nothing therefore but the clothes on their backs, the routed army ran off in the direction of Pamplona, whither we followed close at their heels during three successive days cannonading, skirmishing &c but the country was too mountainous and being able to march along *the road only*, no advantages could be obtained and they never faced [about] for one instant, dropped all their wounded, sick &c and their two remaining guns, getting into Pamplona, [saving] *one* howitzer only. We suffered in one respect equally with themselves, it rained in torrents during the whole period. The roads were ancle [sic] deep in mud & water & supplies of bread for a long time past had become half rations per diem, now they were only issued every other day. This happened in consequence of having outstripped the commissariat & marching without any at all. All the villages moreover were deserted in the track of the enemies retreat, who set fire to several, whilst their inmates fled to the mountains & had their stores, all consequently on our entry was as simply desert[ed] & [a] compleat picture of desolation.

Before Pamplona we halted a day whilst his lordship reconnoitred its fortifications. It is indeed a noble city but very strong & the citadel one of the finest & most compleat in Europe. A most respectable garrison defended the whole place which has double ditches, lots of mines, and every species of obstacle against a besieging force & would cut out two or three months ample bloody work for 20 or 30,000 men.

Leaving this therefore under a close blockade, his lordship bent his course *eastward*, sending General Graham to follow Joseph's broken army & marched to Sanguesa in the confines of the kingdom of Aragon with a view of intercepting General Clausel, who with a corps of 10,000 men was on his route to join the main body, but by the affair of Vitoria had been separated. This general was soon apprized of the hue & cry and first made for Pamplona, but here we were before him, he then made for Jaca, but was again turned. Finding therefore his road to France intercepted, he threw his artillery into the Ebro and ran down indirectly [in] an opposite direction towards Saragossa & put himself in communication with Suchet at Valencia, whither it did not enter into our plans to follow.

11 The 18th Hussars were heavily implicated and drew Wellington's wrath. See Gareth Glover, *With Wellington's Hussars in the Peninsula and Waterloo, The Journal of Lieutenant George Woodberry 18th Hussars* (Barnsley: Pen and Sword, 2018), p.129.

The country to which I have just been alluding towards Arraga [Auzoa] and the Ebro is certainly the fairest portion of Spain we have ever traversed. Not being within the sphere of the operations of either armies, the towns were perfectly uninjured, more opulent & full of inhabitants who seemed highly gratified at our arrival, never having seen the English before & no doubt respecting them for the late achievements. The country is rather flat, abounding in corn, wine and all that is good. To me it appeared a partial return of the Golden age, wine being sold at two pence or two pence half-penny a *pinta* which is about a pint & a half of English measure, and a loaf of the best white bread weighing near four pounds costing eight or nine pence. Such prices are strange indeed to Englishmen, we are used to joke saying that when peace was made this would be the country for half pay officers who might live & fare like princes.

Well, giving up the chase of Monsieur Clausel we retraced our steps and repassed Pamplona and arrived at the positions we now occupy on the French frontier. General Graham in the meanwhile had begun the siege of St Sebastian [San Sebastian], this sea port is very well fortified and possesses a castle at high tide washed on all sides by the sea, excepting where communication with the mainland by a narrow neck of sand & is supposed to be only reducible by famine. After all the necessary approaches had been made a breach was effected against the town alone, but the governor who is general in chief of the engineers of their Spanish army had taken every precaution to give the assailants a warm reception & entrenched himself like Phillipon at Badajoz.[12] The storming party were obliged to wade up to their middles in water, one by one & in mounting the breach found an immense deep *pit dug all across it* in the centre of the bastion, which was [after] losing four or five hundred men, they were forced to give up the attempt.[13]

Whilst all this was going on Marshal Soult arrives with more than post haste from the heart of Silesia at Bayonne, despatched, no doubt by Bonaparte to prop up his shattered affairs.[14] This marshal, gave quick specimens of superior talent by an immediate reorganisation of his army, which he effected by drawing forth all the National Guards and calling out under arms every man from 18 to 30 in the southern provinces; wishing moreover to relieve St Sebastian & Pamplona, he assumed the offensive & commenced by attacking General Hill in the passes of the Maya & Roncesvalles. The mountainous nature of the country most effectually concealed his movements, which were favoured by another singular piece of good fortune, upon which he could not have calculated. The subaltern of the 92nd Regiment who had charge of the outpost did not exercise a sufficient degree of vigilance and his two advanced sentries on the look-out fell

12 *Général de Brigade* Louis Emmanuel Rey commanded the garrison of San Sebastian.

13 An assault was made on 25 July but beaten off with 693 killed and wounded and a further 316 captured.

14 Marshal Jean de Dieu Soult was sent by Napoleon to command French forces in south western France in the wake of the disaster at Vitoria.

asleep on their posts at three o'clock in the afternoon[15]. Soult, as the devil would have it, was in the very act of manoeuvring and thereby was enabled to approach in great force to the pass without any alarm or intimation being given. So compleat was our surprize that the troops had scarcely time to get under arms before he arrived at the summit, took all their tents, baggage &c & gained the pass. To restore this from a superior force was a matter of no small difficulty, it succeeded however, after a most heroic attack by General Hill, with the loss however of near 1,500 men, 500 of whom alone, together with 23 officers belonging to the 92nd,[16] all [of] whom fell a sacrifice to their subaltern officer's un-soldierlike neglect. The Roncesvalles pass however had been forced at the same time & a retreat became necessary. Lord Wellington, for the purpose of concentrating, drew back his right, still blockading St Sebastian with General Graham's troops & took up a position in front of Pamplona, whither Soult followed, with 60,000 men and attacked us, who from the above surprises never could muster more than 40,000. He followed the favourite French method and with 30,000 men in masses, attempted to storm the 3rd & 6th Divisions, from a hill which the latter most nobly defended & where after suffering the most frightful carnage, he was finally repulsed. The second day was employed in burying the dead, carrying off the wounded & on the 3rd the contest was renewed. After another ineffectual attempt on our position, we followed him up, turned the tables & *assaulted his,* the success was most compleat, his lordship & the brave allied army carried all before them and made some thousand prisoners. Soult's retreat was then most precipitate; he attempted a final stand on a very fine position in this neighbourhood, but his dispirited troops were successively driven from one height to another till at length he was finally obliged to take repose in France and from whence he never has since thought proper to move.

During all these affairs, the Light Division was never so much as once engaged, indeed they were altogether detached from the main army for the purpose of keeping open communications to the left, in the execution of this service they had a deal of marching and counter marching by day and night, in short all the toil and lay without a particle of the honour of these days and finally retraced their steps to the ground from which I date the present.

And now adieu my good fellow, I hope you will have patience to wait to the end of this long epistle to form your next. Sincerely & truly G U Barlow.

15 The surprise of the troops at Maya is understandably shrouded in some mystery. George Barlow had obviously heard that a subaltern of the 92nd had failed to sound the alarm, but others state that it was a subaltern of the 71st. Sergeant David Robertson of the 92nd confirms that Captain Archibald Armstrong of the 71st did try to warn Colonel John Cameron but that the latter refused to believe that a French column was advancing until too late.

16 The losses at the Pass of Maya did indeed total 1,488 casualties, the 92nd suffering 343 casualties in total.

To William Barlow Esq, Little Bridge Street, Blackfriars, London
Camp before Vera, 11 August 1811

My dearest uncle,
By the date of the present you will see that we have returned to our old position in front of this pass. I wrote last to all the little girls from Lezaca on the 24th of July & sending them some French letters[17] by Pritchard, who left us for the second battalion in England, to which he is appointed adjutant. Two days subsequent we broke up in consequence of the attack of the French on the Maya Pass.

You will doubtless have seen in the papers all the details which have occurred relating to the transactions of the late most awful, yet honourable period of a fortnight, to the British army. You will perceive by what trifling events the greatest incidents are governed and how much the allied cause might have been endangered by the neglect of merely one subaltern and a detachment of twenty or thirty men, who relaxed their vigilance. This officer of the 92nd walked away from his picquet for the space of half an hour about three o'clock in the afternoon, not dreaming of any mischance & neglecting to patrol regularly around his sentries. During the heat of the day, his two advanced videttes fell asleep, who had been posted on some high ground to give timely notice of the enemy's advance. Soult on his side had previously been determined on an assault, but never could have calculated on such an extraordinary piece of good fortune. He thus was enabled to arrive at the post unseen in open daylight, bringing up an overwhelming mass of force. The picquet officer had scarcely time to give the alarm, so as to enable General Hill to seize his arms, before the enemy had arrived in the very camp, took all his tents, baggage, in short everything he had. The troops had scarcely formed before a most desperate conflict took place in which General Hill finally succeeded in repulsing them, though with the loss of 1,500 men, of which the 92nd lost alone 23 officers & 500 men owing to the neglect of their detachment.

The map will show you how important was this advantage to the French marshal. It gave him a passage, distant but two days from Pamplona, immediately in rear of our right flank & through which he did not fail to pour 60,000 men, having also turned the pass of Roncesvalles. During the month which had elapsed since the business of Vitoria, every means had been taken to reorganize their beaten forces and that admirable engine of French despotism, in the shape of conscriptions & levees en masse put in motion to the fullest extent. All the National Guards to the amount of many thousands were called out & every male from 18 to 35 years of age obliged to take up arms. The whole resources of the south of France were placed at the disposal of Soult & it is well known that he had a genius & talent to avail himself of them to the best advantage. Lord Wellington concentrated his

17 He refers to the letters of *Général de Brigade* Montfort captured at San Millan.

right & took up a position close to Pamplona, whose garrison might behold the efforts made by their friends to bring them relief from the highest steeples. The contest that took place was of the most sanguinary nature, both parties being repeatedly in close contact at the point of the bayonet. 20,000 of their best troops made an attack on one particularly important hill. As soon as one mass was cut up & defeated, another solid body came forward & thus was the assault given five successive times & received as often with the most heroic firmness, till the French officers were seen beating their men with the flat ends of their swords & using the utmost personal efforts to make them advance again, but [torn- with?] no effect.

The next day was employed by both parties burying the dead, carrying off the wounded &c &c and on the 30th the fight was renewed. His lordship was now the assailant though the numbers of the enemy were very superior & their position on these tremendous hills most advantageous. All this however was counterbalanced by the superior spirit of their adversaries, who stormed these heights one after the other & carried all before them.[18] The contest ended at night, leaving in our hands upwards of four thousand prisoners. The pursuit was hot & close during the two following days & on the 2nd instant I saw them attempt another stand on some very fine ground in this neighbourhood, but were driven off as usual, till at length they finally retreated to the passes on the frontiers of their own country, which they now occupy after losing as I am told, near 20,000 men in these late fruitless efforts. In all these affairs our division took no part, having been engaged in a series of harassing, fatiguing marches up & down these mountains, by night as well as by day & being destined to keep up the communications with General Graham, was obliged to conform in its movements with the direction taken by the rest of the army. Had Lord W[ellington] been beaten, our situation would have been critical indeed, as it is, we stare this formidable pass in the face. No notion of ours in advance is at present anticipated until the fall of St Sebastian & Pamplona; previous to which from all accounts, another attack from the enemy may be expected & for which we hear they are making most active preparations, as they are unwilling to resign their last holds in the Spanish territory without another desperate effort.

Two days ago, I received a few hasty lines from you & Fred dated the 21st of July. They are the first I have had since leaving you all in February last and I look forward with much pleasure to the accounts which you both promise me by the next mail. I have a letter from Eliza dated the 5th & two from Dr Amos, who was about to set out for the north on his travels. God bless you all my dear uncle & believe me your ever-affectionate nephew G U Barlow

18 This refers to the two Battles of Sorauren fought on 28 and 30 of July 1813, when the French lost around 4,000 men killed and wounded. Over the entire campaign in the Pyrenees, some 10,000 Frenchmen were killed or wounded and nearly 3,000 made prisoners. Wellington's forces lost some 7,000 killed and wounded.

Time at Vera inevitably hung heavy with little to do, but the stunning scenery was capable of sending George into raptures.

No. 5
To A[ndrew] Amos Esq to the care of James Amos Esq., St Helen's Place, Bishopgate Street, London
Undated (supposed August)

My dear Amos,
So you have been seized with a set for rambling and desirous of breaking through the precincts of our narrow & yet great isle, you quit its hospitable retreats for the wilder dominions of the eastern world? These appear to be the nature of your plans in the last letter which came to hand at [Fuente]guinaldo. For this and one of a former date which I received at Lisbon, I return my best thanks, as well as the precis of politics and news which they contain from the perusal, I look forward with much pleasure to the account of the peregrinations of which they left you in the act of starting. The year 1813 has fortunately seen us both occupied in our respective travels, your promenades have probably been more leisurely conducted & more philosophical than mine, of the latter I send you an epitome annexed from the time of our leaving [Fuente]guinaldo to the present moment among the Pyrenees, although I [have] written to you from the midst of these latter mountains, they are extracted from various meanderings in my journal book regularly kept during the march, and as the *journey is* really very long I thought *these* notes not unreasonable and therefore have added the annexed dates for matter of form, in order to continue unbroken the chain of my correspondence and is a measure I should like to see adopted in yours. Some time since we agreed to institute the practise of numbers but somehow or other there has been a deviation from so methodical a plan, but behold it now again new revived, and Vera among the Pyrenees giving birth to No 5 from the period of our quitting [Fuente]guinaldo on the 19th of May last.

You are doubtless aware of my partiality for professional disquisitions[19] and a certain teasing propensity to force upon others the fruit of reflections not the most valuable or interesting. Our present state of inactivity however offers little to fill up the remainder of this sheet, and I may therefore be pardoned for mounting afresh my favoured hobby horse, within cannon shot of the formidable pass of Vera and staring Messieurs les Francois in the face, whose advanced sentries and our own are posted within two hundred yards of each other, along a little valley through which runs the stream of the Bidassoa and dividing the ridge of our position from that on which theirs is situated. Every drum and trumpet may be distinguished from either camp, and should the foe possess a spy glass, he may perceive

19 Disquiditions – discussions.

me in the door of the tent sitting down to the table just as clearly as I have frequently observed them cooking, washing or employed in their various occupations. The greatest politeness is maintained on both sides, although the Spaniards & Longa's guerrillas are frequently apt to break through the laws of this belligerent etiquette and which specimen of ill breeding the French resent against *them* alone by the exchange of partial shots.

After the unparalleled state of activity with which this campaign has been hitherto conducted, our present repose of near three weeks continuance begins to partake so little of ennui. We cannot venture out any distance from camp as the proximity of the enemy's position might occasion a movement at half an hour's notice. The country moreover offers few temptations for the sportsman's researches, did not the tremendous crags and precipices forbid his excursions. You may perhaps have before perused the unanimous testimonies of delight which travellers of all ages have experienced from the beauties of Pyrenean scenery, whose landscapes have been transplanted into our own soul, as far as the flowers of language would admit, by the magic hand of Miss Radcliffe.[20] They are subjects indeed worthy the descriptive touches of the Enchantress of Udolpho and well calculated to warm the effusions of every romantic's imagination. You begin to descend these hills on the first day's march beyond Pamplona and the commencement of the true chain may be easily distinguished from the more barren ranges shooting forth from Biscay by the beautiful woods which invariably clothe their gigantic sides. Every league afforded an opportunity for the description of the [enchanting?] woods & purling rills, and materials for the heroic in endless progression. On one part of the road which leads over some of the highest eminences, the trees on either side leaning over, grew so thick & were interwoven to that degree as to form a continual alcove for a very great distance through which the passenger when on horseback is obliged to make frequent deviations by reason *of the [height?] of this leafy canopy* and where the scorching heat of a meridian sun still penetrates. Frequently a floating mass of clouds succeeds, occasionally enveloping the tops of the higher eminences, or slowly stealing along their bases for a while, obscure from the more elevated observers the instant prospect of the vale beneath, situated in the latter, may behold the peasants cottage or the rural hamlet smiling resplendence & plenty & begirt[21] with the variegated colours of luxuriant cultivation of the golden harvest, contrasted with the more delicate tints of the vineyard, whilst the gallant array of the British army, which might be seen pursuing the serpentine direction of the road, now diving into the deepest glen and then climbing the arduous rock, sometimes emerging from the bosom of the forest, or crossing the torrent on a mountain bridge in the gaiety of success, sounding a martial strain of harmony formed the tout ensemble of this animated picture.

20 Anne Radcliffe (1764-1823), author and poet, she has been credited with pioneering the Gothic novel, her most famous work being *The Mysteries of Udolpho*.

21 Begirt – encircled.

The natives of these provinces are evidently a distinct race from the remainder of Spain, much fairer in complexion, and to use the language of a French officer, far more civilised.[22] This phrase is certainly not very complimentary to the dons, but the real drift of this, that their customs more resemble our own and those of the French, the houses are more modernized, cleaner & well built, the streets regularly better paved, numerous orchards & gardens may be seen skirting the different villages which the enemy in their rapid flight have not found sufficient time to devastate.

This is probably the first time that an English army or many individuals of that nation has set foot in these unknown recesses. Fame might have trumpeted forth no very favourable reports of our character from the disgraceful conduct of a few unworthy miscreants, these apprehensions were soon removed by the peaceable demeanour and strict discipline observed throughout the army and from that period nothing was more conspicuous than their uniform hospitality & kindness. In one place particularly, I remember that in consequency of a deficiency in the commissariat the regimental quartermaster was compelled to procure the necessary supplies of bread. He offered them money which they generously refused, saying they well knew that we could ill afford it at that period, and signifying that they would be sufficiently content with a paper certificate of the quantity taken & wait till the commissary should think proper to pay for the same. This was no inconsiderable act of liberality shown to perfect strangers, as the bread thus obtained was upwards of one-thousand-pound weight for the 52nd Regiment alone.

Of their orderly deportment they are probably the more sensible when contrasted with that of the Spanish troops whose licentiousness, more particularly Longa's guerrillas are truly flagrant. These last mentioned chiefs of banditry (for such they are both in appearance & behaviour) amount to several thousands, and no doubt have proved very formidable by the French armies, possessing no commissariat their means of subsistence are truly precarious & they are pretty active in levying contributions and plundering their own countrymen to make up for their deficiency, whom in their indignation I have heard to say that the guerrillas were worse than the French. These roaming bands rob & pillage the whole face of the country, British officers even are not secure from their attacks, one of whom the other day going to St Sebastian, was surprised by a volley from some bushes on looking around saw his servant sprawling in the dust, while a party of these gentry rushing forth seized the baggage & forced him to run with all possible speed.

Among our present matters, the agreeable change of climate, which presently in these mountainous regions is one of the most remarkable. We arrived at Salamanca the latter end of May when the summer began to be well set in & the heat most excessive. Many a *cracked lip* and face peeled off

22 They had of course now entered the Basque region.

as to then bore testimony to the ardours of a Spanish sun, which during the months of June, July & August prevails. Both the same terrible uniformity throughout the greater part of Spain, more particularly in the province of Castille & Extramadura, hitherto the chief scene of our operations. Here on the contrary the climate partakes of the, to us, most agreeable uncertainty of England. We are frequently enveloped in clouds, today it may rain, tomorrow shine, so about precisely getting an English summer, which circumstance of course proceeds from the immense chain of mountains, the scene of our present operations makes the season appear to me who left England in March like one unvaried run of constant spring.

One of our greatest inconveniences arises from a total ignorance of the language of these provinces. It may seem very strange, but is not the less true that our army, which has been several years in Spain should be ignorant of the language. You must understand that they do not speak Castillian but lengua Basquesa or Biscayan. The first question we ask a man in these parts is, do you speak *Castillian*, which is the same as if you had said do you speak *Spanish* for Castillians signify & is as often used for Spaniard as Espagnol. Castellan being the purest dialect as spoken by the natives of Castille. Biscayan I think must be a dialect of the Celtic, not having the slightest affinity to Castillian as will appear by the subjoined terms for numerals which correspond in most tongues, but not at all in these two.[23]

Spanish	Biscayan
Uno	Bat
Dos	Bi
Tres	Hiru
Quatro	Lau
Cinco	Bost
Seis	Sei
Siete	Zazpi
Ocho	Zortzi
Nueve	Bederatzi

May not the natives who were descended from the Goths & never fell under the Moorish yoke in these mountains have preserved their native tongue, the… [End of letter torn off]

23 The Basque language has been compared with many others, including Celtic to establish where it came from, but it seems that Basque is not related to any other world language and is described as 'a linguistic isolate'.

To William Barlow Esq, Little Bridge Street, Blackfriars, London
Camp near Vera, 20 August 1813

My dearest uncle,
Your packet of the 24th of July came to hand on the 17th instant affording me the most real pleasure, since from accidents untoward enough, but most satisfactorily accounted for, I have been prevented from having a sight of your handwriting during six very long months. The first budget dated in *May last* was dispatched after me to Santarem from the regiment & never reached its owner. The second sent by Major Ferguson I expect in the course of this week, as I hear that his regiment, the 85th, landed at Passages [Pasajes] this morning.[24] I perfectly agree with you that to send letters by private hands (excepting on some very few occasions) is certainly the very worst method of conveyance & their safety is always questionable and at best their arrival is most tardy & they certainly cannot be committed to a better charge than that of Frederick's franks, which unite both safety and expedition. The non-arrival of my share in the correspondence may be traced to the itinerant mode of life we now lead. Our proper Adjutant General at this moment is at home for the recovery of his health & the officer who for a-while officiates in his stead not belonging to the division, does not trouble his head much about them, or pay that attention to a thousand little nameless comforts which it is in his power to promote, amongst which, that of sending advice when a mail is about to be made up for England at head-quarters & procuring our letters early from thence, constitutes one. As these last are therefore so much exposed to mischance I shall note down all that I have written since the 24th of June, the last which you acknowledge to have received. One to my aunt *from Oronoz* about the 10th or 12th of July, one to little Fanny from this camp *at Vera* about the 18th of July, a packet with some French letters on *the 24th* of the same month by Pritchard,[25] and lastly to you about the 10th of August acknowledging the receipt of your frank of the 21st of July, with an account of the late transactions near Pamplona & in this vicinity. I am sorry that my letter from Aldea Nueva with the postscript of the 6th of June did not come to hand, as it contained a summary of all our proceedings up to that date from the time of our first starting, together with an account of Salamanca and everything I saw therein.

You may my give my best love to my aunt, Miss Page and all the dear little girls for their kind letters, a reply to which was anticipated by mine of the 24th ultimo not forgetting *Mr* Richard, who appears to have set a better example to his elder brother of diligence,[26] than the latter has imitated & who shall not be forgotten for his capital specimen of belles lettres. I think that all the ladies wrote very *good fists,* & Miss Louisa *with care & attention* a free easy running hand.

24 Major James Fergusson 85th Foot arrived in Spain in August 1813.
25 This letter is not to be found.
26 His younger brother Richard Wellesley Barlow born in 1804.

With regard to matters in this quarter, they bear a stationary appearance. The last fleet from England has brought out a new battering train together with ample supplies of ammunition & St Sebastian is to be besieged with redoubled vigour. It is very strong and possesses a castle at high tides washed on all sides by the sea, excepting where it communicates with the shore by a narrow neck of sand and is supposed to be only reducible by famine. After all the necessary approaches had been made, a breach was affected against the town alone. But the governor who is general in chief of the French engineers had taken every precaution to give the assailants a warm reception & entrenched himself like Philippon at Badajoz. The storming party were obliged to wade up to their middles in the water and on mounting the breach found an immense *deep pit across it* in the centre of the bastion, which was effectually separated from the town by traverses. To advance was utterly impracticable and after losing four or five hundred men, they were forced to give up the attempt.[27]

I have every reason to think that his lordship had a general attack in contemplation on this part of the French position about a fortnight since. We were ordered to lay down at night fully accoutred to turn out at a moment's notice and his lordship sent directions to Marshal Beresford, Generals Cole, Alten and all the chief staff officers to meet him by a certain hour on the top of the highest eminence on this side of Vera.[28] Thither they all repaired, but after keeping them waiting the greater part of the day till near six in the evening, he sent a message to say they might all go home. Rumour states that now the reinforcements are landed some attempt will certainly be made. This day his lordship has been abroad peeping and spying and we generally find something of importance takes place after such minute reconnaissance's. If the French allow themselves to be driven by main force from their present heights, they need not take up any more positions. The flanks of the present are protected by two immense ravines where a man cannot climb up scarcely with hands & feet. The assault must therefore be made in front where the ground is very broken & redoubts & abatis commanding the most accessible points; since the [torn – war of?] 1793 between the French and Spaniards, the former picked it out as their secure [torn – base?] which never has been forced.[29] People seem to be of opinion that Lord W[ellington] turning the Maya or Roncesvalles passes & thus manoeuvre them out. Whatever may be the result, depend upon it that the British army will not compromise its recent achievements & high character. The troops are in the best order & state of health, place

27 This first attempt to storm San Sebastian was launched on 25 July, but was beaten back at the breach with the loss of 693 killed and wounded and 316 prisoners.

28 Marshal William Carr Beresford commanding the Portuguese army, Lieutenant General Lowry Cole commanding the 4th Division and Major General Charles Baron Alten commanding the Light Division.

29 Spain joined the coalition against Revolutionary France in 1793, but little occurred in this sphere of operations and a peace treaty was signed in 1795.

the most unbounded confidence in their chief, are animated with the most dashing spirit, in a word you may expect from them everything that men can possibly perform.

Enclosed is a letter for [blanked out] which I transmit you open. Peruse it & decide whether it should be sent or otherwise, which is left entirely at your option to decide. I took this step, in consequence of *his request*, that I would write and let him know of any favourable circumstance which might come to my knowledge. My slight acquaintance with him renders it a delicate affair; perhaps it would be as well if you was to enclose it in a note of your own, stating two or three details which would come with an ill grace from me. There was among us some short time since strong rumours of an immediate peace; it is no means beyond the reach of possibility that such an event might be brought about in the course of a few months; in that case I might continue a subaltern for some years to come & promotion would be out of the position altogether. I have been obliged to draw on you for 160 dollars or at the rate of exchange as now standing for fifty pounds payable to Staff Surgeon Maling, formerly of our regiment.[30] My letter from Aldea Nueva having miscarried,[31] you probably are in ignorance of my mule having been stolen in the night owing to the negligence of the sentinel appointed to take charge of the animals, two days march *from Rodrigo*. No resource was left but to transfer the baggage which it carried to my horse, who was unequal to it & got in consequence a very bad sore back. No mules could be procured but at Salamanca & good strong ones bore a tremendous price. We halted one day & were under orders to march early the next morning. No alternative remained but to leave the best part of my baggage & comfort behind at the very outset of a most active campaign or purchase one on the spur of the moment coute que coute;[32] I could meet but with *one* animal for sale, which I was obliged to buy & pay the sum of *one hundred & fifty dollars* in those gold pieces I procured in London. This pretty nigh ruined me as I had calculated upon the above sum to last certainly to the conclusion of the present campaign. The beast is [a] very good [one] of the sort & my only consolation is that I may regain my money when I find it convenient to dispose of him, as also that my £120 granted by the medical board will pretty nigh cover the £140 drawn upon you & beyond my allowance for the year, which I received on quitting England and which debt upon my father's purse I desire may be liquidated out of the above £120 as far as it will go. Dollars here cannot be procured under six shillings apiece. God bless you, my dearest uncle & with my kindest love to my aunt, Miss Page & all the dear little girls. Believe me your affectionate nephew G U Barlow

30 Maling was now Staff Surgeon attached to the Light Division.

31 This letter has not been found.

32 French: at all costs.

The Storming of San Sebastian, by Denis Dighton. (Public Domain)

> P.S.10 September. By the date of the above, you will see that the present has been particularly unfortunate. I returned two days since from St Sebastian and found the mail had been dispatched in my absence. There is barely time for me to add this short postscript, assuring you that in the course of a day or two, I will send an account of all our late transactions, as yet I continue in the best health & spirit.

His hurried postscript indicated that something momentous had occurred and his next letter brought his uncle fully up to date on the various happenings. San Sebastian had been successfully stormed, but French attacks designed to relieve the fortress had also to be fought off. A feint attack on Vera kept the 7th and Light Divisions occupied, whilst another large French force attempted to drive in the Spanish forces holding San Marcial. Although closely supported, Wellington was glad to see the Spanish troops achieve success, greatly enhancing their morale. The French retired, but heavy rains made the River Bidassoa swell rapidly, cutting off the two fords used by the French to advance that morning. The French sought out the only bridge in the area at Vera, but this was barricaded and controlled by Captain Cadoux of the 95th Rifles and about one hundred men, who held a large fortified house at the end of the narrow bridge. The French were effectively stuck unless they could gain control of the bridge and the fighting was intense. However, the Light Division, standing only half a mile away and fully aware of the situation, had been held back by Major General John Skerrett, who refused to support Cadoux. Eventually Cadoux was overrun and half of his men killed. It is interesting that George was with Skerrett that day and he skirts over the issue. Many others in the Light Division never forgave

Passajes by Batty. (Editor's Collection)

Skerrett and it is probably not coincidence that he decided to leave them soon after. The 52nd were again simply spectators in all this.

George then obtained permission to view San Sebastian only three days after the town had been captured, which was still strewn with the bodies of the fallen and fires continued to rage throughout the town, but while the garrison still continued to hold out in the castle on Monte Urgull and were still being shelled incessantly. After his return to Vera, George heard that the French had finally capitulated at San Sebastian.

> To William Barlow Esq, Little Bridge Street, Blackfriars, London
> Camp near Vera, 10 September 1813
>
> My dearest uncle,
> As the hasty postscript which I was obliged to affix to my last dated from this place August 20th precluded me from entering into any details of our late proceedings, I shall resume the thread of my story which left us quietly posted at Vera in expectation of an attack from the enemy. St Sebastian was known to be very hard prest [sic] & an attempt for its relief hourly expected. I was returning one morning, drowsy enough, as you may suppose from being on picquet the whole night in Vera, when at first dawn several massy columns were seen formed on the opposite hills & hourly increasing in numbers, till at length the imposing spectacle of 20,000 in two solid heaps

might be seen assembled. One party of these directed themselves against two Portuguese regiments and a brigade of the Seventh Division on our left, who were overpowered by such superior forces, but retired gradually disputing every inch of ground, until they arrived at a strong position where a sufficient force was drawn up ready to receive the assailants, who made a dead halt and at that moment, news arriving of St Sebastian having been carried by storm, whilst General Giron's Spanish Division having most gallantly beaten off another corps which attempted to cross the Bidassoa lower down near Irun, they did not attempt to proceed any further.[33]

In the meanwhile, the remaining half commenced their operations against our brigade by driving the picquets out of Vera and clearing that bank of the Bidassoa, came down upon the bridge with the seeming design of attacking us & crossing it. But viewing the steady countenance which our brigade preserved, drawn up in the best order upon some very advantageous heights, they thought proper to leave it unmolested. After some smart skirmishing about the river in which the 95th distinguished themselves, they passed on in a different direction leaving a sufficient force to watch our movements. We had no artillery, or they would have been handsomely paid all this while. As it was we were forced to see them pass under our noses at half cannon shot without giving them the slightest annoyance & our inferior numbers were obliged to remain stationary on the heights. They had moreover brought up various guns in advantageous positions which would have compleatly commanded us in the event of any forward advance.

Night came on, whilst a heavy rain rendered the fords nearly impassable, which circumstance coupled with the ill news they had received from their right determined their retreat and early next morning previous to daybreak, they made two or three attempts to carry the bridge of Vera but were resisted with the utmost effect & bravery by two companies of the 95th under Captain Cadoux,[34] who was charged with the defence of the same. He maintained it from three o'clock till five, when light dawning discovered to the enemy the inferior numbers of their opponents. Led on by General Vandermaesen & Lamartiniere,[35] they made a final & most desperate rush in great force and forced the two companies to retire, not however until the latter had trimmed them most handsomely, mortally wounding the first named officer & very badly the second under cover of their guns, the remaining troops crossed over, when the whole withdrew to

33 This refers to the Action at San Marcial on 31 August, where Wellington was happy to see the Spanish troops repulse a French attack in an attempt to relieve San Sebastian, thus greatly boosting their morale.

34 Captain Daniel Cadoux 2/95th Rifles, was killed at the action of Vera. Cadoux's company of some 60 men held a fortified house overlooking the Bridge at Vera and was apparently supported by a company of 3/95th under Lieutenant Travers. They held until dawn, but then had to retire, having lost some sixteen men.

35 *Général de Division* Eme-Martin Vandermaesen commanded the rearguard, he was killed at the Action of Vera. *Général de Division* Thomas Mignot de Lamartiniere was also wounded at the action at Vera and died at Bayonne five days later.

their old positions & might be seen slowly dragging up the tremendous pass of Vera, in the most wretched plight after two days of incessant marching & countermarching, drenched with the most violent & incessant rains which perhaps I have ever witnessed.

Such has been the result of Marshal Soult's second attempt at invasion. Our regiment stood in position during the whole time without firing a shot. It happened however to be my lot to attend General Skerrett as a sort of officer in waiting,[36] to carry orders to the different corps, which caused me to be present in these various affairs, which were nothing more than skirmishing, but certainly some of the sharpest that has ever fallen within my view.

On the morning of the 2nd instant I obtained permission to take a trip of excursion to St Sebastian. You should be previously informed that in consequence of the former failure at that place, a picked party from the 1st, 4th and Light Divisions were ordered thither for making a second attempt on the breaches. To the senior subalterns were allowed the choice of volunteering from each regiment & ours of course went; its proportion being one major, one captain and one lieutenant. The papers will have informed you how compleatly the assault succeeded, but with severe loss. Poor Harvest being killed after having been twice previously wounded & refusing to quit his station, whilst Major Hunt & Captain Campbell were each severely wounded together with twenty-five out of thirty-five men composing the party which accompanied them.[37]

On arriving about half way, the object of my journey might be discerned from afar, marked by a tremendous volume of smoke arising from the conflagrations of this unhappy city and so eager was I to discover the shortest route that upon attempting to cross a narrow arm of Passages [Pasajes] harbour at low water, where footsteps might be seen in the mud and three marks of direction, my mule was swamped up to his belly & there stuck. After being extricated from this plight I arrived safe enough at St Sebastian. You approach it by a very long and beautiful avenue of trees, which would make a very pretty promenade for any of our sea bathing places, the sands are extensive and the country round about delightful. It was necessary for me to pass close to the batteries at that time, in full volley; but my mule stood fire like a veteran. Being pretty well jaded by a journey of twenty miles in very mountainous roads; the city stands of a narrow neck of land running out into the sea and forming on either side two very

36 Major General John Byne Skerrett, commanded a brigade of the Light Division.

37 Brevet Lieutenant Colonel John Hunt and Captain Robert Campbell were both severely wounded, whilst Lieutenant Augustus Harvest was killed. Some three sergeants and 35 privates volunteered for the Storming Party. Two men were killed (Privates Thomas Conway and John Delaney) whilst 16 were wounded (Sergeants Hugh McCurie and D. McKay, Corporals Samuel Armstrong, Henry Read and James Henderson and Privates Joseph Anderson, Patrick Breen, Edward Casey, Denis Campbell, William Cochrane, Marbro Crump, George Duggen, Philip Fox, John McAvoy, David McGlinn, and Charles McLaughton).

picturesque bays, outside of which might be seen Sir George Collier's squadron at anchor.[38] The castle forms a very striking object in the picture & together with the heavy bombardment would form one of the most beautiful panoramas you can imagine, partaking of which the ground moreover presents peculiar facilities.

I took up my quarters with a brother officer in the Convent of St Bartholomew,[39] terribly ruined by our cannon, whilst approaches [were] approaching the suburbs, and on this occasion [now] converted into an hospital for our wounded. After putting up my mule, I went immediately into the town and passed over the breaches. It was the third day subsequent to the storm, but its melancholy victims might be seen strewed all over them and in their vicinity, English and French, German or Italian, promiscuously mixed and their numbers attesting the gallantry shown by either party during the combat. The main breach was a most gigantic one, very easy of access, but had most formidable defences within, was well traversed, so that on mounting you found yourself exposed from head to foot to a line of troops firing from behind parapets about twelve yards in rear, themselves being well protected & posted in ruined houses. A battery of six pieces from the castle played terribly on the ramparts as soon as you gained their height. The streets were also well entrenched, deep pits cut and every precaution taken by a skilful foe to maintain his posts, their troops encouraged by former success, fought most obstinately & certainly with every advantage. But the assault of our people was irresistible, whilst the Fifth Division, not a little piqued at the detachments of the 1st, 4th & Light being called in to their support, exhibited I am told, the most devoted gallantry. A mine was sprung upon them with great effect, but still no hesitation displayed itself and a fresh swarm succeeded to the place of their unfortunate comrades, till at length such powerful exertions were attended by their merited success and 1,200 men, all that remained of originally 2,500 driven into the castle.

As is customary amidst such scenes of carnage & disorder, various conflagrations quickly broke out in several parts of this unhappy town, already well sacked by the French garrison previous to our attack. All our attention, even on the third day, was directed to the carrying off the wounded, burying the dead & bombarding the castle. During this period, no attempts were made to arrest the flames, which on the contrary, feeding on the dry timber & nourished by a succession of brisk sea breezes raged with the utmost fury. On the day of my return from thence, I left the two principal streets and market place on fire from extremity to the other, whilst the houses were falling in every direction and I really think that scarcely one stone can be left standing on another.

The poor garrison now cooped up in so small a space, with little or no cover, caught a terrible pummelling. 2,016 shells alone were thrown in

38 Commodore Sir George Ralph Collier Royal Navy commanded the squadron on the north coast of Spain in 1813.

39 The Convent of San Bartolome still stands on a hill dominating the city of San Sebastian.

every twenty-four hours, which ploughed up its interior & prevented the garrison from returning a shot.[40] In this pitiable state, they held out yet five days longer, when a breach in the castle walls being pretty night effected & dreading the effect of a second storm, when no mercy could be expected, nor any refuge at hand, they surrendered on the afternoon of the 8th instant, after a defence of nearly two months, which entitles to the governor, the praise of one liberal enemy to another in having so ably performed his duty.

The weather has of late undergone considerable changes for the worse, attended with high winds and deluges of rain, which renders our linen habitation on the tops of these high mountains not the most agreeable. We must wait however until another desperate effort has been made by Soult for the relief of Pamplona, for which all accounts agree, that he is making every preparation. It must be his last, as the garrison is already reduced to the greatest extremity, I trust however that the campaign will be closed with the same brilliancy with which it has been commenced & hitherto carried on. People seem to be [torn – of the] opinion that the Light Division will not go into winter cantonments this year, but sent eastward into Catalonia, where Suchet yet keeps his ground. I know not on what authority this intelligence rests, but nevertheless consider it as highly probable.

God bless you all, my dearest uncle and with kindest love to all the dear little girls, my aunt, Miss Page & other friends, believe me your most affectionate nephew G U Barlow

Another short note to his uncle saw George back in San Sebastian again.

To William Barlow Esq, Little Bridge Street, Blackfriars, London
By favour of Lieutenant Colonel Hunt
St Sebastian, 15 September 1813

My dearest uncle,
I have just time to write a few lines by Lieutenant Colonel Hunt of our regiment who is going home to England on account of the wound received at the storm of this place & to whom I took the opportunity of paying a visit of enquiry on the occasion of coming to *Passages* with a detachment to procure corn. This is a lucky circumstance as it passes for my turn of duty and prevents me from going *to Lisbon or Bilbao* to take charge of the regimental hospitals at one of those places, which must have been the case in a few days. With regard to Lord Teignmouth's letter which arrived with your last packet,[41] I have acted as you recommended & burnt the same, not needing any introduction of the sort.

---

40 This equates with 1.4 shells being fired every minute.

41 John Shore, 1st Baron Teignmouth (1751-1834) had served as Governor General of Bengal from 1793-7. He had clearly forwarded a letter of introduction to some senior officer with the army, but which was now deemed by George as useless.

San Sebastian from the top of Monte Urgull 1814. (Editor's Collection)

I am very well & in the best spirits. A mail has arrived with papers & letters up to the 31st of August & I have great hopes of receiving some from you on returning to the regiment. I wrote a long letter to you & *Richard* on the 10th of this month, which I hope will arrive safe; it has an enclosure for Greenwood &c. God bless you all and believe me your most affectionate nephew, G U Barlow

[PS] I write this in an old ruined house, which has but one room remaining and the inhabitant of which has been good enough to lend me this scrap of paper.

George went over the same news to his friend, but revealed more information, including how close he had been to being hit by a shell burst at Vera.

[No.6]
To A[ndrew] Amos Esq, to the care of J[ames] Amos Esq.
Vera, 24 September 1813

My dear Amos,
No.5, I think, left our noble chief again recognized the favourite shield of victory, and beheld from the tops of the Pyrenees his routed foes drawn back to their own limits with shame and dismay. This recent triumph was

the more enhanced from the circumstance of the enemy having anticipated a very different result, by bringing an overwhelming force to one particular point. For a while they enjoyed an ephemeral success and forced the centre to march a retrograde movement. Conceiving therefore that the tide of war had now undergone the desired turn, they ordered from Bayonne both cavalry & artillery, arms that do not suit these mountainous regions. His lordship, still interposed between them and Pamplona & by the 28th July had concentrated in sufficient force to give them battle. The result was a compleat victory. On the 30th his lordship became the assailant and victory again showed how competent he was either for offensive or defensive movements.

All this while St Sebastian was blockaded, although active operations against that fortress had undergone temporary suspension. Immediately however after these recent successes and the two armies had re-ordered their dispositions, the siege was again commenced with great vigour. I must here observe that from the heights of Bayonet[42] the French constantly communicated by telegraph with the garrison & learnt on the 30th of August that the place was reduced to the last extremity and that an assault was about to be made. Soult therefore put himself in motion and attacked the allied forces at the very same hour that the assault was made on the breaches by General Graham. I happened to have been on piquet the preceding night in the town of Vera, which our outposts occupied within musket shot of the French advanced guard and was not a little surprized at the first dawn of light, when about to be relieved, to see a large mass of their troops drawn up on the face of a hill within cannon shot & their numbers every moment increasing, they at last presented the imposing spectacle of 20,000 men drawn up in two solid masses who quickly, under cover of their cannon drove the picquets out of the place. In the affair which ensued I happened to attend by rotation on General Skerrett, to carry about his orders and accompanied him to a part of the position which the enemy were smartly cannonading and very nearly had my head broke by the explosion of a shell which burst close to my horses' feet before I could say *Jack Robinson*,[43] whilst I beheld the *arm of a soldier* as high as the elbow come flying by me through the air. Neither in this affair, nor in a desperate attack which they made against the Spanish troops did Soult succeed in piercing our lines & penetrating to St Sebastian & learning at the same time that the town had been carried by storm, he forthwith retired, abandoning the remainder of the garrison, who had shut themselves up in the castle to their fate.

I will now proceed to give you some particulars of the memorable assault, which on the 30th day of August was made against that devoted city. English and French were alike covered with glory and the poor citizens with inevitable ruin. I visited the trenches the succeeding day, whilst

42 He means the heights above Vera, which included the Bayonette ridge.

43 A phrase denoting a very short period of time. Its origins are unclear, but it was in use by 1778 and is recorded in the *Dictionary of the Vulgar Tongue* of 1811.

our batteries were continually playing upon the castle and being on the spot, could form a tolerable idea of the progress of recent operations. The breaches were washed by the sea and therefore could only be stormed at low water. The garrison were some of the elite of the French army, being the same that defended Burgos last year,[44] as I have previously informed you were animated with their success in repulsing our recent assault and moreover had their energies seconded by the skill & talents of the French chief of engineers, General Rey.

On the other hand, the 5th Division under General Leith, who had formerly miscarried, were eager to revenge their first defeat & moreover felt just a little hurt at the arrival of a party of volunteers from the 1st, 4th & Light Divisions, to try the breach. A request was made & granted, that these last new-comers should not be permitted to lead the way. I will not fatigue you with a minute selection of the particulars of this desperate affair. The assailants showed the most heroic devotion, more especially the officers, who were mowed down successively one after the other. As the attack was made at noon day their individual exertions were manifest to the whole army and attracted most particularly the enemy's fire; 170 of these fell out of 250 who were on the breach. Several mines & explosions took place on either side & for two hours the victory hung in suspense. At length the breaching batteries were opened over our own troops [heads] and directed with the nicest precision, every shot passing within a few yards of their heads and sweeping down the garrison who lined the walls. This decided the day; we got firm footing on the rampart and then rushing into the city overcame all. The contest was however by no means discontinued but continued from street to street, which had been previously fortified and blockaded for that purpose and on passing through these, I could not help remarking that the brave grenadiers of the garrison had unknowingly imputed the conduct of the sacred Thebans band. They lay every man at his post, and died each in their rank as they had fought EYHCOUaNXUagh MGSWV[45] ten or twenty alone survived out of two or three companies who defended the breach.

Driven from the town, the remnant of the enemy retreated into the castle, which something like Windsor, is situated on a very steep hill, but of infinitely more difficult [of] access than the latter, whilst the city was delivered a prey to various raging conflagrations. These had been kindled previous to our entering the place by the French themselves, who had also pillaged & plundered it pretty handsomely during the course of the siege, particularly when the inhabitants towards the latter end had fled. Our troops committed serious excesses which it was impossible to prevent in the fury of the storm, but certainly not to the extent that certain miscreant Spaniards affirm. When

44 This is incorrect. Oman states that the garrison of Burgos consisted of two battalions of the 34e and one of the 130e Ligne. The garrison of San Sebastian consisted of one battalion of the 22e and 34e Ligne, two battalions of the 62e and elements of the 1er and 119e Ligne. Hence it can be seen that only one battalion of the 34e can have been at both sieges.

45 Presumably this is some form of personal cypher.

I entered the town the English were employed in various military works & operations along the walls and also in bombarding the castle, so that it was impossible to extinguish the flames which were fed by a very brisk breeze springing up from the sea & raged in various quarters. Whole streets were actually flaming and the tremendous volume of smoke, the crash of falling houses, added to the thunder of our batteries, formed a picture of horror which it is almost impossible to describe. We continued for the space of five days, throwing 2,000 shells into the castle every twenty four hours and there being no bomb proof or casemates, the garrison were unable to stand such a terrible fire & at length surrendered, by which time St Sebastian was entirely destroyed excepting *forty houses,* in a street adjoining the grand hospital for the French wounded and but for this latter circumstance they would not have escaped the general destruction & in short one may say here St Sebastian once stood, for at present it exists but in name and is one mournful heap of rubbish & ruins, incapable of affording any shelter to its former tenants. Yours most sincerely G U Barlow.

The situation regarding his father came to the fore once again in George's next letter. Still his enemies continued their campaign against him.

To William Barlow Esq, Little Bridge Street, Blackfriars, London
Camp near Vera, 26 September 1813

My dearest uncle,
Your letter of the 9th instant, reached us on the 24th and mine of the 10th acknowledged, I think, the receipt of yours dated the 26th of July together with those of the little girls, in the intermediate space the War Office cover, enclosing the dissents lately printed came safely to hand. First and foremost it is necessary to return you my best thanks for transmitting this valuable little production, more particularly acceptable to me, so remote from those transactions and who takes so deep an interest in their progress. The preface though short is certainly *multum in parvo,*[46] or in a small space contains much to the purpose & enabling me to proceed immediately to the subject, which is also proportionately concise, will secure the attention of a numerous list of the lukewarm & indifferent tribe, who would be otherwise deterred from the perusal of a larger work.

Two most disgusting features in this work of iniquity must particularly catch the eye of every well-informed reader, on arriving at the 10th page, where close the observations regarding Lord Minto & Sir George Nugent.[47] First that the appointment of Lord Moira by a certain great personage,[48]

46 Latin: 'A great deal in a small space'.
47 Lieutenant General Sir George Nugent (1757-1849) was made Commander in Chief in India from 1811-13. Francis Rawdon-Hastings, 2nd Lord Moira, became Governor General of India in 1813, a post he held for 10 years.
48 The Prince Regent was a very close friend of Lord Moira.

originated in no motive of public good, but rather an individual & *as we know*, pecuniary considerations. Hence the haggling about '*salary*', '*appointments*', '*about which no question was to arise*' thus for *one* favoured character, are *three* others, all equally competent for their stations and certainly his equals in capacity & recorded successes, kicked out *sans ceremonie*. Secondly, the demon-like malice which yet rankles at this distant period with unsatiated bitterness, against the object of their past unsuccessful attempts, in the minds of certain directors. Intoxicated by the good fortune that has so unfortunately turned the scale in their favour, the unworthy chairman seems determined to stop at no lengths to gratify his darling & iniquitous passion. For this is the Governor of Madras, removed with most indecent precipitancy; no successor for a permanency can be thought of, no matter whom, take anybody, General Abercrombie or other person,[49] put in Sir George's place, get him out, away with the hated object no matter by what means & I am satisfied. For this, does the same chairman bow the knee & saddle his constituents with an additional £9,000 a year at the beck of ministers and consent to any measure, that he may be allowed his heart's idol. Pages 12 & 13 wind up in good style the dissent of the four directors & the whole is I think a creditable performance to their character as individuals & statesmen.

Much however as we must applaud the preceding paper, it cannot for ability, language, or argument be compared with the accompanying document of Mr Grant. Like every other literary production of the same gentleman, it is a masterpiece, and I really am at a loss from page 28 to the end, to single out any particular part as deserving of peculiar commendation. The whole is written with singular force and animation, nor could a more eloquent appeal for virtues and honour have been issued, had he been pleading in his own cause instead of the distinguished individual in question. The aggravated heap of injustice done him, page 30 condenses into a mass and sets forth in the most glowing colours and I rest fully persuaded that whatever impression could be effected on the public mind by the press as to the justice of our cause has been already made by the efforts of this gentleman & Mr Buchan[an]; may the due result attend their praiseworthy labours.

Colonel Hunt, to whom I made a call on the occasion of going over to St Sebastian, would convey to you a few hasty lines dated the 14th or 15th written in haste. On returning to camp I found matters as usual. There seems to be no chance of a movement till the surrender of Pamplona, now understood to be suffering in a high degree. Experience however has shown us how hard it is to starve out a Frenchman. They will hold out no doubt [torn – to?] the last extremity and then blowing up the works try to escape.

---

49 Lieutenant General John Abercromby had been Commander in Chief of the Bombay army since 1809. He led the forces that gained Mauritius in 1810 and returned to India as Commander in Chief of the Madras Army and temporary Governor of Madras. The Indian climate had however broken his health and he was allowed to return to Britain in 1813.

We are however aware of their plan & will take measures accordingly. Afterwards I think something must be attempted by his lordship, if it is but to make a diversion in favour of the allies & attract some part of the enemy's attention by entering the south of France. The army is very strong with the exception of one or two divisions that have lately suffered, pontoons are in readiness near Irun, in short nothing is wanting but the word, *forward.* I am ignorant however if the seasons will admit of much longer campaigning & am only certain that our animals *must* starve, if we stop here another fortnight, or three weeks. I wish however that on the receipt of this you would cut out of my old French atlas, all the maps on the southern *half* of France, or in other words *everything* south of a *line* beginning at the seaport of *La Rochelle* or *Rochefort,* drawn from thence to *Orleans* & then running across, so as to include the whole of the province formally called *Franche-Comte,* capital of which is Besancon, 'touching the frontiers of Switzerland & Italy'. If it could be contrived to send them out under cover of three or four War Office franks, they would be most valuable as no one possesses any map of France however bad & mine are singularly good.

You may thank my aunt for her kind postscript, I cannot however make out to whom *No. 8* alludes, & in her letter by Major Fergusson the *wafer* was unfortunately put upon the *very place* where she *speaks* of the *marriage* of one of the Miss Harris & I cannot make out which is the fortunate lady. Give my kindest love to all & believe me, your most affectionate nephew G U Barlow

PS Frederick's franks are the most expeditious & safe mode of conveyance of letters for which return him my thanks.

The next letter from George was written after Wellington's army had pushed over the French border, crossing the Bidassoa River at a number of points and attacking the numerous redoubts they had built on the French side of the Pyrenees. The attack plan was for the 95th Rifles and the Portuguese Cacadores to advance as a formidable cloud of skirmishers, which would envelop the French redoubts and the 52nd would then storm them in attack column formation. The advance began at 8:00 a.m. on the 7 October, Colborne's brigade passed to the left of Vera and attacked the heights to its front, whilst the other brigade under Major General James Kempt passed to the right of Vera and attacked the heights in their front, a deep valley separating the two brigades during this attack. Exhausted by the climb to the first redoubt, Colborne's men halted to form up just below the brow of the hill, when the garrison of the redoubt came out and attacked the 52nd, hoping to take advantage of their exhaustion. Only five companies had formed up, but Colborne did not hesitate to counter-charge and drove the French off and won the redoubt. At each redoubt the plan of attack was executed perfectly until the main redoubt was reached. Here the garrison had formed line to repel the 52nd with their fire. Colborne again sent the men forward and the French broke and retired at speed leaving three mountain guns behind. The brigade continued its pursuit down the French slopes and captured 22 officers and nearly 400 men prisoners.

Crossing the Bidassoa by Heath. (Editor's Collection)

In this series of assaults, the losses of the 1/52nd was one sergeant and 11 men killed, with six officers,[50] two sergeants, two buglers and 62 rank and file wounded: a low figure, given the strong positions they had captured.

To William Barlow Esq, Little Bridge Street, Blackfriars, London
Camp in sight of St Jean de Luz, 10 October 1813

My dearest uncle,
Since my last a most material change has taken place in our army and instead of writing to you from *Spain*, I sit down to pen a letter from the *French territories* and fairly within their frontier, on the 6th instant a special messenger arrived from England, bringing the glorious news from Germany[51] and at the same time as I suppose orders for our advance and the whole army was put in motion early the next morning. Lord Wellington with the 1st, 5th & a Spanish Division was to cross the Bidassoa in front of Irun among the flats & ours supported by the 4th to make an attack on the enemy opposite to whom we have been so long posted. You have often heard me speak of

50 Major William Mein was severely wounded, Captains Patrick Campbell (slightly), John Douglas (severely) and John Sheddon (slightly), Lieutenant William Hunter (severely) and Ensign John Frazer (died of his wounds 19 October).

51 Following the French victory of Dresden on 27 August, the French suffered defeat at Dennewitz on 6 September.

the formidable heights & pass of Vera, to the natural strength of which, the French had not failed to make great additions by numerous redoubts & entrenchments, and they actually were hard at work with spades & pickaxes to the very last hour of the assault which was directed against them early on the morning of the 7th crowned as you will shortly see with the compleatest success.

About nine in the morning, all the arrangements having been compleated in the most admirable manner, the columns advanced to the post of the enemies position. The right brigade of the Light Division under General Kempt, assaulted the main pass flanked by General Giron's Spanish Division, the left brigade under Colonel Colborne of the 52nd (who acted as brigadier, General Skerrett having left us for England) ascended the adjacent heights, the 95th & Portuguese riflemen climbing up the woods & precipices, in all directions, whilst the 52nd Regiment forming the main attack advanced in close column to storm the main ridge of the enemies position. This latter was so narrow as to allow only of *one single company* passing abreast and we had advanced in one compact & solid mass instead of a line as usual. On the first rising ground stood a redoubt which kept up a very severe & well directed fire. A strong body of troops were formed close in the rear who drove in the skirmishers & showed a disposition to advance down upon the columns. Five companies of the 52nd had arrived about forty yards in front of the work when their brave colonel ordered a charge of the bayonet. This was given with a loud shout in the best manner & the fort instantly carried whilst the astonished enemy turned tail & fled up to their next entrenchments, pursued as fast in our fagged & tired state as was possible. Two other lines of entrenchments were successively carried in the same style, the enemy keeping up a very heavy fire from along the whole line, till the attacking column arrived within charging distance at thirty or forty yards. A general rush & shout was then given & the enemy invariably ran, whilst we allowed them no breathing. Three pieces of cannon were tumbled down the precipices & between three & four hundred prisoners made. Their loss in killed & wounded was very considerable, particularly upon the 9th Regiment of light infantry. The pursuit was very hot & close & had this decided advantage, having left all our men's haversacks in camp, who consequently had the head of the routed enemy, who were driven close to St Jean de Luz in the flat country below the French side of the Pyrenees. The sight that burst upon us on arriving at the summit of the position was most exquisite, the beautiful plain of Guienne extending around for many miles together with Bayonne, St Jean de Luz & many beautiful villages, the country beautifully intersected with hedges, full of farmhouses, corn fields & in short, like the best cultivated part of England. I went into a farmhouse near which my picquet was posted on the morning of the 8th. All the people had fled, leaving however plenty of good hay & corn and fowls & pigs & all that was good. God bless you all my dear uncle, I write in much haste but in the best health & spirits & promising you a more detailed account when more at leisure. Believe me your most affectionate nephew G U Barlow

George also recounted to his friend, his regular fraternisation with French officers at the outposts.

No.7
To A[ndrew] Amos Esq, to the care of J[ames] Amos Esq
Camp in front of St Jean de Luz, 24 October 1814 [actually 1813]

My dear Amos,
During the temporary suspension of hostilities which the blockade of Pamplona obliges us to maintain, I have had two or three opportunities of meeting our gallic neighbours on rather more friendly terms than usual. This was a source of novelty to me who had never encountered them before on any other than those of angry defiance. Possessing some smattering of French, I was dispatched on a mission to their advanced posts with some letters & money for English officers, prisoners of war in France. I advanced accompanied by a trumpeter, holding a white handkerchief in my hand and scrambled up the hill as fast as possible, to gain a view of their position behind. They seemed however to guess at my intentions & spared me that trouble by running down half-way to meet me, five or six in number, all officers; happening to make a stop, one of them held out his hand and said '*doucement*' [gently] adding shortly afterwards '*je suis charme de vous voir*' [I am charmed to meet you] in the true style of a Parisian petit maitre. I soon unfolded the objects of my mission and whilst a report was sent to the general I remained in conversation with them upwards of an hour & a half. They were tolerably genteel young men & seemed much superior to the generality of their officers, at least from what I had been informed. Their corps was the 70th of the Line, I have heard it bears a very high character. A most lively chat ensued interspersed, on their part, with a vast deal of wit and brusquerie, so peculiarly characteristic of their nation. The fair sex in particular were a favourite topic; speaking of their own country women '*quoique elles acent un peu de libertin, elles sent pas les pires pour cela*' [Even though they are a little libertine, they aren't the worse for it] observed one of them, concurring also that I possessed the usual penchant of John Bull for spiritous liquors, they were very profuse of their brandy. A variety of sprightly remarks followed from each in succession and never, I confess, did I pass a pleasanter hour, than in conversation of those fellows, who the next day with just as much readiness [would] have given me a *coup de grace* and myself vice versa. We had talked a good deal about dancing, upon taking leave therefore, one of them expressed his hope to meet some of our nation at a French Ball, at the same time putting his arms & hands in a theatrical attitude & cutting a caper, which caused me to laugh most immoderately.

The weather continues to be most beautiful, though rather cold. It is pretty well adapted however to our present occupations. We have had of late I am ashamed to say, several desertions, in consequence of which the picquets have been everywhere doubled and the outpost duty become particularly severe, keeping me out of bed almost every other night. Our opposite neighbours however seem more to dread an attack, than entertain any idea of paying us a visit. Hundreds of men are daily employed in raising entrenchments & batteries along the whole site of their naturally strong position, which is the identical one marked out in the Revolutionary War of 1793 as their barrier against invading enemies. Just along the top ridge runs the boundary line marked by mile posts, which separate France from Spain, so that you see we are very near violating the territory of the great nation. It will however be a tough job, whenever an attack takes place, as the position is one of the stiffest I ever have seen, independent of the formidable entrenchments with which it is covered & it is more than probable that the *first* man who steps across the boundary will realize the ball.

October 10th

A new era has now presented itself in our operations, a British Army across the sacred territory and within sight of the walls of Bayonne obtains a permanent footing on French ground. Such are the inscrutable decrees of providence, whose finger evidently appears throughout the late continental & peninsula campaigns to have singularly favoured the cause of justice. That army which was to have driven the English into the sea, and threatened at once Cadiz & Lisbon, now is ignominiously chased and forced to seek refuge under the cannon of Bayonne. I will now endeavour to give you an abstract accessing of what share the Light Division bore in bringing about these auspicious events.

About noon on the 6th instant, a confused hum and rumour passed through the camp about an attack on the opposite hills & upon enquiry I soon ascertained its correctness. Every arrangement was made for that purpose, to commence the same at daylight. The dawn broke and was ushered in by the French picquets firing upon the Spanish guerrilla skirmishers & shortly afterwards the whole division moved on and began ascending the hills, the 95th & Portuguese cacadores clearing the way *en tirailleur*, whilst the 52nd Regiment followed close at hand in a solid column. On coming however at a pretty stiff redoubt, the tirailleurs were brought to a flank, but the 52nd hung close at hand to support, charged en masse and carried the redoubt at the point of [the] bayonet. The enemy keeping up a very hot fire till we arrived within thirty yards of their line & upon our giving a loud shout & rushing forward to charge, they turned tail & broke in all directions. Three or four successive lines of entrenchments were thus stormed, one after the other, we moving up in their front under a very severe fire, but upon making a charge, the enemy always yielding. They were driven from every part of their position, losing a great number of killed & wounded & leaving three pieces of cannon, 24 officers and 400 prisoners in our hands,[52] belonging to the 9th Legere & 26th & 47th of the line, which three regiments were immediately opposed to our brigade, as

52 Moorsom, *History of the 52nd Regiment*, p.205, records 22 officers and 400 men captured.

the 34th, 70th & 100th were to General Kempt's.[53] This latter general did not meet much opposition on his side, as the fate of the day was quickly decided by our brigade, which gained the flank of the Vera pass & compelled the enemy to fly, without being able much to oppose his advance.

Early on the commencement of the day, the captain who commanded the leading company was severely wounded[54] & your humble servant during the remainder of it, held the post of honour & for his pains, got a pretty smart rap on the *left arm*, from a spent ball, which rebounded from thence on his breast, but did not further injury. Never did I feel more pleased than by the spirit which our men showed on this occasion & all expressing their wish to close with the bayonet. The brigade lost about 350 men;[55] never shall I forget the animating moment when we first crossed the boundary line & arrived on the summit of these tremendous hills. At our feet lay the fine places of Gascony, stretching as far as the eye could reach, until lost in immensity of. There a little in front was the town of St Jean de Luz, surrounded with a highly cultivated country, abounding in farms, enclosures & cultivation and exactly the picture of the finest counties of England. It was a trial of speed, who had the best legs, during the two first miles we ran into France as the enemy did not observe any order & we gave them little or no rest till they came under the guns of their entrenched camp around St Jean de Luz, two miles from which we are at present encamped & where it is supposed we shall wait the fall of Pamplona, now said to be reduced to the last extremity. Yours most sincerely G U Barlow.

P.S. Of protestations on the frozen hands.

George had time to write to his uncle regarding promotion and also the latest politics. He betrayed a strong fear that the local French population would prove as determined against the army once they entered France, as the Spanish had been against the French invasion. Nevertheless, they would have to advance off the mountains before the winter set in, as they were already virtually under water from the heavy rains.

Camp in front of St Jean de Luz, 8 November 1813

My dearest uncle,
Circumstances as detailed in my postscript to Miss Page's letter of the 1st instant prevented me from more immediately acknowledging the receipt of your kind letter of the 23rd of September, accompanying the French maps enclosed in one of Frederick's franks. You mention therein having delivered

53 Major General James Kempt commanded a brigade of the Light Division

54 This must refer to Captain John Graham Douglas, the only officer of this rank to be severely wounded.

55 The entire Light Division only lost two officers and 49 men killed and 13 officers and 177 wounded at the passage of the Bidassoa.

my letter to [obliterated on purpose by some other hand] but depend upon it I shall entertain no extravagant hopes in consequence of his declarations. Fair promises are a currency so generally in use among subalterns desirous of promotion, that I do not attach any great importance to them, however literally they may be bestowed on me. I have heard however from a very different quarter of Sir S[amuel] Auchmuty's exertions on my behalf, and therefore return you my best thanks for calling on the general and acknowledging the same.

As for the maps they are peculiarly accessible, none bad, good or indifferent being obtainable in this country. The hopes of the most sanguine never could have expected that the campaign which commenced at Salamanca would terminate within the eight miles of the walls of Bayonne, such however are the decrees of providence which throughout the course of this eventful year, has in all quarters favoured in a most marked manner the cause of justice and rendered our noble chief the instrument of its designs. Pamplona, I find has at length surrendered so that now not a Frenchman remains in the Spanish peninsula,[56] excepting a few at its most distant extremity around Barcelona & its neighbourhood.

By the papers, it would seem that none [of] your good politicians venture to chalk out, as heretofore, the line of conduct which his lordship is in future to pursue. The field of conjecture is here as wide, as those of Gascony now under my view. A British army never can invade France, more especially in this distant quarter, with any view of territorial aggrandisement. Nature evidently has placed these hills as the proper limits of demarkation between France & Spain; and the project of restoring the Bourbons is abandoned by all the best statesmen.[57] France under any future Louis or great man would always prove our natural enemy & whether Bonaparte or Bernadotte are its rulers, she must be kept down alike by an equal balance of power among her neighbours. To restore the equilibrium, the labours of our brave allies seem fast tending. Such at least is the tenor of their professions and to promote so laudable an undertaking I should think will be the principal aim of all our future operations. This will be best effected by creating a most powerful diversion on our side, preventing any reinforcements from being dispatched to Germany, besieging Bayonne and advancing eighty or a hundred miles into the country [&] kick up all the dust we can; till at length confined within his natural boundaries and overpowered beneath the gigantic blows of a confederated Europe, the foe is compelled to a form of lasting peace.

Let us now examine what degree of strength England is capable of putting forth, to bringing about so desirable an issue. You have an army limited indeed as to numbers (45,000 of all descriptions present & effective at *the*

56 The French garrison of Pamplona surrendered on 31 October 1813.

57 This is correct as to the prevailing view of the various countries fighting Napoleon, but in the end no viable alternative could be identified and they were duly returned to power, with King Louis XVIII taking the throne.

utmost) but equal, whether in regard to equipment, discipline & science & physical strength to any in the world. These good qualities added as they are by such a general as Lord Wellington, can operate however but to a certain extent. Our cause in Spain to which every good Frenchman might be a well-wisher, assumes a very different complexion when as invaders we enter his native soil. Every heart & hand would then most cordially unite in one great work & every internal discontent be healed up in the main object of getting rid of us. National pride, as well as patriotism would be set at work & we have before our eyes an example of what an armed population can effect against armies twenty times more powerful than our own & enjoying perhaps greater advantages & which amidst this pretty & harassing warfare, have at length frittered away into imbecility & even non-existence.

None of these obstacles however can cramp our impending or more immediate operations. Please God, the same troops who have hitherto stormed so many fortresses & entrenched positions, will obtain a similar success in carrying that upon the Nivelle. Opposite to us I really believe are 70,000 men and most accounts agreeing stating near 80,000. A line of works perhaps as compleat & formidable as ever were seen, redoubts, batteries &c are allotted them for to defend. The country is moreover very woody and everywhere enclosed with strong thick hedges like Surry [sic] or any other part of England, which is very favourable to their constant practise of skirmishing & making long shots. These local advantages to them are of the greatest importance, as speaking most impartially the French army is by no means what it formerly was. To make up its present imposing complement, an unusual proportion of raw recruits & young conscripts have been added. By the emperor's desire, 30,000 were raised in the provinces adjoining the Pyrenees about a month from hence. Of their *morale* (to use Bonaparte's phrase) the late affair on these hills was no very brilliant specimen, any more than a trifling circumstance which occurred the other day, on taking in the flag of truce, after writing the postscript to Miss Page's letter. I went in with no other attendant than a trumpeter & myself perfectly unarmed. The country as I have before said is very enclosed & woody, so that upon turning the corner of a hedge, I suddenly popped upon three of them within twenty yards; standing beneath a large tree at a farmhouse. I called out '*Parlementaire*' & exhibited a white handkerchief, whilst the bugler 'blew a blast' without stopping an instant, the valiant trio took to their heels as fast as they could run & fled to their picquet, one of them discharging his piece to give the alarm. Here I was halted by a large felled tree, the bushy head of which filled up the road & prevented any passage. At length, two old hands whom I spied sneaking & reconnoitring around a hedge came up, presently afterwards followed the officer & then the remainder of the party. They apologized for so uncivil a reception, saying that the sentinels were young troops. This declaration [torn – was?] perfectly needless; the clownish gait & boyish youth of the whole assemblage [torn – with?] one or two exceptions whom it was easy enough to discriminate, so forcibly strong that I enquired of the officer, if they were not of the last conscription, which [torn – he?] acknowledged was the fact. Never was outpost duty or watch kept in a more slovenly manner, nor from the above specimen do I think the conduct of the troops likely to have repaired any hobble into which they might have fallen by a want of vigilance.

Let happen what will, any change for us in our present situation must be for the better. The severity of a Pyrenean climate in winter is very well known & we already begin to feel the effects. Torrents of the heaviest rain constantly fall by night & day attended with violent westerly winds. Our camp though on the top of a hill is a perfect swamp and many of the tents little better than sieves (to use a joke current amongst ourselves), we need not look far for a draught of water. Make a small hole in the ground & a spring rises in the middle of the tent. But speaking seriously, nothing can exceed the misery of being constantly wet both by day & night, with a thermometer almost as low as freezing point; the weather is extremely pinching, the animals half-starved and despite of the double allowances of grog given to the troops, they will soon suffer most terribly if a change into the low country does not very soon take place, this however we know will very soon happen. As for my part I enjoy the very best health though my right arm most sensibly feels the changes of climate & at times expose a very great degree of weakness. This however is always the consequence of so bad a fracture. My good stars prevented me from leaving behind at Lisbon my stock of *flannels* & I now really find them worth their carriage dues this summer. Nothing of that sort or in the worsted way, are to be procured here, some common coarse soldiers stockings which cost sixteen or eighteen pence in England, are sold at eight or nine shillings a pair in Vera some days since.

With regard to the £118 10s 0d you need not open any running account. Upon leaving England, my allowance was paid to the end of 1813 & hence since my arrival in this country I have drawn bills to the amount of 130 or £140 which receipt as in a former letter, I desired is to be paid out of the above issued gratuity as far as it goes; nor if possible will I draw for any further sums during the course of this year.

God bless you all, give my best love to my aunt, for her hand postscript, as well as to all the dear little girls and believe me, your most affectionate nephew G U Barlow

P.S. Be so good as to deliver the enclosure to Frederick for his friend.

George's next letter home announced that he had been wounded again. This time he had been shot in the foot at the Battle of the Nivelle on 10 November 1813. On the night before, the 1/52nd, then commanded by Brevet Major Patrick Campbell, moved silently to a position only three hundred metres from the French line of fortifications on the heights of La Petite Rhune. Advancing at daybreak the troops rapidly outflanked these redoubts and the French hurriedly abandoned them, having offered very little resistance. The brigade remained here, until the objectives set for other divisions were also met and the village of Sarre cleared of French

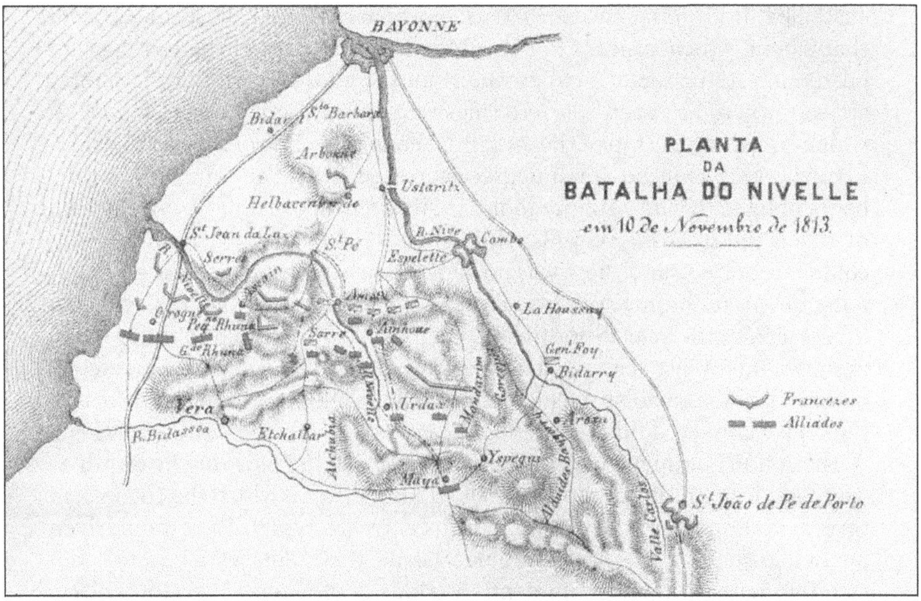

Plan of the Battle of Nivelle. (Editor's Collection)

troops. Initially a number of further redoubts were taken with relative ease, but then the 1/52nd encountered a stronger star fort, from which emanated a heavy fire of musketry. Two efforts to launch an attack by wings were beaten back with heavy losses, the 12-foot-high scarp proving impossible to mount without ladders, and the regiment retired slightly to reform. Luckily successes elsewhere cut off the garrison's retreat over the Bridge of Amotz and they duly surrendered, following a parley. Five hundred and sixty men were captured here. In these attacks, the regiment lost two sergeants and 30 rank and file killed and six officers,[58] seven sergeants, three buglers and 192 men wounded.

To William Barlow Esq, Little Bridge Street, Blackfriars, London
Vera, 11 November 1813

My dearest uncle,
By yesterday's returns you will see that I have again found a place among the list of the unlucky. I am pretty severely touched up but thank God that it was not worse. My left foot is a good deal shattered, a musket ball having entered close to the ankle and passing through the centre of the instep, came out underneath in the hollow of the same. The extent of the injury I have not as yet been able to ascertain, having as yet undergone a very cursory examination and am ignorant whether the above joint has

58 The officers wounded were Captain William Rentall (severely), Lieutenants Charles Yorke (slightly), George Barlow (severely) Matthew Anderson (severely) Charles Kenny (slightly) and Matthew Agnew (slightly).

sustained any injury, though I trust no material one. I suspect however that a bone which appears to bound the inside hollow of the foot has not been quite so fortunate as to escape from the above description. You may conceive there has been a severe smash among the small bones & sinews, which run along the top of the foot, this renders it a case of the most painful nature, which is in no small degree increased by the circumstance of my being obliged to *ride* with my foot dangling five or six miles from the field of action and bleeding very fast. This town is the nearest place where cover could be obtained and there was no alternative between proceeding for it or lying out all night in a solitary ravine at the foot of the Pyrenees, which at this season of the year is not the most agreeable. Jose, I told to follow close to the regiment just keeping out of fire & leading my horse with a greatcoat, blanket & some eatables; he luckily came up to the spot soon afterwards & thus was I conveyed off.

The action commenced at daylight about six in the morning by our division assaulting the lower mountain of La Rhune, upon which the enemy had three battalions in position with various entrenchments. They were driven out of it in such style as not to be able to strike their tents, which were taken standing with all their equipments. Various manoeuvres then took place, while we were kept back during the attack of the Fourth Division on Sarre. As soon as this had made a certain progress, we again pushed forward, our brigade leading. In front was a very strong commanding height, the key of that part of their position which they had taken special pains to fortify the same, with two or three star works, each capable of containing five or six hundred men with three or four entrenchments in advance, half way down the hill, which of itself was of no ordinary steepness or size. We were ascending it & storming these latter defences under a very hot fire when I met with my accident. I saw very plainly the gentlemen to whom I was more immediately indebted for it, but in the same style as usual, they ran away the moment our people arrived at charging distance. It was from the flanking face of one of the entrenchments.

This conquest being affected, another remained of equal difficulty with the former, in a large fort commanding the surrounding country. I beheld the brigade go up to it in the handsomest manner & as soon as it arrived on the glacis, the garrison beat a parley & surrendered to the number of 550 men & we were equally glad to allow them terms, as it could not have been carried without a frightful loss of blood.

Thus far have I detailed all the circumstances which fell under my view till ten o'clock in the morning, the time I was obliged to retire. Marshal Soult I believe had calculated pretty fairly on keeping his ground; he need not now however trouble himself any further in choosing positions or constructing works, since his men will not, with everything in their favour, resolutely defend them.

I am at present very comfortable in a snug house & the people very civil. I feel very weak & of course cannot move an inch but in other respects as

La Rhune Mountain in the Pyrenees by Batty. (Editor's Collection)

to health & spirits perfectly well. God bless you all & believe me your affectionate nephew G U Barlow

I only received *two days* since the nice letter of the dear little girls, give them my very best love & thanks.

George wrote again, informing his uncle that he was being sent to England to recuperate but he no held hope of being home for Christmas.

To William Barlow Esq, Little Bridge Street, Blackfriars, London
Vera, 10 December 1813

My dearest uncle,
I take every opportunity of dispatching a line when anyone proceeds to the regiment, not knowing when another may occur. In my last to little Anne[59] dated the *1st of this month* I stated that the Medical Board had granted me leave homewards, but it was afterwards discovered that our chief Asclepius had not drawn up the proceedings in *proper form*;[60] another board was therefore held on the 5th, my leave renewed. Owing to the most unaccountable delays however, the certificates were not dispatched to headquarters until this morning and I can form no idea when they will be returned with the official approvals as the army are now in motion along the whole line &

59 Anne Caroline was a younger sister born in Calcutta on 16 March 1803. This letter has not been found.

60 Asclepius was the Greek God of medicine, hence he refers to the chief surgeon.

his lordship of course is gone to the front & has at present something else to think about than signing sick certificates. As yet we have had no authentic particulars either of yesterday's or today's actions,[61] though I entertain no doubt as to their favourable issue. By this time we have probably crossed the Nive & compleatly invested both the town & citadel of Bayonne.

As for myself, I am just in the situation of a man who has been confined to his bed a month & living upon low diet, whom a fly could utmost upset. I have however nothing to complain of, as my foot will now permit one to lie on my back & turn on the left side; which is truly a comfort, after a gathering had broke on my right hip from constant pressure.[62] Three or four days ago I put on my clothes and yesterday by way of a wonderful feat, I put my leg into a sling and thus crawled with my crutches into the kitchen.

In truth, I long very much to partake of the comforts of an English fireside; nothing of the sort is known here. The weather is now very cold & you may imagine my situation, unable to take exercise or quicken the circulation of the blood & as for the charcoal pans, they always annoy me with headaches.

A mail has arrived from England with papers & letters up to the 25th ultimo, I know not at present whether there are any from you as [I am] not with the regiment. I have seen your advertisement of the publication against Marsh & long much to peruse it.[63]

From what I have before stated, it is impossible to fix with any certainty the period of my embarkation at Passages [Pasajes] & there is no chance of my eating my Christmas dinner with you at Streatham as I could have wished and indeed shall think myself lucky if I come in for a slice of the twelfth night cake. As for my father, I suppose we need not expect him till the ensuing February or March.

God bless you all and with my kindest love to my aunt & all the little ones, believe me your most affectionate nephew, G U Barlow

No.8
To A[ndrew] Amos Esq, to the care of J[ames] Amos Esq
Vera among the Pyrenees, 13 December 1814 [Actually 1813]

My dear Amos,
Long ere this my good fellow will you have seen me numbered among the unfortunate. It is indeed rather unlucky that a shadow like mine should so often get in harm's way and it reflects some credit on the French tirailleurs

61 The Battle of the Nive was fought between 9-12 December 1813. The 1/52nd was not heavily involved in this fighting, losing only 4 rank and file killed, with six officers and 15 other ranks wounded and four more returned 'missing'.

62 He describes a bed sore.

63 William Barlow had employed no less than the poet Robert Southey to write a rebuttal of Marsh's claims. Southey wrote a pamphlet entitled *An Exposure of the Misrepresentations and Calumnies in Mr Marsh's Review of Sir George Barlow's Administration at Madras. By the Relatives of Sir George Barlow* (1813).

for having hit so small a mark. Nevertheless, I cannot murmur, where many others have fallen never to rise again, possessing also the consoling opinions expressed by the best medical advice, that my cure though painful and one probably of great tedious steps, will nevertheless be compleat. In other words, it was a plunging shot fired in a perpendicular direction as we were ascending a hill & entering close to the left ancle [sic] bone on the top of the instep, passed through the foot & came out at the sole underneath, carrying gaiter, stockings & all in its course. The old saying of a miss is as good as a mile may be applied to my case. The ball grazed close by the ancle [sic] & my injury to which would probably have rendered amputation necessary, or at all events would have been succeeded by a stiff joint. My temperate habits, aided by a naturally good constitution have as in former instances served very conspicuous. Past experience as you well know, must have taught me what I had to expect & suffer. My mind was therefore made up for this repetition of former calamity. The first few days I experienced a deal of pain and though nature was uniformly kind throughout, three small splinters were extracted from the orifice & several still however yet remained. My foot would admit of but one posture, namely that of laying stretched at full length on the right side. Nor could I as much as once turn on my back, or left hip. Thus, for the space of three weeks, did I keep my bed, until reduced to a wretched state of weakness so as to be unable to stand and having an abscess formed on the right hip bone, by such considerable and constant pressure during the above period. I am at present a miserable object and have only put on my clothes within this last day or two & changed my hated posture from the right side. My foot in the meanwhile is propped up with a mountain of pillows & bolsters and this to continue to sit on my bottom & write to you and amuse myself. In the meanwhile, a board of surgeons have sat on my case and recommended me for leave to England, whither I propose proceeding as soon as I am capable of being moved.

It is necessary now to resume the thread of my narrative, where it was broken off and which I think left us in daily expectation of the fall of Pamplona. The citadel of this place is the work of Vauban, and one of his masterpieces and deservedly may be reckoned the key of Spain on this side. General Casan with 4,000 men was shut up in the place.[64] To reduce him by force would have cost a multitude of lives, especially as the glacis was separately mined and it being a notorious fact that the place was not sufficiently provisioned, in consequence of the unexpected Battle of Vitoria and our subsequent rapid pursuit, his lordship most wisely determined on starving him into submission. For that purpose, Don Carlos' Spanish army had ever since kept it in strict blockade.[65] Soult had, as has been seen, made various desperate efforts to raise the siege as well as that of St Sebastian but with uniform ill success. At length he abandoned it to its fate with directions

64 *Général de Brigade* Louis Pierre Cassan commanded a garrison of around 3,800 men.

65 The blockade of Pamplona was initially commanded by General Henry O'Donnell and later by General Carlos de Espana.

however, to hold out to the last extremity, an order which the governor most literally obeyed, since the longer he held out, the longer was Lord W[ellington] prevented from executing any scheme of invasion against France or Soult.

About the 6th instant, he had the impudence to propose a capitulation on condition of returning with his garrison to France. This was of course rejected & three days afterwards, surrendered at discretion with these fine few troops unconquered & unbended, having done everything that was capable within the walls.

In this interval the British army lay quiet in the position which had been taken up immediately on our passage of the Bidassoa, in the affair of the 7th of October; the right at Roncesvalles and the left touching the sea. The Light Division was posted towards the centre, attacking the last ridge of the Pyrenees, previous to entering the flat country, from hence we had a minute view of the enemies positions & force & another officer had offered our services to watch their movements; so that alternately, every other day, from exercising till night with my glass consistently in hand, was I perched on top of a high Pyrenee for that purpose. The season was particularly inclement, such as no period of time will ever efface from memory. The thermometer must have been almost as low as freezing point which rendered the incessant deluges of heavy rain & hail almost insupportable. Mighty gusts of wind would sometimes start up on a sudden at midnight and blow down our tents whilst companies & squadrons poured out the full measure of their pitchers upon our miserable camps. Day & night did these torrents run through everything and we might be termed contemptuous [of] living as we lived more in water than on land. These tempests were succeeded by heavy falls of snow which pretty nigh buried General Hill's picquets alive near Roncesvalles & rendered the way impassable, so that all the hours of passing a winter encamped on the top of the Pyrenees began to stare us in the face, when an order arrived on the 9th instant for a general attack along the enemy's whole line. For this prospect we quitted our camp about dark and favoured by the tremendous inequalities of the ground, arrived about half past eleven underneath a small ridge within cannon shot of the enemy's advanced division. Here we drew up en-masse and lay in ambush all night, ready to surprize the foe at dawn. Every man lay down in his ranks and no noise or any fires were allowed. The plan was, I understand suggested by our excellent Colonel Colborne & was certainly most admirable. The position of the foe was rendered strong both by nature & art and little did he dream of our being so close on his flank, I might almost say in his rear. At daylight, upon the firing of a certain number of cannon, the battle commenced by General Kempt's Brigade and the 43rd Regiment moving up most handsomely in front of their entrenchments & storming the same, whilst our brigade rapidly dashed to get in their rear. These joint manoeuvres proved incontestable. The enemy broke like a flock of sheep & every man endeavoured to save himself as well as he could, this was indeed the best plan, so had they endeavoured to afford their retreat in any degree of order or method they would have been intercepted to a certainty. As it was, their escape was most narrow, *five minutes* more & we should have had them snug enough. But being obliged to keep our ranks in pursuing them, the trial of speed was unequal, they ran the gauntlet however, under a pretty smart fire, from the whole division & we took all their tents, stores, baggage &c. I cannot conceive any operation done in a more prompter, soldier-like manner, everything to use the French gasconading term was carried at the *pas de charge*. Having attained these objects, we halted for a couple of hours & beheld the rest of the army engaged from our elevated position, as far as the sea on one side and the Maya pass on the other. When they had arrived upon nearly the same advanced line as ourselves, the 3rd, 4th & Light Divisions directed on the village of Sarre, the key of the French position, where their chief force was concentrated. It fell to the lot of our brigade & the 52nd Regiment to attack the redoubts & entrenchments on its right. We advanced up to their teeth under a most severe & well directed fire. On arriving [at] about thirty yards, I beheld several men pop their heads above the parapet & fire in the direction where I then was, immediately several musket balls fell close to me & at the same time was pinned through the foot. I did not fall and finding it impossible to be able to proceed & being in the thick of a very hot fire, in the confusion of the moment, I made shift to move to a hedge about twenty or thirty yards & there dropped.

My Portuguese boy Jose, followed close out of fire with my horse & blankets. I was lifted up on *Lancelot* my charger & moved up a road to the place, a distance of five or six miles. The effort I knew must cost me great pain, but there was no alternative between that or laying out in the fields all night, which prospect among the Pyrenees and in the month of November I by no means desired. I therefore came back and took up quarters in as much comfort as I could, where I am now. Yours Sincerely G U Barlow

10

A Change of Regiment

George left the Peninsula at the end of December 1813 and he was never to return there, as whilst he was in England he finally achieved his ambition and was gazetted to be a captain, but in a different regiment. On 30 December 1813 it was announced that George was to be the captain of a company in the 2nd Battalion 69th Regiment of Foot (South Lincolnshire), by purchase, vice Captain the Honourable John Allen, who transferred into the 45th (Nottinghamshire) Regiment of Foot. His father had clearly supplied the additional funds to purchase George the captaincy, requiring no less an outlay than £950.[1]

Clearly however, George could not venture to join his new regiment, which was serving in a force under the command of Sir Thomas Graham in Holland, until he had recovered from his wound. He was perhaps particularly fortunate in this enforced delay as the 2nd Battalion was heavily involved in the disastrous attempt to capture the fortress of Bergen op Zoom, across the frozen moat, on 8 March 1814. Initially successful, the French garrison rallied and eventually forced the British troops who had entered the fortress to surrender. The 2/69th lost their colours during the confusion, a major disgrace.[2] The battalion lost one officer and eight men killed and four officers and 23 men wounded, but it is recorded that another two officers and 89 men were missing. A Return of the forces in Holland on 25 April 1814 state that the 2/69th only mustered 210 men.[3]

On 13 April 1814, following the fall of Paris, Napoleon agreed to abdicate and Europe celebrated the end of 21 years of almost interminable war finally coming to an end.

In June, the Allied sovereigns visited Britain together, before they left for the continuation of the Congress of Vienna. It is almost certain that George would have witnessed their visit to London and the great festivities that ensued, but unfortunately we have no knowledge of his life during this period as he and all of his family

1 The captaincy cost £1,500, but £550 could be recouped by the sale of his lieutenancy.

2 There are a great number of conflicting reports regarding how many colours were lost by the 69th at Bergen op Zoom and it is impossible to be certain if they lost one or both Colours there. We know for certain that the battalion had two colours during the Waterloo campaign, but do not know if one or two were new replacements. Given that the colours held in Paris are unidentifiable because of damage, I tend to favour the fact that both colours of the 2/69th were captured and were replaced before the Waterloo campaign.

3 Quoted in Andrew Bamford *A Bold and Ambitious Enterprise* (Barnsley: Pen and Sword, 2013), pp.276.

were now resident in England, precluding the need to write. We do however, gain a glimpse of George in August 1814, when he wrote to his father, whilst visiting his Uncle Robert and family at Chatham, but he still failed to make any comment as to when he would be fit enough to join his new regiment.

To Sir G H Barlow Bart KB, Streatham, Surrey
Chatham, 19 August 1814

My dearest father,
Annexed I transmit you Captain Talbot's letter to my uncle respecting Charles and am only concerned that my pleasure rising from his good conduct should be so much qualified by unpleasant accounts as to the state of his health, amounting even to the question of his further continuance in the service.[4] That the liver should show itself at the poor little fellow's tender age and with such decided symptoms is most afflicting and appears somewhat strange. Nevertheless, even in the absence of all other information, I cannot help entertaining hopes that the nature of his complaint, may have been mistaken.[5] Boys of his age are generally more or less delicate & changes of climate added to a salt provision diet, together with much exposure to weather, perhaps have a little disorganised his health, though I trust not to the extent stated, of a liver affliction. My uncle however in anticipation of your wishes has secured a berth for him on a nice new frigate commanded by a Captain James now fitting out, it is supposed for the American station,[6] should his continuance in the profession be deemed advisable & Captain Talbot have not otherwise provided for him.

The Admiralty folks quitted us this morning for Sheerness, after dining with us yesterday. On such an occasion my uncle studiously avoided bringing Lord Melville's notice to your affairs during the evening,[7] however he was greatly surprised at his lordship calling him aside to a separate corner of the room & bringing [up] himself the subject, in the hopes in the course of conversation my uncle noticed Peter's letter,[8] which Lord M[elville] expressed a desire to see and has been promised a copy. The sooner one is made out & transmitted to my uncle the better, who writes himself to forward it [to] Lord M[elville], my uncle then observed that you bore your lot with equanimity & that the late proceedings [torn – have?] not annoyed you in any over-great degree. His lordship replied that 'they need not, or [torn – believes?] you would have no occasion to be so' or words to that effect. Here the conversation suddenly ceased, as if his lordship thought

4 This must refer to Captain Sir John Talbot Royal Navy who commanded HMS *Victorious*, which was then blockading the busy whaling port of New London in Conneticut.

5 His younger brother Charles Anstruther Barlow eventually became a captain in the Royal Navy and lived until 1855.

6 Captain Joseph James RN was then fitting out the fir-built HMS *Tanais* of 38 guns, for the Jamaica station.

7 Robert Dundas, 2nd Viscount Melville, was First Lord of the Admiralty from 1812-27.

8 There is no obvious candidate as to who Peter was, he was not family.

that he had rather committed himself too far. From these and several other hints thrown out in the course of the interview my uncle is inclined to believe that your 'refutation' has been already under the serious discussion of the Cabinet, that the ministers are favourably disposed, although nothing fell from Lord Melville on which any certain or specific conjectures could be grounded, as to the particular manner in which their good offices could be exerted.

All the good folks [&] uncle in kindest love to you & my mother & in extreme impatience for your proposed visit & with my love to all the school room. Believe me your dutiful & affectionate son George Barlow.

P.S. My uncle desires that his communication with Lord Melville may be considered as most confidential.

With the war ending, the British troops were moved into Belgium to help guard the border against French incursions. The 2/69th were at Tournai on 15 September 1814 when Lieutenant General Henry Clinton reviewed them. That day they consisted of 18 officers and only 388 other ranks and were commanded by Lieutenant Colonel George Muttlebury in the absence of Lieutenant Colonel Charles Morris [sic].[9] It is fair to say that Clinton was not impressed, stating that 'There is nothing in the appearance of this regiment which marks attention in a commanding officer'.[10]

Clinton inspected them again on 6 January 1815 when he found that they numbered a much healthier, 25 officers and 505 other ranks and he found the troops free of almost all of the faults he had picked up previously. The battalion monthly returns show an increase in numbers in May 1814 to 436, presumably with the return of the prisoners and the wounded who had recovered from Bergen op Zoom. In October 1814 the Return suddenly increases by nearly another 100 men to a figure just under 500 men. It is not known where this large draft of men came from. What was of concern, however, was that Clinton stated that Colonel Morice was 'much at a loss in moving his battalion'.[11]

We do not know exactly when George arrived with the regiment at Ypres, but it is likely that he arrived there in October 1814. The first letter we have from George's time with the 2/69th was sent from their cantonments at Ypres near the French border only five days after this second review, which he does not mention. What George thought of his new regiment is not clear, but he must have found it a very different experience to the 52nd. George was appointed to the command of No. 10 Company, which at Waterloo had a strength of only 59 men. The entire battalion was half the size of the 52nd and many of the men were extremely young and inexperienced. The numbers of the men who joined this regiment when under 18 years of age was inordinately high at 159, and the average length of service in the battalion

9 Lieutenant Colonel Charles Morice – not Morris, as Clinton had spelled it –had been wounded at Bergen op Zoom and he was to be killed at Quatre Bras.

10 Gareth Glover (ed.) *The Correspondence of Sir Henry Clinton in the Waterloo Campaign* (Godmanchester: Ken Trotman, 2015) Vol.1, p.49.

11 Glover (ed.), *Clinton*, Vol.I, p.166.

was only 3½ years, indicating that they had regularly supplied drafts to the first battalion which had been serving in India for the last ten years.[12] In fact, the 2/69th had not left the shores of Britain during the entire Napoleonic wars, until it was sent to Holland in late 1813. This may help to explain its indifferent performance both at Bergen op Zoom and during the Waterloo campaign.

George wrote now to his mother and father who were back in England and recounted that his father's name was known here. He spoke about Belgian customs and also that Louis XVIII had closed the frontier to British troops and some officers had been arrested for crossing the border during an innocent ride. The Belgians were also unhappy in joining the Dutch in the new Kingdom of the Netherlands.

To G H Barlow Bart & KB
Streatham
Surrey
Ypres, 11 January 1815 (annotated received 22 January, answered 9 March)

My dearest father,
The commencement of the New Year was agreeably ushered in by the arrival of yours, my mother's & Robert's letters of the 23rd & 24th of December, which came to hand on the 5th instant.[13] To each of the contributors on the family budget, return my best thanks for their respective stores. The length of time which elapses ere the army packets reach their destination is owing to mail being sent to Harwich, from where it is conveyed to Helvetloeys[14] & then making a tour through Holland, it stops at Brussels, our grand headquarters. The letters are then assorted for the different regiments & forwarded to each cantonment, among which Ypres is one of the most distant, about seventy miles from Brussels.

Some vague rumours are at present about respecting a change of our cantonments. This I trust will in practise, not take place, now that we are beginning to feel so comfortably settled in our present quarters. I have two rooms tolerably comfortable & pretty well furnished for forty franca per month, which is rather dear, as to the average rate of lodgings & were I not John Bull in the place, it would be even an unreasonable price. You may tell Miss Page that I have not been able to stumble upon anything equal to the half-crown per week concern in Bloomsbury which has so often afforded us a laugh as you may perhaps remember.

There is a singular custom prevalent in this place and as I am told common to all Flanders, a stranger upon his arrival, without any introduction or

12 Martin Aaron, '2nd Battalion 69th (South Lincolnshire) Foot during the Waterloo Campaign, *Napoleon Series*, at www.napoleon-series.org/military/organization/Britain/Infantry/c_2-69Waterloo.html, reports that it was more normal for under-18s to amount to less than 20 in a battalion.

13 Presumably he refers to his younger brother Robert: he cannot mean his uncle, as he does not use his title. His brother became a judge in India, but he may well have been in England at the time.

14 Actually the Dutch port of Hellevoetsluis, some ten miles from Rotterdam.

previous acquaintance, pays the first visit to the inhabitants, who then in turn make calls & send him invitations. This seems a singular anomaly at least to our ideas of etiquette. I have however, as is always the wisest plan, confined myself to the practise of those among whom I live & made the first advances. My idea in travelling is to gain all possible information and enlarge my stock of intelligence, wherever it is to be obtained. I was both surprised and pleased at the following circumstance, which happened the other day. The gentleman to whom I had paid a visit, demanded my address upon taking leave. I pulled out my card & presented the same. He took it & read, Barlow. Repeating the word once or twice, 'surely I know that name, it comes from the East Indies'. 'Yes', answered I, 'I was born there'. Captain Hobhouse,[15] who accompanied me, then put in a word & mentioned who you were & the station you had filled, upon which the gentleman signified his recollection of the circumstance. You may imagine, my dear father, how pleased I was to find that your well-earned fame had secured a carrier in Ypres. It is now pretty well known among the Beau Monde of this place and I could wish it were equally current in our London circles, at least among those it ought to find a place. Captain Hobhouse of the 69th, son of the Carnatic Commissariat, was present & can vouch that I never gave any clue or had any conversation which led to this circumstance. Now that we are on the subject of English politics, I cannot omit to mention the high character our country has obtained throughout these provinces. Every tongue is ready to do justice to our exertions in the cause of civilised Europe and everyone regards us as regulators of the balance of the scale of politics. Independent of these considerations, the Flemmings [sic] are very partial to our nation, whose customs & manners they have so considerable a resemblance to their own & both are an agricultural & commercial people. They are by no means partial to their present government, the Dutch & cannot but fear the French, but would prefer returning to their old sovereigns, the House of Austria, or to be under the protection of England.

I propose taking a tour for a few days on my newly purchased steed, to Namur & Liege, with a view of seeing the chief frontier towns. To a military man they offer nothing worthy of notice as the works of these and most of the other border towns have been completely ruined & destroyed about fifteen years since by an order of their former governor, the Emperor Joseph,[16] who apprehended some disaffection among his Flemish subjects. To Lille, Douay and the French territories, we are most positively forbidden to pass, without special leave given. As sufficient proof of their politeness to travellers & strangers, who have crossed the line of demarcation without

15 Captain Benjamin Hobhouse, 69th Foot, was the second son of Sir Benjamin Hobhouse of Fort William, Bengal, chairman of the committees for supplies and first commissioner for investigating the debts of the nabobs of the Carnatic. He acted as orderly officer to Sir Colin Halkett at Waterloo where he was killed.

16 Emperor Joseph II (1741-1790), Belgium was then known as the Austrian Netherlands and formed a part of the Holy Roman Empire.

passports, by putting under arrest four English officers who passed it, for the purpose of visiting a fine convent on the road to Valenciennes.

As this reaches Streatham, my dear father, you will have entered your 53rd year. God grant you many happy returns of its 20th instant and may each bring with it an exercise of happiness & that health which I am happy to find you yet continue to enjoy.[17] Give my kindest love to my mother with my hopes that she no longer feels any inconvenience from the accident in her right hand. Present the same to all your dear little school room and remember me also most kindly to Miss Page and believe me to be my dearest father, your most dutiful and affectionate son. G U Barlow.

P.S. Wednesday afternoon. I wrote the above this morning & on returning from my ride, I find a mail with papers to the 3rd instant. Dear little Louisa's nice long letter of the 26th December, for which offer her my kindest love. It is charmingly written.

George apprised his father that the heavy snow and ice was thawing and he was still having to be extremely careful with his injured foot. All the talk was of war between the great powers of Europe over disagreements at the Congress of Vienna, but as George rightly pointed out, all of the continental powers were bankrupt following the wars and without British finance they could not even contemplate another.

To GH Barlow Bart & KB, Streatham, Surrey
Ypres, 29 January 1815 (annotated received 10 February, answered 29 March)

My dearest father,
I wrote to you about a fortnight since and take up my pen again being post day, although I have little more to tell you than that the late severe frost has happily broken up. A very heavy snow has covered the ground for nearly a fortnight past and I have not consequently bestrode my horse during that period. Sledge driving appears to be the principal transport, but I have not ventured to hazard my neck, or rather my foot on any of their vehicles, which being only supported on two pieces of wood resembling skates are very liable to be overturned if any large stone or lump of ice encounters them.

Wars and rumours of wars are very current in these parts, you however who live in England generally get at the real truth and have better information respecting our proceedings than those who live nearer to the scene of negotiations. I rather think that those who delight to fish in troubled waters would not be sorry to see Europe in arms again. France is the common enemy of all the great potentates and would not be unwilling to see one against the other and then come in at the last for the great intention after

17 His father had been born on 20 January 1763, making him 52.

each has been sufficiently destroyed to pay. Money however, the main siren of war wanting to the whole continent; John Bull is the only man to supply their needs & he would I believe be most interested to control their purse strings, to such an end has long been the [hope?] of things & tender olive branches then; is the most desirable, because of laws & fair play.

Two or three engineer officers are lately arrived from Antwerp and the dilapidated fortifications of the place are to be again put in a state of repair, at this the burghers are set against, among them are several genteel families where acquaintance is really necessary. I have complied with the singular custom of making the first advance and pay my respects to all the inhabitants that [are] in the place. Some of them have travelled in England and on the whole, they are much attached to our nation. I enter into their society with a view to improve my French and extend the [depth of?] my knowledge of the world & mankind, should I travel over all the globe, nothing will be able to change that laudable and rational preference to the manners & customs of my own country, which every successive example and everyday experiences convinces me they so justly deserve.

I drew a bill on Frederick for fifty-five pounds,[18] the price of my horse, about a month since, should my funds not be in the way to reimburse him for the same, I would feel much obliged to you covering his demand and my Uncle William will pay you the amount.

Give my kindest love to my mother and all the schoolroom, telling them that I will write soon and believe me to be ever my dearest father, with every sincere wish for your health and happiness, your most dutiful & affectionate G U Barlow.

Ypres, 25 February 1815 (annotated received 28 February, answered 29 February)

My dearest father,
An officer of the regiment being on the point of leaving us for England tomorrow, I avail myself of the opportunity of enclosing a few lines for Fanny. I have nothing particular to tell you except that I leave this place on the 1st March for Brussels on an excursion of pleasure & shall positively return by the 10th of the month & then hope to receive some accounts of you all, my last are of the 24th & 26th December. I have taken the liberty of drawing a bill on you at *Glyn's* dated the 24th instant & payable to our Paymaster Mr Vyvian[19] on his order for thirty pounds if you will have the goodness to accept it, my Uncle William will refund you the amount;[20] I draw on you as my uncle may be at a distance from town, the bill is payable

18 It is unclear who Frederick was, beyond a horse trader.
19 Paymaster Philip Vyvian.
20 The bank of Glyn, Mills & Halifax until 1851 is now fully incorporated within Royal Bank of Scotland.

soon after sight. Give my dearest love to my mother & accept the same my dearest father of your most affectionate son, G. U. Barlow

The battalion moved from Ypres to Menin in March. Europe, having been apprised of Napoleon's sudden departure from Elba and following the shock of his regaining the throne of France, everything was being prepared for war once again. The regiment was to receive a surprise visitor, as Louis XVIII and his small entourage crossed the border at Menin and they saluted him as he passed on his way to Ghent, many more following his tracks in the ensuing days.

On 21 March Sir Henry Clinton wrote to Lieutenant General Calvert, confirming that the troops were improving and that 'Some of our 2nd battalions are in tolerable order and in a state soon to become efficient if their ranks were only filled. The best are the 30th, 33rd, 35th, 44th, 52nd and 69th, the 52nd is a mere skeleton'.[21] A muster on 1 April recorded the 69th at 39 officers, 18 sergeants, 19 drummers and 490 men present, with an additional 37 men sick.

George wrote of the recent excitement, when Louis XVIII passed through Menin into renewed exile.

Menin, 24 March 1815 (annotated received 3 April, answered 16 May)

My dearest father,
We do indeed live in an extraordinary age, each succeeding year teems with fresh wonders, more outstanding even than those that are just gone by, and which have yet scarcely ceased to excite amazement. Surely we are awaking from some long dream in which a Louis on the throne of France was a mien a-greatly beguiling the imagination, but the dream scene having now flitted past, we arise alive to the painful reality of finding a Napoleon [back] in his place, scarcely will our senses allow of believing that this usurper has taken possession of a throne with as much ease & rapidity, as a lawful owner enters upon the enjoyment of his estate. Did not the events of yesterday, afford too melancholy and irresistible a proof of what would otherwise stagger credulity and of which I myself was a painful witness.

It will be necessary to tell you that Menin stands precisely on the boundary line dividing Flanders from France & is situated upon the little River Lys, here about thirty yards in breadth & over which is thrown a small bridge; the frontiers following the course of its stream.[22] I had just returned express from Courtrai, having been sent thither with the *Moniteur* of the 21st containing the news of Bonaparte's first entry into Paris & his proclamations.[23] Having been thoroughly drenched to the skin by the way & almost in the act of changing, a rare hubbub on a sudden ran through the

21 Glover (ed.), *Clinton*, Vol.I, p.166.
22 This road is now designated the N32b and is known as Rijselstraat as it enters Menin. The original small bridge has been replaced by a much larger modern construction.
23 *Le Moniteur Universel*, to give its full title, was the official newspaper of the French government and was renowned for its inaccuracies.

town and a French general came galloping in; he announced that Louis the eighteenth was close at hand escorted by a party of cuirassiers. We had scarcely time to stand to our arms when the cavalcade appeared & stopped at the bridge. Upon arriving, the king desired his escort would return into Lisle [Lille], which they I am told were very unwilling to do; but his majesty insisted & their parting was very affecting; many of the soldiers rode up to the window & kissed his hand, whilst several in the most determined manner declared they would accompany him; whether he would allow them or not & a few are therefore permitted to enter.

The 69th were drawn up in the main street and received the cavalcade with all due honours. It was composed of but four carriages, that of the king leading, drawn by six very indifferent post horses, the traces being of rope. Upon arriving at the Colours, close to where I stood, it stopped and he let down the window. The commanding officer desired me to step up to the carriage and enquire what were His Majesty's wishes and which I accordingly did. There were no post horses in the town, and as he expressed a desire to proceed to Bruges I offered to go on in advance and prepare the requisite number [at] Roeselare which he thanked me to do. The commanding officer however thought proper to send forward two dragoons and thus I was saved some hard riding, in addition to that of the morning. The remaining carriages were filled with his suite, consisting of different noblemen, among whom was the Prince of Neufchatel & Wagram, Marshal Berthier, the old friend & companion of Bonaparte, whom he has attended throughout all his campaigns & of whose success he is supposed to have been one of the most efficient causes.[24]

I will leave you to conjecture my dearest father, what were my feelings on beholding this unfortunate monarch again rejected from the bosom of his ungrateful country, to seek an asylum in a foreign land, and with what cordiality I joined in the shouts of 'Vive le Roi', which were rather more sincere than those he has of late been accustomed to hear. From the little opportunity I had of judging, he seemed very resigned, though the noblemen in his carriage were much affected at once more entering upon a state of exile & shed tears.

Ever since, both by night and day carriages belonging to his suite & friends are continually passing through this town and as we are but nine miles from Lisle [Lille], everyone is obliged to undergo strict examinations, at several of which I have been present. General Drouet, a notorious partisan of Bonaparte has been released from confinement & commands at Lisle [Lille] a numerous garrison and we feel rather awkwardly situated,[25] not being able to push any posts into the French territory for the purposes of observation & the people of this town are said to be unworthy of trust as

24 The Prince de Neufchatel and Wagram were both titles held by Marshal Berthier.

25 *Général de Division* Jean-Baptiste Drouet, Comte d'Erlon commanded a corps in the Waterloo campaign.

spies; everyone therefore sleeps in his clothes [fully] accoutred, so as to turn out at a moment's notice.

We quitted Ypres on the 21st instant after having passed in it four very pleasant months; our departure I may say with all truth was much regretted, as the conduct of the troops throughout that period was most exemplary & good, and the sum of money put in consideration by a pretty numerous garrison was such as to keep the bourgeois in good humour, had they even been otherwise inclined. Ypres was never before so considerable a military cantonment and the good conduct of the 52nd & 69th Regiments has I believe contributed to leave rather a favourable impression [of our?] national character.

As for myself I am perfectly well & in good spirits but shall be obliged to do my duty on horseback as *the foot* although *certainly better &* stronger, is not yet capable of active service. Could the smallest idea have been entertained of what has of late so marvellously come to pass, I should have fitted myself out rather differently, but for this, there is at present no remedy, and as we are in a Christian-like civilised country I trust to be able to contrive matters pretty well.

God bless you, my dearest father and all beneath your kind roof, give my very best love to everyone & accept the same of your dutiful & affectionate son, G.U. Barlow

The battalion was soon moved again to Courtrai and then Tournai in late March and was then inspected at Ath on 5 April by Clinton, who recorded the battalion as having numbered 22 officers, 33 Sergeants, 18 Drummers and 449 Rank & File. He apparently saw little improvement in the battalion since his last inspection in January and was particularly scathing of Colonel Morice, stating that 'the neglected state of the appointments and of the ammunition is sufficient to mark Colonel Morice, who commands it and has done so for many months, as a man totally unfit for his situation.' But the regiment also came in for some stern criticism, stating that 'This regiment is bad from beginning to end, the officers do not do their duty & the men are loose & unsteady'.[26] The regiment then continued on to Soignies.

The Duke of Wellington had been given command of the allied army in Belgium and was to work in close co-operation with the Prussian army of Field Marshal Blucher, but they were to await the arrival of Russian and Austrian armies on the French borders, to allow a co-ordinated multi-pronged invasion of France.

A small public house near Soignies, 22 April 1815 (postmarked received 28 April, annotated answered 16 May)

My dearest father,

Your kind letter of the 29th of March from Streatham came to hand whilst the regiment was in the act of marching out of Tournai on the 4th instant.

26 Glover (ed.), *Clinton*, Vol.I, p.230.

In times like these and in our situation, nothing affords me greater comfort & happiness than hearing from those we love and esteem. It is therefore needless to mention what kind of reception any arrival from Streatham meets with from me. As you make no particular mention, I think that you continue to enjoy your usual good health & spirits, these are too constant. I think you have for ever engaged in your interests and it makes me happy, I think that they never can desert you.

In reply to your enquiries regarding my foot, I have only to repeat that it continues in much the same state, as long as we continue on a fine flat road it does very well but if our march should be across a ploughed field or difficult ground I could no longer keep pace with the rest and have therefore obtained permission to do my duty on horseback. This being the case I propose looking out for some country beast, that which I ride at present being far too good to expose to the chances of war and should any mishap befall it, I am entitled to no recompense whatever.[27]

I thank you for accepting my bill, on our paymaster, it is I presume the last of the two drawn by me upon him. It was for thirty-two pounds dated I think on the 14th February, the former was for fifty-five pounds in payment of the horse & was addressed to Frederick; should you have honoured them both in consequence of my uncle being out of town, the latter I have requested when convenient to reimburse you in their joint amount.

I am most obliged by your offer regarding an introduction to any general officer, but really am at a loss to fix upon one in the view you mean, everyone is anxious to provide for his friends and the peninsular war now brings forward a host of claimants. Brussels I am told is crowded with these gentry and the list was quickly filled up as soon as opened; in these circumstances we must lay upon our [arms and await?] the turn of events.

Since writing last from Menin we have consecutively been to Courtrai, Tournai, Ath & lately moved to the cantonments we at present occupy after having spent a few days at each of the above mentioned. I have now made an excursion to Mons, the regiment is dispersed about in the neighbourhood of Soignies, a small town nearly half way between Castries and Mons. I am quartered alone at a small ale house by the roadside such as you would probably see in England on the highway with the sign of the Leg of Mutton and Turnips. The people however are the civilest creatures in the world, and as they furnish me with a clean bed I require nothing further.

God bless you my dear father, and those belonging to you require my most affectionate love to everyone and believe me ever your dutiful & affectionate son G. U Barlow

Again, they moved, this time to Lens, with everyone expecting the campaign to begin, with them invading France at the end of May.

27 A comment which should be noted. His best horse was too good and too expensive to lose in battle without compensation. Presumably, most officers thought similarly and rode their 'second' horse in battle.

Lens, 6 May 1815 (postmarked UK 12 May)

My dearest father and mother,[28]
We shifted our quarters from Soignies yesterday afternoon to this place, a town half way between Ath and Mons on the great high road. I am as usual lodged in a town house about two miles out and riding by accident into the village where the Adjutant General resides, learn that the post for England will be despatched in the course of the afternoon. I lose therefore not a moment in giving you some account of our proceedings up to the very last opportunity of consequence, although thrown together in a very hasty manner imagining that these would be more satisfactory than nothing at all.

It is now pretty generally understood that the campaign will commence about the latter end of the present month; at least everything will be in perfect readiness for that purpose, unless pacific arrangements at Vienna or Frankfurt should settle what has now every appearance of being decided by the sword. Cavalry, infantry, artillery, commissariat are all in motion along this frontier and the country unmercifully crammed with troops. I am in a very small farm together with the two officers of my company[29] and twenty-five men lodged in the chief barn; such are the delightful consequences of an army of seventy or eighty thousand men being assembled in one's neighbourhood.

Pray offer my best remembrances to Miss Page for her very kind letter which I received near Soignies on the 25th last month; she informs me of a circumstance which till then I had never heard, namely my aunt's recent indisposition at Brighton; this in some degree accounts for my not having received any advices from my uncle or herself in answer to the letters I have severally addressed to each.

On the 24th of last month I wrote a bill on you for twenty-five pounds payable to the order of Mr Vyvian our Paymaster; I have money enough in my uncle's hands to answer this as well as all my former demands & only trust that the advances which you have been so good as to make me from time to time will not occasion you any inconvenience. I would draw on my uncle's at Glyn's but as he is now out of town & my bills are at ten days sight, I am necessitated to trespass on your goodness, as being more immediate[ly] on the spot.

Give my kindest love to my mother as well as all the dear little girls, remember me also to Miss Page and believe me to be my dearest father, your most dutiful & affectionate son, G.U. Barlow.

[PS] The money I have drawn is for a fit out and various expenses attending preparations for campaigning.

28 This is the only letter addressed to his two parents together and was at the point when they were about to divorce, his mother having had a child by another man.

29 George commanded No. 10 company; the identities of his subaltern officers are unfortunately not clear from the records.

George wrote again on the last day of May, from another new location, informing his father that all was ready for the invasion of France, but they were still waiting for the Russians to draw closer. The area around Mons had also been inundated to guard against any possible French attack.

Neufvilles,[30] 31 May 1815 (annotated received 6 June)

My dearest father,
Your kind letter of the 19th instant came to hand on the 26th and imposes on me the agreeable trick of returning you my best thanks for the affectionate sentiments therein expressed; offer also my love to dear little Fanny and Anne for their respective shares in the acceptable packet and to the latter my congratulations on her improvement in letter writing, the style and turn of which were very prettily expressed and particularly attracted my notice.

I am much concerned at your message respecting my aunt's health, it is really melancholy to terminate ten long years of sickness and find oneself in nearly the same state as at the commencement of the mournful period, this is sufficient to break the stoutest hearts, or the very best spirits; I am sorry at thus accounting for the long silence to the letters some time since written by me to each, but trust that a repetition of the warm sea bathing, which produced such wonderful good effect last year, will in like measure be now attended with similar beneficial consequences; I propose writing again in a few days to the same quarter.

Contrary to general expectation, you see, we have thus long remained tranquil without hostilities being committed, on either side. Report states us to be only awaiting the arrival of the hardy sons of the north, previous to finally throwing aside the scabbard. In the meanwhile the enemy remains by no means idle and is employing every method to meet the impending storm; he has put in requisition all the horses of the gendarmerie throughout France to remount his cavalry & laid hands on all the carts, wagons & beasts of burthen throughout French Flanders; their peasants are therefore coming over to us daily with their vehicles in order that they may not fall within this undiscriminating seizure. Desertion alone among his soldiery are also very numerous & the only hope of success left to him is to [cause?] dissensions among the allies and raising insurrections in this country or Germany where an unfortunate sequence of events has created for him a considerable number of partisans & [particularly?] Saxony & Poland; it will be hoped however that [the side?] of justice will finally prevail.

In the meanwhile, we are passing our time very pleasantly in the different farmhouses and cottages around the little village of Neufvilles; the country people are extremely hospitable and obliging throughout, nothing wanting to complete their happiness, but a continuance of that tranquillity which

30 Neufvilles is half way between Soignies and Lens.

they have recently been enjoying some months past & which is now so lamentably about to be attacked. Already has the work of destruction commenced, 12,000 acres of fine rich land having been flooded around Mons, to secure the works of that place from a hostile attack.

And now I must conclude with desiring you to offer my very best love to my mother and all the good folks of the school room and that God may ever bless you all is the sincerest prayer of your most dutiful & affectionate son, G. U. Barlow

11

The Waterloo Campaign

All was peaceful in early June, but the fighting broke out in earnest with Napoleon's forces attacking the Prussian forces centred around Charleroi and driving them back. The surprise was complete, with Wellington and Blucher struggling to quickly assemble their strung-out armies before their forward elements were completely overwhelmed.

The 2/69th was in the 5th Brigade of Major General Sir Colin Halkett in the 3rd Division, along with the 2/30th, 33rd and 2/73rd. They were encamped around Soignies on the night of the 15th, General Halkett having heard rumours that the French had crossed the border that morning. They marched at 2:00 a.m. on the 16th for the general assembly point at Nivelles and continued on to Quatre Bras, where they arrived at around 5:00 p.m. The fighting at Quatre Bras continued to rage and Wellington's infantry were barely holding on against the French onslaughts. The troops were therefore deployed immediately on their arrival: exhausted by a long march in very hot weather, the 2/69th now found themselves in fields of rye so tall that it towered over their heads, unable to see the enemy and totally reliant on their senior officers on horseback to guide them to their positions and to warn them in the case of an attack. The brigade was placed a few hundred yards south of the cross-roads in the narrow strip of fields to the west of the main Charleroi road which ran up to the great wood that formed the western flank of the battlefield. The 2/69th were stood opposite La Bergerie farm and in a slight dip that protected them from the worst of the French cannon fire. Here the troops were constantly agitated by skirmishers and the occasional cannon shot and they remained in line to reduce the casualties suffered, but being effectively 'blind' because of the crops, they remained very nervous and vulnerable to a sudden cavalry attack.

Major General Halkett later recounted discovering a large body of cavalry moving by sections as if going to water the horses. Halkett stated that he sent orders to the 2/69th to form square as he suspected the cavalry was about to attack. The 2/69th did form square but the Prince of Orange appears to have ordered Colonel Morice to reform in line as he could not see any cavalry. The French cavalry attack went in against the infantry to the right of the 2/69th and they remained unaware of them as they continued to reform line. Suddenly the cavalry turned towards them and the cry 'Cavalry' rang out. As the regiment was already half way through reforming into line, the urgent cries to 'form square' simply caused panic and confusion. The square was partially formed, but three companies could not arrive to complete the formation before the cavalry arrived. Major Henry Lindsay commanding this

Wellington at Waterloo by Hillingford. (Editor's Collection)

isolated force unfortunately chose to make his men stand and fire on the cavalry rather than running into the main square. Having discharged their weapons, the men were vulnerable to attack and a number were cut down and the rest fled. The troops in the main square, watched this awful scene and aware that their formation was incomplete and very vulnerable to the cavalry, the young soldiers broke and fled on mass for the protection of the nearby wood or like George, they 'played dead' as the French Cuirassiers rode by. During this confusion and in uncertain circumstances, both ensigns in charge of the colours managed to lose them, although neither were actually wounded. Ensign Ainslie, carrying the Regimental Colour was apparently knocked over and Volunteer Clarke caught hold of the Colour, he reputedly killed three Cuirassiers but sustained twenty-three wounds during the fighting and eventually collapsed to the ground with the Colours underneath him to save them.[1] What happened to Ensign Henry Keith is more obscure, but the King's Colour he was carrying was captured by the French while he was unscathed. There were numerous claimants in the 8e Cuirassiers for the honour of capturing the Colour and we cannot be certain who did capture it.[2]

This was certainly a mess and the regiment was shamed by the loss of another colour in less than a year, but it was far from the massacre that is often claimed. In

1 He was granted a commission in the 42nd Foot afterwards, but lost the use of one arm.

2 The history of the King's Colour after the battle is a strange one. In 1909, a Captain Jeffcock of the Inniskillings, saw the Colour for sale at Azay-le-Rideau and bought it for £24. The Colour was given back to the regiment and is now on display at the military museum at Cardiff Castle.

fact, one officer, four sergeants and 33 men were killed, four officers, six sergeants, one drummer and 103 men were wounded and none recorded as 'missing' at Quatre Bras from a total of 516 men.[3] This is a casualty rate of around 28%, which is certainly not the highest percentage suffered at Quatre Bras.

Having suffered the long march back to the position before Waterloo on the 17 June with little food and coupled with the torrential rains of that night, few of the men of the 2/69th would have arisen that Sunday morning well rested and in perfect condition to fight a battle.[4] The men spent the morning drying their clothes, searching out a morsel of food and preparing their equipment for the battle which was sure to come. The 2/69th and the rest of the brigade, formed near the centre of Wellington's line, just a little north of the position of the Lion Mound which was built there afterwards. Their reduced numbers after Quatre Bras led to two battalions forming squares together throughout the 18th of June, the 2/69th joining up with the 33rd Foot. These regiments were not given a starring role this day, but they did their bit, holding the line stoically against the incessant and punishing artillery barrage whilst taking heavy casualties, forming squares against the thousands of French cavalry that swarmed the allied ridge in the afternoon and facing the might of the Imperial Guard in the final, decisive, moments of the battle. At times there is some evidence that they buckled slightly and there is no doubt that their collective stoicism was pushed to the limits, but they did not break and they did not flee. They did what was asked of them, to hold their ground no matter what. With the defeat of the Guard, they were simply too exhausted to join in the final advance and they sank to the ground where they had fought and slept soundly whilst surrounded by the mangled corpses of the dead and the screams of the wounded. The 2/69th ended the battle with a 'butcher's bill' totalling four officers[5] and 14 men killed, three officers[6] and 50 men wounded and two drummers and 13 men missing.[7] On the 19th the army began its march on Paris.

George's hurried note was actually penned whilst still sat on the battlefield, at sunrise the day after the Battle of Waterloo. George had been lucky enough to survive both battles without a wound, particularly at the Battle of Quatre Bras, where he was ridden over by the French cavalry. He also lost his best horse which was stolen from his servant in the rear, his servant being dreadfully wounded. This meant that he had to walk all of the retreat to Waterloo despite his painful foot.

---

3 The officer killed at Quatre Bras was Lieutenant Edmund Wightwick who died of his wounds on the 17th. The officers wounded at Quatre Bras were Major Henry Lindsay, Lieutenant Brooke Pigot, Lieutenant Christopher Busteed and Lieutenant John Stewart. Unit strength from Captain William Siborne's *History of the Waterloo Campaign* (London: T and W Boone, 1848), p. 555.

4 During the retreat it is recorded that the 2/69th suffered one sergeant and two men wounded; see Siborne, *Waterloo Campaign*, p.558.

5 The officers killed at Waterloo were Lieutenant Colonel Charles Morice, Captain Benjamin Hobhouse, Captain William Curzon, and Captain Robert Blackwood.

6 The officers wounded at Waterloo were Captain J. Lewis Watson, Lieutenant Henry Anderson, and Ensign Edward Hodder.

7 Siborne, *Waterloo Campaign*, p564.

Field of Battle, eight miles from the [torn-City of?] Brussels, 19 June 1815 (annotated received 23 June)

My dearest father,
I am writing a few lines in haste on my knee, it is now sunrise and I take therefore the earliest opportunity of informing you that an all kind providence has preserved me in two most sanguinary conflicts on the 16th & 18th instant. That of yesterday was perhaps one of the severest ever fought, Bonaparte commanding in person & the Imperial Guards both horse & foot having made the most desperate & repeated attacks to force the Allied army from their present ground, but all to no purpose. The enemy were the assailants and their cavalry commanded by the King of Naples,[8] elated by some trifling success on the 16th,[9] made repeated charges, more especially the cuirassiers upon our infantry formed into squares, but never succeeded in breaking any one of them.[10] These charges were made in the most daring manner up to the bayonets of the infantry & the muzzles of our cannon, but every attempt was punished with frightful loss. The artillery on both sides was very well served & numerous and that of the British particularly so, as the present scene alas too desperately bears witness; this field is strewed with helmets, cuirasses & horses. Seventeen guns are taken [on this?] part of the field & I believe many more in other directions. The combat terminated only with the night, which I believe alone saved the routed remains of the enemy as our cavalry followed in full pursuit & many prisoners have been made although their numbers I know not. The field is covered with the [bodies of the] Imperial Guard, who were the forces chiefly employed in this direction.

As for poor George, providence saved him on two or three occasions in the affair of the 16th. A large body of cuirassiers charged the 69th before they could form into square & consequently before they could resist their attack & therefore dispersed them; the cavalry rode over George, who was incapable of running on account of his foot & therefore he lay on the ground till they passed by & then getting on his legs & he rejoined the 42nd who had not been attacked & were formed in square a short distance to the right. He is yet very lame in consequence of the exertions of yesterday.

I am sorry to inform you that I must draw a bill in consequence of the casualties of yesterday. My horse attended by my servant was in the rear of the army in a village about dusk when a Dutch soldier whom I have not been able to discover, attacked & wounded him most severely & took the horse from him by force; my poor servant has had his arm amputated in

---

8 This was untrue. He refers to Murat, King of Naples, who was not present at Waterloo although many rumours stated that he was.

9 This is somewhat of an understatement, given that the 69th lost a colour at Quatre Bras. Perhaps understandably, George skirts over this fact.

10 Here he talks of Waterloo, where no allied square was broken, despite French claims to the contrary.

Lieutenant Colonel Muttlebury escaping the French cavalry on 16 June, by Charles Warren. (Anne S.K. Brown Military Collection)

consequence, such you see is the consequence & confusion of this general action. God bless you, & with my love to all, believe me to be your most affectionate son, G. U. Barlow

The march to Paris was largely uneventful for the 2/69th as they were not involved in the couple of short sieges along the way. Paris fell to the allies on 7 July and the following day King Louis XVIII was reinstated as monarch. Napoleon went to Rochefort in an attempt to escape to America but was foiled and he finally surrendered to Captain Maitland onboard HMS *Bellerophon* on 15 July and was eventually sent to St Helena.

Entering the capital on the 7 July and encamped in the Bois de Boulogne on the edge of Paris, George was able to furnish a fuller account of his part in the recent battles. He also sent news that he was temporarily acting as brigade major.

Camp near Paris, 7 July 1815

My dear father,
It is now the 7th of July and since the few harty [sic] lines written to you & ever since the 19th June I have scarcely had an hour which could well be called my own. Excepting on the 23rd we have been making daily forced marches & these rapid strides brought us on the 1st of July in sight of the great city of Paris. I have moreover [been] of late pro tempore filling the

situation of brigade major and undertook it at a period of no ordinary difficulty.[11]. Upon the loss of every adjutant but one,[12] most of the sergeant majors and the absence of all the regimental books, rendered it rather a troublesome office.

So decisive was the tremendous blow struck on the 18th ultimo that tyranny has never been able to recover from its effects, which are best seen by our rapid progress this far, but for a wonderful celerity the march has resembled a triumphant progress rather than an invasion of a hostile country. Not a shot has been scarcely fired since the business of Belle Alliance, & here we are on the 7th of July encamped in the Bois de Boulogne.

To attempt a description of these wonderful events would exceed the limits both of my time & paper. I will therefore as briefly as possible recapitulate the chief circumstances which have occurred since the opening of the campaign. We left Soignies on the 16th of June & marched to Nivelles in the direction of Fleurus; Bonaparte having concentrated his army at Maubeuge on the 14th, entered Belgium and drove the Prussians from Charleroi on the 15th. Marshal Blucher then resolved to give him battle on the 16th notwithstanding a large corps of his army under General Bulow was not yet arrived. This took place at Fleurus and the Prussians after a most gallant resistance against very superior numbers being worsted, were obliged to retire with severe loss both in men & cannon.

As I have said before, we moved from Soignies on the same day to their succour, but on reaching Nivelles there was ample work enough for ourselves. Marshal Ney had penetrated within a league of that town. Our division (General Alten's)[13] hastened forward & found General Picton's division with some Belgic troops engaged against very disproportionate numbers, which the arrival of our reinforcement by no means equalised.[14] It was a fine summers evening about five o'clock when we first came into fire & we soon found ourselves under a heavy cannonade. The division was then formed into squares of regiments, a measure which the proximity of the enemy's cavalry and the total absence of that species of force on our part, rendered absolutely necessary.

The scene of action lay upon ground diversified with little dales & gently rising slopes, covered throughout with rye & wheat which here grows

11 Captain Walter Crofton, 54th Foot, brigade major to Sir Colin Halkett, was killed at the Battle of Waterloo and George stood in.

12 Of the Adjutants in Sir Colin Halkett's Brigade, Lieutenant Matthias Andrews of the 30th Foot, Ensign William Thain of the 33rd Foot, and Ensign Patrick Hay of the 73rd Foot were wounded. The only Adjutant in the brigade to escape injury was Lieutenant Henry Oldershaw of the 69th Foot.

13 Lieutenant General Baron Charles Alten commanded the 3rd Division, which consisted of Major General Sir Colin Halkett's 5th British Brigade (which included the 2/69th), Colonel Baron Ompteda's 2nd King's German Legion Brigade, and *Generalmajor* Graf von Kielmansegge's 1st Hanoverian Brigade.

14 Lieutenant General Sir Thomas Picton commanded the 5th Division; he was killed at Waterloo.

extremely high, between five or six feet. In the course of manoeuvring the 69th for a moment found itself at the bottom of one of these little dips & being formed in square was perfectly secure. A certain personage, who shall be nameless, sent down an order that the 69th should deploy into line.[15] It was obeyed & scarcely done when a strong body of French cuirassiers as if by magic showed themselves close in rear of our flank at about fifty yards. As I have before mentioned, we happened to be in a small hollow commanded on every side with high gentle hillocks & the height of the surrounding corn precluded a view of everything beyond the close distance.

The enemy taking advantage of it, approached close to the regiment unperceived, & rushed at us from an ambuscade on the flank of the line, a situation which rendered us perfectly defenceless. An attempt was made to form square, but the proximity of the cuirassiers and the instantaneousness of their attack, rendered it impossible. In a flash they rode through & over our little battalion of 400 men. One Colour was taken in the confusion which ensued, the other was preserved.[16] Many of our unfortunate men were sabred & wounded but no prisoners made, as the neighbouring regiments taking warning from our example quickly threw themselves into square & before the cuirassiers could reform, they kept up such a terrible fire that the greater part of our gallant enemies perished on the spot.

Night falling, the whole of the French army retired into some neighbouring woods and we bivouacked upon the field of battle.

I have been thus circumstantial in my details as the event of losing a standard has been blazed in the French papers and I have therefore attempted to account for such a circumstance & presume this case to be one of misfortune rather than dishonour; perhaps almost unavoidable. This opinion formed upon minutely examining the very spot next morning; whither curiosity by the circumstance interested me to proceed & which I coolly dispassionately surveyed.

As for George, when he saw that the game was up & resistance at an end & some of these armour-bearing cuirassiers at his back, he had [the] presence of mind to throw himself down on the ground and the enemy passed by & over him. He had heard before of this species of ruse & being incapable of running, no other resource was left to him; he waited a while & then getting on his legs made the best of his way to the square of the 42nd Regiment & was thereby rescued.[17]

15 This refers to the Prince of Orange.

16 This confirms that both colours were at Quatre Bras.

17 It is recorded in Rev. William Leeke, *The History of Lord Seaton's Regiment (the 52nd Light Infantry) at the Battle of Waterloo* (London: Hatchard & Co, 1866), p.13, that Colonel Hall 52nd Foot had informed Leeke that: 'Near Nivelles we overtook Barlow, captain in the 69th. He had been promoted from the 52nd about a year before. Through the fault of the Prince of Orange, the 69th, in the act of changing position, had been charged by French dragoons [cuirassiers]. Barlow, and many others, lay down and escaped hurt, except from the trampling of the horses. He was limping along, very sore and lame, and feelingly declaimed against the common notion, that a horse will not tread on a man lying on the ground. His

Towards dusk George returned to the spot where he had left his servant & horse. Upon my arrival I learnt that some Belgic, Brunswick or foreign hussars had attacked my poor servant & wounded him so desperately in the arm, that the arm was obliged to be amputated next morning, taking away at the same time my much-valued horse [the?] good *Barossa*. Never since have I ever been able to obtain any tidings or sight of her; the thief probably went direct to Brussels & disposed of his ill acquired spoil, thus was I left destitute for the march & retreat of the ensuing day, the 17th, deprived also of my coat & cloaks to keep out the heaviest rain which it has been my lot perhaps ever to witness. Will you credit that on the 17th I walked between thirteen & fourteen miles to the position of Waterloo in country cross roads of the most execrable description.[18] The circumstances of the occasion however kept me up & I was determined to hold out to the last; as towards evening the enemy's cavalry came on along the pavé & made many prisoners of those who had straggled or stopt [sic] behind the march of the columns.

Night came on & with it the flood gates, it however seemed to be opened as it poured in torrents without intermission. We had no canopy but the sky, nothing to eat, thus hungry; drenched & sleepless around a fire which barely emitted heat & would scarcely burn, did we await in a cornfield the dawning of the 18th of June.[19]

The tendency of all our movements the preceding evening and having before witnessed the system of our great chief all conspired to make me think that a general action would ensue the following day for the possession of Brussels. The Prussians made a corresponding movement in retreat on Wavre & the whole English & Hanoverian army during the evening & night of the 17th by various routes & different columns, marched into the position of Waterloo, our force as near as I can ascertain being rather more than 80,000 men of all sorts & descriptions including the Prussian division of General Bulow, but of course not the remainder of Marshal Blucher's army.[20]

The position of Waterloo upon which the battle for the destinies of Europe was about to be fought, was nothing more than a range of moderate rising ground, touching upon the right the pavé leading from Nivelles to Brussels & extending on the left to the high road from Genappe & conducting to the

---

jacket was blackened with the marks of horse shoes. I suppose in such a case the horse has no choice and cannot pick its way.'

18 The direct road from Quatre Bras to the position at Waterloo is just under ten miles, but George seems to indicate that he made the journey via by-roads and it may well have been longer. It certainly would have felt longer given the pain in his foot.

19 It is a strange fact that although the corn and rye at Quatre Bras had grown over six feet tall, the crops at Waterloo were no higher than waist high. Not one of the thousand odd eyewitness statements from the Battle of Waterloo mention head-high crops, whereas every one written about Quatre Bras remarks on them.

20 In fact Wellington's Allied Army numbered around 67,000 men, whilst eventually Bulow's, Ziethen's, and Pirch's corps were involved totalling around 30,000 Prussians.

same metropolis. Here two routes formed the summit [of] an angle, meeting near Braine l'Alleud, to which the position of the British army served as the base, or third side, its flanks leaning upon & thus covering either approach. It was fine commanding open fighting ground, but traversable in all directions by cavalry & cannon. The French artillery lined the whole summit of these heights. The army was drawn up in order of battle behind them a little way down the reverse of the slope so as to be perfectly concealed from the enemy who could by no means get sight of its force or disposition and according to his own, confirm he was kept in perfect ignorance of its intentions.

To get the anxiously desired peep behind, it was necessary to come up to the muzzles of one hundred & fifty pieces of cannon placed in different directions, steady troops in their rear & the French position of a corresponding order & parallel to our own. The party quitting their [position] therefore laboured under certain disadvantages, which however the superiority of the assailants, in this case ought to have counterbalanced; one corps being left to watch the Prussians. Bonaparte brought the remaining four entire and the whole of the Imperial Guard (itself about twenty thousand men) and upwards of two hundred guns against the Duke of Wellington's army.

The day became fair about eleven & the cannonade on both sides commenced. An impetuous attack was first made against the right, where the Guard and German Legion held some loop-holed houses & a small cypress coppice;[21] the Germans quitted their post after making an admirable defence. The enemy having set fire to the building, the Guards were fortunate in having maintained theirs against repeated assaults & very much distinguished themselves. Abattis thrown across the road impeded the enemy much & after sending parallel efforts they directed themselves against the centre where General Alten's corps was posted.[22]

This happened about two o'clock when our friends, the cuirassiers again showed themselves, who by the rapidity of their advance forced our artillery men to quit their guns; these last however galloped away with the limbers & traces so that the enemy had no means of carrying them off over the ploughed ground; those on foot took shelter in the squares of infantry, which had been formed in that order since the commencement of the attack & were a short distance in rear, all perfectly prepared. The cuirassiers & dragoons then attempted to pierce the squares but were received with such a terrible fire that they were thrown into the greatest disorder & obliged to fly with all possible speed.

Such was the result of the first attack of the cavalry which I had conceived to have been a reconnaissance on the part of the enemy, but to my great surprise, this was succeeded by a second on the left, then a third and

21 He describes the farm of Hougoumont and La Haye Sainte, which acted like small fortresses in front of the allied line.

22 Abattis: a military term for a hastily made obstruction built from trees, undergrowth, and farm implements, usually used to block a road.

afterwards by a variety of others, during the course of these hours till five o'clock on every part of the division & Lord Hill's corps these attacks were reiterated in the most daring manner. Their officers we saw [urging them] on in a very gallant style and their men followed up the example; but the squares stood firm throughout and not one of them was for a moment disordered. The enemy cavalry repeatedly dashed into the centre of the British centre and at each attempt were received with such destructive vollies [sic] from the surrounding squares to excite my astonishment at such useless destruction, nor were they discontinued till the flower of the French cavalry both in men & horses were almost wholly destroyed and the remainder could not be brought to act with any effort at a period shortly afterwards when their service were most arguably required as will be presently related.

Between six & seven o'clock Bonaparte ordered forward his infantry; several large masses were put in motion and began to ascend the British position in various directions covered by the fire of their batteries and [the] cannon were then ordered to be poured against them to retard their advance. As soon as they had arrived at the proper distance the infantry commenced and after a very heavy fire on both sides succeeded in making them retire. Eight o'clock came and found the battle yet undecided, for shortly afterwards four solid masses of the Imperial Guard infantry advanced and made a most formidable attack. These fellows came up with carried arms and in the most determined manner to within seventy or eighty yards of the heights along which our infantry were placed and poured a terrible fire, two pieces of cannon accompanied them and being placed affront our brigade, which was formed en masses, raked it most severely with grapeshot as did shells from some more distant howitzers. This was indeed the crisis of this eventful day, both armies were in close contact and hot action and the cannonade really tremendous along the whole line as the entire artillery of either army were in full play to support their respective parties in an effort which was to decide the fortune of the battle, an effort worthy of the great stake for which each contested.

P.S. I have received yours of the 27th of June, as also Robert's letter and the maps &c &c.

12

Paris and the Army of Occupation

The armies remained in the vicinity of Paris for a considerable period, until 20 November 1815, when the Second Treaty of Paris was signed. An army of 600,000 men would remain in France at French expense, for five years (reduced later to three) under the command of the Duke of Wellington, to ensure that the massive financial reparations ordered against France were paid in full. George, like all the other British troops, took the opportunity to explore Paris and its surroundings and report on the sights and the people. It must be borne in mind that France had virtually been a 'no go' area for the last 23 years and there was a great clamour to discover more about it. George was happy to oblige. Eventually the allies left Paris and their troops were cantoned in the north and eastern edges of the country, forming an effective barrier between French forces and Belgium and Germany.

To G H Barlow Bart GCB, Streatham, Surrey
Paris, 27 July 1815 (annotated received 31 July, answered 1 August)

My dearest father,
After an interval here of some few days I again resume my pen for the purpose of giving you a description of those objects worthy of notice which have come within my observation during that period. Paris has the character of being a city containing more for the inspection of foreigners than perhaps any other in the world and my own private opinion is much inclined to subscribe to the justice of the same remark.

From the telegraph on the top of the heights of Montmartre you have a delightful view of the surrounding country, and at one scope take in nearly the furthest limits of this great metropolis. It is said to stand on more ground than London, but I question much the accuracy of such a statement. Paris possesses however, one advantage over its rival, namely in point of appearance. The exterior of the houses being chiefly white and as at this season of the year there are so few fires for which also fire wood is used, the clearness of the atmosphere formed a pleasing contrast to that sombre, smoky darkness which hovers over the site of our metropolis; but this latter impresses the stranger with far greater ideas of opulence and national prosperity. Here the eye ranges with delight over the variety of spires & public edifices. Uncertain how to decide the preference amid so pleasing & numerous an assemblage, here it remains fixed on two or three objects, the Hotel des Invalides, the Pantheon, the Church of Notre Dame, the only things of the kind and not equalling St Paul's, Westminster Abbey &c &c.

Descending from thence you find yourself on the boulevards, which *are* peculiar, I believe to this city alone. Fancy an avenue of fine large trees similar to that which runs by Madame [Pirzzi's?] house but the road of which is twice the breadth, circumventing almost the whole of Paris and with the chaussee's branching off to every quarter of the kingdom planted for the post two or three miles all along their sides in the same fashion and it will give you some idea of the avenues to this capital. Previous however to entering, it is necessary to pass a Barrier, here your vehicle is generally met & detained by a douanier or custom house officer & here the precautions of an arbitrary government are most visible. These Barriers are in fact as many Guard houses planted at convenient distances with which to communicate between each, so that no carriage or cart driver can pass; consequently in times of trouble, Paris may be most strictly blockaded.

And now were a stranger to be blindfolded on his arrival at these gates and the bandage not removed until he was set down somewhere near the Tuileries and if you should restrict his walks within a circumference of almost three miles of which the above palace was the centre, he would most assuredly pronounce Paris to be the first & finest city in the world, a city laid out by someone [of] comprehensive mind which had uniformly kept a new elegance & regularity of structure throughout and had selected this spot to exhibit a chef d'oeuf of its taste whose completion it had superintended and witnessed. The Seine is here nearly of the same breadth as the Thames about Kensington and which with three or four bridges of very light & elegant structure, is highly ornamental. Near its banks close to the Pont de Concorde stands the magnificent palace of the Tuileries, a habitation worthy the monarch of a great nation. Behind are three celebrated gardens, always open to the public, divided into parterres, shrubberies & walks, with fountains in the centre, the whole laid out with a regularity & care too uniform to be natural & consequently differing from our English notions of taste, but they are nevertheless very striking and correspond with the princely edifice to which they appertain. After beholding these, I no longer wonder at a foreigner's surprise on being shown St James or Carleton House as the residence of our sovereign's edifices, insignificant in comparison with that which I have already described.

On going out of the gardens of the Tuileries you cross the Place de Louis Quinze,[1] celebrated as being the place of execution to his unfortunate successor and then enter upon the Champs Elysees which is planted thick with fine trees & resembling Kensington Gardens & is pretty enough, extending nearly to the Pont de Jena; this is a new bridge extremely beautiful, built by Bonaparte and has a delightful appearance conducting to the Champ de Mars. When the quays that are now building along either banks

1 Now known as the Place de la Concorde.

of the Seine are complete, the tout ensemble of all the above objects added to the House of Commons and the venerable Hotel des Invalides with its gilt dome & cupola crowning the whole will constitute to produce an admirable effect.

Hereabouts Paris is certainly beheld to the best advantage and variety of design seems to pervade every part, and what was so magnificently planned and commenced by the Louis's has with similar ability been continued by a Bonaparte, for this assuming despot neglected nothing which might contribute to pamper the Parisian vanity in seeing their city enlarged and enriched. The arbitrary imposts which have impoverished the outposts & ruined the commerce of France have in some fashion been expended on the Imperial residence, and thus whilst at Marseilles, Bordeaux & Rochefort, the character of the man appeared in its true light of an oppressor, at Paris it at least shone in the fictitious glass of a benefactor.

But step not over the prescribed limits of this pleasing circle, for beyond its boundaries the contrast is most disagreeable & unvarying. You traverse throughout narrow dirty streets, wretchedly paved & having no walk for foot passengers. The shops are neither so numerous or magnificent as in London; that pleasing bustle & hurry of business, that superabundance of population is wanting and a dull stupid mediocrity pervades the whole, partaking neither of the commercial activity of the city, or the elegance & quiet of the West End of the town. To this observation, the interior boulevards form a pleasing but the only exception; they are planted with trees precisely the same as those I have described in a former part, and present to an Englishman the singular spectacle of avenues of foliage, in the middle of a large city, with houses on either side & paved streets, a mixture which at first sight seems rather unnatural, though custom may in some degree reconcile it to the eye. Setting these aside a small region whose limits are very circumscribed, Paris cannot bear any comparison with London, in the one excellence, however great, is confined to one inconsiderable space, in the other it is more generally, though not so strikingly at first sight diffused.

In attempting thus to draw something of a parallel between these two cities, I have studiously endeavoured to avoid any undue influence or natural prejudice. The acquisition of knowledge and the enlargement of one's ideas which thereby enables us to form a more correct judgement of things by the making of comparisons, is one of the great advantages of travelling. The insular situation of Great Britain, added to a peculiar series of political events have contributed to exclude her inhabitants from the continent during the greater portion of the last fifteen years and thus doubtless you may find a greater portion of that natural lies amongst us than perhaps any other race of people. There are few who feel a greater attachment to their native soil than myself, I am desirous therefore on all occasions of counteracting in a certain measure the influence of such sentiments so that they may not attain too great a degree of sway, being assured that they will always maintain their due preponderance.

A description of the interior of all those edifices & buildings before mentioned shall be reserved for some future letter, in the meanwhile my dearest father, in answer to the latter part of yours of the 10th instant, I have to observe, that if you could contrive to get me confirmed in my present situation, an important point would be gained. I am not yet eligible for a family,[2] this five or six weeks, but am at present pro tempore filling the situation of brigade major to this brigade & have held the same ever since three days integument to the Battle of Waterloo.

General Halkett who is [lying] wounded at Brussels recommended a friend of his own, but the appointment was not confirmed. Colonel Elphinstone commanding the 33rd Regiment & then senior officer together with the Adjutant General of this division have written to headquarters on my behalf a month since, but no notice has been taken of it; perhaps these documents have been mislaid or lost. In the meanwhile a new brigadier has superseded Colonel Elphinstone and another general succeeds to the division pro tempore, to him both I & Colonel Evans [are] utter strangers.[3] General Halkett is now duly expected here & will no doubt in time have some friend of his own appointed. This General Halkett is a very anxious man, he is acquainted with my Uncle William and with Mr Clarke's brother in law,[4] notwithstanding this he has never taken any notice of me whatever for particular reasons.

I most positively request that neither you nor my Uncle William will make any representation whatever & Mr & Mrs Clarke on my behalf; sooner than this I should prefer returning to my duty in the 69th; any other channel, particularly addressed to headquarters would be acceptable.

I have drawn a bill on you for twenty-seven pounds dated I think July 20th payable to the order of Major Evans 5th West India Regiment.[5] This is on account of a horse I was obliged to buy at the same time, saddle &c as that which poor Blackwood was bringing up to me was all lost & plundered after the battle of the 18th,[6] the sum total of the animal & his equipage amounted to sixty-seven pounds, forty of which I have given myself. It was impossible to procure anything fit for a brigade major to be seen upon at a parade as it would have looked so disreputable to see a Staff officer mounted upon a miserable animal, a country pony, and to have thus marched past Lord Wellington & all the emperors as indeed the day before yesterday & I fear that it may yet be necessary to make some farther trespass on your liberality, for as the losing of my horse has made my expenses beyond my

2 The aide de camps and the staff of generals were often referred to as their 'family'.

3 Major De Lacy Evans became a lieutenant colonel immediately after Waterloo and he would appear to mean the same man here although he refers to him as major at the end of the letter.

4 This would appear to be Sir Simon Haughton brother in law of Mrs Catharine Clarke (nee James); they were distant relatives of George.

5 Major De Lacey Evans was extra aide de camp to Sir William Ponsonby at Waterloo. He is associated with the so called 'Delancey Disposition' which purports to show the dispositions of Wellington's troops early on 16 June, his copy being the only version extant.

6 Captain Robert Blackwood, 69th Foot, was killed at Waterloo.

means, but I will avoid doing so if possible. Were I confirmed, in my present situation such necessity would no longer exist & until such confirmation is made I am not entitled to any pay whatever. With my love to all, believe me to remain your most dutiful & affectionate son, G U Barlow

Paris 10 August 1815 (annotated received 15 August, answered 29 August)
In the Bois de Boulogne, Paris 10 August 1815

My dearest father,
I received your two kind letters of the 4th together with its enclosures on the 8th instant and have to assure you how much I feel this new proof of your kindness in addition to the many former instances which you have shown, as early as I can recollect, in my behalf. The encomiums bestowed on the little narrative of the 7th of July, are really more than such a thing can merit; it was drawn up with no particular care, as I had never imagined that the letter would have gone beyond the circle of the family, or perhaps of one or two friends; otherwise it might have received a further degree of attention, previous to falling into such high hands.

Yesterday there was a Grand Review of the Russian Imperial Guard and the Duke of course fully occupied in the society of emperors & kings; today or tomorrow therefore I will deliver to him your letter; I shall take care also to write to Greenwood according to your instructions.

Give my love to Richard for his very nice letter and assure Miss Page how kindly I take her half of the sheet of paper. It gives me great pleasure to hear that she is doing as well & advancing towards a perfect recovery. I will shortly send each of them answer, Mr M. shall also be remembered.[7]

Last week we daily expected orders to quit this metropolis for the purpose of being cantoned in Picardy or Normandy to which provinces all our cavalry are already marched and are anon stationed in the neighbourhood of Rouen. But these rumours have died away and it is reported that our stay here will be protracted for some further time, until things become a little more settled. As for any disturbance of consequence in this city, it is out of the question during the presence of our army; but what new revolutions might take place when it is once marched off, no one can conjecture. Paris is full of officers & soldiers from the disbanded army on the Loire, & after what we have already witnessed of the fickle character of this nation [we?] should be prepared for anything.[8]

In the meanwhile, Paris begins to swarm with English bucks & families; among them we have Sir John Malcolm;[9] the Duke has received him with

7 It has proven impossible to be sure who he refers to here.
8 The new French government, desperate to reduce spending to be able to cover the allied reparations, ordered a massive reduction in the size of the army.
9 Colonel Sir John Malcolm had served in the East for many years; Wellington knew him from his India days and was a close friend.

great attention & lent him a carriage &c to drive about this place, which piece of intelligence I gained the other day from a friend & relation of his.

I am in much haste and must conclude with desiring you to present my best love to my mother & all the school room & believe me to be, your most dutiful & affectionate son, G U Barlow

Paris, 1 September 1815 (annotated received 7 September)

My dearest father,
For the first time in my life do I feel under an embarrassment when sitting down to write to you, the ever-ready pen seems now at a loss for a commencement, but silence any more would be criminal and be it mine to remove that veil of delicacy, which would be misapplied in sheltering any longer the enormities of guilt.

Alas, my dearest father you have had but one fault, one of the most amiable, a guileless hue in too much kindness in that goodness which has led you to judge of others by yourself. Letters shown me some years back by that unpalatable woman on whom the laws of nature and the fetters of speech yet free me to impose the name of mother and acts themselves infinite in number & more powerful than words have convinced your son, who it was that alike deserved to be called the best of husbands as the best of fathers. The forward glance of iniquity shall regard the transactions of twenty-six years & seek in vain for one instance to the contrary, has it ever known a want or a wish ungratified has me frown ever obscured the ray of habitual and all melting tenderness & patience. But for you I would be ashamed of the blood that flows in my veins, of an existence derived from such demon like origin.[10]

But it is done, the work of enormity is complete and nought remains but to assume that attitude which the laws of justice and our country so fully authorise. The die is cast and we must accommodate ourselves to the result. I candidly acknowledge that my own personal sufferings regarding the miserable object in question are little indeed, for alas I never knew the sound of maternal fondness, no not even the slightest whisperings from my earliest period of being able to be acquainted with them. It is for you alone (& that a great God is witness). I do really feel how sincerely I adopt your sorrows and make your situation my own.

One source of comfort still remains, may it be superabundant and perennial, may you ever find it in the midst of that family whom providence has bestowed & trust but to make amends for the conduct of their unnatural, their guilty mother; stand in the middle of us and as the church service tells us, never will you have reason to be dismayed. The world and its affairs will

10 His mother Elizabeth (nee Smith) was guilty of adultery and his father applied for and gained a divorce by act of parliament on 30 April 1816. This was in consequence of the birth of George's brother Frederick, on 23 May 1810, who was apparently not the child of Sir George.

frequently call particular members from the united society. They I trust, will however never be found wanting to the present head; while those whom sex and circumstances more especially allow of being encircled around, you will (God be pleased) be destined to afford constant subject for consideration & comfort; that may thus God bless you most respected & beloved of fathers will be the constant prayer of your most dutiful & affectionate son G U Barlow

Paris, 25 September 1815 (annotated received 29 September)

My dearest father,
It occurred to me the other day, when on the point of writing to Mr Greenwood regarding the matters connected with your kind letter of the 29th of August, that the subject would receive more attention coming from you, than from myself, the immediate object of such a communication. Under this impression I was induced to decline entering on any correspondence with Mr G[reenwood], who from his situation is no doubt fully surcharged with similar applications from every quarter and one originating with so humble an individual as myself, would gain nothing perhaps, but a civil answer. As you have therefore so kindly offered to speak on my behalf, I will thank you to do the same at a convenient opportunity. The point in question is one of great importance and the attaining of it has always been attended with considerable difficulties, which are now doubly augmented by the present state of things, so large a portion of the army being employed on actual service and the inefficient part of it now at home being so soon about to be reduced on half pay.

As for my brigade major-ship, it is already decided that I should keep it no longer; a letter from General Halkett at Brussels has just been received, stating that the nomination of the brigade major having been placed at his disposal, he had recommended a Brevet Major Love of the 52nd Regiment for that situation.[11] With this officer I am very well acquainted, he is at present wounded & somewhere in the rear, I believe Brussels & has previously been attached to the general in the same capacity; this does not occasion me therefore any surprise. Every man will naturally provide for his own friends & acquaintances. I shall therefore very quietly descend from the major into a minor situation whenever my successor arrives.

As for the Duke, he is extremely taken up with the various important military & political arrangements now making between France & the allied powers. I paid him a visit the other day & encountered the hero with a great bundle of papers in an anteroom. He stated having a perfect remembrance of you, asked if I was not on the Staff; my reply was that I held a temporary situation. 'Let me see you to dinner at six o'clock'; with these & a few hasty words I took my leave & repaired thither at the appointed hour, when a large party was assembled & of course nothing more could then pass between us.

11 Captain James Frederick Love received four wounds at Waterloo but survived.

Give my kindest love to all [the?] little girls as well as to Miss Page for her letter; [torn – tell ?] Louisa that I have sent Lady Hobhouse two excellent catalogues of the pictures & statues in the Louvre.[12] With Sir Benjamin Hobhouse you are of course acquainted by character. He & his family have been making a short visit to Paris & the death of a beloved son who was in this regiment and fell at Waterloo, a particular friend of mine, was the melancholy means of making me known to him.[13] They promised to take charge of any little packet & deliver them safely. I wish you would call on Sir B[enjamin] for his civility & attention towards me. He expressed also *a particular desire* to become acquainted with you & I wish it also very much. Lady H[obhouse] is a charming agreeable woman & so indeed are the four daughters, who accompanied them. God bless you my dearest father, believe me ever to be your most dutiful & affectionate son. G U Barlow

[PS] We have every reason to believe that the British Army will winter in this country. I shall therefore endeavour & pay you a visit in the course of the autumn & am not without hopes of being able to succeed.

George clearly managed to get leave, as his next letter explains that he had just arrived back in Paris from London.

Paris, 5 November 1815 (annotated received 11 November, answered 18 November

My dearest father,
I take this, the earliest opportunity since my arrival here of presenting you with some account of my proceedings. The beginning of the journey was not attended with very auspicious circumstances; that is to say the stage broke down about four miles on the London side of Cuckfield.[14] We were fortunately about to descend a hill & proceeding rather slowly when the axle tree of one of the fore wheels snapped; it was fortunately a moonlight night and the driver immediately perceived the accident and drew up; another step & we would have been upset. The horses were immediately taken from the carriage & the guard proceeded on and returned with two post chaises from Cuckfield; into which we put the luggage and passengers & thus we arrived at Brighton on Tuesday morning.

At two o'clock the same day the packet sailed and after a very tempestuous passage we all landed at Dieppe on Wednesday noon, about twelve o'clock. At *two* the diligence set out for Rouen; by this therefore you will see that I had not time to write a line with the information of my precious self, having been safely conveyed across the water, that short space having been

12 Lady Amelia wife of Sir Benjamin Hobhouse, 1st Baronet.
13 Captain Benjamin Hobhouse, 69th Foot.
14 Cuckfield is one mile west of Haywards Heath.

occupied in clearing our baggage from the custom house, breakfasting &c, besides there is a regular English post by way of Dieppe.

Thursday, I spent at Rouen in rambling all over the town, which is a sad dirty place & contained nothing worthy of notice but a fine cathedral. I left it at night by the diligence & arrived here on Friday morning. Upon enquiry I found that the whole army had broken up from camp and was gone into cantonments, my regiment is at a small village about nine miles from hence on the road to Orleans called Visus [Wissous] & whether I shall proceed this day.

Yesterday about twelve o'clock I waited on the Adjutant General, upon announcing my name and being ushered in, he immediately remembered my business and without any preamble he said that the Duke proposed to put me on the Staff, in the event of a favourable opportunity offering itself; nothing therefore remained for me to say, but that I had taken the earliest opportunity of waiting on him (the Adjutant General) to thank him for his kind advice and to show [torn – that?] I had paid to it every possible attention, [torn – and a?] trifling conversation followed and then I took my leave, such therefore is the present state of affairs.

I am writing at present in much haste and in a coffee room which is a perfect Babel among a sad confusion of tongues; present therefore my very best love to Miss Page and all the dear little girls and accept the same my dearest father, your most dutiful & affectionate son, G U Barlow

George was now becoming fearful that the 2/69th might be disbanded very soon, causing him to have to go on Half Pay.

Paris, 19 November 1815 (annotated received 23rd November, answered 24th November)

My dearest father,
We are now fast approaching to the conclusion of the present month, and from certain intelligence which has lately come to my knowledge, I am strongly led to believe that we shall return to England ere the ensuing Christmas. The long-contemplated measure of reducing the inefficient second battalions is shortly about to take place and the present state of politics admitting of such a step, there is every reason to imagine that it will be no longer delayed. From a person who has the means of procuring good information, I learn that all the necessary arrangements had actually been made and were about to be published in the General Orders, when an officer arrived from England and prevented the same being put in execution. The report at present in circulation is that the British Army will not move from the neighbourhood of Paris until that article of the treaty has been fulfilled which stipulates that certain fortresses shall be put into the hands of the allies. These are expected to be delivered up in the course of the ensuing week and then the British Army will be put in motion for the frontiers of Belgium, and that portion which it is intended to send home is

to take the route of Dieppe, which is only 120 miles from this metropolis. Sir H[enry] Torrens arrived three or four days ago and no doubt his journey is in some degree connected with the important arrangements which are shortly to be made.[15]

In my last I omitted to mention a circumstance of which it will be therefore necessary here to notice Sir B[enjamin] Hobhouse repeated his former kind offer of using his interest in my behalf and alluded to Lord Sidmouth by name, who is a particular friend;[16] I of course returned my best thanks. Possibly by this time you have been so fortunate as to meet him; he is generally to be found at the Carnatic Office in Manchester Buildings, Westminster,[17] about twelve o'clock; it is the last house on the right-hand side of the street & as it were suspended over the water. He expressed a strong wish to become acquainted with you; in the event of his coming to Streatham let the armour be put out of sight and everyone be cautioned against mentioning either my name as connected with Waterloo or anything relative to those transactions.[18] That subject is yet a fertile source of affliction and is the source of correspondence between me & his relative Mr H[enry] Hobhouse.[19] It was only this morning that I received a letter from Mr H[obhouse] respecting a gun, the property of my late friend; & his accounts I have yet to [obtain?] from Sir B[enjamin] [from whom] I have also lately heard. He of course relates on other subjects and gives me a very entertaining account of the journey homewards; he corresponds like any young friend of my own age, rather than as one who is old enough to be my father; so much notice does he take & so grateful are his feelings for a circumstance which really merits nothing like the consideration that it has received.

The winter has now commenced in earnest; we have had two falls of snow, not very heavy and the mornings become extremely cold, so as to impede your usual walk before breakfast. There is no temptation here to practice that beneficial custom, the roads in general being so very bad and execrably muddy.

Offer to all the school room my very best love and accept the same, my dearest father, of your most dutiful & affectionate son, G U Barlow

George wrote that his battalion was to be sent home and would surely be disbanded. He continued with his efforts to gain a last-minute staff appointment, but he did not hold out much hope.

---

15 Major General Sir Henry Torrens was Military Secretary from 1809-20.

16 Henry Addington, 1st Viscount Sidmouth, politician and previous Prime Minister.

17 The Manchester Buildings, at Cannon Row in Westminster was the former town house of the Montagu family, who had been created Dukes of Manchester in 1719. It had long been divided up into separate flats and houses. Since 1807, No. 11 Manchester Buildings had been rented by the East India Company, to house the Commissioners for investigating the debts of the late Nabobs of the Carnatic.

18 It would appear that George had taken some relics home from Waterloo, perhaps a cuirass?

19 His son, Henry William Hobhouse, was in the Honourable East India Company Service.

Paris, 7 December 1815 (annotated received 12 December)

I have to acknowledge the receipt of your two kind letters dated the 22nd & 27th & which I have thus long deferred answering for the purpose of being able to communicate the result of those steps which you recommended me to take. I shall commence a detail of my proceedings with transcribing the following letter written & left by me early on Monday morning left at General Barnes' house.[20] 'Sir, at moments like the present, when the time of his Excellency the Commander in Chief is doubtless sufficiently occupied, it is with some diffidence I bring myself to intrude either upon his or your attention, in soliciting you to call His Grace's notice to anything concerning an individual so humble as myself. His kind intentions however, which you were so good as to signify in a letter dated the 30th of September last, induce me to address you on the subject of the present communication. My regiment being under orders to proceed to England during the course of the ensuing week, this circumstance, I trust will excuse the liberty I take in requesting to be informed, whether any opportunity is likely to offer for the fulfilment of those kind intentions'.

I am writing the present in a very noisy coffee room and from memory commit the above to paper, it is almost word for word the same as the original which you shall shortly see. Today (Thursday) is almost passed by & I have not received any answer whatever; this application is not therefore likely to meet with success, the more so as instead of any augmentation being made to the Staff, a reduction of no less than twelve or fifteen officers has taken place in the Adjutant & Quarter Master General's departments & my old brigade, Sir P. Belson's is likewise broken up.[21] Upon calling to pay my respects to General Torrens, I found also that he had quitted Paris ten days previous. To Lord Hill I presented my letter and had the honour of dining with his lordship yesterday. He said however nothing calculated to inspire any hopes & after some trifling conversation regarding Lord Teignmouth & one or two other personages known to himself & me we parted.

It now remains for me to add that the regiment marched off from hence this morning for Boulogne & I shall follow in the course of an hour or two. We shall reach the sea coast on the 20th instant, Dover is to be the place of our debarkation or Harwich I have yet to learn.

Remember me most kindly to Miss Page for her letter of the 7th December [and her?] little difficulty.[22] I am glad that circumstances placed me some distance from home when this affair came before the court, even in reading Miss Page's letter I was agitated by a thousand conflicting emotions, that it

20 Major General Sir Edward Barnes, Adjutant General of the Army of Occupation.
21 Lieutenant Colonel Sir Charles P. Belson, 28th Foot, took command of the 8th Brigade after Waterloo.
22 The governess Miss Page was obviously caught between his warring parents.

would be in vain for me to attempt to describe but no more of this horrible subject.

I have taken advantage of your goodness also to draw upon [a] bill at ten days [only?] for fifty pounds payable at Messrs Glyn & Co. and will feel much obliged by your honouring the same, but more of this when we next meet. Give my kindest love to all, accept the same my dear father of your most dutiful & affectionate son. G U Barlow

13

India

As George remained in England for the next few years, he had no reason to write and his correspondence ceases. He did however marry his first cousin (Uncle Robert's daughter) Hilare Barlow on 27 February 1817.

George had gone on Half Pay in the 69th Foot in 1816, soon after the second battalion returned from France in December 1815. He eventually exchanged into the 22nd Light Dragoons vice Captain George Davyson on 17 August 1820 but his new regiment was disbanded that year and he remained on half pay. However, having transferred into the cavalry he was then able to transfer into the 4th (Queen's Own) Light Dragoons on 5 April 1821 vice Captain Charles Wood which put him back on full pay, as the regiment was ordered for India. Therefore on New Year's day 1822 we find his correspondence resumes, when we find him awaiting transportation to India. He had embarked with the regiment on the *Dunira* on 31 December 1821, accompanied by his wife Hilare, arriving in India on 16 May 1822.

To Sir George Barlow GCB, Oakwood, Chichester
Dunira at Gravesend, 1 January 1822[1]

My dearest father,
We all came on board yesterday at noon, the last day of the old year. The troops arrived from Romford at Tilbury Fort, where I was in waiting to join them, and about an hour afterwards my beloved Hilare accompanied by dear William alone, came off to the ship. Our, I will not say, little cabin was perfectly ready for her reception, owing to the kindness of my good uncle, who had previously dispatched the yacht's crew to prepare matters so that we had all the chests, table, chairs ready lashed & secured & could have encountered immediately a gale of wind. As far as depends upon externals, we want nothing that can contribute to comfort thank God & *your* kindness & liberality, my beloved parent, to whom I owe so much & indeed everything. The cabin is eighteen feet long so as to afford a little promenade in bad weather and possesses everything that can make a ship tolerable. Added to all this, Mrs Forbes has brought on board the Ayah,[2] of whom we

1 The *Dunira* was an East India ship of 1,325 tons, which was in commission from 1817 to 1833.
2 An Ayah was an Indian servant girl. It has proven impossible to identify Mrs Forbes with any certainty.

have been so long in expectance. Mrs Forbes has taken the trouble to come all the way from Cheltenham to Gravesend for the purpose of putting in person this woman on board. She speaks of her, I may say, in terms of affection & at the same time gave me a written character of which the following is an extract, 'You will find her strictly honest, sober, modest, and cleanly to a degree of delicacy compared with other natives of India. She is remarkably diligent & active, but her exertions are always quickened by a desire of pleasing. She has been in my service nearly two years & I have not yet had occasion to remind her of any part of her duty or find fault with an awkward performance of it. Her disposition is so amiable that we all regard her with affection & part with her with sincere regret. I beg you to observe that she is of the Mussalman[3] persuasion which forbids the eating of beef or pork. Will you be kind enough to desire the steward to provide her daily with a clean mess of rice and curry of mutton, fowl or fish, and to give her clean white biscuit with her tea.' These testimonials are very strong and as the poor woman is never sick at sea I doubt not but that she will prove a valuable acquisition to my dear Hilare. We set down every day to dinner *forty persons* among whom eight are ladies. Everything is conducted in the most handsome and elegant style and although the party is as large, there is no confusion in the attendance & we have quite sufficient space. Tomorrow we drop down to the lower Hope[4] & the next day tend to reach the Downs, from whence we shall sail with the very first fair wind, since the Purser is already come onboard with the final dispatches & the owners of the vessel are obliged to pay thirty pounds a day for demurrage [to?] the Company for being behind the appointed time, as the wind has been constantly fair. Besides getting ashore about a week since, on Saturday last she experienced a second accident, another East Indiaman '*Harry*' ran foul of and carried away her jib boom, which has occasioned a still further delay.[5] I will not say a word as to our present feelings, you are all too well acquainted with all the dear folks at Chatham not to fancy their distraction, as well as our own: it is enough to make a stone weep, what we went through, however no more. I am obliged to finish this hurried letter, being perpetually interrupted by details respecting the troops & the ship just now is a scene of confusion that exceeds [anything?].

A thousand loves to all your dear circle, to all of whom I will write respectively in the course of the voyage. God ever bless and protect those who so well deserve Heaven's choicest gifts, is the most comprehensive form of words that I can use at the present heart-breaking moment & now ever will be the prayer of your most dutiful & affectionate son, G U Barlow.

3 A Muslim.
4 Presumably Stanford-le-Hope, a village near the mouth of the Thames.
5 Possibly the '*Henry Porcher*' which served with the Honourable East India Company between 1818 and 1831.

[PS] I have received Mr Money's packet of letters, for which pray do not forget to thank him most kindly if I have not time. I have several letters to write.

George's next letter announced their arrival in Bombay after a very rapid and pleasant voyage.

To Sir G Barlow Bart GCB, Oakwood near Chichester
Bombay, 14 May 1822 (annotated received on 8th October, replied on 23rd December)

My dearest father,
We are now within a few day's sail of our destination, I shall therefore prepare these lines in readiness for the first conveyance to be dispatched, please God, on our anticipated arrival some ship may be found on the eve of sailing, at a moment when we are occupied with vicious weather attendant upon present landing then I shall not have time to be so circumstantial as could be wished. To say everything in as concise and comprehensive a form of words as possible, know then that our voyage has been most delightful, even beyond the most sanguine expectation. Not a single day of bad weather since leaving England, and with the exception of a few hours off the Canary Islands (as mentioned in my letter by the French man of war brig *La Pintade*[6] to dear Anne) an open boat might have come all the way throughout, such is the opinion of the sailors, and therefore conclusive enough on that score, they declare that such an uninterrupted series of fair weather during four months is rarely experienced without some tempests of rain or thunder in these tropical climates thus far depended upon the Almighty; there is not a single individual either young or old among the forty persons who sailed & sat down together at table whose conduct form an exception to the above remark and when I add that constant good health had pervaded every part of our little group the description is compleat. The Master has ably set us towards the latter end of May and Colonel Dalbiac[7] is exceeding anxious to have the regiment sent up to Karnak [the Carnatic] previous to that period, if the government accedes to his wishes our stay at Bombay will be short indeed, probably but a few days, barely sufficient to transmit such messages as may be absolutely necessary and provide those articles of furniture, apparel &c indispensably requisite before we are sent into Guzerat [Goojerat]. In that case we shall see little of our friends and the various introductions will procure about as many dinners & nothing more. I must confess myself desirous of making a few weeks sejour[8] was to form connections and acquaintances that may hereafter turn to some account.

6 I have been unable to discover anything about this brig.
7 Colonel Sir James Charles Dalbiac of the 4th Light Dragoons, was brigadier general of the Goojerat District of the Bombay Army from 1822-4.
8 French: Stay

Such are my wishes which in all probability will not be fulfilled. It is generally supposed that in a week or ten days after arrival, we shall be shipped on to coasting vessels which will put us ashore at Bombay, distant about thirty-six miles from the cantonments & bring back the regiment that we are about to replace.

I have sent to Chatham a small roughly sketched chart of our track from which you will be able to follow. We have touched nowhere since departing land previous to the line, have made the land on two occasions for the purpose of rectifying the chronometer, the first time at the island of Tristan da Cunha and the second at Rodriguez near the Mauritius.[9] On the 13th of last month we crossed the line;[10] the latter part of our passage has been hot as was expected and as it always is the case at the present season. Continued light winds & variable currents constantly prevailing in these latitudes. We have had a pretty good introduction into hot weather. The thermometer in our cabin never weakening below 82 [28 C] at any period of the twenty-four hours and in the shade during the day generally rises to 85 or 87 [31 C] with all the windows & ports open. Thank God both dear Hilare & myself are remarkably well. Those who appear to be most annoyed by the heat are two or three old Indians. They affirm that when we all set down together forty in number at dinner, in the cuddy which is nearly six feet six inches high & pretty well crammed,[11] without any punkas,[12] the temperature is more oppressive than even in India. The fumes of so many hot cups of tea at breakfast, and an equal number of temporary decks always make the thermometer rise higher than at other times.[13]

We can never be too thankful for that kindness which has enabled us to procure such excellent accommodation as our present cabin. Without it we would have been uncomfortable indeed. According to my notions there is no other suitable for ladies and we are as private as if in our own houses with ample space for the trunks & furniture and above all so delightfully cool. I must not omit to mention that the Ayah has in every respect proved worthy of the high character given by Mrs Forbes. Mrs Nepean[14] has been sadly troubled by her English maid whereas the Ayah has been most useful, good, composed, hones & clean to a nicety. I wish much that she could be persuaded to accompany us to Kaira[15] but that I fear is out of the question, as she has local ties at Bombay, such as two children &c. She is a Mohammadan woman of a very good cast & most respectable.

9 Tristan da Cunha is a small group of volcanic islands in the South Atlantic, Rodrigues is an outer island of the Mauritius group being some 350 miles east of Mauritius.

10 The equator.

11 A small compartment on a ship.

12 A canvas frame, pulled by a 'punka-wallah' to act as a fan.

13 He presumably means temporary partitions for the various passengers preventing a through draught.

14 The wife of Captain William Nepean, 4th Light Dragoons.

15 Kaira is also known as Kheda and is 22 miles from Ahmedabad, it lies on the banks of the Vatrak and Shedhi Rivers.

I shall not secure my pen for the purpose of concluding the present until we are safely landed at Bombay. We trust in a few weeks afterwards to have some accounts from dear England and Oakwood by the March ships.[16] It really seems quite an age since hearing from those we hold dear & which concentrates our greatest preservation. On board the ship there is still both internal & exterior mourning observed, for Robert had been obliged to take a voyage for the recovery of health to the Cape, having had a severe illness in consequence of snipe shooting, hog hunting &c.

Henry also had been obliged to take a voyage to the Cape so that I am now literally the only son that you have in India.[17] Thank God, Hilare is in good health and I through perpetuity [of] fagging both by land & water understands a vertical line from morning till night & almost worried to death, yet am quite well & remain with love to all your most fond, dutiful & affectionate son G U Barlow

George's next letter announced their arrival at the cantonment for the regiment at Kaira, which had been ceded to the British in 1803 and was used as a military station until 1830.

To Sir GH Barlow Bart GCB, Oakwood near Chichester England
Marked prepaid 3Q[Quarter Anna?] 10R[upees][18]
Kutcherry Kaira 14 June 1822 (Annotated received 14 November, answered 23 December)

My dearest father,
My last from Bombay was concluded in some haste and announced to you our speedy departure from the presidency after a short stay of only four days. A small armed vessel belonging to the Company called the *Chaser* mounting four guns with twenty men,[19] was given up solely to us and Captain & Mrs Kerr,[20] no troops being put on board. This was tolerable accommodation composed with that enjoyed by other who went on board large open other boats. Although having the option of remaining during the monsoon for four months at Bombay, and Mr Warden kindly offered us his house in the fort,[21] during his projected excursion for some months on the Dekan [Deccan], I chose to accompany the regiment, having no particular friends or other inducements to remain at the presidency. Four days

16 Oakwood House, built in 1811 stands two miles from Chichester, it is now a Prep School.
17 Robert and John Henry were both in the Bengal Civil Service.
18 The coinage in India was not unified between the three Presidencies until 1835. The Bengal Presidency coinage was – 1 Mohur was equal to 16 Rupees, an Anna being 1/16 of a Rupee and a Quarter Anna being 1/64 of a Rupee. An Anna was worth 4 Pice or 12 Pie.
19 The *Chaser* was a small 160 ton vessel in the Bengal Pilot Service of the Honourable East India Company. She was built in Batavia in 1778.
20 Paymaster Robert Kerr and his wife 4th Light Dragoons. Paymasters were granted the regimental rank of the most junior captain.
21 Mr Francis Warden, a member of the Bombay Council.

The Rosa at Kaira by Robert Pouget. (Editor's Collection)

was too short a period for comfortably transacting our business, many of the introductory letters I was compelled to forward by post with the necessary apologies and I was obliged to go about, often walking under a vertical sun & be a great deal afloat, to superintend the shipment of my baggage from the *Dunira* to the little ketch. I procured however servants, cooking utensils, stock for the second voyage and in short did as much as was ever transacted within the same time, personally superintending everything. I think I told you of my having breakfasted & dined at the governors, the Commander in Chief's & the last day the Wardens had a grand dinner party, at which we met Mr More the Collector of Kaira who kindly offered us the use of the Kutcherry till we could procure a habitation for ourselves and being absent on leave himself at Bombay,[22] he wrote to have the house made ready for our reception; from whence I write the present and where we have resided ever since our arrival at this place on the 3rd instant.

To resume however the thread of the narrative, we sailed from Bombay on Thursday afternoon the 16th of May and after a most tempestuous passage of three days & nights, during which our little bark so unlike the *Dunira* was terribly tossed about, going under a close reefed foresail only. We [torn – arrived?] at the mouth of the Chadur & soon & threaded [torn – through?] hills into the Gulf of Cambay [now Khambhat] about twelve or fifteen miles to the north of the celebrated Numbuddah [Narmada] River. Dear Hilare again underwent all the horrors of sea sickness and in that

22 A Kutcherry refers to government accommodation.

weak state was conveyed to the camp about two miles distant. After a day's halt we proceeded to Jumboosur [Jambusar] in the Collectorate of Baroche and from thence three marches to Baroda,[23] the residence of the Guckwar where we have a subsidiary force on this route to Kaira became necessary on account of the swollen state of the fords of the Mhye [Mahi] River.

This march so immediately following the sea sickness added to the unusual method of a palanquin during the night which prevented sleep, and the extraordinary heat of the weather during the day when we halted. The thermometer standing at 105 of Fahrenheit [41 C] in our tent made dear Hilare very ill. I also, who ought to have known better, but from extreme anxiety, to superintend & see everything right, would run about under a vertical sun, paid also forfeit though not very heavily, being seized with a sick headache & stomach, which required some appropriate doses of medicine that soon however set all to rights.

We remained at Banda [Bhavda?] four or five days in the bungalow of a Mr Young surgeon of one of the Sepoy battalions,[24] who kindly made us the offer of his house, which we accepted & where a little rest & quiet quickly restored us both, so that with our animals we were able to make this place in two nights journeys from Banda of about eighteen Coss each.[25] Mr Williams the resident at the latter city, being kind enough to furnish us with a couple of horsemen in passing through the Guckwar's territory as an escort for ourselves & baggage. Our cantonment is about two miles distant from this town & reckoned one of the best in India. The bungalows well built and that which I have purchased, small but very comfortable, requiring no repairs, possessing a very pretty garden & some furniture, such as chairs and tables & beds. So that as soon as the present occupant can find shelter for himself & wife, we hope to take possession previous to the rains that are now hourly expected. We have had a few momentary showers and the usual signs of change. We are to have the 17th Dragoons with us during the monsoon of which I am rather sorry in point of *society* both male and female, they cannot bear any comparison with the 4th.[26] As soon as I am a little settled and able to look about, I shall write more fully to you and your dear circle on a variety of matters. The present must be concluded as a hasty compendium thrown together because the ships sail so soon. This is the 14th of June, a letter is always *six* & sometimes during rains, ten days going from hence to Bombay & towards the end of the month the ships sail for England so that I must be concise. Our latest advice from England are by the Company's ship *Macqueen*[27] up to the 25th of January last. Hilare

23 Baroda is now called Vadodara, it was under the control of the Gaekwad Dynasty.
24 Surgeon Archibald Young served in the HEIC army from 1820-7.
25 A Coss was a unit of land distance in India which unhelpfully ranged from 1 to 3 miles in length.
26 The 17th Light Dragoons were officially nominated as lancers in 1822 but did not learn of this change until they arrived at St Helena on their way home the following year.
27 The *Macqueen* East India Company Ship of 1,333 tons served between 1822-1831.

begs me to say that when a little more settled and composed, she will write to the dear girls, so will I.

We have a letter from my cousin Robert[28] at Ghazeepore [Ghazipur] dated the 18th of May announcing the loss of his little girl Hilare & the birth of another named Caroline Penelope.[29] He was unacquainted with our arrival but wrote in the anticipation. There has not been time to hear from Charlotte and whether it is my brother Henry or Robert, or both, that have been forced to go to the Cape on account of illness. It is a pity that civilians who are never exposed to the climate & who know their prospects so exclusively depend upon health, should take so little care of it. Military men must occasionally run risques [sic]. I must as usual conclude with my emphatic sentence of 'God Bless you all' & that the present may find you as it leaves us in good health & happiness. Hilare unites with me in kindest love to all the dear circle, and believe me to be, my dearest father, your most dutiful & affectionate son, G U Barlow.

To Sir G H Barlow, Bart GCB, Oakwood (redirected to H M Dockyard, Chatham, Kent)
Kaira, 1 August 1822 (annotated answered 10 March 1823)

My dearest father,
I received the day before yesterday yours of 1st of March last bearing the Madras postmark 4th July. It announced for the first time to my great entertainment and concern, the circumstances of dear Harriet's peculiar illness;[30] about six weeks ago we received a letter from Chatham dated the 4th of March which was utterly silent on so melancholy a subject and as no news is good news we had fondly hoped that all our beloved relations at Oakwood and elsewhere might be considered as enjoying that most invaluable of blessing, health. Even at this distance of time, when we are assured that all danger & anxiety is overspent, it can feel as much as if the fatal crisis was actually impending. To read that 'for two or three days you were almost without a shadow of hope that she would recover' really makes me shudder; for what new trials my dearest father must we be reserved? Oh, may it please the Almighty to think that our branch of the family have already drank sufficiently deep of the bitter cup of affliction, may it please him to spare us a renewal of sorrow yet too recent. It is an example by all this, of how little real use all human precautions, when can one be sure to be safe[?] I should have thought that your habits of life at such a place as Oakwood would have been a suffice to guarantee against the gangers of the maladies which

28 His cousin Robert was the son of Uncle Robert.

29 Hilare Elizabeth Barlow died 21 September 1821 aged 6 years 6 months. Her parents were Robert and Catherine Barlow at Ghazipur. Caroline Penelope was baptised on 26 October 1821. Robert and Catherine had also lost George aged 14 months on 20 July 1817.

30 It would appear that Harriet had contracted Smallpox despite have been inoculated previously.

usually affect crowded cities. As for myself I am notwithstanding all that has passed, the friend of vaccination although more of professional men can properly be said to be able to form an opinion on the subject, I cannot help thinking once on the unanimous opinion of the College of Surgeons where such a host of medical names & all the first talent of the country may be seen. Opposing in such unqualified terms, the reoccurrence in some persons from peculiarity of constitution or from ale [sic] or what is perhaps more frequent than either from some defect in the malady of the matter the inoculation perhaps does not take effect to the desired extent. Several cases are on record which were under Dr James's[31] more delicate superintendence wherein the smallpox rash essentially appeared on the patient & died but millions of instances may be cited of an opposite nature for one of this description attended to, our only regret that the sixteen cannot be reduced to a few only as it really is to an almost convenient certainty.

God be praised we are both of us in the enjoyment of the best health. You know I always tell the truth, there is a good deal of sickness in the regiment among the men chiefly owing to their over indulgence, the same may be said of the officers that exposure to vertical sun may also weaken the best constitutions, but presently I am called to scrawl mails and I can safely say that the greater portion of the sufferers have none but themselves to blame. To tell you the truth from what I have latterly seen of Guzerat [Gujarat] the present season of the rains is quite delightful. These are strictly speaking but tropical showers and although they have been more extensive than usual I have never been prevented from taking my exercise either in the morning or evening since their commencement about six weeks ago. The above account applies to this part of India alone, there being no hills, at Bombay however & in the Dekan [Deccan] I am told the rains are incessant and violent. As for the mortality among the Europeans, I am not at all surprised. They drink to an excess which excites in me the greatest horror. At home a man is obliged to content himself with porter, with now and then a little gin, but here unfortunately they receive double pay and the arrack is in the same proportion cheap.[32] Moreover, the rules of the service as it were, patronize intoxication since the Company allow two dram per diem per man at the same time as his rations. When on hard service it might perhaps be proper enough, but when they are all day in quarters it actually engenders disease. Liberties of this nature cannot be taken with impunity in this climate, but it is all in vain to talk. A military outstation is not most assuredly the best sinecure in the world. Young men who are not possessed of superior minds know not how to kill time & go out in the heat of the day, they dare not, possessing no internal resources of amusement, no books, no good companions & so forth, they generally take to smoking and drinking even in the middle of the day. That repast differs [little] is also very pernicious. People sit down

31 This would appear to be Surgeon Joseph James who was in the HEIC Medical service from 1784.

32 Arrack or Arak is a distilled drink made in India, not to be confused with the beverage produced in North Africa.

to a compleat dinner, drink a great deal of wine & never feel hungry at the great meal about seven o'clock, then again Madeira and Claret being placed before them the temptation is irresistible. I do readily believe that matrimony is the saviour of man in India, it saves his health, it spares his pocket & improves his manners and makes up for the want of society which after all is the greatest privation in India; hence the terrible ennui of which most of our people complain & which already has determined several of them to return to Europe immediately. As for me I have found India exactly according with preconceived expectations. Those I deem were certainly formed upon superior information & correct standard. In many respects it is even more agreeable, nothing disgusts or disappoints me & should dear Hilare & I continue to enjoy that necessary health, we shall be very comfortable. An opportunity offers for me to go round to Calcutta in charge of a detachment of dragoons who have volunteered for regiments at that presidency. However pleasant such a trip might prove, and a strong one to touch at Madras, spend three or four months with my brother Henry, see Robert my cousin who could come down from Ghatpoor [Ghazipur] & so forth, I have not allowed inclination to get the better of prudence & steady to those views which have brought me out to this continent, I shall keep perfectly quiet. My house is very comfortable & contrived to get very good servants, good horses and establish a system of things which would be utterly deranged by any travelling expeditions and incur some expenses that at this moment would be unacceptable.

A few days ago, I wrote to dear Fanny; perhaps this person may be in time for the same conveyance to Europe. I think it would be as well to establish an intercourse with some of the clerks about the India House in Leadenhall Street who are charged with making up the letter bags, to give you and all our dear family about a fortnight's notice previous to the sailing of the *Freetraders* who are sailing at all periods of the year & thereby could transport out the most recent accounts from home.[33] This suggestion is worthy of your attention.

God bless you my dearest father, may the same Almighty superintendence vanquishes [the] troubles of all beneath the same roof. Give my kindest love to all and with every sentiment of duty & affection, believe me to be your most fond & affectionate son, G U Barlow.

To Sir G H Barlow Bart GCB, Oakwood, near Chichester
Kaira, 3 November 1822 (annotated Received 10 April 1823, Answered 16 February 1824)

My dearest father,
I see by the papers that a ship named the *Bombay Merchant* is advertised to sail on the 10th instant;[34] should the intelligence be correct the present will

33 The demand from British merchants at home for the freeing of trade by removing import dues was gaining acceptance and the government began dismantling the Navigation Acts.
34 This was not an East India Company ship.

arrive just in time to convey the latest intelligence from Guzerat [Gujarat], as a letter would not move there in five or ten days going between this & the presidency, since the rains have subsided. Separated as we are from home by such an immensity of space in a climate not reputed the most healthy, my first care shall always be to commence with the important article of health, and I pray God that it may be in my power to set at rest your anxious hearts in these few yet expressive words 'All is well' as literally is our present case. We have just passed through what is considered the only unhealthy season on this side of India. This period commences about the middle of September at the termination of the rains, continue throughout the month of October & ceases about the present time. Up to this, we have lost three officers and about fifty men. Great as the loss may seem, the 20th Regiment which had been two or three years at St Helena and from there to the Cape, and landing at Bombay shortly after ourselves, remained there during the monsoon, has suffered to a considerably greater extent,[35] so that the mortality is not peculiar to Guzerat [Gujarat], of which however the people & the presidency have a great horror. The civilians dislike coming beyond Surat. The causes of this annual mortality are common to the whole of this side of India. After the cool refreshing period of the rains, which cease about the middle of September, the sky again becomes cloudless and the sun breaks forth with increased power. During the first week of October the thermometer on the coolest, shady part of the interior of our house generally stood at 92 [33 C], there was not a *breath of wind.* On the mean whole, a scorching sun draws out of the ground well saturated with the recent rains, a very great vapour, whether it is at Kaira or Bombay or elsewhere, which is more particularly visible at sunrise & sunset. Those who after the sultry heat of the day, sleep on verandas or with doors & windows wide open or in fortunate draughts of the night breezes or like our poor soldiers, lie down on the grass with scarcely any clothes, generally catch a terrible fever which often terminates fatally. All these disadvantages are aggravated by the lives many people lead. The dragoon sees it in his power to indulge his dreadful propensity of drinking at a trifling expense & those who should know better, commit all sorts of errors in diet, which with the superior pay and allowances of the country afford great encouragement. For the heartfelt gratitude to God, dear Hilare & I can say that we have always felt uncommonly well. We have not found any peculiar cautions necessary beyond those that constitute our daily habits of life. Early rising and exercise in plenty at proper hours; regular living, *three o'clock dinners* & at nine to Bedfordshire.

We are now approaching the delightful period of the cold season; already the number of sick in the hospital begins to decrease, and the general temperature with the exception of two or three hours in the middle of the day is become very pleasant. Early in the morning at sunrise, when I go out to take my ride, or attend the drills, a blue cloth jacket is very acceptable; the thermometer being at 65 [18 C] during the day, however, it generally

35 The 20th Foot (East Devonshire).

mounts to 83 or 84 [29 C]. The fineness of the weather during the last three or four weeks has permitted me to make various little alterations in our bungalow, which I had some time since contemplated. We have enlarged the bedroom by making an arch in the wall of the house & taking in the veranda. The sitting room & parlour are both laid down with fine marble [churam?][36] so as to look beautifully white & cool. The kitchen garden has been tolerably well stocked & [is] supplying us at present with French beans & spinach & by Christmas I hope to have a plentiful crop of most European vegetables, green peas, cauliflower & potatoes besides the usual productions of this country; it is indeed the best in the cantonment.

Remember however that in all these proceedings I have never for a moment, lost sight of *economy*. My improvements have cost *a few hundred of rupees*, but *that* is only known *to myself*, much *show* is made for the money which independent of the comfort & style that it furnishes to me now, will hereafter return into my pocket, since the little old man acquires an increased *reputation for* value. With the exception of *timber*, materials for building are not expensive. *Labour however is very dear*. When you pay a man for a *day's work, he commences at nine and leaves off at five o'clock*. Nothing can persuade a Hindoo to alter these hours & after all, his performance during that stated period does not amount to near half what one of your fine sturdy Sussex labourers would do in the same time. As it is I am obliged to be my own burser as well as architect & keep master Blacky to his stable,[37] otherwise working by the day would be a losing chore.

I have however been more than usually fortunate in the settlement of my household. The head servant is an uncommonly active, clever fellow who well understands his business. I keep him however well in hand & my daily expenditure convinces me that he is [torn – no greater?] rogue than the remainder of his fraternity. By maintaining this salutary check & making as small as is possible consistently with propriety, the scale of our own private expenses, I am enabled to maintain an elegant appearance & see company in as good style as the commander of the cantonments. All this moreover is accompanied with a surplus of income which is monthly set aside to defray the marginal cost of my journey up to the place, the bungalow, horses &c. However, all these are details which should be made known in some future letter.

My last letter from Oakwood [received here is?] dated 17th of May which refers to some *former* letters that have not as yet come to hand. This correspondence must account for my friend's silence, as to any of their kind letters. Two ships, the *Barkworth*[38] & *James Sibbald*[39] have been long

36 This means pass or valley in hindi. I presume he means the marble is used as floor tiles.

37 His horse Blacky.

38 The *Barkworth* was an East India Company ship of 500 tons in 1816-17 but appears to have continued plying the Indian route.

39 The *James Sibbald* was an East India Company ship of 670 tons between 1811-17. It appears to have continued plying the Indian route.

expected, the former I believe sailed from England as long ago as April last, perhaps has put into the Cape [of Good Hope] or some other port on the passage. I am in anxious expectation of the next account, to hear how you all are, as well as the dear general & Miss Page. With humblest love to all in which dear Hilare unites acceptance, my dearest father, your most dutiful & affectionate son G U Barlow.

[PS] The papers mention the death of *Mrs John Neave* in Weymouth Street after a long & easy illness. Is it our acquaintances?

To G.H. Barlow Bart GCB, Oakwood near Chichester
Kaira, 18 January 1823 (Annotated received 1 July, answered 16 February 1824)

My dearest father,
Since writing to Miss Page on the 5th instant, another opportunity offers for the conveyance of letters to Europe which I shall not neglect. Ships arrive at & sail from Bombay every month, but when homeward bound they generally touch at the Cape so that accounts from us can never be very recent. We are thank God both quite well, to us newly arrived Europeans this cool season is charming. The poor natives however, seem quite petrified and never stir without their heads & faces being quite muffled up. During the whole of the last week there has prevailed a sharp north easterly breeze and on turning out to exercise yesterday morning I had the curiosity to expose my thermometer in the open air when the mercury fell as low as 45 of Fahrenheit [7 C], this was at day break, and I am informed rather an unseasonal temperature for this part of India. It is likely however to last but for a very few days and even now the glass rises to 75 or 80 [26-27 C] towards noon. For the next six weeks pleasant weather may be expected and till the middle of March when the sun approaches pretty near the line and the hot weather commences.

We are anxiously awaiting the next advices from England, which will decide where our dear friends at Chatham propose turning their steps. By a letter from Maria dated in the end of June we had the comfort of learning that her dear good father was considerably in health & sports and beginning to feel somewhat more reconciled to the approaching changes. After a residence of fifteen years, the idea of him is so associated with Chatham that I cannot fancy anyone else commissioner at that place. We hope that his retirement from the situation will be marked by some public act of official approbation, such as the restoration of his name to the list of vice admirals.[40] Independent of other considerations, the accumulated weight of business, or rather drudgery, rising from the reduction of some of the subordinate departments would render it advisable for him to relinquish

40 Uncle Robert retired as a rear admiral in 1823 and enjoyed a long retirement in Canterbury until 1843.

the situation. His life & health to us is most precious and the primary consideration. Three of his children are provided for, and he may seek *otium cum dignitate*[41] whilst an adequate case is made out to the world for his proceedings. I am glad of being furnished with so good a foretext which will spare us & you all many sacrifices of feeling on accounting for so unexpected a resolution.

Lord Londonderry's melancholy end would have afforded good subject for such a spineless as Johnson.[42] What a sad reflection upon our nature, that such a man, possessed of all that this world could cover or afford should thus quit it. We speculate here upon someone else being appointed Governor General in place of Mr Canning whose parliamentary talents in the House of Commons must absolutely be necessary to ministers, a circumstance which will overcome the personal dislike that is entertained towards that gentleman in a higher quarter and give him preference even to Lord Wellesley who sit in the upper chamber.

I am glad to hear that Richard has come off with so much eclat from the college examinations. Just now he is on the point of leaving you all. Poor fellow, my parting trial is yet too recent not to make me feel for what he must shortly undergo. It is a sad qualification to all the advantages of the Company since that so long a separation from one's native country must take place ere any of their servants can return home. That one circumstance in my mind suffices to counterbalance the extraordinary advantages that it otherwise holds out. A civilian who does not at first get into debt, may leave in affluence and return to England at the end of twenty years upon an income of two thousand pounds per annum whilst yet in the prime of life. I can aver that a humble captain of dragoons may keep a most elegant establishment, entertain in the handsomest manner and at the same time enjoy every comfort whilst making outwardly so great a show, upon half his pay, while the remainder may be placed in the strong box. We have now kept house six months, in the manner which we always propose to do and therefore can pretty well speak as to our annual expenditure. Making a due allowance for the article of extraordinaries, I can have a surplus of three hundred rupees per month or about four thousand at the end of the year. This estimate is formed from the experience of the period just past, wherein I have been paying for my new furniture, horses, additions & alterations to the bungalow & such other charges as are not likely again to occur. It will never be necessary for me to draw a shilling upon England; with all this we have the reputation of having the nicest, most elegantly fitted out house & giving the best parties in the cantonment. Nothing but a little good management is required for this purpose. I neither interfere with my cook or head servant, the latter of a hon[our] keeps the keys of my little cellar, all my horse, plate &c &c. But then he is forced to give *a daily* account of

41 Latin: 'leisure with dignity'.

42 The politician Robert Stewart, 2nd Marquess of Londonderry, more often known by his previous title as Lord Castlereagh, committed suicide in 1822.

the expenditure by which means it is impossible to play any tricks. His perquisites were from a certain allowance that the shop keepers make on the monthly payment of my bills. What that allowance is I neither know nor care, whilst satisfied with the actual amount of the disbursements, which are as moderate as I could wish.

Our little society including the civilians, is generally about fifty persons. When Mrs Dalbiac & Mrs Hay now on the voyage from Europe, Mrs Fendall coming from Bengal,[43] arrive we shall have fifteen ladies; which makes it pleasant for Hilare. Kaira is the head quarters of the northern division of Guzerat [Gujarat], consequently we have the whole of the staff, a troop of horse artillery, a regiment of native infantry; a judge & collector, each with two assistants, a chaplain & a church, the only one out of Bombay. This building will be completed in a few months & has cost John Company not a few rupees. This a proof that the station in permanently established and that I may consider my present dwelling as a perfect home, an advantage we possess over Bengal where the king's cavalry change cantonments every three years between Cawnpore [now Kanpur] & Meerut.

My cousin Robert is desirous of arranging an interview with us at Calcutta, whither he is coming down to send another little boy to Europe. Charlotte wishes us to touch at Madras. Such a trip would accord much with my own private feelings in every point of view as well as Hilare's. We should be received with open arms at both presidencies by your numerous friends & our own relations. I have however not permitted inclination to get the better of more sober judgement. In quitting the cantonment I must resign all the comfortable allowances, which render a troop more advantageous than any staff situations in the country and retain alone my personal pay which would by no means counterbalance the expenses of a voyage & the maintenance of my establishment of servants, grooms who are the best of their kind & which I should with reluctance part; unless we take the field I am resorted to remain a fixture at Kaira. Dear Hilare is perfectly of the same opinion, here in the middle of our comforts & little society to whom I know we are not unacceptable, in the enjoyment of health, we are as contented & happy as India can possibly render us. Should such a state of things continue, I may with advancement in my profession, be enabled to realize as much as will enable me to be comfortable hereafter & provide for whatever may occur in the different changes & chances of this mortal life.

Dear Hilare desires me to add her most affectionate love to you all. As I write, it is unneccessary for her to take up the pen till the next opportunity, which will be about the middle of February. Remember us to all our kind friends & relations for whose names I cannot here add space & double letters must be avoided, every single sheet whether to or from Bombay costs us a rupee. Write to us therefore always on a sheet of foolscap if you have anything more than usual to communicate or the dear girls wish to be very

43 The wife of Captain William Fendall, 4th Light Dragoons.

chatty. Believe me ever to remain my dearest father, your most dutiful & affectionate son G U Barlow.

[PS] Major Onslow of our regiment is arranging an exchange with a Major Wyndham of the 67th Regiment who is a son of your great man at Petworth and who is recently come out to join his regiment in this country on promotion.[44]

To Sir G H Barlow Bart GCB, Oakwood near Chichester
Kaira, 20 May 1823 (Annotated received 15 October, answered 16 February 1824)

My dearest father,
The present letter will chiefly be devoted to the detail of some little financial arrangement that I have in contemplation after which it will be necessary to give you a few hints on the subject of my promotion, the period of which although not exactly arrived, yet I think cannot be very far distant.

We will proceed first to money matters. I left England in January 1822 having drawn our dividend for that month, and closed accounts with Messrs Glyn & Co. I left with my cousin William at Chatham, an order on them for about sixty pounds to pay for the piano forte & another little saddler's bill, this was to be furnished by the dividend of July 1822. About twenty pounds would then remain, which added to twenty more arising from the dividend of January 1823 would settle the debt of forty pounds that I owe to my good uncle at Chatham, a debt which I had hoped the sale of my carriage would have covered. The vehicle I understand fetched little or nothing. To the best of my memory I do not owe any other individual in England a sixpence. In January 1823 Glyn would have in hand about sixty pounds, in July one hundred & fifty and in January 1824, two hundred & forty pounds, since you have been so truly kind as to let me have the interest of the sum that was laid out to effect the exchange into this regiment.

Now in this country I was obliged to borrow money off Messrs Forbes & Co.[45] at the rate of nine & ten percent for the purchase of my house, horses &c. Some time elapsed before it was possible to pay off any of the principal by monthly instalments as I am now doing, but the ten percent is a great drawback all the while. An opportunity however very advantageous to me in consequence of the rate of exchange is just now offered and I have therefore given a bill upon you for two hundred & forty pounds payable thirty

44 Major William Onslow, 4th Light Dragoons, actually transferred into the 42nd Foot and immediately retired on half pay, his place as major being taken by Major George Brown of the 8th Light Dragoons in May 1824. Major Charles Wyndham of the 67th finally gained a lieutenant colonelcy in the infantry (unattached).

45 John Forbes set up a business at Bombay in 1764 trading cotton and later became official banker to the Bombay Presidency. The company has continued to grow and is now a huge international conglomerate.

days after sight, as a period that will not be very distant from January 1824 when the said sum will actually be in Messrs Glyn's hands. A gentleman, one of the civilians at this station is also desirous of remitting to England a sum of about three hundred pounds. He cannot get more than one shilling, nine pence halfpenny for his Bombay Rupees, which intrinsically are worth two shillings & three pence. Now were I to accept his offer, long ere this reaches you, my accounts with Messrs Forbes & Co. would be balanced and the ten percent mill-stone no longer felt. I am only hesitating from an apprehension that the proceeding might occasion to you some embarrassment by drawing for stock & sum in advance on account of our little dividend for receiving which I believe you to be provided with a power of attorney. In this transaction I gain a sixpence on every Rupee and clear myself of a debt bearing ten percent entirely. Do not therefore be surprised if a second bill should be presented to this effect. The advantages to me are very considerable, but I weigh them with the reflection that to you they may be the source of embarrassment. Oh what would I give to be within the distance of a week's post, upon this & many other occasions.

I now come to the second chapter on a [linked?] subject, directly or indirectly with the first. Major Onslow of this regiment went home on 20th April with the intention of selling out, should the promotion be allowed to go in the regiment Captain Fendall, the senior captain who is willing to purchase, will gain the step. Now mark Captain Pratt the second senior is at present in England with the depot & is supposed to be making an exchange, not wishing to come out to this country.[46] It is therefore by no means improbable that I may become immediately senior captain of the 4th [Light] Dragoons.

Such a circumstance to me would be most advantageous, as I should then have a chance of obtaining a Majority in the regiment without purchase or expense independent of my extraordinary exaction of interests, on the contrary as a matter of right. Now our senior Lieutenant Colonel, Colonel Dalbiac becomes a Major General on the very first Army promotion. Major Sale, an officer of nearly thirty years' service will most assuredly succeed;[47] and your humble servant of senior captain stands some chance of stepping into Major Sales' place. You must therefore occasionally take a peep at the Army List & be on the watch at home as to what takes place. The moment I become senior captain it would be as well to muster what little interest we possess and endeavour to obtain something like an assurance beforehand from the good folks at the Horse Guards that I shall succeed to the vacant majority. My name at the head of the list, a captain of between ten and eleven years standing, & with some claims of service & so forth is very well. The weak side of my case is being so young a cavalry officer. They may make it a pretext to bring in somebody else at home, where there are many applicants, whilst I not being on the spot could not make any remonstrances.

46 Captain Henry Pratt, 4th Light Dragoons.
47 Major George Sale 4th Light Dragoons.

I would therefore be as well to beg in feeling the way as soon as I become senior captain and the moment an army promotion is announced, a journey to Town[48] & every exertion should be made to secure me so important *a step without purchase:* such an opportunity may never again occur, for the attainment of what in some degree brought me out to this country. Believe me your dutiful & affectionate son G U Barlow

[PS] May 20th
We have just received a letter from *Gates* dated the 4th of December last.[49] It is the only one since that which Maria wrote from Chatham dated 20th of September. Several intermediate ships that were to have sailed in October & November. No less than *four* in number are still missing by which I presume you have written. The China fleet had not arrived at Bombay on the 14th instant.

George wrote at length in his next regarding his Uncle Robert's enforced retirement from Chatham and his disgust that he did not receive a promotion on his departure.

To Sir G H Barlow Bart GCB, Oakwood near Chichester
Kaira, 10 June 1823 (Annotated received 22 November, replied 16 February 1824)

My dearest father,
I received yours of the 23rd of December last on the 3rd instant. The China ships this year made but an indifferent passage. The first of them not reaching Bombay until the 27th of May although she left the Downs on the 8th of January, all their political intelligence had been anticipated by overland accounts of some days more recent date than those which they conveyed to Hilare & myself, however they brought domestic news of the deepest interest. Anything is better than a state of uncertainty & even though hope may not be auspiciously realised; we are now in some measure enabled to conjecture what will be the future fate of those we love. Hard indeed seems the lot assigned to so much excellence & goodness. Such at least is the first exclamation of short sighted humanity, apparently hard does it seem that the declining years of one, whose life has been one scene of so much active worth & benevolence, dedicated to the fulfilment of every public and private duty, should then be visited by affliction of the severest kind. Such must be considered anything like impairment of the faculties, under which it is alas too evident that the dear object of our regret now labours. Hilare in common with myself sufficiently appreciate the tender feelings which have hitherto occasioned silence on this distressing subject. To you the subject must almost be as painful as to ourselves. Who could have believed it possible that the dear man would ever have become an

48 London.
49 I have been unable to identify this person.

instance of one of providences most severe desperations. When I consider his delightful uninterrupted state of good health, that natural innate flow of spirits which seemed to proceed from a perpetual spring rather than any temporary reservoir. When I think upon his Christian-like frame of mind, which although one of the most feeling description, has so patiently in so exemplary a manner submitted to the chastening hand of the Almighty, a mind haunted by no remorse for the past, neither overloaded with occupations of the present or cares for the future. I must [torn – be one?] of the very last who appeared likely [torn – to out?] reach of that particular certainty.

Under all circumstance his removement from office should see [torn – the government?] bring about his wanted peace of mind the receipt of rank unattended as it is by a corresponding equivalent pension is worth the object. He will remain a dear. We are all as ever, if he can think himself happy we must needs become so likewise. One could have wished that in quitting the dockyard his name had been returned to its place in the list of vice admirals, or that a baronetcy (which according to the newspapers seems not unlikely to fall to his successor in the approaching launch of the three decker & the attendance visit of his majesty to Chatham) had been betoken as a decisive acknowledgement of his brilliant services. Such are my ideas whilst writing at a distance from the scene. I am painfully anxious to hear how he has been able to get over the trial of quitting Chatham after a residence of nearly fifteen years.

Endeared to him by so many recollections [torn – he will by me?] and his whole family be missed, requires [torn – no words, but still I?] can scarcely fancy a reality. What a [torn – great change?] of one short twelve month?

A ship [torn – is due?] having nearly two months [torn – of mail and who sailed?] for this, proceeding either in August or September last is not yet arrived. She was obliged to put into Madeira and remained still there when the January ships passed that island. This accounts for the blank between dear Fanny's & Edward's joint letter of the 19th of July & Fanny's of the 13th of November.

Hilare & I thank God continue quite well. The hot season is just closing and we are now daily in expectation of some of those delicious showers that precede the regular setting in of the rains, which the gathering clouds & tempestuous winds assure us cannot be very far distant. Up to this moment however, we have not experienced a single drop of the genial bounty of heaven, which comes rather unusual for this side of India. The *Loo* still prevails.[50] One day I had the curiosity to open all the doors & windows so as to admit a thorough current of air through the house. The thermometer in the shade about the centre of my dining room, where the sun never penetrates immediately rose to 105 of Fahrenheit [41 C]. Several tragical cases of coup de soleil have occurred within the last fortnight among the thoughtless soldiery when in a state of intoxication returning out of doors.

50 The *Loo* is a strong, dusty dry summer wind blowing from the west in India.

Although the days are so exceedingly hot, the nights in general are cool & the early part of the mornings as delightful. It is on these two latter respects that we have a great advantage over the *quips* Robert writes from Ghazeepore [Ghazipur] that when the hot winds blow at *eight & nine in the evening!!!* They go to bed with a *Punka* moving over their heads, which spot & little mattresses at Guzeratee [Gujarat], who till within the last two or three weeks have seldom experienced anything like such oppressive nights. This advantage in some measure arises from our comparative vicinity to the sea, from which in a strait [sic] line we are nearly thirty miles distant at Cambray.

It gives us both the sweetest consolation to think that all at Oakwood are in the enjoyment of good health. A ray of comfort beams upon us from that quarter amid the gloomy intelligence which has reached us from dear Chatham. They all write in the most affectionate terms of your kindness in repairing to the scene of affliction with the design of affording the advice & support, so necessary in their forlorn wretched state. Since writing the above the missing ship *Melpomene*[51] has arrived bringing [torn – the missing letters which?] reached us at the same time from various correspondents [torn – a number of?] answers to letters written on our first landing in this country [torn – and their good wishes?] will be conveyed to the Piggott's[52] [torn – and the rest. A ship is due?] to sail about the 25th of the present [torn – month by which answers may go?]

I have before requested that my congratulations may be offered to Charles on his promotion.[53] It gave me pleasure to see his name to the few words announcing Richard's honours which must assuredly pave the way to his future advancement in the country. I shall write to Henry with a view of securing for him all that assistance which an older brother who has bought experience so dearly might so afford. Henry I believe is fully sensible of all his past errors, but it is to be feared that this correction comes rather late. It is now of ten years standing in the service, as many more must elapse ere his debt will be discharged, and thus instead of being able to return home with a competency like some of his more prudent contemporaries, he will scarcely will be worth a rupee more than on first landing in India. Robert is not so deeply involved, but both have alike suffered losses of health, which no prudence or time perhaps can repair. What a pity that the accomplishments of two such young men, occasioning them to be caressed in every society, should prove the bane of their interests. I am sorry to learn that Henry's wife has again experienced a relapse of ill health, so soon after her return to this country.

51 HMS *Melpomene* was a 38-gun frigate originally captured from the French.
52 I have been unable to identify the Piggotts.
53 Charles had gained promotion to Lieutenant on 1 July 1822 whilst serving on HMS *Despatch*.

[torn – Pray receive?] another [torn – letter, with best wishes sent?] in kindest love to all your dear circle. Believe me to remain my dearest father, your most dutiful & affectionate son G U Barlow.

To Sir G H Barlow, Bart GCB, Oakwood near Chichester
Kaira, 5 July 1823 (annotated received 5 February 1824, answered 16 February 1824)
By *Royal George*[54]

My dearest father,
The *Scaleby Castle*[55] which left Portsmouth on the 13th March brought me yours of the 10th of that month. Like all the ships which sail from Europe about the same period, she made a most excellent passage of ninety-seven days. It really is quite a comfort to have such regular & speedy intercourse with dear England. It seems as if one was merely in some distant part of the continent of Europe. Besides at any period of the year except in the three monsoon months we are able to leave this place & by embarking at Lambay [Khambhat?] can reach the presidency in eight or ten days, so that the situation of Kaira is possessed of many advantages.

A twelve month has passed since we arrived here and I am in the same good humour with this spot as ever. It certainly is not an Elysium but contentment & good health render it tolerably pleasant. We must conform to circumstances and taking everything into consideration I do not see how we could be better situated. No staff situation would be equal to my regimental appointments, nor is there any society female or otherwise superior to that which Kaira can produce. Without vanity, it may be affirmed that we are popular in our little circle; friends with everybody & yet avoiding too strong intimacies that in small societies so often terminate in disagreement. In short, we completely see our way and have taken the most effectual steps to render the period of sojourment both pleasant & useful.

The monsoon this year is unusually late. Up to the present time (the first week in July) some slight sprinklings not deserving the name of showers have as yet alone descended on the thirsty soil. The crops are almost a month behind hand & stand much in need of rain. This year the hot winds & weather continued until the latter end of June, on the 18th of which the thermometer stood at 106 [41 C] in the coolest part of Colonel Dalbiac's house, which is one of the largest & best bungalows that any quarter of India can produce. Cold & heat as you must well know deposed entirely in comparison. I now am writing in a most delicious temperature (98) [37 C] with a soft southerly breeze blowing in at the venetians.[56] The state of my feelings is such as I could fancy in England on a fine day in the month of May with a temperature of about 65 or 70 [21 C]. To all appearance one

54 The *Royal George* was an East India Company ship of 1,333 tons, serving from 1802-25.
55 The *Scaleby Castle* was an East India Company ship of 1,242 tons, serving from 1807-34.
56 Venetian blinds were introduced to Europe from Persia in 1760.

would say that the climate must be healthy, no conclusion can be drawn from the casualties of an European regiment which are generally greater in their barracks than in the field. For instance, I have lost four men in my troop during the last month, but with the exception of one who died of an organic disease of the heart, the others were determined dram drinkers, though in other respects extremely robust, stout men.

I am glad yet sorry at the same time that Charles continues at Oakwood, sorry for the cause, as well as for the resignation of his appointment under Sir B[enjamin] Hallowell, yet happy to think that he is in such good care, as likely to regain that most precious of belongings health. Endeavour if possible to put an old head on young shoulders, draw his attention to some of Abernethy's golden maxims applicable to every situation & climate. He will laugh at first as I myself have often stood [much?] at his age, when any person gave me advice on similar subjects, which I treated as nonsense. God be praised, my folly was never very severely punished, but on reflection as to what might have been the probable consequences, I do not the less condemn it.

Richard as you will have long since learnt has made a very fine passage to Madras. He landed on the 7th of June and on the very next day wrote to us enclosing dear Fanny's letter of the 21st of February to Hilare. As his stay would not be prolonged beyond a few weeks, nearly three of which had elapsed ere the letter came to hand, I directed my answer to Bengal. The tenor of it was such as you have requested me to adopt in my correspondence. Henry I should also hope, would keep him in a steady course, by telling him to take warning from the example of an elder brother now feels the consequences of past follies. Mr Elphinstone has pretty strongly marked his sense of such conduct on the part of the young men who have not attained the required degree of sufficiency. Two or three that I will not name still continue in the most insubordinate situations with small salaries, often having been on the establishment three or four years whilst more junior but diligent candidates have been put over their heads & succeeded to higher situations.

About two months since I wrote to advise you of the changes about to take place in the regiment. Major Onslow sailed for England on the 20th of April last with the intention not to return to the country. He will not however sell out by an exchange or by any reasons till pronounced. I presume that soon after arriving at Bombay he must have written to England on this subject otherwise it could not have been known at home. To speak of Fendall's appointment is therefore somewhat premature as from a letter received this day previous to sailing, which says that he has not anything pledged, subsequently the question of which will be accepted for consideration on reaching England. Should however someone succeed him by the exchange, I have some chance of proceeding with the majority without purchase; for although another should compleat, the promotion cannot be verified without the permission of our much-vaunted Colonel Dalbiac a major general and brigade major (late) an officer of great standing and most probably succeed to the second lieutenant colonelcy and thinks I also should get the second majority. If I become a senior captain at home there would be time to make some plans. Any letter of mine to Sir Herbert Taylor could achieve nothing more than I have so frequently wrote in my correspondence & achieve however little in my interest my case might rest upon his desk.[57] Sir B[enjamin] H[obhouse] after all has never been able to effect anything on my behalf & his friend has retired from office altogether. You might yet perhaps deign to write a letter to Sir H[erbert] Taylor simply stating my service, wounds, length of standing, now on for a step &c. As soon as I become senior captain should anything be said to the effect if silence although it might be very preferable, occasions me to be passed over.

In continuing with my letter of some time since, I have drawn on your funds only once, last September for the 24l[58] I sent a bill for two hundred and forty pounds payable to the regimental agents Messrs Hopkins & sons [rest illegible].

I retain too fond hopes that the next accounts of, I was going to say dear Chatham, may prove more agreeable. Your silence as to all our dear hopes in that quarter was so sadly conclusive. To use an expression of Commissary Fraser's[59] 'I should as soon have expected that the stars would have fallen as that such a calamity would have befallen this once happy world'.

Hilare unites with sincere kindness & love to all the dear party at Oakwood together with my dearest father, your dutiful & affectionate son
G U Barlow

That was George's last letter. The following extract of a letter from an un-named officer in the 4th Dragoons to his sister states.

Karai 1 July 1824
Sent to us by Colonel Hugonin[60]

Would to heaven I could send a better account of the health of my companions, or that our scourge had taken its departure. Alas! I have to report another victim and such a loss not only to society but to our regiment, we can hardly hope to replace for some time. We buried Captain Barlow this morning. In him we have lost a soldier, a gentleman, a sincere Christian, a kind friend, in short a character to stamp respectability in a regiment and one to which every officer might look up as a pattern.

He has left a most amiable woman whose present state of mind you may imagine. No two persons could have been more truly attached [to each other?] than they were, living a most domestic life and only happy in each

57 Major General Sir Herbert Taylor had been private secretary to George III from 1805-11 and was now Ambassador to Berlin.
58 24 guineas.
59 Deputy Assistant Commissary General Archibald Fraser.
60 Colonel Frederick Hugonin, 4th Light Dragoons.

other's company. They were first cousins, he was a son of Sir George Barlow and she a daughter of Sir Robert Barlow; they had I may say fortunately no family. To add to the distress Mrs B[arlow] has no female friend to perform those little attentions so much required in her present melancholy situation. Her intimate friend Mrs Nepean left this before the rains for Bombay to send her little boy off to England, and does not, indeed cannot return, until after the monsoon. Mrs Burrows is too great an invalid.[61] In this case Captain Nepean has performed the part of an affectionate brother, he was unremitting in his attention during the short period of poor Barlow's illness was with her when the melancholy event took place, and immediately had her removed to his own house and attended by most superior woman of the regiment, the wife of a sergeant while he took up his quarters at an officer's bungalow close at hand, and has performed the last sad offices with the greatest kindness and delicacy. He will feel the loss sincerely, they were much together and had been long friends, Captain B[arlow] was at my house the day he was taken ill, in high spirits and to all appearance in the best of health; he was particularly careful of himself, did not expose himself to the sun's, was extremely temperate. I had a note from Mrs Daly[62] the day before his death, in answer to my enquiry after his health, he was then supposed to be doing well, he was sensible to within a few hours of his death, which he was aware was approaching and assured Captain Nepean he had no fear of death but had hoped to have died in a more honourable way. What satisfaction it must be to his friends and relatives to know that few people (whether in the army or not) could have been better prepared for the awful change. Both Mrs B[arlow] and himself were constant in their attendance in their religious duties, and in that truly necessary act could hardly have been excelled by you my dear sister and your good husband, nothing perhaps could have given a stranger a stronger proof of the irreparable loss we have sustained, than the deep gloom impressed upon every countenance at the melancholy service of this morning and at the conclusion, no one felt inclined to address another; a solemn silence prevailed and each I may say departed sorrowing. I shall feel his loss severely (he was my coadjutor, in the concerns of the library). He had been educated at Eton and served with the highest credit in Spain in the Light Divisions, where he was wounded severely several times and was at Waterloo. I had looked forward one day to have seen him in the command of the 4th, where he would have been *an ornament* to the service, but regrets are useless; may we all be enabled to take his character and life for a pattern and example and say, 'May I die the death of the righteous and may my last days be like his'.[63]

61 Catharine, the wife of Captain Robert Burrowes of the 4th Light Dragoons.
62 The wife of Lieutenant Francis Daly, 4th Light Dragoons.
63 Reference MSS Eur F176-65.

The year had proven a particularly unhealthy one for the 4th Light Dragoons, which buried 89 officers and men at Kaira that year along with numerous wives and children.

George died without issue on 29 June 1824 aged 33 years, at Kaira and was buried at St George's Church there on 1 July – the church no longer exists. A tablet was apparently erected there to his memory from his fellow officers, although it strangely appears to quote an incorrect middle name for him of Hilliero rather than Ulric and incorrect date of death. This probably indicates that George's wife was not involved in the production of the inscription.

The inscription was transcribed by a Doctor Buist appearing in *Dr Buist's Notes on a Journey* in the *Transactions of the Bombay Geographical Society* for 1857. It apparently read:

> *Sacred to the Memory of George Hilliero Barlow, Capt. H.M. 4th Dragoons. Eldest son of Sir George Hilliero Barlow, Bart. Governor General of India. Ob. 13 June 1823. Etat 33.*

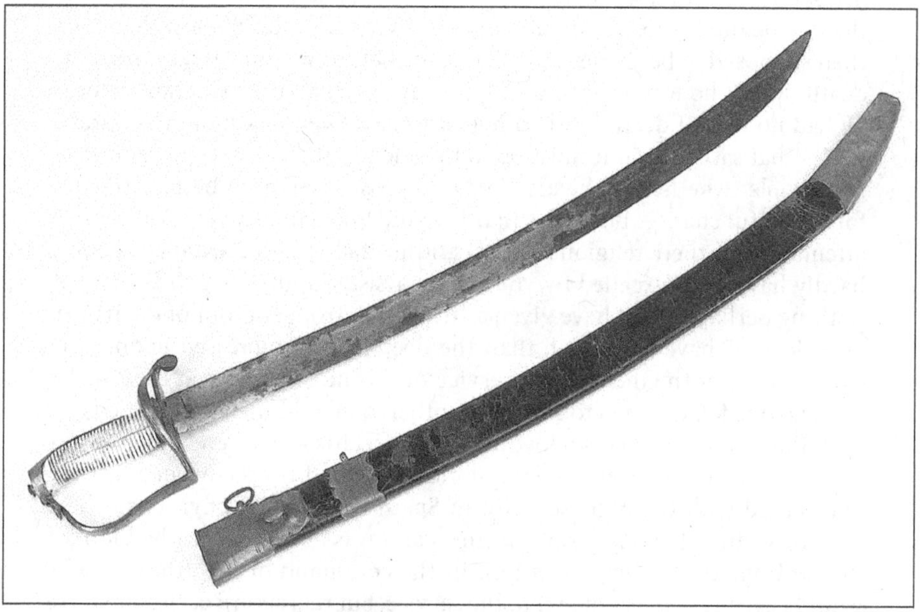

George Barlow's sword. (Editor's Collection)

14

Those that Remained

George's wife Hilare eventually re-married William, Earl Nelson, the elder brother of Horatio Nelson and became Countess Nelson, Duchess of Bronte on 26 March 1829. Earl Nelson then died on 28 February 1835. Hilare married for a third time on 7 February 1837 to Mr George Thomas Knight Esq. but she had no issue from any of the marriages. She died on 22 December 1857.

Sir George Barlow lived until 22 December 1847 when he died at Fir Grove in Farnham aged 84 years old.

Of his Aunts and Uncles:

Admiral Sir Robert had married Elizabeth (nee Garrett) and had seven children (Elizabeth Anne, Robert, William (he became a clergyman), Frances Harriet, Hilare, Maria and Caroline), he lived until 1843.

William (of Streatham) had married Harriet Fleming in 1798 but she died in 1802, he then married Louisa Harris in 1803 but they never had children. He lived until 1839.

The Reverend Thomas William had married Frances Bockett in 1798 and they had four children (John, Thomas, George and Anne Frances). He lived until 1821.

Samuel Barlow (never mentioned) had died unmarried in 1791.

Frances Charlotte (never mentioned) married Mr Thomas Coulthard in 1784 but never had children. She died post-1813.

Harriet Hilare married Henry Mauning of Sidmouth but there do not appear to have been any children. She died in 1846.

Of George's siblings:

Elizabeth Harrie, Viscountess Exmouth had her marriage dissolved to Pownall-Bastard Pellew in July 1820 after having 3 children by him (Edward, Percy Taylor, and Juliana Sarah) and she died in 1833.

William had died in 1811.

Charlotte married a Major Fletcher Balmain and had four children (James George, Eliza, John Henry, and William), she died in 1872.

Sir John Henry Barlow married a Miss Robertson but had no children, he succeeded to the baronetcy but was widowed. He continued as a Bengal Civil Servant and died in 1841.

Sir Robert succeeded as the 2nd baronet. He continued in the Bengal Civil Service, he married Augusta Seymour and they had three children (George Henry, William Charles, and Morison), he died in 1857.

Louisa died unmarried on 22 August 1821.

Captain Charles Anstruther RN never married and died in 1855.

Frances died in 1887.

Anne Caroline never married and died in 1887.

Harriet – not known.

Richard Wellesley married a Miss Maria Nott in 1835 and had two children (Richard Wellesley and Maria Charlotte). He became a magistrate and deputy collector in India, he died in 1839.

Edward Frederick – not known.

Emma Drury died on 8 August 1818.

Frederick was not Sir George's son and was the cause of their subsequent divorce. His later whereabouts are unknown.

Bibliography

Aaron, Martin, '2nd Battalion 69th (South Lincolnshire) Foot during the Waterloo Campaign, *Napoleon Series*, at www.napoleon-series.org/military/organization/Britain/Infantry/c_2-69Waterloo.html

Abbott, Philip, *'Every Implement of Destruction was used against Us' The lives of Henry and Charles Dawson 52nd Regiment of Light Infantry* (Privately published, 2015)

Anon., *The Transactions of the Bombay Geographical Society Vol 13* (Bombay: J. D'Gama, 1857)

Bamford, Andrew, *A Bold and Ambitious Enterprise* (Barnsley: Pen and Sword 2013)

Booth, J., *Additional Particulars to the Battle of Waterloo By A Near Observer* (London: J Booth, 1817)

Burnham, Robert, *The British Army against Napoleon* (Barnsley: Pen and Sword, 2010)

Connolly, T.W.J., *The History of the Corps of Royal Sappers and Miners* (London: Longman, 1855)

Dalton, C., *The Waterloo Roll Call* (London:Eyre & Spottiswood, 1904)

Dobbs, Captain John, *Recollections of An Old 52nd Man* (Staplehurst: Spellmount, 2000)

Drew, Robert (ed.), *Commissioned Officers in the Medical Services of the British Army, 1660-1960* (London: Wellcome Library, 1968).

Glover, Gareth, *A Hellish Business, the letters of Captain Charles Kinloch 52nd Foot (1806-16)* (Huntingdon: Ken Trotman, 2007)

Glover, Gareth, *The Peninsular War Diary of Captain John Frederick Ewart, 52nd Light Infantry (1811-12)* (Huntingdon: Ken Trotman, 2010)

Glover, Gareth (ed.), *The Correspondence of Sir Henry Clinton in the Waterloo Campaign*, 2 vols. (Godmanchester:, Ken Trotman, 2015)

Glover, Gareth, *With Wellington's Hussars in the Peninsula and Waterloo, The Journal of Lieutenant George Woodberry 18th Hussars*, (Barnsley: Pen & Sword, 2018)

Hall, John, *A History of the Peninsular War Volume VIII* (London: Greenhill, 1998)

Hay, William (Ed. Mrs S. Wood), *Reminiscences 1818-1815 Under Wellington* (London: Simpkin, Marshall, Hamilton, Kent & co.,1901)

Jones, Maj. Gen. John T., *Journals of Sieges carried on by the Army under the Duke of Wellington in Spain during the years 1811 to 1814* (London: John Weale, 1846)

Leeke, Rev. William, *The History of Lord Seaton's Regiment (the 52nd Light Infantry) at the Battle of Waterloo* (London: Hatchard & Co, 1866)

Maurice, Maj. Gen. Sir J.F. (ed.), *The Diary of Sir John Moore* (London: Edward Arnold, 1904)
Moorsom, M.S., *History of the 52nd Regiment 1755-1816* (London: Richard Bentley 1860)
Napier, W. *Passages in the Early Military Life of General Sir George T Napier KCB* (London: John Murray, 1884)
Oman, Sir C., *A History of the Peninsular War* (Oxford: Charles Chadwick 1922)
Park, S. & Nafziger, G. *The British Military 1803-15* (Ontario: Rafm Co., 1983)
Siborne, Capt. W., *History of the Waterloo Campaign* (London: T. and W. Boone, 1848)
Summerfield, S., & Law, S., *Sir John Moore and the Universal Soldier* (Huntingdon: Ken Trotman, 2016)
Wilson, J., *Wellington's Marriage* (London: Weidenfeld and Nicolson, 1987)

Index

Note: Members of the Barlow family are identified by their relationship to the writer.

From Reason to Revolution series – Warfare 1721-1815

http://www.helion.co.uk/published-by-helion/reason-to-revolution-1721-1815.html

The 'From Reason to Revolution' series covers the period of military history 1721–1815, an era in which fortress-based strategy and linear battles gave way to the nation-in-arms and the beginnings of total war.

This era saw the evolution and growth of light troops of all arms, and of increasingly flexible command systems to cope with the growing armies fielded by nations able to mobilise far greater proportions of their manpower than ever before. Many of these developments were fired by the great political upheavals of the era, with revolutions in America and France bringing about social change which in turn fed back into the military sphere as whole nations readied themselves for war. Only in the closing years of the period, as the reactionary powers began to regain the upper hand, did a military synthesis of the best of the old and the new become possible.

The series will examine the military and naval history of the period in a greater degree of detail than has hitherto been attempted, and has a very wide brief, with the intention of covering all aspects from the battles, campaigns, logistics, and tactics, to the personalities, armies, uniforms, and equipment.

Submissions

The publishers would be pleased to receive submissions for this series. Please contact series editor Andrew Bamford via email (andrewbamford18@gmail.com), or in writing to Helion & Company Limited, Unit 8 Amherst Business Centre, Budbrooke Road, Warwick, CV34 5WE

Titles

No 1 *Lobositz to Leuthen. Horace St Paul and the Campaigns of the Austrian Army in the Seven Years War 1756-57* Translated with additional materials by Neil Cogswell (ISBN 978-1-911096-67-2)

No 2 *Glories to Useless Heroism. The Seven Years War in North America from the French journals of Comte Maurés de Malartic, 1755-1760* William Raffle (ISBN 978-1-1911512-19-6) (paperback)

No 3 *Reminiscences 1808-1815 Under Wellington. The Peninsular and Waterloo Memoirs of William Hay* William Hay, with notes and commentary by Andrew Bamford (ISBN 978-1-1911512-32-5)

No 4 *Far Distant Ships. The Royal Navy and the Blockade of Brest 1793-1815* Quintin Barry (ISBN 978-1-1911512-14-1)

No 5 *Godoy's Army. Spanish Regiments and Uniforms from the Estado Militar of 1800* Charles Esdaile and Alan Perry (ISBN 978-1-911512-65-3) (paperback)

No 6 *On Gladsmuir Shall the Battle Be! The Battle of Prestonpans 1745* Arran Johnston (ISBN 978-1-911512-83-7)

No 7 *The French Army of the Orient 1798-1801. Napoleon's Beloved 'Egyptians'* Yves Martin (ISBN 978-1-911512-71-4)*

No 8 *The Autobiography, or Narrative of a Soldier. The Peninsular War Memoirs of William Brown of the 45th Foot* William Brown, with notes and commentary by Steve Brown (ISBN 978-1-911512-94-3) (paperback)

No 9 *Recollections from the Ranks. Three Russian Soldiers' Autobiographies from the Napoleonic Wars* Translated and annotated by Darrin Boland (ISBN 978-1-912174-18-8) (paperback)

No 10 *By Fire and Bayonet. Grey's West Indies Campaign of 1794* Steve Brown (ISBN 978-1-911512-60-8)

No 11 *Olmütz to Torgau. Horace St Paul and the Campaigns of the Austrian Army in the Seven Years War 1758-60* Translated with additional materials by Neil Cogswell (ISBN 978-1-911512-72-1)

No 12 *Murat's Army. The Army of the Kingdom of Naples 1806-1815* Digby Smith (ISBN 978-1-912390-09-0) (paperback)

No 13 *The Veteran or 40 Years' Service in the British Army. The Scurrilous Recollections of Paymaster John Harley 47th Foot – 1798-1838* John Harley, with notes and commentary by Gareth Glover (ISBN 978-1-912390-25-0) (paperback)

No 14 *Narrative of the Eventful Life of Thomas Jackson. Militiaman and Coldstream Sergeant, 1803-15* Thomas Jackson, with notes and commentary by Eamonn O'Keeffe (ISBN 978-1-912390-12-0) (paperback)

No 15 *For Orange and the States! The Army of the Dutch Republic 1713-1772. Part I: Infantry* Marc Geerdinck-Schaftenaar (ISBN 978-1-911512-15-8)*

No 16 *'Men who are Determined to be Free': The American Assault on Stony Point 15 July 1779* David Bonk (ISBN 978-1-912174-84-3)*

No 17 *Next to Wellington. General Sir George Murray. The Story of a Scottish Soldier and Statesman, Wellington's Quartermaster General* John Harding-Edgar (ISBN 978-1-912390-13-7)

No 18 *Between Scylla and Charibdys: The Army of Friedrich August II of Saxony, 1733-1763. Part I: Staff and Cavalry* Marco Pagan (ISBN 978-1-912174-89-8)*

No 19 *The Secret Expedition: The Anglo-Russian Invasion of Holland 1799* Geert van Uythoven (ISBN 978-1-912390-20-5)

No 20 *'We Are Accustomed to do our Duty' German Auxiliaries with the British Army 1793-95* Paul Demet (ISBN 978-1-912174-96-6)

No 21 *With the Guards in Flanders. The Diary of Captain Roger Morris 1793-95* Peter Harington (ISBN 978-1-911628-15-6) (paperback)

No 22 *The British Army in Egypt 1801. An Underrated Army Comes of Age* Carole Divall (ISBN 978-1-911628-17-0)*

No 23 *Better is the Proud Plaid. The Clothing, Weapons, and Accoutrements of the Jacobites in 1745* Jenn Scott (ISBN ISBN 978-1-911628-16-3)*

No 24 *The Lilies and the Thistle. French Troops in the Jacobite '45* Andrew Bamford (ISBN 978-1-911628-17-0)*

No 25 *A Light Infantryman With Wellington* Gareth Glover (ed.) (ISBN 978-1-911628-10-1) (paperback)

* indicates 'Falconet' format paperbacks, page size 248mm × 180 mm, with high visual content including colour plates; other titles are hardback monographs unless otherwise noted.

